AF510077

The Colombo Plan

Conceived in 1950, the Colombo Plan for Co-operative Development in South and Southeast Asia was a unique experiment in foreign relations. Meeting annually across what we now know as the 'Indo-Pacific', talented administrators facilitated foreign aid provision and promoted development fuelled state-making, internationalism and experimental regionalism across postwar Asia. David Lowe argues that this new setting and dynamic international cast created an unusually productive diplomatic environment of development internationalism. The Colombo Plan did not escape power politics or Cold War divisions. However, it did run according to its own rhythm, and, unlike other experiments, it endured, continuing today in a much reduced form.

David Lowe is Chair in Contemporary History and Director of the Centre for Contemporary Histories at Deakin University, Victoria.

Global and International History

Series Editors

Erez Manela, *Harvard University*
Heather Salter, *Northeastern University*

The Global and International History series seeks to highlight and explore the convergences between the new International History and the new World History. Its editors are interested in approaches that mix traditional units of analysis such as civilizations, nations and states with other concepts such as transnationalism, diasporas, and international institutions.

Titles in the Series

David Lowe, *The Colombo Plan: Development Internationalism in Cold War Asia*
Thomas Gidney, *An International Anomaly: Colonial Accession to the League of Nations*
Lydia Walker, *States-in-Waiting: A Counternarrative of Global Decolonization*
Erez Manela and Heather Streets-Salter, *The Anticolonial Transnational: Imaginaries, Mobilities, and Networks in the Struggle against Empire*
Ismay Milford, *African Activists in a Decolonising World: The Making of an Anticolonial Culture, 1952–1966*
Florian Wagner, *Colonial Internationalism and the Governmentality of Empire, 1893–1982*
Sarah C. Dunstan, *Race, Rights and Reform: Black Activism in the French Empire and the United States from World War I to the Cold War*
Agnieszka Sobocinska, *Saving the World? Western Volunteers and the Rise of the Humanitarian-Development Complex*
Kirwin R. Shaffer, *Anarchists of the Caribbean: Countercultural Politics and Transnational Networks in the Age of US Expansion*
Stephen J. Macekura and Erez Manela, *The Development Century: A Global History*
Amanda Kay McVety, *The Rinderpest Campaigns: A Virus, Its Vaccines, and Global Development in the Twentieth Century*
Michele L. Louro, *Comrades against Imperialism*
Antoine Acker, *Volkswagen in the Amazon: The Tragedy of Global Development in Modern Brazil*
Christopher R. W. Dietrich, *Oil Revolution: Anti-Colonial Elites, Sovereign Rights, and the Economic Culture of Decolonization*
Nathan J. Citino, *Envisioning the Arab Future: Modernization in U.S.–Arab Relations, 1945–1967*
Stefan Rinke, *Latin America and the First World War*
Timothy Nunan, *Humanitarian Invasion: Global Development in Cold War Afghanistan*
Michael Goebel, *Anti-Imperial Metropolis: Interwar Paris and the Seeds of Third World Nationalism*
Stephen J. Macekura, *Of Limits and Growth: The Rise of Global Sustainable Development in the Twentieth Century*

The Colombo Plan

Development Internationalism in Cold War Asia

DAVID LOWE
Deakin University

CAMBRIDGE
UNIVERSITY PRESS

CAMBRIDGE
UNIVERSITY PRESS

Shaftesbury Road, Cambridge CB2 8EA, United Kingdom

One Liberty Plaza, 20th Floor, New York, NY 10006, USA

477 Williamstown Road, Port Melbourne, VIC 3207, Australia

314–321, 3rd Floor, Plot 3, Splendor Forum, Jasola District Centre, New Delhi – 110025, India

103 Penang Road, #05-06/07, Visioncrest Commercial, Singapore 238467

Cambridge University Press is part of Cambridge University Press & Assessment, a department of the University of Cambridge.

We share the University's mission to contribute to society through the pursuit of education, learning and research at the highest international levels of excellence.

www.cambridge.org
Information on this title: www.cambridge.org/9781009600736

DOI: 10.1017/9781009600729

© David Lowe 2025

This publication is in copyright. Subject to statutory exception and to the provisions of relevant collective licensing agreements, no reproduction of any part may take place without the written permission of Cambridge University Press & Assessment.

When citing this work, please include a reference to the DOI 10.1017/9781009600729

First published 2025

Cover image: Colombo Plan conference, Wellington, November 1956. Hill, Morris James, 1929-2002: Negatives of Wellington, and national events and personalities.

A catalogue record for this publication is available from the British Library

A Cataloging-in-Publication data record for this book is available from the Library of Congress

ISBN 978-1-009-60073-6 Hardback

Cambridge University Press & Assessment has no responsibility for the persistence or accuracy of URLs for external or third-party internet websites referred to in this publication and does not guarantee that any content on such websites is, or will remain, accurate or appropriate.

To our two recently departed mothers, Jan Lowe and Beverley Shimmen.

Contents

Figures

Acknowledgements

The journey behind this book has been an adventurous one, taking me to archives around the world, courtesy of financial and institutional support and the efforts of many people. I am sure it has also tested the patience of those closest to me. I emerge indebted in a multitude of ways, and I can only hope that I can acknowledge them at least partially here.

I have benefited from the financial support of Deakin University's Centre for Contemporary Histories in ongoing ways throughout the course of preparing this book. The Centre has been a source of modest, recurring financial support for big projects such as this one. From 2017 to 2019, the Australian Research Council provided funding that covered some of the Australian and Canadian dimensions of this work. A Smuts Fellowship in 2018–19 at the Centre for South Asian Studies, Cambridge, UK, was the other important source of financial and institutional support. Being based at the Centre for South Asian Studies and at Clare Hall in Cambridge enabled me to make use of the Royal Commonwealth Society's (RCS) collection of Colombo Plan materials in the Cambridge University Library. My thanks go to RCS curators past and present, Rachel Rowe and Sally Kent, for assisting in all ways possible. While I was at Cambridge, Professors Sujit Sivasundaram, Simon Szreter, David Reynolds and Saul Dubow provided intellectual hospitality and enabled my participation in seminar series such as the South Asian and World History seminars. I also enjoyed friendship and support from Lizzie Collingham and Thomas Seidl, and Farzana Haniffa and Mushtaq Fuad, who made my stay in the UK all the richer. Other visiting fellows at Clare Hall provided welcome company (but I do not thank the squirrel who gleefully sabotaged my daily efforts to attract birds to my balcony there).

Archivists and librarians are unsung heroes in many historical research projects, and this project is no exception. Over several years, staff at the National Archives of Australia and the National Library of Australia in Canberra have provided all assistance possible, in spite of their diminishing resources. Similarly, archivists and librarians have assisted at the Library and Archives, Canada, in Ottawa, the (UK) National Archives and the British Library in London, the (US) National Archives and Records Administration in College Park, Maryland, the National Archives of India and Nehru Memorial Museum and Library in New Delhi, Archives New Zealand and the National Library of New Zealand in Wellington, and the Japanese Diplomatic Archive in Tokyo. At various times, the Australian Department of Foreign Affairs and Trade has taken interest and shown support for this project, and I extend my thanks to those officers in Canberra, and the High Commissions in New Delhi and Kuala Lumpur who assisted me. My gratitude also extends to all members of the Cambridge University Press production team.

Among those fellow academics whose patience I have especially tested by periodically discussing some of the main features of the book are Chris Waters, Joan Beaumont, David Ekbladh and Fazal Rizvi. While I was based at the University of Tokyo for six months in 2019–20, I benefited from discussions with Hiroyuki Ogawa there and from Shigeru Akita at the University of Osaka and Ed Vickers at Kyushu University. More generally, the support of my colleagues in the Centre for Contemporary Histories at Deakin University has also been crucial. The research culture fostered by fellow members of the executive, Cassandra Atherton, Clare Corbould, Carolyn Holbrook, Tony Joel, Mia Martin-Hobbs and Andrew Singleton, is a precious commodity in a higher education environment capable of caprice as well as rewards. Other members of the group who have endured some proximity to this project include Jonathan Ritchie, Jemma Purdey, Anna Kent, Michelle Verso and Brad Underhill. Two of the centre's doctoral students, Liam Detering and Hirokazu Matsui, assisted with the manuscript's preparation. For their friendship and unerring capacity to bring a sense of perspective to all matters academic, Rohan Bastin, Tony Joel, Phillip Deery and Chris Waters earn additional thanks. On several occasions, they rescued me from project myopia. And for stimulating and encouraging conversations early in the piece, I thank Srinath Raghavan, David Walker, Frank Bongiorno, Kate Darian-Smith, David Lee and the late Chris Bayly. None of these listed should be held responsible for anything I have written.

It grieves me that my mother, Jan, did not live to see this book in print, but she and my late father, Myles, provided the kind of love and continuing interest in the endeavours of their four sons that keeps reverberating. My brothers, Rod, Barry and Tim, and their families have all, in various ways, provided ongoing love and support. My cousin Brendan Kelly has helped periodically to recharge the batteries.

My greatest debt is to my partner in life, my wife, Andrea Shimmen, whose work with international students in higher education was a welcome bridge to some of the themes explored in this book and enriching for us more generally. Above and beyond that connection is Andrea's capacity to absorb the consequences of projects like this book and to continue to provide constant love and inspiration in the ways of life. Our two boys, Ben and Tristan, are a source of joy and admiration. In their twenties, they teach their parents more than they know. They have probably lived with the Colombo Plan as a shadowy, hopefully benign, thing at the periphery of their worlds. It is also the reputation that the Colombo Plan has enjoyed with many, and which this book aims to correct.

Introduction

Consider a diplomatic moment in October 1957. The Colombo Plan for Co-operative Economic Development in South and Southeast Asia reached a milestone that year when it marked the end of its first series of six-year economic development programs for countries of the region, and its members declared their collective willingness to see the Colombo Plan continue. The annual meeting of the Colombo Plan's Consultative Committee was held in the Republic of Vietnam. When President Ngo Dinh Diem rose to welcome representatives of the twenty-one nations present in Saigon, he faced something of a test, as this was the first time the Committee had met in a non-Commonwealth country. The British had not believed that it would be possible for the Vietnamese to handle such a meeting.[1] Diem, however, was up to the task. He offered greetings that included now-familiar references to East–West bridge-building and celebration of linguistic and cultural diversity. He put particular store on what he saw as the informal, organic quality of the Colombo Plan and its logical genesis in the Commonwealth:

> We all share in the uniqueness of the Colombo Plan. Like the great Commonwealth of Nations which gave it birth, the Plan is a voluntary and flexible arrangement, imbued with the practical idealism of raising man's lot to a higher station. I note with pleasure that the Plan is not encumbered by formal treaties; its hallmarks are the more enduring and universal values of good-will and free

[1] Memorandum of Conversation, Jack Corbett, US Department of State and J. R. A. Bottomley, First Secretary, British Embassy, Washington, 8 February 1957, decimal series, 890.00/2-857, United States National Archives and Records Administration, College Park, Maryland, US (hereafter USNA).

FIGURE I.1 President Diem addressing delegates of the Colombo Plan's Consultative Committee in Saigon, 1957.
Source: The National Archive (UK) DO 35/5733.

participation, of learning from each other, of helping each other, and of forging lasting friendships.

As no other institution, the Colombo Plan demonstrates that dominance, arrogance, and imposition can be replaced by mutual respect, free negotiation, and cooperation. I can conceive of no better way to draw nations together.[2]

Diem is better remembered for his controversial rule of the Republic of Vietnam from 1955 to his assassination in 1963. But some of the key concepts he highlighted in 1957 made the Colombo Plan distinctive at the time and also somewhat enigmatic. His emphasis on the lack of formal treaty, and his sense of cumulative learning through meeting and relationship-building were as accurate as they might now seem woolly (Figure I.1).

Diem's remarks also set the scene well for this book. New histories of development and histories of international organizations are revealing overlooked aspects of twentieth-century international and global history.[3]

[2] Address by Ngo Dinh Diem at Inaugural Session of Ministerial Meeting of Consultative Committee on Co-operative Economic Development in South and South-East Asia, Saigon, 21 October 1957, RG 25 vol. 7360 11038-5-c-40 Pt 2 FP2, Library and National Archives Canada, Ottawa (hereafter LAC).

[3] Among many synthesizing works on the history of development, see Corinna Unger, *International Development: A Postwar History* (London: Bloomsbury, 2018); Stephen

Until relatively recently, stories of how decolonizing Asia negotiated relationships of North–South or South–South character had been viewed mostly through two lenses. One was the tussle between a great power view of the world as being divided into two Cold War camps versus the perspective from the emerging Afro-Asian bloc. Herein the Bandung Conference of 1955 loomed large as the foundational moment of post-colonial solidarity, disrupting Cold War polarity and the Euro-American system of international relations. The second lens, generally used in conjunction with the first, was the bilateral gaze, focusing on relations between two nations, for example, India and the United States.[4]

J. Macekura and Erez Manela (eds.), *The Development Century: A Global History* (Cambridge: Cambridge University Press, 2018); Joseph Morgan Hodge, 'Writing the History of Development (Part 1: The First Wave)', *Humanity: An International Journal of Human Rights, Humanitarianism and Development*, 6, 3 (2015), 429–63; Joseph Morgan Hodge, 'Writing the History of Development (Part 2: Longer, Deeper, Wider)', *Humanity: An International Journal of Human Rights, Humanitarianism and Development*, 7, 1 (2016), 125–74; Stephen J. Macekura, *Of Limits and Growth: The Rise of Global Sustainable Development in the Twentieth Century* (New York: Cambridge University Press 2015). Among works on the histories of international organizations, see Eva-Maria Muschik, 'Towards a Global History of International Organizations and Decolonization', *Journal of Global History*, 17 (2022), 173–90; Amy L. Sayward, *The United Nations in International History* (London: Bloomsbury, 2017); Daniel Maul, *The International Labour Organization: 100 Years of Global Social Policy* (Berlin: DeGruyter, 2019); Nicole Eggers, Jessica L. Pearson, and Auroa Almada e Santos (eds.), *The United Nations and Decolonization* (Abingdon: Routledge, 2020); Glenda Sluga and Patricia Clavin (eds.), *Internationalisms: A Twentieth-Century History* (Cambridge: Cambridge University Press, 2017); Guy Fiti Sinclair, *To Reform the World: International Organizations and the Making of Modern States* (Oxford: Oxford University Press, 2017); and the earlier but seminal, Akira Iriye, *Global Community: The Role of International Organizations in the Making of the Contemporary World* (Berkeley: University of California Press, 2002). And key works that combine these two themes include, Marc Frey, Sönke Kunkel, and Corinna R. Unger (eds.), *International Organizations and Development, 1945–1990* (Basingstoke: Palgrave Macmillan, 2014); Corinne A. Pernet and Amalia Ribi Forclaz, 'Revisiting the Food and Agriculture Organization (FAO): International Histories of Agriculture, Nutrition and Development', *The International History Review*, 41, 2 (2018), 345–50 (and other contributions to this special issue); Eva-Maria Muschik, *Building States: The United Nations, Development, and Decolonization, 1945–1965* (New York: Columbia University Press, 2022); Olav Stokke, *The UN and Development: From Aid to Cooperation* (Bloomington: Indiana University Press, 2009); Daniel Gorman, 'Britain, India and the United Nations: Colonialism and the Development of International Governance, 1945–1960', *Journal of Global History*, 9, 3 (2014), 471–90.

[4] Good examples include David C. Engerman, *The Price of Aid: The Economic Cold War in India* (Cambridge, MA: Harvard University Press, 2018); James M. Carter, *Inventing Vietnam: The United States and State-Building, 1954–1968* (New York: Cambridge University Press, 2008); Suzanne Moon, *Technology and Ethical Idealism: A History of Development in the Netherlands East Indies* (Leiden: CNWS Publications), 2007.

This book builds on the momentum built by newer research into histories of development and of international organizations. My focus is on the overlooked multilateral organization that Diem celebrated in 1957 and was created to promote development, the Colombo Plan for Co-operative Economic Development in South and Southeast Asia. The Colombo Plan took shape in 1950–51 and boasted twenty-one members from the Global South and Global North by the end of the decade. It operated as a loose umbrella under which mostly bilateral aid agreements were struck between so-called developed and developing nations, but members also sought to foster statehood and modest forms of regional organization. This book recovers the Colombo Plan as a laboratory of what I call 'development internationalism', a term that captures the mission behind the Colombo Plan and draws on some of the recent research into different forms of internationalism and development.

Development internationalism comprises three inter-related themes. The first is the conjoining of state-making and economic growth, a priority of governments in decolonizing Asia. This necessarily involved working both with and against the grain of power exercised by others. New, post-independence governments, enterprising bureaucrats and experts constantly evaluated former colonial means of exercising power, and they mediated rather than rejected the development assistance offered by imperial powers. The second theme is internationalism, a work-in-progress ideal that was malleable, drawing from the United Nations in principle and practices, and also from other sources, state-sponsored and transnational. In the case of the Colombo Plan, one distinctive source of internationalism drew on the ideas and workings of the postwar British Commonwealth. The Commonwealth was the organization that initiated the Colombo Plan, before the plan membership quickly expanded beyond Commonwealth countries. Like the auxiliary organizations connected to the UN, the Commonwealth invited non-state transnational exchanges as well as governmental action. And thirdly, development internationalism also consisted of experimental regionalism, exploratory and often guarded attempts to find common ground among the post-colonial nations of what was known as South and Southeast Asia.

While there is no neat evolutionary line between organizations and ideas of the 1950s and 1960s to the present day, the Colombo Plan finds echoes in the present. Its consensus-driven approach to members' meetings anticipated some of the interactions at Bandung in 1955, and beyond this, the practices in the Association of Southeast Asian Nations (ASEAN), an important regional organization since its formation in

1967.[5] The Colombo Plan's embrace of Japanese membership in 1954 enabled the return of Japan to regional political and economic decision-making, paving the way for Japanese leadership in the formation of the Asian Development Bank in 1966. Further, the region covered by the Colombo Plan's membership in the early 1960s approximates one of current geopolitical prominence, the Indo-Pacific. And finally, the Colombo Plan has become an important 'site of memory' for some governments and institutions. This is especially the case in Sri Lanka, Australia and New Zealand, where governments and educational institutions are eager, for reasons of reputation and economic opportunities, to find continuity between the people-to-people connections of the 1950s and today.

Historians such as Glenda Sluga and Sandrine Kott have successfully led a path towards a more sustained analysis of international organizations.[6] The explanatory potential of these organizations lies not only in their capacities as 'international actors', to use the language of international relations scholars, but in their functioning as exploratory laboratories – what Kott describes as 'open social spaces through which we can observe exchanges and circulation located at the intersection of, and interfacing with, international networks, but also specific groups and milieus within different national and local societies'.[7] Both the set-piece occasions for verbal exchanges, such as plenary sessions of meetings, and the bureaucracies sustaining the work of organizations between and during meetings, reveal a broad mix of actors negotiating power imbalances and nationally and internationally shaped objectives. They also enable us to observe how the formation of networks of influence and expertise negotiated and crossed conventional lines of binary division such colonizer/colonized, Capitalist West/Communist East and North/South. In short, international organizations have recently emerged as shaping agents in global history, including as interpretive lenses on twentieth-century themes such as decolonization, development, internationalism and the Cold War, all of which feature in this book. At the

[5] For Bandung, see Amitav Acharya, 'Studying the Bandung Conference from the Global IR Perspective', *Australian Journal of International Affairs*, 70, 4 (2016), 349–50.

[6] See especially Sluga and Clavin, *Internationalisms*, including Sandrine Kott's chapter, 'Cold War Internationalism', pp. 240–62.

[7] Sandrine Kott, 'International Organizations – A Field for Research for a Global History', *Zeithistorische Forschungen/Studies in Contemporary History*, 8 (2011), 446–47.

same time, these international organizations have rightly been 'developing a life of their own'.[8]

This complements another prominent theme among the many historical works on twentieth-century development: the importance of administrators and experts. According to historian Eva-Maria Muschik, technical assistance enabled the United Nations Secretariat to reconcile the great tension between its position as an arbiter of the universal and as a defender of nation-states, including those emerging from colonial rule. Technical assistance for economic development helped nations to help themselves, as a UN General Assembly resolution confirmed in December 1948. It safeguarded the sovereignty of recipient governments by enabling them to control what forms of external assistance they accepted.[9] As the functions of governments became more capacious in the 1950s, driven both by government-identified needs and by rising citizen expectations of improved social and economic conditions, skilled administration as well as technical expertise was needed. The transitions from colonial government to post-colonial governing would be aided by bureaucratic heft. Thinking through the need for administrative assistance for post-colonial governments took various forms, including an imaginative proposal in 1956 by UN Secretary-General Dag Hammarskjöld for an International Administrative Service. The plan was much-debated and ultimately much-pared back.[10] While some of the UN ventures in administrative support focused on South America and North Africa, the call for administrators also rang out across Asia. A recurring refrain from some donor governments involved in the Colombo Plan was the need for more 'non-commissioned officers', more men (the ideal administrator was gender-specific as well as shaped by Western government and military traditions) skilled in the arts of high-level organization and public administration.[11]

The Colombo Plan also took shape in relation to the Cold War in Asia. With good reason, historians of international relations have commonly framed studies of postwar change in Asia according to the power politics of the Cold War. Similarly, the theme of modernization has guided or joined with the Cold War in shaping how postwar politics and development might be understood. Big interpretative themes such as these two are indispensable for anyone interested in the ideology and realities of power

[8] Muschik, 'Towards a Global History of International Organizations and Decolonization', 190.

[9] Muschik, *Building States*, pp. 2–4, 167–71 and passim.

[10] Ibid, pp. 167–97.

[11] See Chapter 2, p. 91.

as it informed the negotiations and forms of aid to a decolonizing world. The Cold War, the globally spreading ideological competition between East and West, complicated the ongoing process of decolonization past the moments of state independence in ways that scholars continue to explore.[12] It also generated security alarms, including fears of nuclear war, and yielded opportunities for Asian governments playing off East against West in trade, investment and development initiatives.

In what follows, these features of 'Cold War Asia', while fundamental, are not the primary focus. Grand-scale framings such as Cold War and modernization tend to prioritize perspectives of the West from whence they evolved, and they operate at the expense of views closer to the ground (even in excellent studies where the agency of actors in the South is made clear).[13] Being too beholden to an interpretive lens of Cold War or modernization risks obscuring the range of possibilities in play as foreign aid programmes unfolded. It can mask the significance of international organizations and administrators and the exploratory and the relationality in new diplomatic and informal encounters between and among the Global South and Global North nations.

As Frederick Cooper has argued, grand interpretive themes risk flattening out the dimensions of *process* in the messy business of decolonization. These dimensions include the instability of boundaries shaping concepts of inclusion, exclusion and difference.[14] Others have joined Cooper in reminding us of the agency of state leaders prior to their independence from colonial rule, and then contests over what sovereignty should look like in the period following independence.[15] Leaders

[12] Good multi-perspective examples are: Leslie James and Elisabeth Leake (eds.), *Decolonization and the Cold War: Negotiating Independence* (London: Bloomsbury, 2015); and Christopher E. Goscha and Christian Ostermann (eds.), *Connecting Histories: Decolonization and the Cold War in Southeast Asia, 1945–1962* (Stanford, CA: Stanford University Press), 2009.

[13] For example, see Engerman, *The Price of Aid.*

[14] Frederick Cooper, *Colonialism in Question: Theory, Knowledge, History* (Berkeley: University of California Press, 2005), pp. 3–32. Cooper, focused on decolonizing French Africa, has also reminded us of the federated possibilities there that competed with any neat transition from colony to nation-state, and the debates on post-independence citizenship that drew from French imperial experience but imagined other ways of thinking about rights and obligations: Frederick Cooper, *Citizenship between Empire and Nation: Remaking France and French Africa, 1945–1960* (Princeton, NJ: Princeton University Press, 2014).

[15] See, for example, Tomoko Akami on inter-colonialism: Tomoko Akami, 'Imperial Polities, Intercolonialism, and the Shaping of Global Governing Norms: Public Health Experts in Asia and the League of Nations Health Organization, 1908–37', *Journal of*

of nations gaining independence in South and Southeast Asia, primarily but not exclusively Anglophone, were arguably more 'statist' minded than those of Cooper's focus in Francophone Africa, but they shared an interest in world-making as well as state-making.[16] A new class of post-colonial elites expected increasing mobility and imagined that they would be capable of brokering new ideas with their populations. Decolonizing South and Southeast Asia had neither uniform colonial history nor strongly articulated forms of a unifying regional future, but its leaders grappled with shared questions about post-independence development, state-making, internationalism and ideas of region.[17] Their efforts to work through the political, economic and collective possibilities of post-independence, internally, with neighbours and with former colonial metropoles and great powers, are afforded closer consideration by means of their regular gatherings and exchanges as members of the Colombo Plan.

In the hands of historians to date, the Colombo Plan is not unknown but is persistently under-appreciated. One part-exception and one of the earliest scholarly studies, without the benefit of government archival sources, is Lalita Prasad Singh's 1966 investigation of how Asian international organizations grappled with economic cooperation.[18] Singh was especially interested in the work of the UN's Economic Commission for Asia and the Far East (ECAFE), the Colombo Plan and the South East Asia Treaty Organization (SEATO), for how they fostered regional cooperation or illustrated impediments to cooperation. A book that is

Global History, 12, 1 (2017), 4–25; and Sarah Stockwell on the non-state, institutional aspect of drawn-out decolonization: Sarah Stockwell, *The British End of the British Empire* (Cambridge: Cambridge University Press, 2018). John Agnew's work on 'sovereignty regimes' rather than sovereignty defaulting to the singular nation-state can apply to the postwar years: John A. Agnew, *Globalization and Sovereignty* (Lanham, MD: Rowman & Littlefield, 2009). And for the case study of the postwar Commonwealth, see Daniel Haines, 'A "Commonwealth Moment" in South Asian Decolonization', in James Leslie and Elisabeth Leake (eds.), *Decolonization and the Cold War: Negotiating Independence* (London: Bloomsbury, 2015), pp. 185–202.

16 Drawing on Adom Getachew's *Worldmaking After Empire: The Rise and Fall of Self-determination* (Princeton, NJ: Princeton University Press), 2019.

17 Daniel Gorman suggests, in a study of Anglo–Indian relations at the UN in its early years, that they confirm the conjoining of 'the imperialism of internationalization, conceived of as the growing global imperative of internationalism as a governing concept, and the internationalization of imperialism, most notably through the challenge of progressive ideas to colonial powers ... ' Gorman, 'Britain, India, and the United Nations', p. 490.

18 Lalita Prasad Singh, *The Politics of Economic Cooperation in Asia: A Study of Asian International Organizations* (Columbia: University of Missouri Press), 1966.

even-handed in its exploration of regional politics and deft in the use of multiple public sources, Singh's *Politics of Economic Cooperation in Asia* is also characterized by a tone of 'thwarted regionalism'. Differences in politics, economics and psychology, argued Singh, prevented the realization of the more ambitious visions of regional cooperation and restricted working regionalism to a few cooperative ventures in transport and waterways sponsored by ECAFE. Notably, the Colombo Plan did not rate a mention in Singh's concluding summary of the retarded state of regional cooperation and integration.[19]

Scholars of Britain and the Cold War in Asia, and/or Britain's postwar financial difficulties have traced the hopes of Foreign Office and Treasury officials to the Colombo Plan. Like the officials, these historians of Britain in world affairs have been left mostly disappointed with what resulted. Tilman Remme's study of *Britain and Regional Cooperation in South East Asia, 1945–49* reveals a broad range of British strategic, foreign policy and financial concerns channelled towards a climactic meeting of Commonwealth Foreign Ministers in Colombo in January 1950; but such plans and hopes were too much for the meeting and the new Colombo Plan to bear. The story of British regional policy thereafter, argues Remme, is best understood according to the exigencies of the Cold War.[20] In a slightly different but complementary interpretation, Nicholas Tarling highlights British statesmanship in the making of the Colombo Plan despite the British being unable to bring substantial resources to the table of regional planning.[21]

Given that membership of the Colombo Plan helped pave the way for Japan's diplomatic re-emergence in Asia in the mid-1950s, it is not surprising that Japanese scholars have shown interest in it. An edited collection of essays edited by Shigeru Akita, Gerold Krozewski and Shoichi Watanabe in 2015 examines the Colombo Plan in relation to national interests, especially those of Britain, Japan and the United States, and the interwoven effects of the Cold War, decolonization, foreign aid and international organization activities in postwar Asia.[22] Collectively,

[19] Ibid, pp. 227–36.

[20] Tilman Remme, *Britain and Regional Cooperation in South-East Asia, 1945–49* (London: Routledge, 2016 [1995]).

[21] Nicholas Tarling, *Britain, Southeast Asia and the Onset of the Cold War, 1945–1950* (Cambridge: Cambridge University Press, 2007 [1998]), especially p. 412.

[22] Shigeru Akita, Gerold Krozewski, and Shoichi Watanabe (eds.), *The Transformation of the International Order of Asia: Decolonization, the Cold War, and the Colombo Plan* (Abingdon: Routledge, 2015).

the thirteen chapters make a compelling case for approaching the Colombo Plan in multidimensional ways and for research that cuts across specialized fields of inquiry. In the hands of different authors, the Colombo Plan becomes far more interesting than merely an episode in Britain's management of decolonization. At the same time, a multi-author, multi-perspective collection dissects components in relation to particular governments or events and views from varying angles better than it understands the Colombo Plan as an international organization and as a form of international relations I am calling development internationalism.

Writing about the Colombo Plan from Australia comes with advantages and challenges. The advantages grow from there being plenty of archival and press material readily found. This arises from contemporaneous efforts in the 1950s and 1960s to maximize publicity for Australia's contributions, as a positive narrative about Australian engagement with Asia, and a counter-narrative to the racial barrier posed by the persistence of Australia's restrictive immigration settings, the so-called White Australia policy. As I and historian Daniel Oakman have suggested, to a significant extent, Australian governments succeeded in promoting their membership of the Colombo Plan as a counter-narrative to the 'White Australia policy' and as a means of managing relations with a rapidly changing region.[23] At the same time, Australians tried to appropriate the Colombo Plan, highlighting in particular their strong efforts, relative to the efforts of other members, in sponsoring Asian students and trainees for educational and training experiences in Australia. This boast was not without some justification and meshes well with recurring arguments that Australians punched above their weight in this type of cultural diplomacy. Furthermore, this story has been reinvigorated over the last ten years. In 2014, the government launched a 'New Colombo Plan', providing funding for reverse flows of students: Australian tertiary students funded to spend time in Asian and Pacific educational and other institutions as a means of building capacity for greater Australian–Asian connectedness.[24] An Australian historian writing about the Colombo

[23] David Lowe, 'Canberra's Colombo Plan: Public Images of Australia's Relations with Post-colonial South and Southeast Asia in the 1950s', *South Asia*, 25, 2 (2002), 183–204; Daniel Oakman, *Facing Asia: A History of the Colombo Plan* (Canberra: Australian National University Press, 2004).

[24] Details are available on the Australian Department of Foreign Affairs and Trade website: www.dfat.gov.au/people-to-people/new-colombo-plan (accessed 1 February 2023). And for connections between 'old' and 'new' Colombo Plans, see, David Lowe, 'Australia's

Plan therefore has a ready audience waiting to see it interpreted according to selective, student-focused activities and with a nationalist lens applied to Australia in world affairs.

Today the word 'development' raises instant concerns about who is doing what to whom under what economic assumptions, and how imbalances of power can easily be accentuated by external assistance rather than ameliorated. The concept of development also meant different things to those embracing it in the early 1950s, but there was a generally shared commitment to what Colombo Plan literature described as a 'the stupendous effort' being made by the peoples and governments of South and Southeast Asia 'to raise their standards of living and to break out of the vicious cycle of poverty'.[25] Other shared assumptions about development were its centrality to governments concerned with state-making and its giving shape to international and regional orders. The Colombo Plan featured capital and technical assistance. As Singh observed, the capital aid was logically divided into two categories: governmental aid that was channelled through another organization such as the World Bank, Export–Import Bank (of the United States and then Japan) or the US Development Loan Fund; and capital assistance provided directly by donor members, initially Canada, Australia, New Zealand, India (both donor and recipient) and Britain. The British liked to include their repayments of sterling debts owed to India, Pakistan and Ceylon with other instances of capital aid provided, but they knew that some distinction was diplomatically necessary.[26]

The lack of formality and the acceptable variations in how achievements were reported were important features of the Colombo Plan. This book focuses on the long 1950s, a period stretching from the start of the decade, 1950, when the Colombo Plan took shape, to 1962, the year marking the start of systematic statistical reporting on foreign aid by the Development Assistance Committee of the newly formed Organisation for Economic Co-operation and Development (OECD). Taken in conjunction with the formation of specialized aid agencies in countries such as Canada (1960), the United States (1961) and Japan (1961), this marked a new professionalization and bureaucratic embedding of foreign

Colombo Plans, Old and New: International Students as Foreign Relations', *International Journal of Cultural Policy*, 21, 4 (2015), 448–62.

[25] Colombo Plan Bureau, *The Colombo Plan Story: Ten Years of Progress, 1951–1961* (Colombo: Colombo Plan Bureau, 1961), p. 3.

[26] Singh, *The Politics of Economic Cooperation in Asia*, pp. 170–72.

aid as a function of the modern state. Prior to that time, those in government departments such as External Affairs reporting on development efforts enjoyed considerable licence. They were able to move between statistics, case studies and mobilizing narratives of growth more easily. Importantly, too, it would be the middle of the 1960s before the first detailed, non-socialist critiques of development projects in Asia emerged.[27] The Colombo Plan in the long 1950s therefore escaped both the rigours of standardized, professional reporting and the fall-out from sustained, scholarly critique.

Two further aspects of this period attest to its distinctiveness. The first was the enduring significance of the Commonwealth. As Diem reminded, the Colombo Plan began as a Commonwealth venture in 1950 but quickly added non-Commonwealth members to its ranks including the United States and Japan, as donors, and the Philippines, Burma, Thailand, Vietnam and Indonesia as regional members. The Commonwealth was regarded by most members as a loose-fitting source of strength, part-model and partly entwined with how the Colombo Plan grew and functioned. Ideas informing how an expanded Commonwealth should situate itself in international affairs, especially ideas developed by new Asian members, have attracted little historical attention to date.[28] The Commonwealth's potency and exemplary status diminished from the early 1960s in the wake of both external forces and internal divisions, especially the racial issue that led to South Africa's withdrawal in 1961.

Secondly, the long 1950s was the period of maximum exploratory work in diplomacy in and about Asia when Asia seemed to command world attention. The period includes the famous Asian-African Conference of 1955 held in Bandung, but the longer timeframe also enables a productive shift away from Bandung's gravitational pull. The Colombo Plan Consultative Committee's recurring annual meetings of between three and four weeks were attended by eighteen members by the mid-1950s and by twenty-three members in the early 1960s. For the historian, they offer rich pickings beyond the one-off gathering of twenty-nine African and Asian nations for one week in 1955 in Bandung (which did not reconvene at government level until 1961).

27 This is excepting novels by Graham Greene, *The Quiet American* (London: William Heinemann, 1955); and William Lederer and Eugene Burdick, *The Ugly American* (New York: W. W. Norton, 1958).

28 An exception is Paul Tonks and Laavanyan Michael Ratnapalan, 'Ideologies of the New Commonwealth', *The International History Review*, 43, 4 (2021), 887–905.

Although convention at Consultative Committee meetings meant no grand announcements and no resolutions, or rather *because* they involved no grand announcements and resolutions, they became regular safe spaces for negotiating between Cold War divisions and new priorities, including those featured at Bandung. At the Committee's 1957 session, as with previous ones, the air was thick with references to friendship, national growth as maturation and a broader conceptualization of economic development that embraced values and dignity.[29] Among the other ministerial opening remarks, Australia's External Affairs Minister R. G. Casey reflected that one under-appreciated benefit of the Colombo Plan's operation was the holding of its annual conference in a different country each year. He added that between the first meetings in 1950–51 to this one in 1957, the number of ministers and officials attending had grown, in line with new memberships, from around 50 to around 150. This, he said, 'gives us all opportunities to meet the leading personalities in Governments and see the people that they represent in their own particular home and environment'.[30] For the historian, these annual conferences therefore invite a narrative that does not settle for too long on the view from any one of the members of the Colombo Plan. This is partial compensation for a historian facing huge archival unevenness among members of the plan and for my linguistic limitations as an English speaker.

As Diem pointed out, the Colombo Plan was flexible and its meetings laboratory-like in their enabling learning. It had no coordinating secretariat but relied on these annual meetings of the Colombo Plan's Consultative Committee for the work of reporting on current projects and embarking on new ones. Otherwise, a very modest bureaucracy around technical assistance grew, in fits and starts, in Colombo. From 1951, there was a Colombo Plan Council overseeing the technical assistance side of the Colombo Plan (i.e. scholarships for training and the provision of experts) and supported by a Bureau. In 1953, a small Information Unit was created, also in Colombo; and from 1957, these two were merged into an enhanced version of the Bureau that enabled the ramping up of information activity. If the Colombo Plan had been a 'plan' with only a small 'p' in the early 1950s, its enterprising information

[29] See comments by Shri B. R. Bhagat, Deputy Minister of Finance, India, and Hon. U. Raschid, Minister for Mines, Burma, 21 October 1957, RG 25 vol. 7360 11038-5-c-40 Pt 2 FP2, LAC.

[30] Comments by R. G. Casey, 21 October 1957, ibid.

bureaucrats then got to work on making it more of a capital 'P', elevating their claims for the collective aid efforts.

Those interested in questions of new diplomacy, foreign aid and regionalism in decolonizing Asia gain much from analysis of the Colombo Plan's laboratory of development internationalism. In addition to the three components of development internationalism outlined, namely, state-making harnessed to growth, internationalism and experimental regionalism, each of the chapters in this book features common threads underpinning the 'laboratory' nature of the Colombo Plan. One of these threads is a focus on under-appreciated officials who networked effectively and whose careers flourished with this new international organization. The increased mobility provided by air travel, and the dependence of politicians on seasoned bureaucrats for advice in an expanded diplomatic sphere gave a cohort of officials influence which they happily seized. Profiling their work and influence builds on the work of Kott, Muschik and others who have argued for the significance of international organizations and the networks of professionals they fostered. It also helps to provide insights into another feature identified by David Engerman as crucial to understanding histories of development politics, namely development as practice, including the nitty-gritty of recipient–donor interactions.[31] After the initial focus on establishing the plan in Chapter 1, each of the following chapters includes profiles of selected enterprising officials whose careers intersected significantly with the Colombo Plan. Officials from India, Ceylon, Canada, Australia, Japan, New Zealand and Britain feature in detail, while a broader cast of internationalists and experts ranging from demographers to women hosts of Colombo Plan students appear throughout the book.

Another constant focus of the chapters is the annual meetings of the Colombo Plan's Consultative Committee. These were attended by officials, who reviewed progress towards development plans and discussed problems and opportunities, and by politicians from each member country. Sometimes dismissed as excessively long and benign in character, these annual meetings were both socializing for how they shaped diplomatic behaviour and enabling for the exchange of ideas and networking

[31] David C. Engerman, 'Development Politics and the Cold War', *Diplomatic History*, 41, 1 (2017), 1–19. Engerman also stresses the significance of development as networks of influential players who moved within and between state power and international organizations.

by officials.[32] I argue for the importance of place and practices, especially in relation to the meetings of the Consultative Committee at different locations throughout the region. Hosting a Consultative Committee meeting was, for nations older and new, important for international standing and maintaining a non-confrontational behaviour at meetings was essential to their success. Such meetings also illustrated how development worked as rhetoric, allowing ideas for new conceptualizations of international relations and idealistic visions of the future.

The high publicity around both meetings and certain development or training projects meant that some features of the Colombo Plan were bound to stand out more than others. Case studies ranging from grand hydroelectric and irrigation ventures such as the Gal Oya scheme in Ceylon to steel-making at Durgapur in India, and the training of Asian students in Australia and New Zealand were all highly publicized. As the following chapters show, these case studies revealed both ambitions and problems. Projects that involved building, industrial and agricultural works, or even students and trainees undergoing training and donor country experts in action, were located in particular geographies and in the hands of experts and organizations over which the state had limited control. Legacies of colonialism and new Cold War imperatives shaped some projects more than publicity and official reports suggested.

Finally, the above features connect to a sub-theme of cultural history developed throughout the book – the development information campaigns launched through multiple forms of media. In the hands of skilled publicists, both in Colombo and in member countries, the production of stories and images, in formats ranging from pamphlets and posters to film and photography, enabled the Colombo Plan to assume grand proportions – for a time. The efforts of the Bureau constituted something of an official history written even as the Plan unfolded.

This study is based partly on the use of a wide lens. It draws on the libraries and archives of Commonwealth countries, Australia, Britain, Canada, India and New Zealand, and other plan members, the United States and Japan, and official UN records. It benefits from my access to official Colombo Plan newsletters and booklets, the biggest collection of which is part of the Royal Commonwealth Society collection at the

32 Somewhat similarly, Alanna O'Malley has argued that socializing space was one of three dimensions of United Nations diplomacy: Alanna O'Malley, *Diplomacy of Decolonisation: America, Britain and the United Nations during the Congo Crisis 1960–64* (Manchester: Manchester University Press, 2018).

University of Cambridge Library where I was able to spend time in 2018–19 as a Smuts Fellow. The book is also informed by newspapers, photographs, films, booklets, postage stamps and creative writing. As my focus is on the context and production of development policy and diplomacy, generously defined, the main agents can be called 'elites', but these elites include mid-tier officials, journalists and advisers who have rarely figured in international histories of the 1950s.

Six chapters and a shorter, concluding Coda, organized broadly by chronology, follow this Introduction. Chapter 1 focuses on the meeting of Commonwealth foreign ministers in January 1950 in Colombo, which gave rise to the Colombo Plan. It outlines how ministers and their officials met at a time of hardening lines in the Cold War and questions over how postwar recovery plans might transition to development of a longer-term nature in Asia. The organizers, the British, saw the Colombo meeting as a great chance to tie together strategic and imperial interests, hoping also to trigger US spending for Asia in a manner akin to the Marshall Plan for postwar Europe. The Colombo conference, and a follow-up in Sydney in May 1950, disappointed them, although the fulsome US response to outbreak of the Korean War offset some of their concern. But the Colombo Plan was born, providing for six-year development plans and a separate arm of technical assistance, notwithstanding the big gap between the finance needed and what was promised. The Indian and Ceylonese governments, eager to seize diplomatic and regional leadership, conceived of themselves as providers of technical aid as well as recipients, and set about planning how the Colombo Plan might mesh with national and regional ideas taking shape.

Chapter 2 considers the growth of the Colombo Plan from a Commonwealth experiment of uncertain duration to a loosely knit organization including the United States, Indonesia, Burma, Nepal and the French Associated States of Laos, Cambodia and Vietnam by the end of 1953. The extent to which the Colombo Plan might take up the mantle of economic and political regionalism was uncertain. In covering three annual Consultative Committee meetings in Ceylon, Pakistan and India, 1951–53 and an extravagant Colombo Plan Exhibition, the chapter demonstrates the importance of diplomacy around place, format and hospitality for new nations establishing their legitimacy and authority. It recognizes the agency of Asian elites in searching for ways around the gate-keeping efforts of the United States and Britain in economic activities encouraged; and the importance of development entrepreneurs and civil servants, who played significant roles in the early years of the Colombo

Plan. Chapter 3 covers the middle years of the long 1950s, during which membership expanded further to include Japan, the Philippines and Thailand from 1954. By the mid-1950s, annual meetings of the Colombo Plan's Consultative Committee had settled into a pattern of alternating between a recipient and a donor nation host. All of these annual meetings grew bigger in numbers and in social and related activities. These years also saw the rise of organized provision of information about the Colombo Plan, including special attention to photographs (including an exhibition in Wellington) and journalist tours. A Colombo Plan Information Unit was established in Colombo, further enabling the Colombo Plan to be drawn in images, and to redraw maps of Asia according to Colombo Plan membership.

By the late 1950s, the Colombo Plan had assumed prominence in foreign aid bureaucracies of Commonwealth members. As Chapter 4 outlines, it did not gain public prominence in countries such as India, where locally produced Five-Year Plans were preeminent, but it continued to prove valuable on account of its regular diplomatic opportunities and its flexibility. There were reminders that at times the Cold War was a near-inescapable operating framework, but members of the Colombo Plan continued to find compelling reasons for their cooperation in ways that might circumvent the East–West tensions. Significantly, this was the case for both donor and recipient governments. These themes are revealed in the three Consultative Committee meetings covered in this chapter, held in Saigon (1957), Seattle (1958) and Djakarta (1959). They also informed distinctive development projects and training initiatives that were well-publicized in donor countries as means by which to engage with decolonizing Asia, finding problems in common while reinforcing distinct identities. Chapter 5 focuses on the early 1960s, including the celebrated tenth anniversary of the Colombo Plan in 1961, an occasion prompting mostly favourable evaluations by member governments. The three meetings of the Consultative Committee examined are those held in Tokyo (1960), Kuala Lumpur (1961) and Melbourne (1962). This chapter considers the significance of membership of the plan for Japan, in the lead up to, and after Tokyo's hosting the Consultative Committee. It shows that membership was an important element in Japan's re-emergence in international and regional societies, helping pave the way for initiatives in regional development and finance. The chapter also analyses some of the iconic projects held up as Colombo Plan success stories. In its capacity to foster ideas about regionalism, promote a new mode of diplomacy and chart development progress that was vaguely measurable, the Colombo Plan reached its upper limits in the 1960s, before beginning a slow decline in status. While annual meetings of the Consultative Committee continued, it was generally acknowledged that the Colombo Plan was being overtaken by new initiatives at the international and regional levels in development assistance for Asia. The chapter concludes with the story of the near demise of the plan in the 1980s and its rebirth in diluted form thereafter.

Chapter 6 considers how the Colombo Plan was projected as a unique experiment in international relations. It focuses on the extraordinary levels of publicity information produced and circulated, paying particular attention to the Information Unit (later part of the Bureau) in Colombo and the history of the Colombo Plan Newsletter/Magazine that it produced from the mid-1950s to the end of the 1960s. Something of a climax in information activity was reached in the early 1960s, in the aftermath of the Plan's tenth anniversary, when photographic exhibitions, celebratory postage stamps and documentary films circulated.

The Colombo Plan still exists in a much-reduced capacity, running regional training programs in niche areas. These activities do not reflect the grander ambitions behind the Colombo Plan in its first twelve years, nor its complicated but significant achievements. So, rather than a Conclusion, the book ends with a Coda. It considers the extent to which official information efforts, past and present, have led to the Colombo Plan becoming a 'site of memory' for some members. This is the case for Japan, Malaysia and Canada, and even more so for current and recent Australian and New Zealand governments keen to attract international students to their higher education institutions while gesturing to their past sponsorship of Asian students. The new Colombo Plan version II Secretariat in Colombo is also invested in the original version of the plan. Thus, the Colombo Plan is remembered selectively, in ways that have obscured other legacies that this book has uncovered and which are broadly consistent with development internationalism.

Such legacies include its significance for postwar diplomacy in Asia, including the reputation-making theatre of meetings and the consensus-based decision-making that has continued, in a new form, to underpin the new regional organization of ASEAN from 1967. The organization also gave rise to talented administrators who built effective networks. A new cast of actors facilitating crash courses in foreign aid provision and basic understanding between Asian and Western diplomats gained prominence through the workings of the Colombo Plan. In addition, the plan's legacies include cautious but continuing thoughts about regionalism in a globalizing world. The term 'Indo-Pacific', in circulation at the start of the 1950s, and sitting neatly with the Colombo Plan's membership, has now become a central means by which the international order in Asia and the Pacific is conceived. This book makes the case for remembering an unusually productive diplomatic environment of development internationalism in postwar Asia. It did not escape power politics or Cold War divisions, but it did run according to its own rhythm, and for those involved, this made it a worthy experiment into new possibilities in international relations.

1

A 'Miniature United Nations' at Colombo, 1950

When the foreign ministers of eight Commonwealth countries met in Colombo in January 1950, they were establishing a new forum: this was the first time foreign ministers of the Commonwealth had met separately. The agenda was, in broad terms, to examine the global state of international relations, the economic and security conditions of Asia, including the recently declared Communist victory in China and the yet-to-be-signed peace treaty with Japan, and to continue financial discussions relating to the sterling area. This last topic was one of the thorniest. During the war, the sterling area had provided for the pooling of the Commonwealth's hard currency, chiefly dollars, in Britain while the British offered credits for them in sterling to the contributing countries. Canada, a dollar-area country, was an exception. The system enabled Britain to make huge war-need purchases in dollars but at the expense of an enormous sterling debt after the war. At the same time, dollars were overtaking sterling as the most essential trading currency. While sterling had been made non-convertible into American dollars during the war, it was a condition of the large US postwar loan to Britain that sterling become convertible. Around £2.5 billion was owed to sterling-area countries; and countries such as India and Pakistan were especially keen to draw down some of their owed sterling to commence ambitious development plans and offset trade deficits. This, however, risked Britain's own balance of payments, as was spectacularly revealed in July 1947 when the run on the British pound was such that convertibility had to be suspended. Just what Indian and Pakistan governments might be able to expect by way of access to their huge sterling balances was a question that loomed large.

Given that Australian, Canadian, Ceylonese, Indian, New Zealand, Pakistan and South African governments all sent representatives to Colombo, it was not surprising that sterling and other weighty issues also exposed differing views among those gathered. How this unfolded is explored in this chapter, as is the process by which, after two further meetings in Sydney (May 1950) and London (September–October 1950), something called 'The Colombo Plan for Co-operative Economic Development in South and Southeast Asia' took shape. What follows outlines how the mix of competing ideas and aims making up the Colombo Plan featured both common objectives and different expectations that threatened either to overwhelm or underwhelm those involved.

In January 1950, that first meeting of Commonwealth foreign ministers in Colombo pivoted on the mid-point of the twentieth century. For those involved, it also marked what seemed to be a more multifaceted sense of transition: from colony to independent members of the Commonwealth in the case of India, Ceylon and Pakistan; from a European–North American pattern of diplomacy to one that embraced Asia and other parts of the decolonizing world; from forms of aid generated by pre-war colonial welfare and then postwar reconstruction in Europe, to something that might better apply to circumstances in Asia; and from a Cold War taking shape in Europe to a struggle that might be developing more global characteristics.

The Cold War dimensions of the build up to the foreign ministers' conference in Colombo were a powerful influence on the British approach and have received the greatest historical attention.[1] In 1948, the British grew alarmed at spikes in communist activities and successes in several locations in South and Southeast Asia. They also noted that from 1947 the region attracted the interest of the Cominform, Moscow's new organization attempting to coordinate overseas communist groups. From the start of 1949, it looked increasingly likely that Mao Zedong's communists would triumph in China over the Nationalist forces led by Chiang Kai-Shek. Of most immediate concern to the British was the new level of Malayan Communist Party violence directed at rubber planters and British administrators. This led London to respond with martial law and the declaration of the so-called 'Malayan Emergency' in 1948, which enabled a strong military response to what could be

[1] See especially, Nicholas Tarling, 'The United Kingdom and the Origins of the Colombo Plan', *The Journal of Commonwealth & Comparative Politics*, 24, 1 (1986), 3–34; Remme, *Britain and Regional Cooperation in South-East Asia*.

described as local, militant communism. Importantly, it also maintained rubber production, an essential, dollar-earning component of Britain's postwar recovery, and it buttressed the privileged place of Malays provided in the Constitution of the Federation of Malaya (1 February 1948) at the expense of Chinese and Indian populations.[2]

Throughout 1949, British diplomats in Asia and their colleagues in London stressed the urgency of taking the lead in political and economic policy aimed at shoring up South and Southeast Asia against further communist successes. With the French struggling to govern Indo-China and the Dutch attracting international criticism for their desperate military actions in Indonesia, Whitehall was convinced that they were the only enlightened colonizers up to such a task. The French and Dutch had been 'slower to appreciate the inevitable march of events in Asia'. 'South-East Asia', according to a Foreign Office assessment endorsed by Cabinet, was 'an area in which the United Kingdom is already vitally involved and where her influence can best be brought to bear both directly and through the Commonwealth connexions.'[3] The British had already been 'the pioneer of regional co-operation' by establishing a Special Commissioner for the UK in South-East Asia in Singapore in 1946, which was absorbed by the Commissioner-General for the UK in South-East Asia in 1948, headed by former politician, Malcolm MacDonald.[4] In March 1949, MacDonald was imploring his colleagues in London to understand that it was 'no exaggeration to say that this [Southeast Asia] region has assumed a vast importance in the world-wide struggle between the Democratic and the Communist causes, quite out of proportion to its industrial and political development'; and that any constructive policy would only be effective if 'the problem of South East Asia is considered as a whole and collectively by all those concerned.'[5]

While acknowledging huge differences on the ground between Europe and Asia, the actions they considered reflected wartime initiatives and

[2] See Karl Hack, *The Malayan Emergency: Revolution and Counterinsurgency at the End of Empire* (Milton Keynes: Open University, 2022); Souchou Yao, *The Malayan Emergency: A Small, Distant War* (Copenhagen: Nordic Institute of Asian Studies Press, 2016); Amrita Mahli, 'Race, Space and the Malayan Emergency: Expelling Malaya Muslim Communism and Reconstituting Malaya's Racial State, 1945–1954', *Itinerario*, 445, 3 (2021), 435–59.

[3] P.U.S.C. (53) 'Regional Co-operation in South-East Asia and the Far East', 20 August 1949, FO 371/76030, TNA.

[4] Ibid.

[5] Malcolm MacDonald (Singapore) to Ernest Bevin, Foreign Secretary, Despatch no. 16, 23 March 1949, FO 371/76033, TNA.

recent postwar successes in Europe. The Second World War provided recent lessons on what had worked (and not worked) in juggling the gathering and transportation of essential resources while keeping populations fed. In addition to conceiving of Southeast Asia as a strategic region, one of the more heralded British-Allied stories was the Middle East Supply Centre, which, during the war had balanced the tasks of feeding populations while harnessing strategic materials so effectively that, for a time, it was seen as a form of regional coordination that might persist into the postwar era. An Eastern Group Supply Council, headquartered in New Delhi, had similarly coordinated the supply of war materials east of Suez. Neither body endured beyond the war. Nevertheless, this model of emergency-led regional cooperation was in the minds of those tasked with putting flesh on the bones of ideas about coordinating aid and development in a strategic context.[6] What might be needed in Asia was therefore subject to different interpretations of what was happening there and ideas about the best models to adapt or build for regional economic development and cooperation. Further, while the British set the agenda for the meeting of Commonwealth foreign ministers in Colombo, they would not be the only ones who brought ideas about the best models to use for regional economic development and cooperation.

IDEAS AND ORGANIZATION FOR ASIA IN POSTWAR DIPLOMACY

In the years following the end of the Second World War, conferences in Asia addressing both regional and global issues gained new international profile. This reflected the rest of the world's attention turning towards Asia more than it did because of novelty in major meetings within Asian countries, where non-government level conferences had already been hosted successfully in recent years. It also reflected new expectations attached to so-called 'summit diplomacy' arising from the leaders'

[6] See Martin W. Wilmington, *The Middle East Supply Centre* (New York: State University of New York Press, 1971 [1961]). The supply councils' mode of operating by continuous session was the model for the Colombo Plan Bureau initially suggested by New Zealand and Australian governments. An adapted version of this eventually prevailed – meetings were far more frequent (monthly) than the 'once or twice a year' approach favoured by the British: David M. Johnson, Canadian High Commissioner, Karachi, to Secretary of State for External Affairs, 11 August 1950, RG 25 vol. 6598 11038-D-40 part 1, LAC.

meetings during the war.[7] There was too an eagerly sought aspect of international recognition attached to the successful hosting of an international conference featuring new and old nation-states. This applied to both before and after the formal transfers of power for those states gaining independence, and it also applied to other countries in the region such as Australia and New Zealand experiencing less of a colonial transfer of power than a sense of new regional agency in a more interconnected world. Conference diplomacy in postwar Asia continues to attract scholarly attention but has been weighted less towards recurring meetings than high-profile gatherings such as the Asian Relations Conference in New Delhi in 1947, another New Delhi Conference on Indonesia in 1949, the Colombo meeting of 1950 and especially the Bandung Conference of 1955.

The Bandung Conference logically attracts special attention for its breadth and ambitions: its joining of African and Asian ambitions, overt rejection of Cold War polarity, solidarity in the ongoing struggle against imperialism and heralding what would become the non-aligned movement and the language of the 'third world'. International relations scholar Amitav Acharya has drawn a line between Bandung and the trajectory and style of Asian regionalism as it took greater shape in the Association of Southeast Asian Nations (ASEAN) formed in 1967. He suggests, 'the informal, interpersonal and consensus-driven nature of the interactions among the top leaders at Bandung might have presaged the "ASEAN Way" – the non-coercive and non-legalistic modes of interactions that marked the formative years of ASEAN'.[8] Tentatively put, as Acharya does, this conclusion is hard to argue with. But Bandung's gravitational pull, based on cultivated remembering as well as celebrated outcomes, risks consigning other Asian conference activity to the status of precursor or marginal.[9]

[7] See David Reynolds, *Summits: Six Meetings that Shaped the Twentieth Century* (New York: Basic Books, 2007).

[8] Acharya, 'Studying the Banding Conference from a Global IR Perspective'.

[9] For examples of Bandung's enduring attraction for historians, including anniversary reflections, see Kweku Ampiah, *The Political and Moral Imperatives of the Banding Conference of 1955: The Reactions of the US, UK and Japan* (Folkstone, UK: Global Oriental, 2007); See Seng Tan and Amativ Acharya (eds.), *Bandung Revisited: The Legacy of the 1955 Asian-African Conference for International Order* (Singapore: National University of Singapore Press, 2009); Derek McDougall and Antonia Finnane (eds.), *Bandung 1955: Little Histories* (Melbourne: Monash University Press, 2010); Naoko Shimazu, 'Diplomacy as Theatre: Staging the Bandung Conference of 1955', *Modern Asian Studies*, 48, 1 (2014), 225–52.

Research on the less-studied Asian Relations Conference held in New Delhi in March–April 1947 reveals the processes of exchange and circulation of ideas, including articulations of difference and commonality, in large meetings of this kind. As twenty-eight participating countries (plus six other contingents) took up Prime Minister-in-waiting Jawaharlal Nehru's invitation to advance Asian relations, the sense of the moment was driven by scale as well as international circumstances. Earlier articulations of pan-Asian federation were also in play, including Nehru's thoughts on the role of Asia in 'one-worldism', on Asia being at the centre of an evolving world federation.[10] He welcomed delegates with a sketch of world history in which a thriving and fruitfully connected Asia and Africa had fallen 'static' as Asia 'became just a field for the rival imperialisms of Europe, and Europe became the centre of history and progress in human affairs'. He continued, 'A change is coming over the scene now and Asia is again finding herself. We live in a tremendous age of transition and already the next stage takes shape when Asia takes her rightful place with the other continents.'[11] Nehru's historical sketching, including his briefest of glances at the colonial era, provided something of a template not only for pan-Asian gestures, but also for information pamphlets and other materials generated by the Colombo Plan in the 1950s.

As an exercise in showcasing the Indian leadership, the Asian Relations Conference was a spectacular success. Possibly 10,000 gathered for the opening session on 23 March, and the 193 delegates spent the next nine days in round table and plenary sessions grouped under seven main headings: national movements for freedom; racial problems and inter-Asian migration; transition from colonial to national economy; agricultural reconstruction; industrial development; labour problems and social services' cultural problems; and the status of women and women's movements.[12] Under the free-flowing discussions on these themes lay an unresolved tension between a form of internationalism that transcended the

[10] There is a significant literature on Indian imaginings of its role in a future, decolonized Asia. See, for example, Ali Raza, Franziska Roy, and Benjamin Zachariah (eds.), *The Internationalist Moment: South Asia, Worlds and Worldviews, 1917–1939* (New Delhi: Sage India, 2014); Manu Goswami, 'Imaginary Futures and Colonial Internationalisms', *American Historical Review*, 117, 5 (2012), 1461–85; and Sugata Bose and Kris Manjapra (eds.), *Cosmopolitan Thought Zones: South Asia and the Global Circulation of Ideas* (Houndmills: Palgrave Macmillan), 2010.

[11] *Asian Relations*, being *Report of the Proceedings and Documentation of the First Asian Relations Conference, New Delhi, March–April 1947* (New Delhi: Asian Relations Organization, 1948), p. 21.

[12] The statistics are those from the official report/book produced: *Asian Relations*, p. 1.

state-based postcolonial 'moments' of independence, and a form that assumed state sovereignty as its basis. The conference took place some five months before the British transfer of power and creation of independent India and Pakistan. Both pre-independence and sovereign state versions were supported robustly, if vaguely at the Asian Relations Conference.[13] Indeed, in avoiding difficult political questions and choices, there was much that was unresolved. Taking its cue from the Institute of Pacific Relations' interwar conferences promoting forms of cooperation among nations of the Pacific rim, the conference deliberately avoided resolutions. As a grand concept filled with constructive dialogue that looked to future meetings, however, Nehru hailed it as a success. Significantly, he also saw its benefits domestically, writing that, 'The conference has left an abiding impression in India and made large numbers of people Asia conscious. It has broadened their horizons and made them feel that India is rapidly developing into a country which influences Asian and world politics.'[14]

Following the Asian Relations Conference of 1947, Nehru and his officials in New Delhi continued to sketch ideas for a growing connection between Asian diplomatic activity and the progress of decolonization. In January 1949, Nehru hosted representatives from fifteen Asian countries to discuss the situation in Indonesia, where the Dutch had recently launched their 'Second Police Action', a brutal military offensive to defeat Indonesian Republicans seeking to throw off Dutch colonial rule. Delegates were critical of enduring forms of Western colonialism in general as well as calling on the Dutch to hold elections in Indonesia in October 1949 and transfer sovereignty to the United States of Indonesia by 1 January 1950. These recommendations were fed into the UN Security Council resolution then being drafted by Indian, Australian and Indonesian Republic representatives, and helped force the Dutch to comply with the UN resolution, transferring sovereignty on 29 December 1949. Nehru also took the opportunity to encourage further consideration of machinery that might enable future policy coordination among those represented.[15]

[13] See Vineet Thakur, 'An Asian Drama: The Asian Relations Conference, 1947', *International History Review*, 41, 3 (2019), 673–95.

[14] Nehru to K. P. S. Menon, quoted in ibid, p. 16.

[15] UK High Commission in India to CRO, no. 220, 5 February 1949, F2191, FO 371/76031, TNA; A. K. George, 'Asian Regionalism and India's Early Initiatives: The Two Asian Conferences', *India Quarterly: A Journal of International Affairs*, 27, 3 (1971), 238–43.

In the new United Nations, however, the great powers set limits to early ventures in regional planning for postwar Asia. As the United Nations prepared for research and administrative organization to address the urgent problems of postwar Europe in 1946, Asian representatives led by Chinese (Guomindang) P. C. Chang successfully campaigned for something similar to address the needs of Asia. They were conscious of the imminent shutting down of the UN Relief and Rehabilitation Agency (UNRRA), which had been funded overwhelmingly by the British and Americans. UNRRA was, as historian David Ekbladh notes, recognized as a hugely successful aid story, enabling the rapid recovery of Europe through industrial reconstruction and attention to agriculture and public health. From an American perspective in particular, it tutored those continuing to work in international development and drove home the importance of technical assistance in any programmatic planning for societies.[16] The proposed UN Economic Commission for Europe (ECE), a commission reporting to the UN Economic and Social Council (ECOSOC), took up from where UNRRA left off and then connected with the European Recovery Program administering Marshall Plan efforts. Neither the British nor Americans, however, were keen to see an Asian equivalent of the ECE. As something of a compromise, the Economic Commission for Asia and the Far East (ECAFE) was created, ostensibly as a research organization. ECAFE's charter was research, investigative, evaluative and advisory in relation to problems and development within the region, but its main objective always made possible bolder and regionalist activities: 'Initiate and participate in measures for facilitating concerted action for the economic reconstruction and development of Asia and the Far East, for raising the level of economic activity in Asia and the Far East and for maintaining and strengthening the economic relations of these areas both among themselves and with other countries of the world.'[17] From 1947, ECAFE produced an annual regional *Economic Survey*, and from 1950 also a quarterly *Economic Bulletin for Asia and the Far East*. In their early years, both publications struggled to garner the kind of comparable and reliable data needed for robust surveys about food, fertilizer, energy etc., but they quickly grew stronger in quality and reliability.

[16] David Ekbladh, *The Great American Mission: Modernisation and the Construction of an American World Order* (Princeton, NJ: Princeton University Press, 2010), pp. 87–88.

[17] UN Economic and Social Council Resolution 37 (IV), 28 March 1947, Document E/405, 4th Session, 1947, UN Digital Library, https://digitallibrary.un.org/record/211438?ln=en (accessed 5 July 2019).

FIGURE 1.1 Palamadai S. Lokanathan.
Source: UN Economic and Social Commission for Asia and the Pacific: www.unescap.org/former-executive-secretary/lokanathan

Conscious of European reconstruction grabbing most attention and resources, Chang and Indian delegates persisted in trying to make ECAFE more like a Marshall Plan for Asia.[18] ECAFE's Executive Secretary, Indian economist Palamadai S. Lokanathan (pictured Figure 1.1), proved influential in both ECAFE and Colombo Plan work, and his work is discussed further in Chapter 3. He shared Chang's ambitions for a more expansive ECAFE, but great power obstruction and developments within the UN stymied this. Particularly circumscribing were ECOSOC's reluctance to give Lokanathan anything resembling control over resources, and the creation of a new UN department keen to garner its own power, the Technical Assistance Administration (1950).[19]

[18] David Wightman, *Toward Economic Cooperation in Asia: The United Nations Economic Commission for Asia and the Far East* (New Haven, CT: Yale University Press, 1963), pp. 12–20.

[19] Ibid, pp. 40–49.

Undeterred, Chang, Lokanathan and others set out to make ECAFE an imaginative diplomatic and research forum that would become too important to marginalize. What constituted 'Asia and the Far East' for ECAFE was work in constant progress. The original ten members meeting in Shanghai in March 1947 were an incomplete list of those facing the current and prospective consequences of regional decolonization: Australia, (Nationalist) China, France, India, the Netherlands, the Philippines, the Soviet Union, Thailand, the United Kingdom and the United States. By September 1950, Burma, Indonesia, New Zealand and Pakistan had also joined.

Early ECAFE meetings facilitated familiar colonial-nationalist jousting and Cold War posturing. They threw together new groups of diplomats and planners in novel meeting spaces. For example, the Australians joined the new Asia-focused conference circuit in hosting an early meeting. The fourth session of ECAFE was held at Lapstone, in the Blue Mountains near Sydney, from 29 November to 11 December 1948. Like other early meetings of ECAFE, this one was a mixture of research and liaison work plus efforts to add definition and goals. Many questions hung over ECAFE's future, including where its permanent headquarters might be and whether it would survive beyond its initial period of commission. ECAFE was less shaped by the work of antecedent organizations than its sibling, the ECE. At Lapstone, Chinese and Indian delegates invited the Americans to produce something akin to a Marshall Plan for Asia (envisaging a five-year reconstruction plan costing some $13.6 billion)[20] but were rebuffed by the Americans. Asian nations, they said, would have to rely on private investment and government loans, and would be unwise to develop grandiose plans for industrialization when they should be focusing on addressing living standards.[21] Although it did not stop regional members of ECAFE from continuing to press for capital assistance, this meant defining ECAFE by its limitations and a deliberate hosing down of Asian hopes. In the words of one commentator, 'They wanted help and got sermons.'[22] The conference was also a mixed blessing for its Australian hosts, who might have been stung by some of the press reports that highlighted the lack of sufficient centralized accommodation for the 120 guests. In the absence of one or two large hotels capable of taking this

[20] Dawn editorial, 2 March 1951, in J. R. Hunt (CRO) to Francis (FO), US11037/1, FO 371/95817, TNA.
[21] *Canberra Times*, 6 December 1948, p. 2.
[22] Wightman, *Toward Economic Cooperation in Asia*, p. 44.

number, delegates were farmed out to multiple smaller hotels throughout the Blue Mountains, some staying as far as 65 kilometres from the Lapstone Hotel where proceedings were held.[23]

Yet, ECAFE was wired into an Asia in transition and was the carrier of Indian hopes for a burgeoning regional consciousness. In the wake of the next ECAFE session, in Bangkok, March–April 1949, the Indian Ministry of External Affairs' assessment of the commission was that it represented a light-touch 'system of regional cooperation in Asia'. Indian representative B. N. Adarkar wrote that 'every successive session of this body serves to strengthen and consolidate the system'.[24] He and other Indian officials were happy to be seen as leaders in this kind of regionalism, and keen to promote the emergence of new diplomatic platforms enabling more Asian members to find their international voices. What was needed was a form of leadership that also preserved the distinctiveness of India's Five-Year Planning, and guarded against possible regional over-demand for Indian training and its emerging industrial resources.[25] Over the next year, Indian diplomats maintained this position of welcoming a new organization that would enable regional members to become more active, diplomatically, while preserving a distinctive standing for India, including a capacity to seek development assistance separately if necessary.[26]

Thus, while ECAFE later gained a reputation for being a relatively innocuous research-focused talking shop, in its early years it proved an important testing ground for the diplomats of newly independent Asian nations accumulating diplomatic experience and laying ground for tentative forms of regional cooperation. Much was unsettled about ECAFE initially, including the relative weight it gave to tasks of gathering and reporting data, detailed analysis of the data, coordinating with other UN bodies and embarking on economic planning. Its headquarters moved from Shanghai at the end of 1948 to Singapore, and then to Bangkok where it remained. Nor was it guaranteed to survive past 1951. This was the year specified by ECOSOC for its review, to determine whether the new organization enjoyed sufficient support for its continuation.

[23] *Argus*, 7 December 1948, p. 2; *Sydney Morning Herald*, 2 December 1948, p. 2.

[24] Report of Indian Delegation to ECAFE Meeting of Whole, Bangkok, 28 March–5 April 1949, by B. N. Adarkar, DEA, 1(20)-UN-1/49, National Archives of India, New Delhi.

[25] Ibid.

[26] UK High Commissioner to India to Commonwealth Relations Office IV Department, no. 306, 15 May 1950, relaying instructions for Indian delegation to Sydney meeting of Consultative Committee, DO 35/2923, TNA.

Running partly parallel and partly intertwined with these events were several tests for the functioning of the postwar Commonwealth. As is well-told elsewhere, the last three years of the 1940s were marked by an extraordinary level of diplomatic and constitutional work in London, and with members of the Commonwealth, that would enable the continued vitality of the Commonwealth (minus the 'British' appellation) while accommodating Indian/Pakistan independence, Ceylon's independence and then Indian republican status.[27] At the same time, all members tested out ideas about the levels of agency that might best transition the Commonwealth into the circumstances of the postwar world. At successive conferences British officials cautiously encouraged the idea of devolved responsibility in the new Commonwealth, with regional members assuming new leadership for Commonwealth affairs according to geography. As was evident in the Asian Relations Conference, the Indians stretched their diplomatic muscles even before formal independence. In the latter part of the Second World War, the Australians had also agitated for greater agency and revised lines of communication between Commonwealth capitals and London, drawing on high commissioners in a broader range of roles.[28] While part-observing and part-participating in the two Asian conferences organized by Nehru,[29] the Australians took the lead in Commonwealth regional defence planning through the secret ANZAM Agreement, covering the area defined by its full title, the Australia–New Zealand–Malaya arrangement, signed at the beginning of 1949. But there was growing unease in London at Indian, and to a lesser extent, Australian efforts to lead regional policy development in the late 1940s. The dominions, old and new, could not be counted on to strike that special balance needed between careful calibration of Britain's sterling reserves, on the one hand, and dexterous management of other allies, on the other. Wielding these

[27] Recent work by Harshan Kumarasingham explores this in detail. See his, *A Political Legacy of the British Empire: Power and the Parliamentary System in Post-colonial India and Sri Lanka* (London: I. B. Tauris, 2013); and 'The "Tropical Dominions": The Appeal of Dominion Status in the Decolonisation of India, Pakistan and Ceylon', *Transactions of the Royal Historical Society*, 23, 6th series (2013), 223–45.

[28] See David Lowe, 'From War to Postwar: Ted Williams in Canberra, 1946–52', in Christopher Baxter and Andrew Stewart (eds.), *Diplomats at War: British and Commonwealth Diplomacy in Wartime* (Leiden: Martinus Nijhoff, 2008), pp. 275–93.

[29] See Julie Suares, 'Engaging with Asia: The Chifley Government and the New Delhi Conferences of 1947 and 1949', *Australian Journal of Politics and History*, 57, 4 (2011), 495–510.

skills would enable the British to resume international leadership while others bore more of their economic burden.

At the meeting of Commonwealth Prime Ministers in London in 1948, all members welcomed the prospect of future meetings on subjects such as foreign and economic policy at the ministerial level.[30] Following a special prime ministers' meeting in April 1949, which adjusted the relationship to the Crown to provide for Indian republicanism, Commonwealth Finance Ministers met in London in July to work on problems facing the sterling area. Access to US dollars for India, and from August 1947 for Pakistan, had become the subject of tense annual negotiations. By 1950 the sterling holdings for India, Pakistan and Ceylon had been reduced from £1,218 million in 1947 to £790 million, but they were still by far the highest in the sterling area.[31] What the British needed from the meeting of Commonwealth Foreign Ministers in Colombo was a connection of their financial crisis to a broader economic and security plan for South Asia. They sought to restrict drawings on sterling, by India and Pakistan US dollars instead of Commonwealth reserves should meet South Asian needs and the needs of others in the sterling area. They wanted trade between the West and Asia to resume its promising pre-war momentum. Decolonization should be managed such that the financial importance of former colonies for European metropoles was not greatly disturbed by declarations of independence, and Britain's international solvency might be preserved. 'It was after all', wrote a Whitehall officer more than two years after the Colombo meeting at the beginning of 1950, 'the three cornered trade with the [South and Southeast Asia] Colombo Plan area which enabled Europe to balance its dollar account with the U.S.A. before the war.'[32]

The British regional thinking in Singapore anticipated the Colombo conference with similarly high expectations. Under Malcolm MacDonald's leadership as Commissioner-General in South-East Asia, Singapore was the focal point for British colonial rule there, and Malaya, North Borneo and Sarawak. MacDonald also assumed responsibility for pro-consul-like policy recommendations for the region. From the late 1940s through mid-1950s, MacDonald's influence in London sparked and spluttered, his lengthy recommendations undermined

30 These events are well-covered in R. J. Moore, *Making the New Commonwealth* (Oxford: Oxford University Press, 1987).

31 Catherine R. Schenk, *Britain and the Sterling Area: From Devaluation to Convertibility in the 1950s* (Abingdon: Routledge, 1994), p. 19.

32 S. J. G. Fingland, (CRO) Draft of interdepartmental memo, 'Publicity for the Colombo Plan', 29 July 1952, DO 35/5754, TNA.

somewhat by his love of cocktail diplomacy conducted in a sultan's palace and his sexual adventures, captured in photographs and well-circulated rumours.[33] But MacDonald's voice was important in the two years leading up to the meeting in Colombo. He was both insistent on the severity of the threat from communism and on the need to respond with policy that was regional rather than country-specific. While always adding that Asia was different, he still pushed for 'Asian equivalents of the Marshall Plan and the Atlantic Pact'.[34] His colleagues in the Foreign Office thought similarly, arguing for a neo-colonial British leadership in the region, based on the assumption that only Britain had the ability to 'knit the South East Asia region together'.[35] They were also cautiously enthusiastic about the subject of regionalism. A meeting convened in Nanking by the British Ambassador to China, Sir Ralph Stevenson, in March 1949 resulted in a memorandum reflecting the views of Stevenson and his American, Indian and Australian diplomatic counterparts. The group spoke of a 'confederation of South East Asia with a planned and integrated economy' as 'the ultimate solution' to the challenges posed economically and by communism.[36]

Thus, the British saw the meeting of foreign ministers at Colombo as the chance to tie together several formidable policy challenges: to regain and retain leadership in foreign, economic and strategic policy planning for the South–Southeast region; to ensure discipline in drawings on the sterling balances in order to avoid another devaluation debacle; to encourage economic development and technical training especially in ways that increased dollar-earning exports; to lay bare the gap that lay between the region's development needs and the capacity of the Commonwealth to assist in a manner that would encourage the US government to join in the generous provision of capital for development; and to then to shape the delivery of the anticipated US aid in ways that maintained sterling-area discipline and moderated the demands of countries such as the South Asian dominions on London. It was an ambitious set of goals that accompanied the British to Colombo, even allowing for

[33] For further details described by his biographer, see Clyde Sanger, *Malcolm MacDonald: Bringing an End to Empire* (Montreal: McGill-Queen's University Press, 1995); and the detail of MacDonald's work in Singapore is well-captured in Remme, *Britain and Regional Cooperation in South East Asia*.

[34] Malcolm MacDonald (Singapore) to Ernest Bevin, Foreign Secretary, Despatch no. 16, 23 March 1949, FO 371/76033, TNA.

[35] Esler Dening to Syers (CRO), 4 April 1949, F219/1072/61, FO 371/76031, TNA.

[36] Sir R. Stevenson to Esler Dening, 4 March 1949, F3790/1015/10, FO 371/75745, TNA.

the very considerable unknowns about what the Americans would do and perhaps an understandable sense of optimism that they might react with dollars in the wake of the declaration of Mao Zedong's Chinese People's Republic.

Not surprisingly, the level of ambition bordering on hubris has fascinated historians drawing primarily on British archival sources.[37] When only some of the British revivalist goals were partially met, and none were met spectacularly, the British-led story necessarily sags. What happened after the Colombo meeting became, according to historians who cleave to the view from Whitehall, an anti-climax as the British stitching of finance, strategy, leadership, development plans and American participation/collaboration unravelled, slowly rather than spectacularly. But the demise of overblown British expectations was also the start of a new experiment in development internationalism, characterized by hopes for new forums and forms of international relations, state-making harnessed to plans for economic growth and exploratory forms of regionalism. Loosening the hold that the British record has had, and reading sometimes against the grain of British documents, reveals much more than a meeting in Colombo that failed to meet London's policy aims.

COLOMBO, JANUARY 1950

As well as the first conference of Commonwealth Foreign Ministers, the Colombo meeting was the first meeting of the new Commonwealth in Asia and therefore attracted considerable media attention. Among those who showed the greatest enthusiasm for the possibilities that might flow from the meeting were, not surprisingly, the Ceylonese hosts. The meeting

[37] Tilman Remme set out to write a history of the Colombo Plan but ended up writing only about the journey towards Colombo, January 1950, as this sense of climactic build up was surely the biggest story. Through a very British lens, his inclinations and the writing of some others make sense: Remme, *Britain and Regional Cooperation in South-East Asia*. See also Nicholas Tarling's *Britain, Southeast Asia and the Onset of the Cold War*. The excellence of British record-keeping and archival organization affords English-speaking historians documentary riches attesting to British officials' endeavours and their confidence in being able to square impossible circles. At the end of his study, Tarling concludes that British diplomacy was resourceful at a time when Britain lacked resources. The British sought a continued European presence in postwar Southeast Asia 'working with new regimes that needed their help' (p. 412). That this region emerged in the 1970s onwards as a zone of peace and prosperity owed something to US, Japanese and also British efforts, including, suggests Tarling, 'the British statesmanship of the post-war period, which conceived of and worked towards a region in which the East and West collaborated' (p. 412).

was not Colombo's first major international conference,[38] but it was the first major post-independence meeting. Coming just under two years after Ceylonese independence in 1948, it was a means of displaying Colombo's new international standing. The *Times of Ceylon* made the most of observers' comments foretelling of a momentous meeting, including those by veteran Conservative politician and commentator on empire, Leo Amery, foreseeing Commonwealth greatness through unity in its newly expanded form. Even better was Philip Noel-Baker, Commonwealth Relations Secretary who set out for Colombo saying that this would be one of the most important conferences in the Commonwealth's history and that 'the relations of Asia with the rest of the world were now in the forefront and this was of extreme importance to the Commonwealth as a whole'.[39] *The Times of Ceylon* followed the arrivals and movements of delegates with interest and dwelt especially on the predicaments and achievements of the ailing British Foreign Secretary, Ernest Bevin. Such was his doctor's concern for Bevin's heart that the Foreign Secretary had to travel by sea from Suez to Colombo, and his activities on board the light cruiser, *HMS Kenya*, were front page news.[40] When he arrived in Colombo, awaiting him was a specially built chair that could be carried up the two flights of stairs, which was needed for his attendance in the Senate Building, where the conference was held. Much to the fascination of reporters, Bevin chose to walk up the stairs for the morning session of the first day, taking seven minutes to negotiate those two flights (but he opted at subsequent sessions to be carried in his chair). Equally prominent on page one of *The Times* was a summary of London press reports demonstrating the high profile of the conference and of other events in Asia.[41]

Eleven plenary meetings were held between 9 and 14 January. Subtle adjustments of practices reflected the place and the changed dynamics within the Commonwealth. Prior to Colombo, the order of speaking at Commonwealth conferences had been based on seniority: the British going first, then followed by Canada, Australia and others. At Colombo, the order varied according to the topic under discussion, with India or Britain leading off, depending on whether the topic was Asian or European/global focused, followed by Ceylon and Pakistan,

[38] Colombo hosted the Pan-Asiatic Labour Conference in 1934.

[39] *Times of Ceylon*, 5 January 1950, p. 1.

[40] Ibid, 7 January 1950, p. 1.

[41] Ibid, 9 January 1950, p. 1.

then others.[42] Otherwise, there was less subtlety in the inclination of British and white dominion representatives to interpret events in Asia through the lenses of recent developments in Europe. The minutes of the discussions revealed a recurring divergence between Nehru and British/white dominion approaches to communism in Southeast Asia: where the British and others saw the extension of the Cold War and analogized in hydraulic terms of 'flows' and 'spreads' of communism in locations such as Indo-China, Nehru maintained that embracing some form of nationalism and the expectation of social-economic betterment were the starting points for understanding what was occurring and how best to respond. Only just below the surface was the Indian Prime Minister's insistence, with some support from his Ceylonese hosts, that Asia's problems could not be interpreted as some form of spill-over from Europe's problems and the responses they generated (though Ceylonese Prime Minister Senanayake tended to extol both Asian distinctiveness *and* the dangers of communism being checked in Europe and therefore expanding to Asia).[43] On some analyses of situations in Asia, such as Malcolm MacDonald's positive appraisal of the French-supported Bao Dai government in Vietnam, Nehru flatly disagreed. His information suggested that Bao Dai was unlikely to enjoy broad-based legitimacy among the Vietnamese, a prediction that proved accurate.[44]

Dominion delegates (pictured in Figure 1.2) varied considerably in their approaches to the meeting. In the months leading up to the conference, the Australians had produced analyses of change in Southeast Asia that challenged their government to respond with greater trade and other forms of engagement in the region, in order to help establish a buffer of secure governments between themselves and the Asian mainland, taking into account Mao Zedong's recent victory in China. In these analyses, they focused in particular on Indonesia, recently recognized as independent and which Australian External Affairs Minister Percy Spender and his party visited en route to Colombo.[45] The Canadians, led by External Affairs

[42] Lester Pearson to Heeney, via Canadian High Commissioner in the UK to Secretary of State for External Affairs, 21 January 1950, DEA/50081-40, *Documents on Canadian External Relations*, volume 16, 1950, p. 1197.

[43] FMM (50) 1st meeting, 9 January 1950, CRS A10617 1950/1, NAA.

[44] FMM (50) 5th meeting, 11 January 1950, CRS A10617 1950/1, NAA; FMM (50) 6th meeting, 11 January 1950, ibid.

[45] 'Discussions on Asia with Representatives of the United Kingdom and New Zealand at Canberra, 10–11th November 1949', unsigned, mid-November 1949, CRS A 1838 item 532/5/1, NAA; 'Australia and South-East Asia' by John Burton, External Affairs,

Commonwealth Foreign Ministers at Colombo Front Row: Lester Pearson (Canada), Percy Spender (Australia), Ghulam Mohammed (Pakistan), Jawaharlal Nehru (India), Ernest Bevin (U.K.), Frederick Doidge (New Zealand)

FIGURE 1.2 Commonwealth Foreign Ministers gathered in Colombo, January 1950.
Source: The Colombo Plan, Facebook page, The Founding Fathers, www.facebook.com/photo?fbid=355093371177605&set=a.355091987844410

Minister Lester Pearson, did not expect to be embarking on a program of ongoing development aid for the new Asian members of the Commonwealth but were committed to making the new Commonwealth work, and, like the British, concerned about the potential of the Cold War to flow into Asia.[46] The New Zealand External Affairs Minister Frederick Doidge was similarly unprepared for more than discussions about China, progress on the Japanese Peace Treaty and other well-flagged issues of Commonwealth concern.[47] South Africa's representative, Minister for

13 November 1949, CRS A 621 item 753, NAA; Summary of Record Discussions between Representatives of the Departments of External Affairs, Commerce and Agriculture, and Australian Representatives in South East Asia, 14 November 1949', CRS A 1838 (TS) item 532/5/2/2, NAA; This work was completed under the Chifley Labor Government which lost power to Robert Menzies' Liberal/Country Party coalition in December 1949.

[46] Canadian High Commissioner in United Kingdom to Secretary of State for External Affairs, Ottawa, forwarding report by Lester Pearson, Colombo, 21 January 1950, telegram 131, DEA/50012-40, *Documents on Canadian External Relations*, vol. 16, 1950, no. 652.

[47] Undated paper (May 1950) by Alister McIntosh (New Zealand Secretary of External Affairs), 'Colombo Plan', McIntosh Papers, MS6759-182, National Library of New Zealand (Alexander Turnbull), Wellington; Malcolm McKinnon, *Independence and*

Railways Paul Sauer, was there primarily to engage on the issues of European and global strategic importance including measures to halt the spread of communist groups, and was more of an observer than a participant in discussions about Asia.[48] The South African government would not join in later discussions or in membership of the Colombo Plan.

Despite their best efforts, delegates reached no consensus on what forms of recent security and economic architecture agreed for Europe might be applicable or adaptable to Asian circumstances. Spender and Doidge would have welcomed a Pacific Pact including the Americans taking shape in a way that would guarantee their respective nations' security, but they agreed with others that the circumstances in Asia and the Pacific did not approximate those that made the recent signing of the North Atlantic Treaty (NATO) possible.[49] Nevertheless, in the wake of NATO's signing, Bevin was seized of the potential of the Pacific dominions to play the bridging role that might present in the south. As Spender put it in a report back to his Prime Minister, 'He [Bevin] looked to Australia and New Zealand to provide the sort of link between the United Kingdom and the East as Canada provides with the United States.'[50] As if to reinforce the point, Spender was positioned at the very short turn of a long oval table throughout the conference and his Canadian counterpart, Pearson, sat opposite at the other short end.[51]

Similar questions of how European developments might shape discussions hung in the air when the focus shifted to Asia's development needs. This subject was also informed by a paper from Ceylonese Finance Minister J. R. Jayawardene, who, by virtue of speaking first, beat the Australians to presenting a similar paper. When Jayawardene and Spender spoke on Asia's developmental needs, they did not mention it, but they clearly had the Marshall Plan's spectacular start in Europe in mind. By contrast, they found hotch-potch and overall, very little by way of international economic arrangements in place in Asia. Spender mentioned bodies such as ECAFE, the International Bank of Reconstruction

Foreign Policy: New Zealand in the World since 1935 (Auckland: Auckland University Press, 1993), p. 116.

48 This assessment is based on Sauer's contributions to the eleven plenary meetings held in Colombo, official minutes for which are in several government archives. In this case, I have used the Australian copies, FMM (50) 1st meeting to FMM (50) eleventh meeting, 9–14 January 1950, CRS A10617 item 1950/1, NAA.

49 Minutes of the Second Meeting, 9 January 1950, FMM (50) 2nd meeting, ibid.

50 Spender's cablegram to Menzies, 11 January 1950, ibid.

51 Table Plan, FMM (50) 1, 7 January, Arrangements for Meeting, ibid.

and Development (IBRD, soon known as the World Bank) and the United Nations Educational, Scientific and Cultural Organization (UNESCO) but said that none were showing signs of providing the leadership and resources needed; and Jayawardene said that, to date, Southeast Asia was 'a no-man's land' for economic cooperation.[52] By way of brief summary, Jayawardene outlined a need for ten-year development plans; and after a discussion with the Australians, some of Jayawardene's ideas were incorporated into a new, revised Australian paper and presentation. The Ceylonese recommendation was ambitious in recommending that ten-year development programs submitted by Asian members form the basis of donor responses. The Australians adjusted this to a non-specified period for development programmes and were able to elevate to equal prominence the need for a Technical Council providing technical assistance and expertise, one of the more specific recommendations in their original paper. Their stopover in Indonesia en route to Colombo had reinforced for them how welcome such technical assistance might be there; and Ceylon's Prime Minister D. S. Senanayake added that he thought this technical expertise was also Ceylon's most urgent need. The Australians were soon to host a meeting of a new 'Consultative Committee', set up to examine countries' responses to the idea of development programmes.[53]

These were the essential ideas endorsed by other members as the basis for the next steps. They were the bare bones on which future forms of consultation, cooperation and sometimes cajoling would unfold. The tone of communiqués pointing to the need for external capital was generally mildly optimistic, more fast-tracking local development plans than alleviating hunger, but the consequences for North–South relations were nevertheless significant. At the start of the meeting, Nehru declared that India had no desire to interfere in the affairs of other nations and would resist any type of interference in Indian internal affairs. 'A complication', he added, 'was that Asia generally was now undergoing a belated and unnaturally rapid industrial revolution.'[54] Nehru's 'complication' would generate new relations between politics, diplomacy and finance for a broadening group of nations.

There were, in fact, two conferences running in parallel in Colombo's Senate House. Downstairs from where foreign ministers gathered,

[52] FMM (50) 8th meeting, 12 January 1950, ibid.

[53] Ibid; and Final Communique, attached to FMM (50) 11th meeting, 14 January 1950, ibid.

[54] As recorded in minutes of the second meeting, FMM (50) 2nd meeting, 9 January 1950, ibid.

Commonwealth economic experts, primarily Treasury officials, continued the work of the Commonwealth Finance Ministers meeting in London in July 1949, focusing on the problems of the sterling area. In London, the ministers had focused on the need to rein in dollar spending (through drawing on the centrally held gold reserves). In the six months since July, the dominions, and the Indians in particular, had not restricted their dollar spending to the extent agreed, and this had contributed to more pressure on the British pound. The British responded with a sudden devaluation of the pound in September 1949, catching dominion governments by surprise and generating tensions. At Colombo in January 1950, officials continued to assess the worrying balance of payments within the sterling area and worked on measures that might improve the area's accumulation of dollars. Without agreed restraint from Indians in drawing down their large balances, and without restraint by all members in curbing their drawings on the central dollar pool, the viability of the sterling area as a financial system was in danger. There was a real fear in London that increased drawings on sterling for development purposes would lead to a balance of payments crisis. Having been the great banker, Britain was turning into the great debtor nation. Yet it was hard to deny the built-up demand on capital by those governments wanting to move from wartime exigencies to postwar development and harder still to deny the governments of India and Pakistan which pointed to their huge contributions to the war effort and to their urgent needs now. Ideally, from the British point of view, what was required was a new compact that introduced American dollars as development aid in such a manner that reduced the risk of sudden demands on India's and Pakistan's sterling balances held in London. At the same time, London would keep encouraging sterling-area members to increase production of dollar-earning exports, thereby increasing the common pool of dollars available to members of the sterling area.[55] For their part, officials from India and Pakistan arrived in Colombo deeply suspicious of British efforts to tie their sterling needs to a deal done behind their backs with the Americans.[56]

[55] B. R. Tomlinson, '"The Weapons of the Weakened": British Power, Sterling Balances and the Origins of the Colombo Plan', in Akita, Krozewski, and Watanabe (eds.), *The Transformation of the International Order of Asia*, pp. 34–49.

[56] Canadian High Commissioner in United Kingdom to Secretary of State for External Affairs, Ottawa, forwarding report by Lester Pearson, Colombo, 21 January 1950, telegram 131, DEA/50012-40, *Documents on Canadian External Relations*, vol. 16, 1950, p. 563.

The British delegation, led by Bevin, was notable for its complement of senior Treasury officials bent on achieving greater spending discipline and dollar earning within the sterling area; and representatives from finance and economics departments of other countries were of similarly high calibre. The officials wrestling with these problems worked on the lower floor of the Senate House. Occasionally, some of them would ascend the stairs to join as advisors to their foreign ministers, but much of their work remained literally and figuratively below the surface. In contrast to the powerful British concerns over dangers to the sterling area, the communiqué issued at the end of the conference was region-focused and broad-ranging in what might happen next. In addition to examining possibilities for new financial assistance for nations of the region, and to supporting World Bank and UN agencies already active in this space, delegates undertook to consider forms of intra-regional mutual assistance, the possibility of commodity agreements for key products, and they envisaged the establishment of a Commonwealth consultative committee to investigate 'methods of co-ordinating development in South and South East Asia in association with international and regional organizations concerned with the object of raising the level of production and standard of living in the area'. They would consider whether the economic development of the region might be assisted by drawing up 'a coordinated plan of development and by the establishment of special machinery'.[57] Finally, those leaving Colombo looked forward to convening again soon at what would be the first meeting of the Consultative Committee, in Australia.

The Colombo conference was declared by most to have been a success. Senanayake and Jayawardene excelled at conference hospitality, an essential component of national prowess in diplomacy. The Senate House, a Neo-Baroque style building constructed by the British as a Legislative Council in the 1830s, provided a grand setting (Figure 1.3), even if its stairs proved challenging for Bevin. Canadian diplomat Douglas LePan recalled it as 'more splendid and varied' than any other conference he attended. He recalled, with the orientalist adjectives of one entranced by Eastern exotica, an event hosted by Jayawardene, an evening including snake-charmers, musicians and elaborate male dancing.[58] Noel-Baker,

[57] Communique from the Meeting of Commonwealth Foreign Ministers at Colombo, in Cablegram, Spender (Colombo) to Prime Minister Menzies, 14 January 1950, CRS A1838 item 532/7 part 1, NAA.

[58] Douglas LePan, *Bright Glass of Memory: A Set of Four Memoirs* (Toronto: McGraw-Hill Ryerson, 1979), p. 179.

FIGURE 1.3 Legislative Council or Old Senate House, Colombo (now known as the Republic Building).
Source: Public Domain image, Wikimedia Commons, https://commons.wikimedia.org/wiki/File:Repub_building.jpg?uselang=en#Licensing

who had earlier attracted press attention in talking up the significance of the occasion, delighted his hosts again in his vote of thanks and added to the communiqué. He recalled his first diplomatic conference, at Versailles in 1919, and said, 'I have attended scores of meetings since then, and I venture to say that the arrangements for the conference, our meeting room, our Secretariat, and all that has been done, have never been more efficient in the past than they have been here.'[59]

Before departing Ceylon, delegates had the chance to undertake two- or three-day tours to historic and cultural sites on the island. In what became something of a theme for subsequent meetings, they were invited to recall the glories of much older civilizations, such as the BCE Buddhist rock temple at Dambulla, the fortress and palace at Sigiriya, and Polunnaruwa, the capital from the eleventh to thirteenth centuries CE. The famous Temple of the Tooth, the sacred relic of Buddha, in Kandy was the other popular stop.[60] Post-conference tourism ventures mattered for the sources of national/civilizational pride they promoted and the opportunities they created for continuing interactions among delegates.

[59] Proceedings of final, public session, Senate Chamber, Colombo, 14 January 1950, CRS A 10617 1950/1, NAA.
[60] LePan, *Bright Glass of Memory*, pp. 181–86.

Extending the important theme of hospitality, historians have shown how they helped to develop a sense of located diplomacy within Asia and to counter the top-down, grand narrative approach to histories of international relations. More contingency and nuance in human encounters were visible when key actors lingered in particular locations.[61] In this case, tourism also took on broader significance as it reflected some of the official information and media releases about the Colombo Plan taking shape. Very quickly, delegates settled on a compromise message that was non-European – neither colonial exploitation nor modernization – in historical glancing to describe what was happening now in the context of what had come before. While largely avoiding references to recent colonial times, the historical context was one of former civilizational greatness, interrupted for a variety of reasons (including war and conquests, recent and much older), but now recalled to evoke a spirit of restoration and to underline the huge potential that lay ahead with strong plans for economic development.[62] Invoking the Asian tradition was something that former colonial powers could embrace, as it carried two important implications. The first was the rejection of the Marxist alternative prescription for action that sought not to venerate the past but to destroy anything that stood in the way of radical change; and relatedly, reference to tradition and past greatness made possible an ongoing conversation about stages of development and what developmental steps were needed to advance along a path towards modernity.[63]

FROM COLOMBO TO PLAN

In the early months of 1950, the great powers continued to flex their muscles in the shaping of the postwar world, where events in Europe reflected the hardening lines of the Cold War being drawn. Was there, in the wake of the Colombo conference, a chance that the conduct of international relations might work differently in Asia? Much more detail was needed before the scheme for assisting with economic development

[61] See, for an example of 'located' exploration of postwar Australian diplomacy in Asia, David Fettling, *Encounters with Asian Decolonisation* (Melbourne: Australian Scholarly Press, 2017).

[62] See below and the first major Colombo Plan film, *New Horizons: Story of the Colombo Plan*, 1955.

[63] This divide in anticolonial politics is also called the 'nativist' and 'Marxist' division by Odd Arne Westad in *The Global Cold War: Third World Interventions and the Makings of Our Times* (Cambridge: Cambridge University Press, 2005), pp. 79–97.

could be heralded. Would the subsequent meetings of the assembled group live up to early hopes?.

More than the first meeting at Colombo, the follow-up meeting in Sydney in May was marked by impatience, specifically that of Australian External Affairs Minister Percy Spender who harboured ambitions for a tilt at the role of Prime Minister, and therefore wanted results. He needed to make a tangible aid plan emerge from the Sydney meeting in a manner that might also trigger the much-sought American involvement. In addition to putting flesh on the bones of long-term development programmes, he sought the immediate creation of a Commonwealth Technical Assistance Scheme.[64] This would complement the work of recent technical assistance initiatives such as the UN's expanded program of technical assistance and US President Truman's so-called Point Four Program. Announced in Truman's speech in January 1949, this was a global foreign aid programme designed to counter communist influence and impart technical expertise and aid that would lift nations out of poverty. When delegates gathered in Sydney, Truman's programme was making headlines and nearing Congressional approval (5 June 1950). India would be one of the first countries to benefit.

Spender wanted a quick win, and his diplomacy was not that of the subtle, graduated British hopes of bundling all aims into a grand compact with the Americans. Canadian LePan also made the journey to Sydney and observed the differences first-hand. When Spender started by proposing a series of recommendations for establishing aid targets, a Commonwealth Fund, a secretariat and so on, this was counter to his earlier reassurances to delegates that they would not be required to settle on sums of aid, and it provoked a stiff reaction from them. Once in camera, Spender responded with what LePan called 'a tongue-lashing'; and one that was directed particularly at the British for not living up to the promises made at Colombo.[65] He also tried to leverage the fear of

[64] Spender's hopes for the Colombo Plan and for his own career are outlined further in David Lowe, *Australian between Empires: The Life of Percy Spender* (London: Pickering & Chatto, 2010), pp. 103–42.

[65] LePan, *Bright Glass of Memory*, pp. 197–98. British delegates put Spender's behaviour down to his obsession with favourable local publicity, linked to his political ambitions, presumably for Liberal Party leadership and Prime Minister: UK Delegation to Canberra Consultative Committee to Commonwealth Relations Office, no. 304, 16 May 1950, DO 35/2923, TNA. For Canadian accounts, similarly shocked at Spender's tactics, see Canadian High Commissioner in Australia to Secretary of State for External Affairs, telegram 73, 11 May 1950, DEA/11038-40, *Documents on Canadian External Relations*,

increasing communist influence in the region, arguing 'that unless assistance, particularly in fields of public administration and health, could be brought speedily, certain newly formed administrations in South-east Asia, and particularly those outside the Commonwealth, might not be able to maintain their position in the face of opposing groups'. Spender strongly endorsed Malcolm MacDonald's call for Indochinese states to be invited to participate lest they 'be allowed to fall victim to Soviet imperialism'. While it might be very logical to wait until all development needs had been carefully analysed, 'in the real world it was political and individual reactions rather than logic which counted, particularly in South-east Asia at this time'.[66] Diplomats such as LePan and New Zealander John Reid showed nimble skills at softening the effects of Spender's bravura and also manifestations of other tensions, including those between Indian and Pakistani representatives. They helped find paths towards enunciable outcomes, such as a Technical Assistance Scheme administered by the Council in Colombo.[67] Of the ministers who had gathered at Colombo, Doidge (New Zealand) and Jayawardene (Ceylon) travelled also to Sydney and provided some threads of continuity with earlier discussions.

In addition to being horrified at Spender's heavy-handed tactics to get a result, LePan also noted the legacy of recent European cooperation shaping the British approach. The questionnaires envisaged as the start of assessing the needs of regional members were based on those that had informed the Marshall Plan in Europe. They were the basis of regional members preparing six-year economic plans, identifying their most urgent development needs. The chief British Treasury adviser at Sydney, 'Otto' Clarke, had, three years earlier, been one of those most responsible for building the organizational and procedural processes that would make the Marshall Plan work. In Sydney, as LePan saw it, Clarke fell into the trap of seeing the Asian situation in terms of what he had wrestled with in Europe previously. This included an over-optimistic view of how American plans for the region (that remained obscure) might be meshed

vol. 16, no. 664; and Canadian High Commissioner in Australia to Secretary of State for External Affairs, telegram 77, 16 May 1950, DEA/11038-40, ibid, no. 665.

66 Consultative Committee, Fifth Plenary Session, 17 May 1950, Australian Minutes, CRS A10617 1950/6, NAA.

67 Anthony Reid, 'New Zealand's Unexpected Opening to Asia: John Reid and the Making of the Colombo Plan, 1949–52', *New Zealand Journal of Asian Studies*, 21, 1 (2019), 25–31.

with the Commonwealth-led initiative of the Colombo Plan.[68] Clarke and his Treasury colleagues saw an urgent need for something imaginative to take shape, not just for the sake of the region, 'but also because the impending Presidential Election in the United States and the development of the United States economic policy as E.R.P. [European Recovery Programme ie. Marshall Plan aid] approaches its end, make it imperative that the needs of this Area should be authoritatively stated and fitted into the world economic context before the end of this year'.[69] Four months later, US Secretary of State Dean Acheson quashed such thinking. He made it clear that there could be no presentation to the US Congress that tied aid for Asia to the alleviation of Britain's financial position.[70]

Partly owing to Spender's agitations rubbing up against British and also New Zealand and Canadian caution, some of the details around the Commonwealth Technical Assistance Scheme were hammered out later, in July, by a committee working in Colombo. There was to be a Council for Technical Co-operation, headquartered in Colombo, in which each member of the Colombo Plan would be represented. It would be supported by an executive arm, the Colombo Plan Bureau, which would monitor and report progress, keep records, match requests with available resources and liaise with members and other organizations as needed. In broad terms, the aim of these bodies was to assist in meeting the needs of Asian members for technical experts and for training opportunities (and equipment related to training) through bilateral arrangements with donor members and through liaison with UN bodies and the Point Four Program. British, Australian, Canadian and New Zealand governments promised up to £8 million for the first three years.[71]

As had been in the case for journalists in Ceylon, the Australian press embraced the international spotlight brought to Sydney. From security measures such as police checks and coding and decoding telegrams to appearances of the assembled delegates in the Australia Hotel, which 'looked like the set of a Hollywood "diplomatic" film', the event

[68] LePan, *Bright Glass of Memory*, pp. 193–94.

[69] Annex D, 'Report to the [Consultative] Committee by the Preliminary Meeting of Officials. Plan of Development for South and South East Asia', undated, April or May 1950, DO 35/2923, TNA.

[70] Noted in the British Cabinet sub-committee charged with economic development for South and Southeast Asia, ED (SA)(50)110, 19 September 1950, CAB 134/199, TNA. See also, Tomlinson, '"The Weapons of the Weakened"', pp. 40–41.

[71] John R. E. Carr-Gregg, 'The Colombo Plan: A Commonwealth Program for Southeast Asia', *International Conciliation*, 3, 60 (1951), 1–55, pp. 52–55.

encouraged excited journalism.[72] More than seventy gathered for the conference in Admiralty House, the Governor-General's Sydney residence, with commanding views over Sydney Harbour and its famous bridge. Most newspapers aligned generally with Spender in wanting detailed plans of action to emerge, rather than mere lofty ambitions that marked the Colombo conference (As *The Age*, the daily from Melbourne, put it, 'Everyone emphatically agreed that something must be done, and then went home with bulging brief cases.')[73] That the Americans were gearing up for substantial commitments of aid to Southeast Asia in the lead-up weeks underlined both the need for real actions and the excitement around possible US involvement.

The Consultative Committee met in London from 25 September to 4 October to examine the six-year development plans drawn up by the governments of India, Ceylon, Pakistan and on behalf of the British colonial territories, the Federation of Malaya, Singapore, Sarawak and North Borneo. The Burmese and Indonesian governments were still weighing up whether to join while assessing separate US offers of aid, but they enabled their ambassadors to attend as observers. Representatives from the three Associate States of Indo-China accepted invitations to observe and, at the last minute, the Thai government also sent an observing delegation. Encouragingly, the Americans sent a liaison officer. At that time, the Korean War dominated Asian news, providing a dramatic backdrop to discussions. The South Korean capital, Seoul, had just been recaptured from the North by the US-led United Nations force after their successful amphibious landing, but the outcome of the war was uncertain.

Delegates in London noted the two big shortages facing member nations: capital and trained manpower. They acknowledged the need for support from outside the existing membership if the six-year plans were to have a chance.[74] This was the first time that regional members – India, Pakistan, Ceylon, and the Federation of Malaya, Sarawak, Singapore and North Borneo – presented their detailed development plans, indicating where priorities and problems lay and how shortfalls might be addressed. Dato' Onn bin Jaafar spoke for Malaya, as Home

[72] *Daily Telegraph*, 14 May 1950, p. 7; and see ibid, 15 May 1950, p. 10; (Sydney) *Sun*, 15 May 1950, p. 1.

[73] *Age*, 12 May 1950, p. 2; *Canberra Times*, 6 May 1950, p. 1; (Melbourne) *Herald*, 6 May 1950, p. 5; *Sydney Morning Herald*, 9 May 1950, p. 2.

[74] Carr-Gregg, 'The Colombo Plan', pp. 33–34.

Affairs Minister, and C. C. Tan,[75] Legislative Council Member for Singapore, while Malcolm MacDonald covered North Borneo and Sarawak. The needs of India and Pakistan were jaw-dropping for some who were learning fast about the region. How to curb population growth in order to feed everyone, while acknowledging that medical and other technical advances might, in the short term, increase populations, was the subject of earnest, if circuitous debate. India's task ahead, presented by Finance Minister Chintaman Deshmukh, moved New Zealand External Affairs Minister Doidge to enthuse about the impact of the intended print version of the Colombo Plan for popular use: ' ... stories such as the Committee had just listened to would catch the imagination of the world, and ... a romantic picture could be given of the magnitude of the task in hand. If the imagination of the public could be caught in this way, something tangible would have been achieved'.[76] Much of the remaining discussion concerned the provision of technical assistance, how it would be coordinated with other agencies such as the UN and what rates would be paid to experts. This was a conversation that the broader group assembled could join as it was presented as a separate scheme, capable of being accessed without governments necessarily submitting detailed development plans and joining the Consultative Committee.[77]

The ninety-page report arising from the London meeting detailed the needs of each country/territory and the pledges of donor governments, not all of which could stretch to a six-year commitment. In their shape, the plans of the seven countries unfolded under common headings but with different emphases according to the specific needs identified.[78] In the case of India, the biggest spending was for ambitious river valley schemes regulating water flow, enabling irrigation for agriculture, and generating

[75] Popularly known as C. C. Tan, his full name was Tan Chye Cheng.

[76] C.C.L. (50) 4th Meeting, Commonwealth Consultative Committee, Minutes of meeting in Lancaster House, 27th September 1950, CRS A1067 1950. 11, NAA. Summary draws also on C.C.L. (50) 5th Meeting, Commonwealth Consultative Committee, Minutes of meeting in Lancaster House, 27th September 1950, CRS A1067 1950. 11, NAA; C.C.L. (50) 6th Meeting, Commonwealth Consultative Committee, Minutes of meeting in Lancaster House, 28th September 1950, CRS A1067 1950. 11, NAA.

[77] S.E.A.L. (50) 3rd Meeting, Economic Development in South and South-East Asia, Minutes of meeting in Lancaster House, 3 October 1950, CRS A10617 1950/11, NAA; S.E.A.L. (50) 4th Meeting, Economic Development in South and South-East Asia, Minutes of meeting in Lancaster House, 4 October 1950, CRS A10617 1950/11, NAA.

[78] Report by the Commonwealth Consultative Committee, *The Colombo Plan for Cooperative Economic Development in South and South-East Asia*, HMSO, London, September–October 1950.

hydroelectric power. Similar projects lay at the heart of Pakistani and Ceylonese plans, where agricultural production was central. British authorities played a dominant role in identifying the priorities of their colonies in Southeast Asia. Restoring and expanding rice and rubber production were the biggest components of Malaya's plans, education for Singapore and rebuilding communications and expanded training in British Borneo. The version of the London report produced for popular use – in donor nations and in South Asia and British Southeast Asia – was *New Horizons in the East*, some forty pages rich with graphs, maps and photographs (Figure 1.4).[79]

The total cost of development plans for India, Pakistan, Ceylon, Malaya, Singapore and British Borneo was £1,868 million; and the amount of external assistance sought, after taking into account governments' budgeted spending, was more than half of this, £1,085 million. The plan's starting date was set at 1 July 1951. Host government Britain offered £300 million over six years, of which £246 million was the release of sterling balances, thus hoping that, by 1956 the Colombo Plan would have 'virtually solved' the wartime accumulation of sterling by the South Asian Dominions.[80] The Australians, after Cabinet approval in December, offered £25 million, the New Zealanders £3 million during the first three years and the Canadians $25 million during the first year. Assuming similar New Zealand and Canadian contributions for the full six years, the combined total reached only £362 million. The gap between capital needed and what was promised was £723 million.[81]

Press reactions in the member countries varied. Across India, the many English-language dailies gave prominence to the announcements in London but were divided in their levels of enthusiasm. Those such as the *Bombay Chronicle* sensed a chance to extend India's leadership in regional cooperation and a new Commonwealth mandate that was a welcome antidote to the attractions of communism and therefore embraced the Colombo Plan. Those such as the *Times of India* and *Hindustan Times* worried that uncertainty over US intentions, now even harder to gauge with their sudden re-arming for the Korean War, might

[79] HMSO, London, 1950.

[80] British Chancellor of the Exchequer, Hugh Gaitskell, quoted in Tomlinson, '"The Weapons of the Weakened"', p. 41.

[81] Draft paper by Economic Policy Committee, July 1951, DO 35/2774, TNA; Australian Cabinet meeting, decision no. 37A, CRS A 4638/XM1 set NAA. These sums do not include appropriations for the Technical Assistance side of the Colombo Plan.

FIGURE 1.4 *New Horizons in the East*, 1950.
Source: Royal Commonwealth Society, Cambridge University Library

potentially hamstring aid efforts.[82] India's Deshmukh bemoaned that his fellow Cabinet members might be too sensitive to US imperialism for them to acknowledge the importance of US aid.[83] Notwithstanding this concern, most eyes turned to the United States to see what the Truman administration might be prepared to do to meet the gap left by initial aid commitments, now that self-help and due diligence relating to planning was shown. And importantly, having fended off the suggestion of a close connection to Britain's repayments problems, the Americans did agree, in November, to join the Colombo Plan's Consultative Committee. Successive US national security policy papers and the outbreak of the Korean War in June led the Americans to commit to aid for South and Southeast Asia, even if they remained reluctant to allow the Colombo Plan to develop organizational prominence or dictate the nature of their assistance.[84]

Even before the US commitment, the British media was upbeat. A Pathé newsreel described the conference as a great success for British diplomats, highlighting the emergence of the South Asian members of the Commonwealth in world affairs and the creation of a 'miniature United Nations' devoted to assisting with the economic problems of the region.[85] *New Horizons in the East* told of South Asian economies derailed by the war. Using simple images and statistics to compare the poor state of Indian agriculture with that of the United States, its authors looked to modern industry: 'Power and machines are the key to plenty on the land – factories to make implements and fertilizers; machines to till the soil; dams to provide water for irrigation and to control the floods.'[86] The booklet outlined the main features of each country's development plans, with photographs and graphs of current productive activities and projected improvements. In the case of India, the huge river valley projects

[82] As summarized and reported in UK High Commissioner, India to CRO, no. 2278, 1 December 1950, FZ11013/291, FO 371/84595, TNA.

[83] C. D. Deshmukh letter to Nehru, 30 November 1950, Abilekh Patal, Indian National Archives Online, Sardar Patel Collection, file, 'Colombo Plan – Offer of Help from America'.

[84] Andrew Rotter, *The Path to Vietnam: Origins of the American Commitment to Southeast Asia* (Ithaca, NY: Cornell University Press, 1987), pp. 141–64, 208; and see generally, Nick Cullather, *The Hungry World: America's Cold War Battle against Poverty in Asia* (Cambridge, MA: Harvard University Press, 2010).

[85] Pathé newsreel, 19 January 1950, www.britishpathe.com/video/colombo-opens-new-chapter-for-commonwealth (accessed 6 February 2019).

[86] *New Horizons in the East*, p. 11.

featured. Seven of these, including the Damodar Project in Bihar, the Tungabhadra in Karnataka and the Mahanadi in Bengal, were 'already in hand'.[87] The difference that would be made by these and other schemes building factories and improving agriculture could be seen in the lives of ordinary people. 'At present the ration of cereals in many of the towns in limited to 12 ounces a day. *By 1957, as a result of the programme, it is hoped to raise this to 16 ounces. There should also be an increase is consumption of cotton cloth from an average of 15 yards.*'[88] There were similar summaries for the other Asian members, with irrigating, power-generating river valley projects looming large also in Pakistan and Ceylon. All countries were taking up the opportunities to host technical experts, and for their students to train in Commonwealth universities and colleges.[89]

This first popular depiction of the Colombo Plan was thus notable for both the excitement around grand projects and its tone of ongoing colonial development under British tutelage. It side-stepped the bubbling of ideas about how the gathering momentum from Colombo and ECAFE might yield new forms of diplomatic agency for independent Asia. Already, the Indian government was engaged in a balancing act between promoting ECAFE as a venue in which independent Asian voices could emerge under Indian leadership, while making claims about its own capacity to provide technical training.[90] After the Colombo Plan meeting in Sydney, the Indians set up a new unit in the Department of Economic Affairs under Prem Narian to coordinate technical assistance activity with established programs under the US Point Four and the UN Technical Assistance schemes. Immediately, they saw themselves as likely *providers* of such technical assistance under the Colombo Plan as well as potential receivers.[91] Likewise, Jayawardene said that the Ceylonese government would provide technical aid.[92]

[87] Ibid, p. 20. [88] Ibid, p. 22. Italics in original. [89] Ibid, pp. 22–34.

[90] P. S. Lokanathan (Exec Sec, ECAFE) 'Technical Training' to Minister, External Affairs, 21 September 1948, External Affairs File 5 (96) – UNI(48) Activities in Training Section of ECAFE, NAI; Secretary External Affairs telegram 13709 to High Commissioner, Canberra, 30 November 1948, Abilekh Patal, National Archives of India Online.

[91] P. C. Battacharya (Joint Secretary, Government of India) memo, 'Technical Assistance, Sydney Conference Recommendations – Organisation of Separate Unit to Deal with All Assistance Programmes', 24 June 1950, F. 15-1/50-D1 Ministry of Education, Sydney Conference, no. 1 (1) – Tech/50 Ministry of Finance, Abilekh Patal, National Archives of India Online.

[92] *Canberra Times*, 17 May 1950, p. 1.

In the last months of 1950, there remained scepticism elsewhere. The governments of New Zealand and Canadian struggled to see what small amounts of aid might do to alleviate poverty, expecting the United Nations and auxiliary bodies to be better able to grapple with this, and unsure how to respond to Cold War tensions manifesting in Asia.[93] By way of another white dominion perspective, Percy Spender later wrote a detailed memoir dealing with the Colombo Plan and the ANZUS Treaty. In this account, the Colombo Plan assumed a more prominent and holistic role in his outlook on Asia, which he summarized as 'to work with these new and different nations, giving them whatever assistance we could and which they were willing to accept, in order to help them hold fast their new found independence and develop their countries in freedom and peace'.[94] This was more noble-sounding than some of his impatience at Sydney, and some of his more candid, sweeping stereotypical descriptions of new nations (e.g. the Indians, for their determination to cleanse Asia of imperialism, were 'the Jesuits of the Orient').[95] Like many memoirs, it also had posterity in mind. But it was characteristic of the way in which the Colombo Plan would, for Spender and others, also provide for new agency in postwar diplomacy and fill a perceived gap in inter-connected thinking about the region.

Three Commonwealth-Asian focused conferences during ten months from January to October 1950 – Colombo, Sydney and London – brought together ministers and officials in ways that had not been attempted before. The near-continuous work on the Colombo Plan involved senior cabinet ministers from new and older Commonwealth countries repeatedly: Jayawardene, Spender, Deshmukh, Doidge, Mayhew, Malcolm MacDonald and Ghulam Mohammed were all present in London. And,

93 David Webster, 'Developing the World in Canada's Image: Hugh Keenleyside and Technical Assistance', in Greg Donaghy and David Webster (eds.), *A Samaritan State Revisited: Historical Perspectives on Canadian Foreign Aid* (Calgary: University of Calgary Press, 2019), pp. 73–75; Mcintosh, undated memo (May 1950), McIntosh Papers, MS6759–182, National Library of New Zealand (Alexander Turnbull), Wellington (hereafter NLNZ); Jim Rolfe, 'Coming to Terms with Regional Identity', in Anthony L. Smith (ed.), *Southeast Asia and New Zealand: A History of Regional and Bilateral Relations* (Wellington: Institute of Southeast Asian Studies and New Zealand Institute of International Affairs, in association with Victoria University Press, 2005), pp. 32–35.

94 Percy Spender, *Exercises in Diplomacy: The ANZUS Treaty and the Colombo Plan* (Sydney: University of Sydney Press, 1969), p. 206.

95 Hooker A. Doolittle (US Chargé d'Affairs, Pakistan) to US Secretary of State, reporting conversation with Spender, 26 January 1950, RG 84 Canberra, box 86, 1950–52, 28-321, USNA.

in LePan's words, 'Behind them were officials who had been knitted into a kind of free masonry of their own by the events of the past nine months and among whom were many ties of personal friendship.'[96] Officials such as Otto Clarke, Australians Tom Critchley and Arthur Tange, New Zealander John Reid and Ceylon's Rajendra Coomaraswamy had, like LePan, been involved in policy deliberations from the beginning. A Colombo Plan Council for Technical Cooperation convened for the first time in Colombo in December. Comprised of Commonwealth High Commissioners in Ceylon and Coomaraswamy as the first President, its role was to meet regularly, at what became around every six weeks, to assess progress in the plan's technical assistance activities.[97]

Although a seemingly modest remit, the Council also controlled the publicity and accounting engine that was the Colombo Plan Bureau for Technical Cooperation, responsible for the production of reports, profiles and records.

By the end of 1950, the Colombo Plan was also the agreed name for the venture. In the wake of the initial meeting in Colombo, there were other options, and Spender, wanting to make the most of his contributions, did not discourage the notion of the 'Spender Plan' through the first half of the year, including at the meeting in Sydney. But by the time of the London meeting New Zealand, Canadian and Ceylonese officials had mustered consensus behind the city of origin. Spender, too, reluctantly acknowledged the sleepless nights that treasuries would have endured with something called a 'Spender Plan'. A late proposal by India's Deshmukh for SEAPED, the 'South and South-East Asia Plan for Economic Development' was politely ignored.[98] In its naming, the Colombo Plan avoided the recent nomenclature of international plans and pacts for statesmen, such as in the Marshall, Truman Plans and it also departed from acronyms such as NATO.

Transitions are more readily identified in their aftermath, and those attending the Colombo conference could not anticipate Asian events such as the outbreak of the Korean War five months later, the Viet Minh's defeat of the French in Vietnam in mid-1954, or the Bandung Conference the following year. But they were conscious of meeting amid unsettling changes to the world order. Between the pages of dry minutes of meetings

[96] LePan, *Bright Glass of Memory*, p. 214.

[97] The Council was funded by donor members under their technical assistance allocations.

[98] C.C.L. (50) 3rd Meeting Commonwealth Consultative Committee, Minutes of meeting in Lancaster House, London, 26 September 1950, CRS A10617 1950/11, NAA.

and in occasional personal comments and recollections, we can feel a sense of new opportunities for development plans as the possible vehicles for regional-minded diplomacy and enhancing the credentials of newly independent states in Asia.

These ambitions ran up against a British colonial determination to harness development to broader economic needs of a financially buffeted sterling area and to manage the pace of decolonization as best possible. For the historian, two features stand out over the course of the years 1950–51, as the Colombo Plan took shape. The first is a sense of overloaded expectations by the British not being met, especially after the Americans declined to tie their own policy to British plans for sterling debt reduction. Logically, those seeking a British-shaped or US-determined narrative dependent on the conjoining of finance, foreign policy and defence strategy in plans for South and Southeast Asia need to look elsewhere, not at the Colombo Plan. The second is the emergence of a broader range of diplomats, politicians and planners whose work appears marginally in British and US archival records, but from 1950 to 1951 increasingly in the archives of other Colombo Plan members such as Canada, India, Australia and New Zealand. This bigger cast of diplomatic players decouples the Colombo Plan from its British anchoring and enables the agency of others to emerge more fully.

While perhaps not obvious initially, the formative period for the Colombo Plan was also the dawn of a new arena for the conduct of foreign relations. The Colombo conference at the start of 1950, while focused on development needs, also provided a stage for experiments in representation, hospitality and diplomacy. Subsequent meetings that year in Sydney and London elevated the experiment from one that might have been fleeting to something more akin to a moving laboratory. These qualities would be seized on as a welcome, recurring congress for Asian–Western negotiations on development and forms of aid in Colombo Plan meetings ahead.

2

Experimental Regionalism

The six-year development plans of the member nations underpinning the Colombo Plan began officially on 1 July 1951. Beyond this, and the declared intent for annual meetings, much remained unknown. Members' embrace of regionalism as an ideal to be harnessed in the Colombo Plan varied noticeably in the early years of the meetings. 'At the outset', wrote one observer-participant, 'the Colombo Plan took on the flavour and *modus operandi* of a British club'.[1] For the governments of Australia, New Zealand and Canada, the Commonwealth origins of the plan and Britain's strong involvement were especially important in the formative process. As leaders of the Commonwealth and one of the chief sponsors of the plan, the British were determined to shape its parameters in ways that addressed their postwar indebtedness; and it was only as the more ambitious aspects of these efforts gave way that a more exploratory and iterative, multi-party approach to the Colombo Plan emerged. Suggestions that it was a multilateral plan, as some seemed to imply when comparing it to the Marshall Plan, could not be sustained when it functioned more like an umbrella under which bilateral flows of development between donor and recipient governments were negotiated. But the perspective of newly independent governments was also important. Common colonial experiences and shared interest in what kinds of collective actions might unfold lay close to the surface of conversations in the Colombo Plan meetings.

During the course of 1951, the British Treasury shifted only slowly from seeing the plan as a well-defined 'package' of development for presentation

[1] Keith Spicer, 'Clubmanship Upstaged: Canada's Twenty Years in the Colombo Plan', *International Journal*, 25, 1 (1969), 28.

purposes to the Americans. For the same reason, Treasury officials were lukewarm about non-Commonwealth countries joining. Their focus was on a balance of payments approach, linked to the management of their sterling debts, and they did not want British colonies to start pointing to levels of generosity for others that the colonies did not seem to share.[2] Only from mid-1951, when the Americans reiterated that they would not be linking 'free development dollars' to the retirement of sterling debts in the region did Treasury partly relax its control over the British aims within the Colombo Plan – at least in envisaging broader membership.[3]

By this time, the Americans were providing aid to parts of Southeast Asia under their Point Four Program and courting Congress for more money. The State Department felt that the Colombo Plan was best kept separate during this process.[4] The British were tempted to adjust again. They considered trying to limit the Colombo Plan so that it complemented rather than doubled up on US aid starting to flow to some parts of the region. Inviting non-Commonwealth members to join, argued Treasury, had been 'largely a matter of tactics to make the United States give aid to these countries as well as to Commonwealth countries'.[5] Now that countries such as Vietnam and Cambodia were benefiting under US Point Four aid, the case for their joining the plan was weaker; and the British government should not provide aid to governments that had not submitted robust development plans.[6] For more practical reasons, other donor countries also struggled, initially, to look much beyond the Commonwealth. The Canadians did not envisage any aid extending beyond Commonwealth members and were unsure how long the new Colombo Plan might last.[7] New Zealand's initial allocation of financial

[2] See ED(SA)(51), 56, Cabinet Committee on Economic Development in South and South East Asia, 'United Kingdom Assistance to Non-Commonwealth Countries', Note by Treasury, 20 April 1951, CAB 134/201, TNA; ED(SA)(51), 74 (2nd Revise), Cabinet Working Party on Economic Development in South and South East Asia, 'Progress Report for Ministers', by Treasury, 30 June 1951, ibid.

[3] ED(SA)(51), 74 (2nd Revise), Cabinet Working Party on Economic Development in South and South East Asia, 'Progress Report for Ministers', by Treasury, 30 June 1951, ibid.

[4] Copy of letter from B. A. B. Burrows on discussions in Washington between Symon, Boyd, Mackay (UK) and Kennedy, Hamilton, Gold, Fluker, Beale (US) to Foreign Office, 12 July 1951, DO 35/2712, TNA.

[5] ED(SA)(51), 11th Meeting of Cabinet Working Party on Economic Development in South and South East Asia, 30 May 1951, CAB134/200, TNA.

[6] Ibid.

[7] Jill Campbell-Miller, 'Encounter and Apprenticeship: The Colombo Plan and Canadian Aid in India, 1950–1960', in Donaghy and Webster (eds.), *A Samaritan State Revisited*, pp. 28–29.

assistance in 1951 reflected how little they knew of countries beyond the Commonwealth in Asia. Their small sum was simply portioned: one-quarter for India; one-quarter for Pakistan; one-quarter for Ceylon; and one-quarter for the rest.[8]

A number of non-Commonwealth countries thought most likely to benefit from joining hesitated, too. Buoyed suddenly by soaring prices of raw materials such as rubber and tin from the Korean War boom, governments in Indonesia and Burma felt less urgency about development plans and donor aid through 1951. Then the boom suddenly ended. The prospect of extensive Japanese war reparations, yet to be agreed, was another hard-to-judge factor.[9] And it was not until later in 1951 that it became clear that other European powers with colonial responsibilities and/or residual influence, namely the French and Dutch, would not be able to join the Colombo Plan. While the British would have welcomed their joining, they did not want European membership at the expense of Indonesia refusing to join, and this plus Indian and Ceylonese hostility to the French and Dutch put the matter beyond doubt.[10]

This chapter charts the transition of the Colombo Plan from a Commonwealth experiment overburdened by British plans for debt management into a loose-knit group of countries extending beyond the Commonwealth. The expanded membership brought tentative explorations of regional ideation and practice. In the wake of US membership confirmed in 1951, members pursued a careful diplomatic path between Cold War polarities and one that was also mindful of colonial legacies, past and continuing. Aid provision started officially from the middle of 1951. Importantly, a pattern of annual meetings of the Colombo Plan Consultative Committee took shape, hosted each year by a different member government and accompanied by a strong sense of performance. Whether donor or recipient nation, to host a Colombo Plan

[8] Richard Grew (Office of Canadian High Commissioner, Wellington) to Under-Secretary of State for External Affairs, Ottawa, 10 July 1951, New Zealand aid to India under the Colombo Plan, RG 25 vol. 8407 11038-AB-4-40, part 1.1, LAC.

[9] In addition to Burma and Indonesia, the issue of Japanese war reparations applied to most regional members of the Colombo Plan, as it grew during 1950–53, excepting India, which waived the right to reparations in 1952: Hiroyuki Hoshiro, 'Reconsidering Japan's War Reparations and Economic Re-Entry into Southeast Asia', *Diplomacy and Statecraft*, 34, 4 (2023), 673–702.

[10] ED(SA)(51), 17 (2nd Revise), Cabinet Working Party on Economic Development in South and South East Asia, 'Brief for the UK Delegation to the Forthcoming Meeting of the Consultative Committee on South and South-East Asia', February 1951, CAB 134/200, TNA.

meeting was to demonstrate one's credentials for the new phase of diplomacy unfolding.

A PLAN WITH A SMALL 'P'

Politicians' early claims for the Colombo Plan suggested a squaring of several circles: it was to alleviate poverty while fuelling development; it would foster a new community of equal nations while retaining former imperial guidance and embracing newer US forms; and its focus on improving living standards would counter the appeal of communist rhetoric while transcending the language of the Cold War. The opening speech of US delegate and Ambassador to Pakistan, Avra Warren, at the Consultative Committee meeting in Karachi in March 1952, sketched these aims with an emphasis on what he called the 'true mutuality of interests between the United States and the peoples of South and Southeast Asia'. Warren said that:

> The United States Government are [sic] aware of the aspirations of these Asian countries for economic development. It has co-operated in the efforts of these countries to rehabilitate their economies and to push forward their plans for economic development, for my Government believes that only through the energetic development of the resources of the countries of the area can a basis be established for the improvement of living levels, and that such improvement is essential if freedom and peace are to prevail in the world.[11]

His colleagues from Australia, Britain and Canada added in ways that celebrated the 'history-making' efforts of the assembled and the cultural exchange and shared learning that would accompany development. They expressed faith in the organic unfolding of what would happen next. The seeds planted at Colombo could be nurtured to grow strong roots for future cooperation.[12]

At Karachi, the views of the Burmese delegate, U Pe Kin, were, by contrast, a reminder of raw memories of colonialism that could surface should there be any suggestion that what was needed was restoration of the pre-war colonial influence. Speaking of scars left by the Second World War, Kin added, 'I may be forgiven if I observe that long periods of foreign domination and exploitation are in no way less responsible ...'[13] Kin was forgiven as Burma was welcomed as a new member at this meeting. From another angle, the previously supportive *Times of India*

[11] *Dawn*, 25 March 1952, p. 4. [12] Ibid. [13] Ibid.

wondered whether earlier promises had been 'virtually consigned to the limbo of forgotten things', considering new pressures on Britain's balance of payments and what appeared to be token contributions by Canada and Australia to date.[14] For those talking up the virtues of the Colombo Plan, there was a need to strike a balance between the resources and agency of colonial powers and the evident sensitivities of newly independent nations in the region.

It is hard to gauge the depth of early 1950s hopes that development activity might build the kind of regionally minded community that could transcend the experiences of war and colonialism. For governments in decolonizing Asia, the transition from war to peace was accompanied not only by well-founded suspicions of neo-colonial intent but also by belief in a broader concept of economic progress. The elites of imperial governments and those of newly independent nations shared a common faith in science and technology driving development.[15] Indian Prime Minister Nehru was a well-known apostle of science and engineering, in addition to being a fierce opponent of Western plans to wield scientific and development rationalism in ways that would retard India's industrial development and render it dependent on the West.[16] Consensus lay in the broad conviction that rapid economic progress might best unfold through postwar internationalism harnessed to science and social science aimed at alleviating poverty.[17] The devil lay in the detail of how this might be achieved without new forms of dependency settling on the grooves left by older colonial forms of control.

By the time the Colombo Plan officially began, there were other organizations trying to set new patterns of cooperation in Asia. ECAFE had subcommittees working on subjects such as inland transport, and iron and steel production. Other UN auxiliaries such as UNESCO had set up three Asian offices by 1951. There was a UN International Children's Emergency Fund (UNICEF) programme for the Far East, the new World

[14] *Times of India*, 25 March 1952, in Henry Deimel (US Embassy, New Delhi) to State Department, no. 2391, 27 March 1952, 890.00/3-2752, United States National Archives, College Park, Maryland (hereinafter USNA).

[15] Unger, *International Development*, pp. 79–101.

[16] A detailed study of Nehru's embrace of nuclear scientists as architects of development is Robert S. Anderson, *Nucleus and Nation: Scientists, International Networks and Power in India* (Chicago: University of Chicago Press, 2010).

[17] See Glenda Sluga, *Internationalism in the Age of Nationalism* (Philadelphia: University of Pennsylvania Press, 2013), pp. 79–117. Sluga writes that 'mid-century internationalism was fashioned out of economic progress and opportunity for economic equality and democracy in the image of modern industrialization' (p. 111).

Health Organization (WHO) had a regional committee for Southeast Asia based in New Delhi and another committee taking shape for the Western Pacific, and the Food and Agricultural Organization (FAO) had established regional advisory bodies on rice, forestry and fisheries. The fisheries body was the 'Indo-Pacific Fisheries Council', the 'Indo-Pacific' being a term used occasionally since the 1920s before its fulsome political embrace in the twenty-first century.[18]

As made clear by the British approach to the formation of the Colombo Plan, the governments of newly independent nations were justified in their wariness of lingering colonial/war-legacy aims influencing the diplomacy within these organizations. Eleanor Hinder was an Australian-born welfare internationalist and diplomat well placed to observe how recently declared independent nations tried to walk new diplomatic paths of regional cooperation. Hinder had been based in China in the interwar years campaigning for industrial reforms and making representations to the International Labour Organization (ILO), another organization that quickly expanded its reach to South and Southeast Asia after the Second World War.[19] Hinder then worked as a diplomat representing the British on most of these UN-related and other regional bodies from 1947 to 1951. She was the only woman among the small team of diplomats in the middle of 1950 that helped set out the basic workings of the Colombo Plan's Technical Assistance Bureau.[20] When the Foreign Office cut back its staff, ending separate representation for ECAFE in Bangkok in 1951, it brought this part of Hinder's colourful career to an end and prompted her to reflect, from a position of considerable expertise, on the state of play in regional cooperation. She wrote of a possessive attitude by governments in Asia towards regional

[18] The German geopolitician Karl Haushofer used the term 'Indo-Pacific area' in the 1920s. For discussion of the rise of the 'Indo-Pacific' in geopolitical thinking and alliances since 2011, see Rory Medcalf, *Contest for the Indo-Pacific: Why China Won't Map the Future* (Carlton: La Trobe University Press and Black Inc, 2020), pp. 9–26.

[19] For more information on the remarkable life and work of Eleanor Hinder, see Frances Wheelhouse, *Eleanor Mary Hinder, an Australian Woman's Social Welfare Work in China between the Wars* (Sydney: Wentworth Books, 1978); Sophie Loy-Wilson, 'White Cargo: Australian Residents, Trade and Colonialism in Shanghai between the Wars, *History Australia*, 9, 3 (2012), 154–77; Sophie Loy-Wilson, '"Liberating Asia": Strikes and Protest in Sydney and Shanghai, 1920–39', *History Workshop Journal*, 72, 1 (2011), 74–102; Sarah Paddle, 'For the China of the Future: Western Feminists, Colonisation and International Citizenship in China in the Inter-War Years', *Australian Feminist Studies*, 16, 36 (2001), 325–41.

[20] David M. Johnson, Canadian High Commissioner, Karachi, to Department of External Affairs, 11 August 1950, RG 25 vol. 6598 11038-D-40 part 1, LAC.

organizations such as ECAFE. Indians, according to Hinder, equated ECAFE's growth with the garnering of Asian prestige, something that also attracted the governments of Burma, Indonesia, Pakistan and the Philippines. Hinder did not want to see a proliferation of more regional committees, noting how the increased number was already stretching the diplomatic capacities of some nations, but she welcomed the 'close comradeship in common work' that had grown through personal contacts and growing friendships. 'I walked into a hotel in Madras one evening', she wrote, 'to find a circle of men, seated and leaning over, their heads almost meeting. It was the Secretary of the Indo-Pacific Fisheries Council, consulting with the Fisheries officers of South India. There is no substitute for such personal contacts in stimulating enthusiasm and steady work.'[21] While urging London to maintain high levels of representation at such gatherings, Hinder wondered if some of the activities envisaged under ECAFE and the Colombo Plan might be conflated: 'It would almost seem that the best way to commend Colombo politically is to enter into an acceptable collaboration with ECAFE.'[22]

Hinder's British colleague and chief representative on ECAFE, P. J. H. Stent, stood down at the same time and issued a long plea that the Foreign Office invest more energy and enthusiasm in ECAFE, whatever might happen with the Colombo Plan. He found a strong sense of 'Asian solidarity' and pride in ECAFE and argued that its status as an organ of the UN was important to Asian members, 'because through the United Nations they are linked to the rest of the world, and because the United Nations is felt to be a genuinely international organization wherein every member has an equal status'.[23] That two long-term observer-participants in postwar regional organizations saw the Colombo Plan as necessarily adjusting to, and complementing, the earlier-established ECAFE suggested that work was needed to elevate the Colombo Plan's standing among other bodies. But as the decade unfolded, the two organizations established their own space, referring regularly to each other in ways that

[21] Hinder to A. A. Dudley, UN (Social and Economic) Department, FO, 17 May 1951, US11051/1, FO 371, 95820, TNA.

[22] Ibid.

[23] Stent's analysis, perhaps consistent with an orientalist gaze cultivated during his long, earlier service in the Indian Civil Service, also gave prominence to what he called the 'psychological factor' in dealing with Asian feelings, as matter of higher importance than rational logic: P. J. H. Stent, minute, 'The Future of Economic Commission for Asia and the Far East and the Policy of His Majesty's Government Towards It', 2 April 1951, US1104/71, FO 371/95778, TNA.

were more complementary than competitive. The Colombo Plan benefited from a smaller membership that grew, by agreement, incrementally. It thus avoided features of ECAFE meetings such as regular Cold War posturing between Soviet Union representatives and others, especially those from the Republic of China after 1949; the acrimony between the Dutch and Indonesians during 1947–48, drawing in other members and culminating in a Dutch walk-out; and a very loose concept of 'Asia and the Far East' that was always shifting to accommodate membership changes such as Afghanistan's joining ECAFE in 1953.[24]

Several of the other postwar bodies that Hinder joined drew on prewar and wartime beginnings. In the interwar League of Nations and some of its successor bodies, a shared sense of professionalism and technical expertise was brought to bear on the world's problems of poverty, access to resources and sources of conflict. By way of brief illustration, this included the FAO formed in 1943. At Hot Springs, Virginia, where the FAO was born, it was the experts rather than diplomats who led the proceedings, arguing the benefits of expanded agricultural activity linked to new nutritional standards and an embrace of science. In the background, US President Roosevelt's 'freedom from want', among his other three 'freedoms', seemed to foreshadow a new US-led determination to steer international diplomacy into more ambitious directions around universal living standards. But, in a manner anticipating the experience of ECAFE, whether the FAO would be a far-reaching regulatory body, or more modestly a collector of information and source of advice, quickly divided members and remained a source of tension at the end of the decade.

Not surprisingly, the US and British concerns won out over more sweeping plans that would have controlled prices and regulated the supply of essential crops. The FAO would see most of its nutrition-and-science basis for policy ceded to the high ground of international trade, as shaped by the International Trade Organization. For Indian and Chinese members of the FAO, whose countries were wracked by recent famines, this marginalization of health in the trade and industry approach to

[24] These and other aspects of ECAFE's early years are explored in Wightman, *Toward Economic Cooperation in Asia*. See also, Ikuto Yamaguchi, 'The Development and Activities of the Economic Commission for Asia and the Far East (ECAFE), 1947–65', in Akita, Krozewski, and Watanabe (eds.), *The Transformation of the International Order of Asia*, pp. 91–108.

development was especially troubling.[25] Instead, 'technical assistance', training and providing experts and specialist equipment, became a major focus of FAO efforts in agricultural development. Elevating the virtues of technical assistance was part of the FAO's adjustment from its heady initial aims to a shifted emphasis on trade/industry/development and the Cold War realities of the late 1940s.

In parallel, influential economists outmanoeuvred those experts who argued for the view from below, a determinedly social grounding for the task of development. The World Bank, having emerged from the Bretton Woods Conference of 1944 and a consensus around the necessary internationalism of postwar state-mediated capitalism, brought experts and money to the task of development. It worked hard to dispense wisdom, experts and resources, including $953 million in its first seventeen years.[26] Of significance for original Colombo Plan members, one of its most successful acts of economic development and diplomacy was steering the governments of India and Pakistan towards a technically and financially backed water-sharing agreement for the Indus Basin (concluded only in 1960), which had become a source of contestation after Partition. But its decision-making up to the early 1960s was largely determined by a group of elites whose economic assumptions and shared world view circumscribed the scope of international development. They viewed the challenges of regions such as South Asia in the bigger context of stabilizing the world order, and part of this view of stability meant preserving open markets and no challenge to existing centres of economic and trading power or divisions of labour.[27]

It was little wonder, then, that at the end of 1950, after another round of jousting on development priorities between great powers and Asian members in ECAFE, an angry Lokanathan considered moving to exclude

[25] Amy Staples, *Birth of Development: How the World Bank, Food and Agriculture Organization, and World Health Organization Changed the World, 1945–1965* (Kent, OH: Kent State University Press, 2006), pp. 76–104; and Amalia Ribi Forclaz, 'From Reconstruction to Development: The Early Years of the Food and Agriculture Organization (FAO) and the Conceptualization of Rural Welfare, 1945–1955', *The International History Review*, 41, 2 (2019), 351–71.

[26] Staples, *Birth of Development*, p. 45.

[27] As historian Amy Staples has shown, women's labour remained invisible to the male-dominated group of World Bankers, and women were generally regarded as non-productive and/or 'backward'. Ibid, pp. 22–45. For early support for co-operatives and community development projects see, Daniel Immerwahr, *Thinking Small: The United Sates and the Lure of Community Development* (Cambridge, MA: Harvard University Press, 2015).

Western members from ECAFE.[28] While he did not pursue this radical idea, he and his Indian colleagues demonstrated greater bullishness from early 1951 after ECAFE had been reviewed by its parent body, ECOSOC, and renewed as an ongoing regional association. Arguing that 'the time has come when the Asian countries should take their own decisions on their own economic problems', Lokanathan suggested that when a majority of regional members agreed on something in ECAFE meetings, it should no longer be capable of being vetoed by a non-regional member.[29] The Indian government backed this approach and non-regional members agreed informally to follow this principle. Observers wondered how the Colombo Plan might negotiate this Indian-led push for greater Asian agency and a stronger sense of regional identity.[30]

The extent to which the Colombo Plan was an organization that might harness or corral these energies was thus an issue that demanded diplomatic finessing from the outset. Early press releases stressed that the plan was less of a plan than a collection of bilateral agreements under which donor nations provided assistance that addressed the needs identified by individual Asian nations. Yet there was no move to change the title of the Colombo Plan. On the one hand, use of the word 'plan' conveyed commitment and a sense of collective endeavour that all members welcomed. Western commentators, concerned about the spread of communism and the deepening Cold War tensions, seemed to derive the greatest satisfaction from a 'plan's' sense of political solidity, finding an echo of the successful Marshall Plan. British journalist Guy Wint described it as a combination of collective salvage from the 'turmoil' of South Asia's emancipation and an attempt to meet the Malthusian challenge of feeding huge and growing populations while putting the region on a new economic footing. Britain, he wrote, was driven to act in support of Asian nations by London's overarching concern for peace and prosperity: 'it was imperative for Britain to give any aid within its power to help shore up the independent countries of South Asia in their zealous struggles to

[28] R. T. Ledward (UK delegation to the UN) to Leonard Scopes, Foreign Office, 27 December 1950 US1104/1, FO 327/95777, TNA.

[29] P. J. H. Stent (Deputy U.K. High Commissioner, Lahore) to Foreign Office, US1104/40, 4 March 1951, FO 371/95778, TNA.

[30] Stent to Foreign Office, US1104/43, 5 March 1951, ibid; and Stent memo, 'The Future of the Economic Commission for Asia and the Far East, and the Policy of His Majesty's Government Towards It', 2 April 1951, ibid.

organise their new life'. He referred briefly to the 'accumulated vast sterling balances' of the Asian dominions.[31]

For regional members, it was a different story. The Ceylonese understandably embraced the capitalized 'Colombo Plan', celebrating their connection with its origins and the subsequent administrative offices located in Colombo. Both the Indian and Pakistan governments, however, had invested huge reputational capital and resources in respective five- and six-year economic plans, both commencing in 1951 and proclaimed as nation-forging programs of developmental work. There was no great desire for another, multi-party 'plan' to compete with them.[32] To the extent that foreign aid provided under the Colombo Plan helped India and Pakistan, it could do so by being folded into their home-grown plans.

Perhaps not surprisingly, then, the Consultative Committee of the Colombo Plan began with cautious circling around different sets of hopes. For around a year, it was not clear that the Consultative Committee would carry the work and administrative load on its own and that this would shape long annual meetings. The first post-setting-up meeting, held in Colombo in February 1951 (again in the Senate Building), lasted little more than a week, partly because it was at the level of officials only. Representatives from the French Associated States of Cambodia and Vietnam joined as members for the first time, and the governments of Thailand, Burma, Indonesia and the Philippines sent observers. The pattern of observing for one or ideally two meetings prior to seeking membership was set early. Delegates did not vote on whether new members would gain full membership; they agreed unanimously prior to the meeting and then welcomed the new member at an appropriate stage early in proceedings. Having just announced their intention to join, the US government representatives Donald D. Kennedy, Director of the Office of

[31] Guy Wint, *What Is the Colombo Plan?* (Bloomsbury: The Batchworth Press, 1952), p. 11 and passim.

[32] The views of Indian and Pakistan officials were a major factor in the tentative descriptions of the 'Plan'. Such views were reported to London and elsewhere by those who sought to evaluate the impact of the Colombo Plan. For example, Treasury Reporter, 'Notes of a Talk by Mr. Geoffrey Bridson, of the British Broadcasting Corporation, to Information Officers held at H.M. Treasury on Tuesday, 24th February, 1953', DO 35/5755, TNA. Policy for relating foreign assistance to successive Indian Five-Year Plans made clear that foreign assistance was welcome to the extent that it aligned with pre-determined priorities under the plans: Y. N. Sukthankar (Secretary, Government of India Planning Commission) memorandum, 'Consultation with the Planning Commission before Acceptance of Offers of Financial Assistance to Ensure that All Foreign Assistance Is Accounted for in the Five Year Plan', 11 June 1953, Education File 42-20/52-SIR, NAI.

South Asian Affairs in the State Department, and Embassy First Secretary Myron L. Black received the warmest of the welcomes at Colombo.[33] For his part, Kennedy said he had come to try to understand how the Committee would work; 'He gathered that it was neither a diplomatic nor an executive committee meeting. It was a sort of Forum. On that basis they had to look to the present and the future in an exploratory way – not to devise ways and means of getting money from generous people.'[34] This set the tone for the American approach to membership, one that was dutiful and mindful of the public relations value in being associated but always wary of any suggestion of interference with policy set in Washington.

Much of the discussion centred on how much of a secretariat was needed. There were enough 'bones' of organization to know that information exchange and progress reports would take place at regular, possibly annual meetings of the committee, and that the technical cooperation side of the plan logically benefited from a small Technical Co-operation Bureau joining up the needs with donors and ensuring expectations were clear in the provision of experts and hosting of students. But did this bureau need to be bigger in order to act as a secretariat for the Consultative Committee? Might there be a Council for Economic Co-operation (clearly an optimistic nod to the powerful Organization for European Economic Co-Operation dispensing Marshall Plan aid)? Opinions varied. Opening a meeting of ECAFE in Lahore, also in February 1951, Pakistan Prime Minister Liaquat Ali Khan wondered if the Colombo Plan would yield more than the loan of technicians and some scholarships.[35] The Ceylonese in particular, keen to make the most of their identification with the plan, sought the opposite – something like a continuing economic council with an equally strong body overseeing the technical assistance side of the plan and a well-staffed headquarters in Colombo.[36] On any occasion that conversation meandered in a direction

[33] Meeting of the Consultative Committee on Economic Development in South and South-East Asia, Minutes of the First Business Meeting in Senate Building, Colombo, 13 February 1951, CRS A10617 item 1951/1, NAA.

[34] Meeting of the Consultative Committee on Economic Development in South and South-East Asia, Minutes of the Second Meeting in Senate Building, Colombo, 14 February 1951, CRS A10617 item 1951/1, NAA.

[35] *Dawn*, 2 March 1951. The sub-heading of the story was 'Colombo Plan Not Enough', Reported in J. B. H. Stent (CRO) to Francis, Foreign Office, 8 March 1951, US11037/1, FO 371/95817, TNA.

[36] ED(SA)(51), Cabinet Working Party on Economic Development in South and South East Asia, 'Report by United Kingdom Delegation on Meeting of Consultative Committee on

that seemed to question the value to be added by the Consultative Committee, delegates leapt to its defence. Ceylon's Coomaraswamy, his Indian counterpart P. C. Battacharyya, and Australia's Critchley and Britain's M. T. Flett were the most insistent that the Colombo Plan would thrive only through some sort of a strong role for the Consultative Committee.[37]

Despite Kennedy's view, the task of getting money was front of mind for the observers from Burma and Thailand who worried that they might not be able to produce anything like a six-year development plan for some time, yet they needed assistance urgently. After some back-and-forth between Burmese delegate U Kyaw Thein and others, it was agreed that governments did not need a multi-year development plan before becoming members and beginning discussions with donor governments about development assistance.[38]

Under technical assistance, the provision of experts and scholarships/traineeships also began unevenly as donors jockeyed for the limelight. In early discussions, the British were annoyed at the Australians' capacity to appear the most forthcoming and generous, including the range of 100 scholarships they were offering. With more than a whiff of condescension, Whitehall officials wondered whether scholarships for studying music and drama in Australia were what developing Asia really needed.[39]

HOSTS AND HOSPITALITY

One aspect of regional stirring that helped overcome the patchy start to the Colombo Plan was the opportunity to demonstrate international credentials through hosting diplomatic events. The short meeting held in Colombo in February 1951 was destined to be overshadowed by the

Economic Development in South and South-East Asia' held in Colombo, 13th to 20th February 1951, CAB 134/201, TNA; ED(SA)(51) 17 (2nd Revise), Cabinet Working Party on Economic Development in South and South East Asia, 'Brief for the UK Delegation to the Forthcoming Meeting of the Consultative Committee on South and South-East Asia', February 1951, CAB 134/200, TNA.

37 Meeting of the Consultative Committee on Economic Development in South and South-East Asia, Minutes of the Fourth Meeting in Senate Building, Colombo, 16 February 1951, CRS A10617 item 1951/1, NAA.

38 Ibid.

39 ED(SA)(51), 17 (2nd Revise), Cabinet Working Party on Economic Development in South and South East Asia, 'Brief for the UK Delegation to the Forthcoming Meeting of the Consultative Committee on South and South-East Asia', February 1951, CAB 134/200, TNA.

expanded war in Korea and fears of a third world war; but the assembling of a bigger number of interested representatives was significant. Delegates from the original Commonwealth member countries joined representatives from Burma, Cambodia, Laos, Vietnam, Indonesia, the Philippines, Thailand, the United States, all potential new members, and the World Bank. The Ceylonese government invested more resources and hoped to enhance its international profile in a Colombo Plan Exhibition held the following year.

Having hosted the initial meeting that conceived the Colombo Plan, before foreign ministers gathered again in Sydney and London, the Ceylonese had at least wrested the meeting location back to where it began; and the Consultative Committee meetings stayed in South Asia for the next three years, with Karachi hosting in 1952 and New Delhi in 1953. From 1954, when Ottawa hosted, the pattern adjusted to meetings being hosted alternately by donor and recipient nations. Thus, the Colombo Plan was an important vehicle by which newly independent Asian nations continued to accumulate diplomatic and reputational credentials through the convening of international conferences. From 1947, when the huge Asian Relations Conference was hosted by the Indians, through the 1960s was a special period for the frequency of major international meetings hosted in Asian and then African cities. The rapid rise in activity was accompanied by more popular forms of participation in meetings and the embrace of an imagined world gaze settling on the host cities.[40] Pride was at stake for the host nation, as the demonstrable capacity to project national progress became intrinsic to internationalist credentials. When Nehru returned from the Bandung Conference in 1955, for example, his report contained considerable detail on how effective the Indonesian accommodation and hosting was and how deficient Delhi looked by comparison.[41] Conference success was measured not only by bold pronouncements or diplomatic breakthroughs but by the organizational skill in managing large events and the quality of the hospitality offered.

With changing host cities for annual meetings of the Consultative Committee, the Colombo Plan was especially marked by a layer of diplomacy around place, format and hospitality. It could boast some scale in terms of numbers represented at its meetings. As Australian External

[40] Naoko Shimazu, 'Places in Geography', *Political Geography*, 31 (2012), 335–36.

[41] J. Nehru to K. D. Malaviya, New Delhi, 29 April 1955, K. D. Malaviya Papers, subfile 7, NMML.

Affairs Minister Casey noted, from fifty at Colombo in 1950 the number was more like 150 by 1957. Elements of theatre and performance were enhanced by the hospitality expected. The following chapters outline how photographic exhibitions displaying Colombo Plan projects and the development of member nations began to accompany the Consultative Committee meetings. They fostered mild competition, as governments geared up to put their best images of achievements forward.[42] From 1952 onwards, the conference format provided for different forms of exchange: scrutiny and discussion of progress under the agreed six-year development plans of the regional members; feeding in contextual research from members' experts, ECAFE, other UN bodies, scholarly reports and philanthropic foundations such as Ford and Rockefeller; bilateral meetings to identify needs and secure offers of aid; meetings between diplomats on other matters of importance; ministerial plenary and private meetings; and a whirl of social events and post-conference excursions.

Governments of recently independent nations were understandably the keenest to enhance their standing and to consolidate power within the new nation-state through exhibiting their international credentials. Before Diem exceeded expectations when he stood up to welcome members in 1957, other new nations demonstrated their capacity to host large diplomatic gatherings. The Ceylonese United National Party (UNP) government of Senanayake made the most of its hosting the initial meeting and blessing the Colombo Plan with its title by following up in 1951 and then with a Colombo Plan Exhibition in February–March 1952. Just over one hundred years since the first of the great international exhibitions or fairs, the Great Exhibition in London, 1851, these enormous showcase events still had the capacity to confer 'world city' status on those who staged them. For one hundred years, primarily in the Western world, they had displayed evidence of progress and modernity: engines of industrialization, trade, consumer culture, art and design. Grand exhibitions always invited comparisons with previous exhibitions and with neighbouring cities and nations. They could speak to regional identity as well as the more international and universal themes of modernity. And in the hands of newly independent governments such as the Senanayake government, exhibitions could both mobilize and control ethnic groups, shaping a particular construction of a new nation. In 1952, before television began

[42] These are similar to claims made for the much better-known Asia–Africa conference in Bandung in 1955. See Shimazu, 'Diplomacy as Theater', pp. 225–52.

to revolutionize popular viewing, visual and spatial connections to text were crucial to exhibition success.[43]

In their communications with London about the exhibition, Ceylonese government officials pressed British civil servants for the kind of support that would make it a grandiose affair, insisting that anything less would not do. They had in mind the features that made the Festival of Britain so successful in 1951: demonstrating recovery from war while suggesting that both Ceylon's past and its embrace of new industry, science and technology would enable its people to thrive. The Senanayake government would harness modernity to a distinctive, Sinhalese past. It was to be the largest exhibition ever held in South/Southeast Asia with expectations of perhaps two million visitors, including 10,000 from overseas.[44]

These great expectations were not quite met (an Australian estimate put the attendance figure at one million),[45] but the Colombo Exhibition was nevertheless a grand affair, spread out in what was still called Victoria Park, the UNP being firm on the message that Ceylonese independence was matched by proud membership of the postwar Commonwealth. It marked not only the Colombo Plan but also the twenty-first anniversary of universal adult suffrage in Ceylon and partial self-government granted by the British (both achievements featuring in a commemorative stamp, Figure 2.1). By the time British and other members realized the extent to which the Colombo Plan was being used as a vehicle to showcase Ceylonese political achievements in what was an election year, it was too late. They managed, at least, to squash some of the more carnival-like features planned. Jayawardene wanted a circus from Australia and a group of New Zealand Maori dancers he had seen perform during a visit to Rotorua, an idea that the New Zealanders stiffly pointed out 'was typical neither of New Zealand nor of the Maori people

[43] See Paul Greenhalgh, *Fair World: A History of World Fairs and Expositions from London to Shanghai, 1851–2010* (Winterbourne: Papadakis, 2011); and for exhibitions and fairs from 'the margins' of the Western world, see Marta Filipova (ed.), *Cultures of International Exhibitions: Great Exhibitions in the Margins* (Abingdon: Routledge, 2015).

[44] Comment by Ceylonese High Commissioner in London, E. A. P. Wijeyarante, quoted in *Dawn*, 17 March 1952, 3; Anoma Pieris, *Architecture and Nationalism in Sri Lanka: The Trouser under the Cloth* (Abingdon: Routledge, 2013), p. 161. For the Festival of Britain, see, Harriet Atkinson, *The Festival of Britain: A Land and Its People* (London: Bloomsbury, 2021).

[45] 'Australia at Colombo Exhibition', *Overseas Trading* (journal of the Australian Department of Commerce and Agriculture), 4, 12 (1952), 1.

FIGURE 2.1 A 1952 Ceylonese commemorative stamp conflated twenty-one years of universal suffrage and the first anniversary of the Colombo Plan. *Source*: Lankastamp collection, www.lankastamp.com/stamp_details.php?id=3013

today'.[46] While the New Zealanders decided against involvement, the governments of Britain, Australia (without circus), Canada, Pakistan, India, Thailand, Vietnam, Indonesia and the United States joined Ceylon in mounting displays that blended trade promotion with stories of cooperative development.[47]

The architecture and exhibits in Victoria Park suggested a symbolic dialogue between the familiar colonial past and a state-forged modernity for the future. The official Ceylon Pavilion took the form of an ancient Kandyan king's palace, but on the inside were displays about reservoirs, hydroelectricity, higher education, irrigation and urbanization projects. Other Asian pavilions featured a similar contrast between the celebration of a glorious, pre-colonized past and education and excitement in the ways of modernity. Western exhibits ranged from heavy-handed lessons in how to make good of agricultural development and advertisements of mechanical ingenuity to less-than-subtle warnings about the dangers of communism. The Australians noted in their display text that 'It is in countries with low living standards and little hope for improvement in

[46] John Reid, 'Colombo Plan – Exhibition', for Minister of External Affairs, 31 July 1951, EA 1 W2824 118/7/6, Archives New Zealand (hereafter ANZ); Pieris, *Architecture and Nationalism*, p. 161. John Reid, Assistant Secretary in New Zealand's Ministry of External Affairs, played a significant and constructive role in early meetings of ECAFE and the Colombo Plan, often working against the grain of his government's scepticism. See Anthony Reid, 'New Zealand's Unexpected Opening to Asia', pp. 19–38.

[47] The New Zealand decision was taken primarily on the grounds of cost and insufficient notice: John Reid, 'Colombo Plan – Exhibition', for Minister of External Affairs, 31 July 1951, EA 1 W2824 118/7/6, ANZ; NZ Department of External Affairs to High Commissioner, Colombo, 20 November 1951, ibid.

the future that extremist political doctrines find fertile ground.'[48] The exhibition was brought to an early close by the sudden death on 22 March of Prime Minister Senanayake. Celebrated by his supporters as 'the father' of the independent nation of Ceylon, he was also described by some as one of the 'fathers' of the Colombo Plan.[49] A lasting reminder of the exhibition was the Colombo Plan Monument, on what is today the Dharmapala Mawartha-F. R. Senanayake roundabout in front of the Colombo Town Hall. The inscription marking the start of the Colombo Plan is in nine languages: Sinhala, Tamil, Hindi, Bahasa Indonesian, Nastaliq, English, Thai, Vietnamese and Pali.

Karachi hosted the Consultative Committee meeting of 1952. Having declined British offers of secretarial help, Pakistani organizers exceeded the expectations of the British High Commission. Hospitality was again a key ingredient of success, and practical measures such as accommodating all delegates in one big hotel, were important in the fostering of camaraderie and informal exchanges.[50] Karachi seemed to pass the hotel test and more generally won applause, with functions for delegates every evening. After the conclusion of the conference, there was a special train excursion to the ancient site of Indus civilization, Mohenjo-Daro, and development projects, the Sukkur Barrage and the Kotri Barrages, on the Sind River. According to the British delegation's report, it was the social side of the conference that featured in the local newspapers; and the post-conference excursion proved most valuable for enabling further conversations among the ministers from different nations.[51]

Having featured after the initial meeting in Colombo in January 1950, then repeated successfully in Colombo (1951) and Karachi, the post-conference excursions would remain a fixture of annual meetings. This proved the case regardless of the considerable costs incurred by host nations. For example, when the Indonesians hosted the Consultative Committee in 1959, the British paused momentarily before committing

[48] Quoted in Pieris, *Architecture and Nationalism*, pp. 160, 158–62.

[49] For example, see *Daily News* (Sri Lanka), 1 July 2019, www.dailynews.lk/2019/07/01/features/189790/colombo-plan---its-origin-and-significance (accessed 2 December 2020).

[50] Hospitality has emerged as a focus for political geographers exploring flows of power and shifting notions of inclusion and exclusion in the performative aspects of international relations. See, for example, Ruth Craggs, 'Hospitality in Geopolitics and the Making of the Commonwealth International Relations', *Geoforum*, 52 (2014), 90–100.

[51] Sir Gilbert Laithwaite (Karachi) to Marquess of Salisbury, 15 April 1952, DO 35/5786, TNA; Memo by Lord Reading, 'Visits to Karachi and Delhi, 22nd March to 3rd April 1952', April 1952, DO 35/5786, TNA.

their delegation to the post-conference excursion in Bali. This was a time of mounting financial troubles for the Indonesian government; but the British were quick to appreciate the insult that might be taken if they declined to join in acknowledging Bali's markers of the remarkable Majapahit empire civilization from six hundred years earlier. They went on to Bali with the delegations of other nations, noting; 'Every government likes to spend money for national prestige, even when resources are slender; we are certain that the Indonesians would expect to spend money on making a good show, much in the same way as they would spend money on arms for their defence ...'[52]

The meeting in Karachi in 1952 also confirmed the political value to a host government of the international embrace of newly independent states demonstrating their legitimacy and authority. In opening the ministerial part of the meeting, Pakistan's Prime Minister, Khwaja Nazimuddin, pointedly put state power at the heart of expanding economic and welfare activities. 'The reasons that have led to the idea of the welfare state', he said, 'when enlarged to transcend national boundaries, embrace the world as a whole'.[53] Pakistan's Minister for Commerce, Education and Economic Affairs, Fazlur Rahman, strengthened his position in the Cabinet through his adroit chairing of ministerial meetings in 1952, thereby demonstrating that the careers of politicians on the rise could benefit from successful meetings.[54]

The Karachi meeting exceeded nervous expectations. The meeting format settled into what had been envisaged by the previous one: a preliminary meeting by officials from all the countries who pored over and adjusted 'chapter' reports of development progress against the plans set out by individual Asian nations, and another chapter summarizing the efforts of donor nations, which would then all be considered by ministers meeting the following week. Although the quality of various nations' chapter reports varied considerably during these early meetings, this was to be expected, and delegates were at pains to smooth over reporting problems while looking to improvements ahead. Pakistan's English newspaper, *Dawn*, took comfort from the presence of the United States, recently joined as member, and also the World Bank (while noting with approval

[52] J. E. Chadwick (Foreign Office) to H. L. Jenkyns (Treasury), 22 September 1959, DK6/56, FO 371, 152537, TNA.

[53] *Dawn*, 24 March 1952, p. 4.

[54] Sir Gilbert Laithwaite (Karachi) to Marquess of Salisbury, 15 April 1952, DO 35/5786, TNA.

the membership of the French Associated States of Laos, Cambodia and Vietnam).[55] The balance of payments crisis afflicting the British economy and the accompanying shift in British officials' language, away from finance to capital goods, had troubled Indian observers in the lead up to the meeting.[56] Colonial legacies unsurprisingly bred suspicions about forms of aid that might cater to donors' interests more than those of recipient nations. Two Commonwealth statesmen who would become Colombo Plan veterans during the decade, Britain's Lord Reading, Parliamentary Secretary and later Minister of State for Foreign Affairs, and Australia's Casey, led the defence against concerns that forms of aid offered might only be those that did not create competition for British industry. Reading and Casey stressed the high levels of commitment to provide the needed materials as they were identified by recipient nations.[57]

When members re-assembled for the next Consultative Committee meeting in New Delhi, all of the earlier bullishness about raw material and primary product prices had died down. The Committee met in October 1953 when prices for most of the major exports in the region were back to pre-Korean War outbreak prices, if not lower. Unfortunately, the prices of major imported products had not fallen as far. But there was a strong consensus that development plans should proceed as best they could. Both Nehru, who opened the meeting, and Pakistan's Minister for Finance Mohammed Ali acknowledged that all the plans developed to date would require the Asian nations to do more themselves.[58] Their authority as senior statesmen present at the creation of the Colombo Plan lent great weight. The other senior figure who had been at the previous conference was Australia's Casey. Other donor nations sent ministers from portfolios that they felt might be most involved: James Sinclair from Canadian Fisheries and Jack Marshall from New Zealand's Ministry of Health. Indonesia joined the Colombo Plan as a full member at this meeting, adding to the broadening reach of the Colombo Plan.

These newer recipient members were preoccupied with political and economic challenges delaying their submission of six-year programmes of

[55] *Dawn*, 10 March 1952, p. 5.

[56] *Times of India*, 25 March 1952, in Harry Deimal (US Embassy, New Delhi) to State Department, 27 March 1952, RG 59 890.00/3-2752, USNA.

[57] *Bangkok Post*, 31 March 1952, p. 2.

[58] Memorandum by the Economic Secretary to the Treasury, 'The Consultative Committee Meeting in New Delhi', for A. C. B. Symon, Commonwealth Relations Office, 26 November 1953, DO35/5528, TNA.

development. At the New Delhi meeting, the British made it clear that their willingness to provide developmental assistance was not limited to Commonwealth countries and that they welcomed requests from others.[59] This was especially good news to members attending from Burma, Cambodia, Indonesia, Laos and Nepal and an observer from Thailand. The Colombo Plan could no longer be regarded as a Commonwealth club plus the Americans and one or two others. Spending on development had at least risen from the previous year, and delegates registered that it was only from that moment, late 1953, onwards that they might reasonably expect to see returns on investment in the various development programmes underway.[60]

The early meetings of the Consultative Committee were watched eagerly by the international media whose initial expectations of something akin to an Asian version of the Marshall Plan gave way to disappointment and then a simmering anticipation of some new model of East–West collaboration.[61] To the frustration of journalists, meetings of the committee did not produce great announcements but were characterized by the search for unanimity, or at least overwhelming consensus, and the minimization of differences between delegates. At one level, this resulted in a wearying familiarity about the proceedings, but at another level, it took considerable work and shared views about what was at stake. One of the earliest public assessments of the Colombo Plan was published by John Carr-Gregg in 1951. Carr-Gregg, later to become head of the British Information Service, suggested that the committee format would attract critics charging that it was, 'often reducing all constructive proposals to the lowest common denominator fixed by the least imaginative member of the group'.[62] But, he continued, the Committee was an effective method of elucidating differences without their getting in the way of cooperative economic planning. The Colombo Plan model showed that diverse members could agree on practical actions without needing first to agree on political and strategic assessments.[63] One of the last decisions

59 Ibid.

60 Communiqué quoted in Douglas G. Bridson, *Progress in Asia: The Colombo Plan in Action* (London: Her Majesty's Stationery Office, 1953), pp. 24–25.

61 See, for example, Ceylonese newspaper reactions to the London meeting in November 1950, UK High Commission, Ceylon, to CRO, FZ11013/288, 30 November 1950, FO 371/84595, TNA; Canadian newspapers, UK Information Office, Ottawa to CRO, FZ11013/294, 1 December 1950, ibid; and Indian newspaper reactions, UK High Commission in India to CRO, FZ1103/291, 1 December 1950, ibid.

62 Carr-Greg, 'The Colombo Plan', p. 20.

63 Ibid.

taken at New Delhi was to establish an Information Unit in Colombo in order to improve the plan's profile and how it was understood.

At the conclusion of official Consultative Committee business in October 1953, delegates boarded a special train in New Delhi. It took them first to some of India's key development projects underway in the Damodar Valley: the Bokharo Thermal Plant, Konar Dam, Chittaranjan Locomotive Factory and the Sindhri Fertilizer Factory. Then the train returned to Delhi and transformed into a tourist expedition to the sites of civilizational glory, the Taj Mahal and Fatehpur Sikri.[64] From their train coaches, delegates might have had reason to reflect that they had also kept the Colombo Plan on the rails. Up to this point, sources of tension had emerged mostly on account of suspicions of neo-colonial economic intent, the initial clubbishness of the plan's Commonwealth origins and some competitive jockeying for prestige. But the New Delhi meeting had gone some way towards assuaging those who were most concerned about its character. The other issue was Japanese membership of the Colombo Plan, which had surfaced as a thorny issue. The Japanese made clear their desire to join, as soon as the Colombo Plan was born. They saw it as a means by which to re-engage with Asia and to transition from war reparations payments to other forms of economic assistance for the region. At first, Japanese membership was, in the opinion of most, something that might best be avoided on account of recent history and the possibility of Japan's competing with others for US aid.[65] But the British view changed quickly in February 1952, in the lead up to the meeting in Karachi, when they learned that the Japanese were prepared to join as donors and invest dollars in the region in order to hasten the production of raw materials needed by Japan. Thereafter, the British were quietly testing the waters with others, and the Americans testing similarly, for Japanese membership of the Colombo Plan. Others who might have been expected to resist, such as the Australians, also began to re-think Japan's role from the Karachi meeting onwards.[66]

[64] As recalled by C. V. Narasimhan, *The Colombo Plan Newsletter*, 6, 7, 1961, p. 11, Royal Commonwealth Society Collection (hereinafter RCS), Cambridge University Library (hereinafter CUL).

[65] UK Foreign Office briefs for Lord Reading during his visit to Rangoon meeting of ECAFE, 19 January 1952, FZ11011/5, FO 371/101246, TNA.

[66] ED(SA)(52)14, Note by Foreign Office on Japan and the Colombo Plan, 21 February 1952, CAB 134/866, TNA; Minute by J. D. Murray, 22 April 1952, FZ 11014/134, FO 371/101254, TNA.

PROJECTS

Histories of postwar aid and development have stressed both the pre-war and wartime roots of aid thinking and also the missionary zeal accompanying the project of modernization.[67] From the American perspective, there is a rough narrative path from early twentieth-century reconstruction work in the Philippines to the creation of the Tennessee Valley Authority (TVA) (1933), to US-led efforts under the United Nations Relief and Rehabilitation Administration (UNRRA), and to assessing nations according to Walt Rostow's five stages of economic growth (1960). Added to this was the official view, especially after the Second World War, that poverty and hunger in far-flung places long associated with these maladies, had become a threat to the world order.[68] The TVA was especially symbolic: a showcase initiative of US President Roosevelt's New Deal program, drawing on unemployed manpower to build dams and produce high volumes of easily distributed hydroelectric power. It showed how an acceptable form of state-sponsored development (as opposed to the unacceptable communist version of state-sponsored development) might be exported as a model – or at least elements of it – for countries seeking to 'catch up' in the great task of better harnessing resources for higher levels of production, including production of food.

Development was a loosely defined but compelling idea embraced by newly independent governments in Asia, too. Economic and political histories of India in the 1940s acknowledge the jostling of ideas between influential industrial families and the spectrum of thinking within the Indian National Congress. By the time of independence in August 1947, Nehru led a government committed to economic growth in the formal economy, driven largely but not exclusively by a powerful state, and with an emphasis on urgent industrialization.[69] Even this highly generalized sketch excludes much. The grandiosity of land reclaiming, multi-purpose

[67] Two pioneering works outlining the roots and evolution of US policy on international development are Ekbladh, *The Great American Mission*; and Cullather, *The Hungry World*.

[68] Walt Whitman Rostow, *The Stages of Economic Growth: A Non-communist Manifesto* (New York: Cambridge University Press), 1960.

[69] Medha M. Kudaisya, *Tryst with Prosperity: India Business and the Bombay Plan of 1944* (Harayana: Penguin Random House, 2018); Nariaki Nakazato, 'The Transfer of Economic Power in India: Indian Big Business, the British Raj and Development Planning, 1930–1948', in Mushirual Hasan and Nariaki Nakazato (eds.), *The Unfinished Agenda: Nation-Building in South Asia* (New Delhi: Manohar Publishers & Distributors, 2001), pp. 247–307.

hydroelectric, irrigation and settlement programmes or new steel mills has often taken centre stage in those interpreting development in Asia through the lens of modernization. But recent studies have shown that smaller scale community development, sometimes based on local co-operatives, was also being promoted by the Indian government and by the Ford Foundation, among other donors. Only in the early 1950s, in organizations such as the FAO, did officials adopt a more uniformly top-down approach at the local level, based on short-term interventions with technical expertise.[70]

As historian Nick Cullather has argued, postwar development acquired high political-diplomatic cachet through the three related roles that projects played: they served to *display* features of development, they were *models* that might be replicated and they provided the basis for *narratives* on modernizing progress.[71] Under Colombo Plan activity, a series of relationships between and beyond governments unfolded around particular development projects. Most obviously, these relationships operated at the government and bureaucrat level between donor(s) and regional members, but they also embraced those doing the work. For big, multi-year infrastructure projects such as dam-building, power generation, steel mill construction or road laying, the layers in the relationship thickened with expert engineers, trainees and more government departments, regulatory bodies and unions. It became a Colombo Plan ideal to combine capital aid projects with training for local technicians under the technical assistance side of the plan. These necessary engagements constitute opportunities for scholars interested in the production of 'postcolonial knowledge' through their negotiations and different forms of expertise being exchanged.[72] For donor governments at the time, it became hard to control what was happening on the ground, both in terms of progress towards project completion and the relations between the various parties involved. Projects that involved building, industrial, agricultural works or even students and trainees undergoing training and donor country experts in action, were located in particular geographic circumstances and in the hands of experts and actors over whom the state had incomplete control. At the same time, donor governments needed, for

70 Immerwahr, *Thinking Small*; Forclaz, 'From Reconstruction to Development', pp. 351–71.

71 Cullather, *The Hungry World*, p. 5 and passim.

72 As, for example, pursued in pre-independence context, by Chris Bayly in, *Empire and Information: Intelligence Gathering and Social Communication in India, 1780–1870* (Cambridge: Cambridge University Press, 1996).

their electoral welfare, to be able to insert their aid activities into a compelling story about the virtues of such spending. The publicity for Colombo Plan projects needed to be directed internally to the voting publics of donor governments, as well as being distributed throughout the region. To attempt a comprehensive survey of the myriad projects and training opportunities made possible under the Colombo Plan is not feasible here, but some of them assumed special importance for their capacity to shape the narrative of the Colombo Plan.

Many of the projects funded began before the Colombo Plan's start date of 1 July 1951 and some of those examined were not completed within the long-1950s scope of this study. They had taken early shape in colonial circumstances and/or wartime exigencies and therefore bore some of the 'colonial welfare' philosophy that looked to increased colonial productivity and civilian health in the service of empire. Their pre-1951 histories were mostly omitted in Colombo Plan statements. In many cases, their progress to completion took shape over a long period in ways that were tied to local politics and the efforts of Western development experts who often 'reworked' the earlier culture of colonial officers in their practices.[73]

The Colombo Plan then enabled donor governments an opportunity to make 'new' several projects that had complicated, often colonial, pre-1950 histories. Among these, the most ambitious and grandest scale projects supported by Colombo Plan capital were those multi-purpose schemes that promised to transform arid or jungle zones into irrigated, powered areas on which crops could grow and new settlers could thrive. Two examples were the Thal project in northern Pakistan and the Gal Oya project in eastern Ceylon. Both projects had pre-independence origins. Both were celebrated in their early stages for their attracting funding from more than one donor: spectacular projects transcending the norm of bilateral aid flows helped make the Colombo Plan look more like a plan and less a mere umbrella under which two parties reached agreements. The Thal, in fact, became known as the Commonwealth Thal project, as it drew on funding from all Commonwealth donors. Created in 1949, the Thal Development Authority used capital and technical forms

[73] See two works by Uma Kothari, 'Authority and Expertise: The Professionalisation of International Development and the Ordering of Dissent', *Antipode*, 37, 3 (2005), 425–46; and 'Spatial Practices and Imaginaries: Experiences of Colonial Officers & Development Professionals', in Mark Duffield and Vernon Hewitt (eds.), *Empire, Development & Colonialism: The Past in the Present* (Suffolk: James Currey, 2009), pp. 161–75.

of assistance to transform a desert area to the east of the Indus River, around 100 miles from Lahore. The original aim was one million acres of arable land. The result five years later was roughly half that, with some 50,000 families settled.[74]

In Ceylon, the Gal Oya project to irrigate the eastern dry zone of the country and colonize the area with new settlers was the largest of several schemes planned by the Ceylonese government prior to the Commonwealth meeting of foreign ministers in Colombo in January 1950. The project involved massive jungle clearance and colonization by new settlers who would farm new plantations, thus reducing Ceylon's dependence on overseas food sources. The Gal Oya Development Board (based on the US TVA) was established for settling landless peasants, and by 1952 claimed to have made 120,000 acres available through irrigation.[75] The Board also oversaw construction of a huge reservoir and hydro-work for electricity generation and flood control. By the late 1950s, like the Thal project, it had attracted support from all Commonwealth donor countries and also Japan. There was also a Gal Oya Technical Training Institute, for which Australia and Canada provided the early principals.

Donor governments were sometimes able to distinguish their aid provision by distinct activity. The Canadians, for example, were quick to provide aerial surveys for (West) Pakistan during 1952–53, yielding data on mineral deposits and other geological features. They followed up with similar surveys of Ceylon in 1956, accompanied by hydrological and soil studies, and then Malaya in 1957, earning themselves reputation as

74 W. Railston, 'Britain and the Technical Development of Eastern Commonwealth Countries under the Colombo Plan', *Journal of the Royal Society of Arts*, 107, 5037 (1959), 656. For an insider's memory of early days of the Thal project, see Charles George Westwater, 'Foreign Intervention in the Planning and Execution of National Development in an Underdeveloped Country: A Case Study of Pakistan', Thesis for Master of City Planning, Massachusetts Institute of Technology, September 1972.

75 Patrick Peebles, 'Colonization and Ethnic Conflict in the Dry Zone of Sri Lanka, *Journal of Asian Studies*, 49, 1 (1990), 37, and 30–55. Peebles also details the ways in alternative pasts invoked by Sinhalese and Tamils, and framed in ethnic nationalism, have fuelled enmities. The claims made for land made available were subsequently disputed, revised and have proven extremely difficult to verify, as is outlined in a detailed study of Gal Oya's rehabilitation from the late 1970s: Norman Uphoff, *Learning from Gal Oya: Possibilities for Participatory Development and Post-Newtonian Social Science* (Ithaca, NY: Cornell University Press, 1992); Clifford H. McFadden, 'The Gal Oya Valley: Ceylon's Little TVA', *Geographical Review*, 44, 2 (1954), 271–81.

surveying specialists.[76] More explicitly, projects were sometimes branded in honour of their donor. The Indians were told to select projects that could bear a Canadian stamp.[77] By the mid-1950s, Pakistan was building or expanding two cement factories, one called the Maple Leaf Factory at Daudkhaul and the other Zeal-Pak, after New Zealand, at Hyderabad.[78]

From the start, a significant part of technical assistance consisted of training students in host countries. The first example of a donor country hosting students was the New Zealand provision for six dental nurses from Ceylon to train at the NZ School Dental Service. This achievement was all the more notable for the New Zealand government's initial wariness towards Colombo Plan funding. External Affairs officers in Wellington scrambled to produce information briefs designed to let Asian members know of New Zealand's training strengths in fields such as agriculture, education, public health and railways.[79] Providing technical assistance was less costly than committing to big projects like the Thal and Gal Oya, and the Holland government's commitment of £400,000 for technical assistance for the first three years was more readily forthcoming. Initially, it went towards training engineering students from Malaya and Ceylon and the Ceylonese dental nurses.[80] Support for dentistry also played to a strength. Since 1921 New Zealand had supported bringing dental services to primary schools, in order to maximize the coverage of children's teeth. It was one component of the expanding New Zealand welfare state that was a source of national pride, also internationally projected. 'In the social laboratory of New Zealand', ran

76 *Colombo Plan Newsletter*, November 1956, pp. 1, 9, 1-3, RCS, CUL; ibid., January–February 1957, pp. 2, 1, 18.

77 Campbell-Miller, 'Encounter and Apprenticeship', p. 37.

78 *Colombo Plan Newsletter*, October 1956, pp. 1, 8, 3, RCS, CUL.

79 While keen to assist in the task of 'drawing the teeth of communism', Holland and colleagues initially baulked at what they saw as a big gap between New Zealand's capacity and the scope of problems Asia faced: McIntosh, undated memo (May 1950), 'Colombo Plan', McIntosh Papers, MS6759-182, National Library of New Zealand (Alexander Turnbull), Wellington; New Zealand External Affairs Record (NZEAR) 1 (April 1951); J. Reid, Draft report of meeting of Departmental representatives, 'Technical Assistance', 2 May 1951, EA 1W2824 item 118/4/3/1, ANZ.

80 Susan M. Moffat, '"A Bold Experiment": The New Zealand School Dental Service and Colombo Plan', *Journal of the Royal Society of New Zealand*, 50, 1 (2020), 47–66, 50; and see also Jenny Collins, 'Perspectives from the Periphery? Colombo Plan Scholars in New Zealand Universities, 1951–1975', *History of Education Review*, 41, 2 (2012), 129–46. The government realized quickly that it would not be able to fully expend the £400,000 in three years: Draft Cabinet Paper, 'Colombo Plan – Technical Assistance Unit', by EA Minister Clifton Webb, 20 December 1951, EA W2824 118/4/3/1, ANZ.

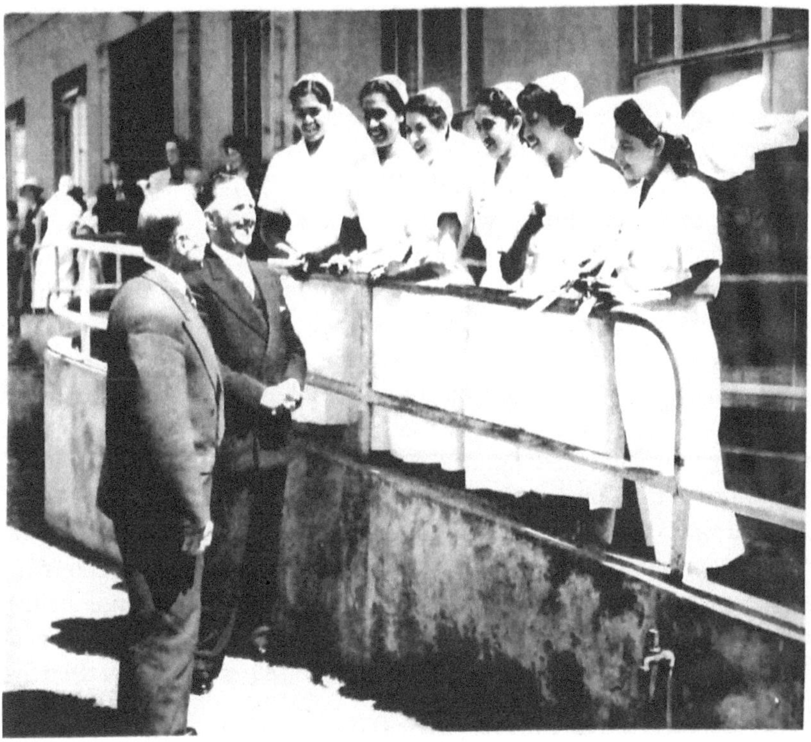

FIGURE 2.2 New Zealand Prime Minister Sid Holland greets six Ceylonese dental nurses in Wellington, 1951.
Source: Public domain.

an account later produced for Colombo Plan publicity, 'it has been shown that State enterprise and private enterprise can operate successfully in the same fields, one acting as a corrective or supplement to the other'.[81] The pioneering nurses arriving in Wellington from Ceylon in 1951 were Chandra Ratwatte, Charmion Drieberg, Kamala Wijesinghe, Eileen Dassanayake, Maheswari Manikawasagar and Kusamawathie Lianage (shown in Figure 2.2). Drieberg later recalled that 'everywhere we went we were photographed and put in the paper and it was just wonderful'.[82]

Such stories elevated the Colombo Plan. They were needed to prevent its being dragged by journalists and critics back towards two narratives

[81] *Colombo Plan Newsletter*, 3, 1, January 1958, RCS, CUL.
[82] Drieberg's recollections in New Zealand Ministry of Foreign Affairs and Trade, *The Colombo Plan at 50: A New Zealand Perspective*, 50th Anniversary of the Colombo Plan 1951–2001 (Wellington: New Zealand Official Development Assistance, 2001), p. 14.

less appealing in much of postwar Asia, namely Britain's indebtedness as a constraint on India, Pakistan and Ceylon having access to funds, and the polarizing tendencies of the Cold War. The Colombo Plan's Consultative Committee gatherings enabled donor countries with less diplomatic experience in the region and in the provision of foreign aid to meet with Asian politicians and administrators to find ways of matching what they had to offer with the needs of individual countries. The initial horizon of six-year development programmes did not encourage very long-term thinking but also prompted workarounds. Where there was no neat match, donors quickly settled on sending surplus foodstuffs such as wheat to generate finance in recipient countries: the sale of wheat, for example, by Asian governments generating what was known as 'counterpart funds' that would be used towards mutually agreed development projects. This suited donor countries such as Australia and Canada (and, outside the Commonwealth, the United States) that often generated such surpluses. Some of the early Australian meetings in New Delhi with Indian Minister for Finance, Prem Narian, explored how counterpart funds arising from gifts of wheat might support the construction of the Tungabhadra Dam and canals in Karnataka.[83] The Australians and Canadians appointed directors of Colombo Plan supplies who had extensive trade and war-supply experience.[84]

In the hands of some, the Colombo Plan remained a Cold War beacon of hope, or at least a rallying call in the great struggle between the Soviets and the West. At a meeting of British information officers in Singapore in January 1953, the Colombo Plan was given an elevated role in the briefing covering the events of recent years and suggesting where to focus information energies. For Sir John Sterndale Bennett, Deputy High Commissioner General for South East Asia, it seemed to be a turning point for the West at a time of grave danger. Sterndale Bennett provided a tale of lonely British defiance as the communist threat in Asia grew in the late 1940s, in a manner evoking a Churchillian interpretation of the early part of the Second World War in Europe. Britain was 'once again' locked in combat with a deadly foe. The years 1949–50 had been the high point of communist success in the region, and there seemed, at that

83 Prem Narian, record of conversation with Francis Stuart, Australian High Commission, and 'J S', 29 July 1952, External Affairs file F.22-5/51-M (m), NAI.

84 As discussed in the following chapter, the Australian was J. B. Todd who was appointed Director of Colombo Plan Supplies in mid-1951 and based in the Melbourne Office of the Department of Commerce and Agriculture.

time, nothing that would stop the spread of Chinese influence to all parts. 'But it was at this darkest moment', he continued, 'that the first glimmers of light began to appear. It was in January 1950 that the first steps were taken to launch the Colombo Plan. This coincided with a similar awakening of interest on the part of the United States'. Sterndale Bennett noted that since then the Commonwealth had rallied around the Colombo Plan and the United States had provided aid to every country in the region, especially after the outbreak of the Korean War.[85] A trite interpretation, even at the time, this narrative probably reflected Sterndale Bennett's military service in the First World War and also the popular reception of Churchill's multi-volume history of the Second World War, published progressively in the early 1950s, including in serialized form in newspapers. Thousands in the English-speaking world were able to read of Britain's courageous resistance to Hitler, according to Churchill's compelling and selective account; and they could also interpret the deepening Cold War through the Churchillian version of the early stages of the previous world war.[86] This Cold War rendering of the Colombo Plan would remain one means by which it gripped popular and planning imaginations, particularly in the donor countries where great struggles and turning points were the stuff of contemporary history.

DEVELOPMENT ENTREPRENEURS

Among the networks of actors who constituted the human faces of post-war aid diplomacy were those officials whose continuous work underpinned international organizations. Again, these networks did not suddenly appear with the end of the Second World War and the creation of the United Nations. The longue-durée approach to the colonial roots of development reveals substantial scientific networks operating within

[85] Opening Statement by Chairman, Sir John Sterndale Bennett K. C. M. G., Deputy High Commissioner, Information Conference, Phoenix Park, Singapore, January 1953, CO 1027/26 INF104/105/03, TNA, accessed through *Cinematic Realism – Documentary Film Website*, The Documentary Film in South and South-East Asia Research Programme, https://digital.lib.hkbu.edu.hk/documentary-film/ (accessed 30 October 2018).

[86] The theme of Churchill's writing influencing interpretations of the Cold War is explored in detail in David Lowe, 'Australia's Cold War: Britishness and English-speaking Worlds Challenged Anew', in Phillip Buckner and R. Douglas Francis (eds.), *Rediscovering the British World* (Calgary: University of Calgary Press, 2005), pp. 361–80.

colonial bureaucracies on food and agriculture well before development acquired its postwar meaning.[87] From the late 1940s, the rise of foreign aid was accompanied by the expansion of bureaucracies, primarily within ministries of finance and external affairs, in both donor and recipient nations. Many experts resumed their interwar missions, some translating from colonial to international organizations, others in newly independent nations welcoming the chance to make a mark in expanding civil services. In all places were careerists, idealists and many who tried to be both.[88]

Several diplomats from the donor countries built careers straddling the boundary lines of administration of Indigenous or 'frontier' peoples within their own national boundaries and consideration of colonial peoples overseas. They therefore embraced a well-established 'development gaze' that not only assumed the virtues of modernization and the progress of science but also drew on experience in taming vast lands and trying to factor Indigenous welfare in this. Prominent Canadians of this kind included Hugh Keenleyside, the inaugural head of the United Nations Technical Assistance Administration, created in 1950, and John W. Holmes and Nik Cavell.[89] Australian officials of similar mind-set who were involved in shaping or working with the Colombo Plan included P. W. E. (Pike) Curtin and Tom Critchley and New Zealanders were John Reid and R. H. (Hunter) Wade. In the case of Britain, the number of Treasury, Colonial Office, Foreign Office and Singapore-based officials was much larger. For the British, the lines of continuity between pre-war policy settings and postwar development, especially those flowing from the 1940 Colonial Welfare and Development Act, were particularly strong. The first Director of the Colombo Plan Bureau, British Treasury official Geoffrey Wilson, was one who straddled these worlds and his work is examined further below.

87 See, especially with reference to the FAO, Forclaz, 'From Reconstruction to Development', pp. 351–71; Benjamin Siegel, '"The Claims of Asia and the Far East": India and the FAO in the Age of Ambivalent Internationalism', *The International History Review*, 41, 2 (2019), 427–50. An important study of earlier officials at work is Susan Pederson's account of the mandates system in the League of Nations: *The Guardians: The League of Nations and the Crisis of Empire* (Oxford: Oxford University Press, 2015).

88 See, in relation to Indian careerists in the FAO, Siegel, '"The Claims of Asia and the Far East"'.

89 See David Webster, 'Modern Missionaries: Canadian Postwar Technical Assistance Advisors in Southeast Asia', *Journal of the Canadian Historical Association*, 20, 2 (2009), 86–111; Webster, 'Developing the World in Canada's Image' , pp. 73–99; David Meren, '"Commend Me the Yak": The Colombo Plan, the Inuit of Ungava, and "Developing" Canada's North', *Histoire sociale/Social History*, 50 (2017), 343–70.

It is hard to quantify the uptake in diplomatic travel and interaction in the late 1940s and early 1950s, but the increased volume and the addition of more mid-level officials and experts to meetings overseas is an important part of what was different. The severed or loosening ties of colonialism, the rapid rise in air travel, and the absence of world war made this possible. Put simply, far more officials, and not merely politicians and senior diplomats, saw new countries for the first time and met new people in similar positions to their own. This applied across the board, often stretching the capacities of recently independent nations in Asia that hosted meetings such as those of the Consultative Committee. It was one of the qualities of the Asian Relations Conference at New Delhi in March–April 1947 that Nehru regarded as so transformational: some of the delegates met with comparable representatives from other Asian countries for the first time. For non-Asian conference attendees, the position was even more stark. Familiar patterns of travel were challenged by these new diplomatic activities focused on Asia. Only one of the six Canadian representatives at the Commonwealth's Colombo conference in 1950 had travelled beyond Europe and North America; such were their travel patterns to date.[90]

The Colombo Plan enabled a broader range of officials to meet and to meet more often. A number of these later moved from government roles to service in UN agencies such as UNTAA or ECAFE (where the money was better),[91] and a few served in Colombo in the Bureau. They cultivated through the long 1950s a blend of networked experience and special status within their respective government departments on account of their modest number. Their special standing would diminish with the rise of the career development expert and the professionalization of development work within new agencies from the early 1960s.[92] Before then, this first cohort played fundamental roles, especially in the early years of the Colombo Plan, in enabling allocated monies to be spent. Without their experience, governments of both donor and regional members would have struggled to translate their initial commitments, broken down to

[90] David Webster, *Fire and the Full Moon: Canada and Indonesia in a Decolonizing World* (Vancouver: University of British Columbia Press, 2009), p. 47.

[91] Unger, *International Development*, 2018, pp. 67–68.

[92] At the same time, the generous educational funding provided by US philanthropic foundations such as Ford, Rockefeller and Carnegie aimed, at least up to the mid-1960s, deliberately at cultivating elites in a the decolonizing world who might share a similar world view: Corinna R. Unger, 'The United States, Decolonization and the Education of Third World Elites', in Jost Dülffer and Marc Frey (eds.), *Elites and Decolonization in the Twentieth Century* (Houndmills: Palgrave Macmillan, 2011), pp. 241–61.

yearly budget expenditure, into assistance that mapped onto regional needs.[93] In profiling some of the key individuals below and in following chapters, their standing as underestimated mediators of Asia–West development diplomacy, and as entrepreneurial aid diplomats capable of shaping policy, emerges more clearly.

Not surprisingly, several of the South Asian officials on the rise had been educated in Britain and had served as Indian Civil Servants prior to independence. One such individual was Chakravarti Vijayaraghava Narasimhan, Oxford-educated, District Officer in Madras and in the early 1950s working in India's Ministry of Finance, responsible for ensuring that external aid was channelled only to projects that had the blessing of India's Planning Commission (shown in Figure 2.3). Narasimhan was a strong administrator who built good relationships with Colombo Plan members and with other international organizations such as WHO, ECAFE and other auxiliary UN bodies. He was at meetings of the Consultative Committee in 1950 to 1955, later recalling these as eye-opening for what he learned of the neighbouring countries. He remembered the Consultative Committee meeting of 1953 in New Delhi as 'my first introduction to other countries in South and South-East Asia';[94] and he recounted fondly India's post-conference hospitality of turning a train into a mobile home for delegates, enabling them to see industrial developments in the Damodar Valley.[95]

Narasimhan led Indian delegations to the meetings of officials in 1954 and 1955, where he proved a skilled diplomat and team leader. He then became Executive Director of ECAFE in 1956 and served with distinction there, overseeing the commencement of ambitious projects such as the Lower Mekong River Basin Development and the Asian Highway. He continued to attend Colombo Plan meetings in his capacity as ECAFE Director.[96] Later, he rose in UN seniority in New York. When he published a memoir in retirement, he reflected on his early career in

[93] Commentator Keith Spicer wrote of Cavell, 'he achieved a tour de force of spending nearly every penny of the $25,400,000 on sensible aid projects in India and Pakistan before the fiscal year deadline of April 1st, 1952, when he was told that his surplus would lapse'. Keith Spicer, 'The Administration of Canadian Colombo Plan Aid', *International Journal*, 16, 169 (1961), 174–75.

[94] Narasimhan, 'Reminiscences of the Colombo Plan from Delhi (1953) to Tokyo (1960)', no date, 1961, RG 25 vol. 5421 11038-5-10-40 part 2, LAC.

[95] C. V. Narasimhan, 'Reminiscences of the Colombo Plan: From Delhi to Tokyo', *Colombo Plan Newsletter*, 6, 7, 1961, p. 11, RCS, CUL.

[96] Singh, *The Politics of Economic Cooperation in Asia*, pp. 98–99.

FIGURE 2.3 C. V. Narasimhan.
Source: UN Economic and Social Commission for Asia and the Pacific, www.unescap.org/former-executive-secretary/narasimhan; Permission granted by UN Photo Library, UNHQ Secretariat, New York.

aid-related work only briefly; but even in the space of twenty-five pages he listed as 'old friends' Canadian aid expert, Nik Cavell, Ceylonese Raju Coomaraswamy, Pakistan's Ambassador to the UN, Said Hasan, UK Treasury official William Armstrong and head of the UN's Technical Assistance Agency, David Owen.[97]

By the middle of the 1950s, Narasimhan's experience with different players in foreign aid was evident in his negotiations with others. He was able to point out the best practices to the Canadians in ways that aligned with his notion of India's interests. When the Canadians began querying risk and insurance liabilities around their transfer of equipment, Narasimhan had the answers. The question was when was the moment that responsibility for new heavy equipment transferred to India for use in

[97] C. V. Narasimhan, *The United Nations at 50: Recollections* (Delhi: Konark Publications, 1996), pp. 4–29.

the Umtru hydroelectric project in Assam. Narasimhan could point to recent contracts struck with the US Technical Co-operation Mission for thermal power stations in Rajasthan as the model.[98] As observer to the Consultative Committee on behalf of ECAFE, Narasimhan was able to inject into discussions ECAFE research on big-picture economic surveys, adding detail to problems of inflation and capital shortage. He kept in play some of the possibilities of greater regional collaboration that bubbled away in ECAFE and were never too far from the surface of bigger thinking in the Consultative Committee. At the Saigon meeting in 1957, he brushed aside suggestions about the supposed lack of complementarity in the regional members' economies and pointed to growing calls for greater economic integration in Europe and Latin America. He ventured that the advantages of closer economic integration of trade and industry in the region would become apparent with what he called 'greater recognition of the inter-dependence of economic development plans'. His illustration was the recent cooperative agreement between riparian states for multi-purpose development of the Mekong River and the ongoing actions this would have.[99]

The Colombo Plan's first Director of the Bureau for Technical Cooperation, Geoffrey Wilson, was an Oxford-trained lawyer who joined the British Foreign Office. Wilson toured India, Burma, China and the Soviet Union with socialist and former Labour politician Stafford Cripps in 1939. Wilson served in the Moscow Embassy, again with Cripps, in the early part of the Second World War. Afterwards, he was engaged by the British Treasury to help manage the massive US loan to Britain and to manage Britain's balance of payments, including sterling-area commitments. He was Secretary-General to the Commonwealth Finance Ministers' Conference of July 1949. A Quaker, Wilson's two years as Director in Colombo, August 1951 to September 1953, deepened his interest in aid, development and the alleviation of poverty. Much of the rest of his career related to this work, including five years as Vice President of the World Bank, 1961–66 and Chair of Oxfam, 1977–83.[100]

98 Under S of S External Affairs to High Commissioner New Delhi, 30 July 1954, RG 25 vol. 6579 11-38-1-2B-40 part 1.2, LAC.

99 Minutes of the Second Meeting of Ministers, Consultative Committee, Conference Room, Hoi-Truong Dien-Hong, 21 October 1957, Attachment 7, statement by Narasimhan, RG 25 vol. 7360 11038-5-5-40 part 2, LAC.

100 Note on Wilson by J. Hunt (CRO) for A. C. B. Symon's signature, 23 August 1951, DO 35/2736, TNA; Guardian Obituary, Dir Geoffrey Wilson, 20 July 2004, www.theguardian.com/news/2004/jul/19/guardianobituaries (accessed 2 July 2021).

In 1951–52, Wilson realized very quickly that he needed to improve the capacity of the Bureau in its advice on the most suitable forms of aid and its ability to project compelling messages about the Colombo Plan. At the end of 1952, he reflected that the bilateral nature of aid provision meant that Australian or Canadian publics were developing pictures of their aid in Asia, but with no sense of what anybody else was doing. 'The result is that the sense of collective effort for a common end is largely lacking and is not nearly as strong as it might be.' Part of the problem was that the Bureau was meant to focus only on technical assistance and not stories connected to the bigger economic development projects. Wilson thought this 'increasingly absurd' and wanted a roving reporter and another Bureau-based writer to write and place news stories on the whole range of Colombo Plan activities.[101] It would take another year, but the need for extra bodies for story-making and the broader remit attaching to the work of the Bureau were endorsed by India's Deshmukh who seized on Wilson's idea of an Information Unit and pushed this successfully to the Colombo Plan members.[102]

Before then, Wilson's personal regional tours and visits to donor countries served as the basis for radio broadcasts and press releases that helped shape the template of messaging to come. Wilson told of great stirrings in India, Ceylon and Pakistan behind dam-building and power-generating projects. There was also a hunger for technical training that current resources could simply not meet. Projected population increases alone would soak up reserves of expertise on the ground. Manual labour was not the issue – there was plenty of that available – but what was desperately needed was the civil equivalent of an army's non-commissioned officers: 'That is the greatest shortage in Asia – men who can be relied on to see the job through, the mechanics, draughtsmen, clerks, electricians, plumbers, the foremen and the supervisors.'[103] These were the gaps that technical assistance aimed to fill.

Among LePan's Colombo Plan 'freemasonry', Nik Cavell (Reginald George Nik Cavell) stood out among fellow Canadians for his advocacy of the Colombo Plan. Cavell had spent twelve years in India from 1913,

101 Copy of letter from Wilson to A. C. B. Symon, CRO, 24 December 1952, DO 35/5755, TNA. Wilson also requested a technical advisory officer and a statistician, but neither of these were supported.

102 Deshmukh agreed to pursue these ideas after meeting Wilson in Delhi in January 1953: Wilson's letter to A. C. B. Symon, 24 January 1953, DO 35/5755, TNA.

103 Undated text of Wilson's broadcast in 'Colombo Plan Publicity' memorandum preparing for Wilson's trip to Canada, 24 September 1952, DO 35/5755, TNA.

first commissioned in the Cavalry Branch of the Indian Army and a further ten years in various business roles in the 'Far East'. Some of this time included his work for electrical and telephone companies based in the UK and Canada. Cavell became chairman of the Executive Committee of the Canadian Institute of International Affairs in 1944 and was one of a small group of Canadians who tried to overcome Canadian conservatives' reluctance to embrace a UN Universal Declaration on Human Rights. He wrote in 1948 that the Atlantic Charter had made a very positive impact in the 'Far East' and that 'the nailing of Human rights flag to the Western nations' mast would make a great stir again and would, I feel, pull to our side a very large number of people in nations who are now wavering on the brink of Communistic connection'.[104] Cavell was appointed Director of Canada's new International Economic and Technical Cooperation Division (IETCD), set up within the Department of Trade and Commerce in September 1951. In these circumstances, and with others around him more inclined to watch and wait, Cavell was well placed to make the running in the early years of Ottawa's grappling with the Colombo Plan.[105]

Cavell could be blunt. 'Here in Pakistan they are in a sad mess', he penned during his regional tour of 1953.[106] A contemporary in the Economic Division of Canada's Department of External Affairs, A. F. W. Plumptre, described him as the kind of prima donna who was right for the times. Cavell used the limelight to ensure growing support, political and from church and community groups, for Canada's aid programme in the mid-1950s. Canadian aid sums might have remained modest, but they were handled and distributed with sensitivity, owing largely to Cavell. Indeed, much of the admiration he attracted stemmed from his capacity to spend nearly all of the early aid allocations voted by the Canadian government, chiefly to India and Pakistan. It is easy to underestimate the importance of spending, and being seen to spend, the entirety of a

104 Cavell's note to John P. Humphrey, October 1948, quoted in A. J. Hobbins, 'Eleanor Roosevelt, John Humphrey – and Canadian Opposition to the Universal Declaration of Human Rights: Looking Back on the 50th Anniversary of UNHDR', *International Journal*, 53 (1998), 336.

105 Jill Campbell-Miller, 'The Mind of Modernity: Canadian Bilateral Foreign Assistance to India, 1950–60', Ph.D. Thesis, University of Waterloo, Canada, 2014, p. 83. An excellent portrayal and appraisal of Cavell is by Greg Donaghy, '"Reasonably Well-Organized": A History of Early Aid Administration', in Donaghy and Webster (eds.), *A Samaritan State Revisited*, pp. 53–65.

106 Cavell (Karachi) to Ed Ritchie, External Affairs, 8 May 1953, RG 25 vol. 6577 11038-40 part 11.2, LAC.

Cabinet's aid allocation on ostensibly sound projects. Early commitments included chassis and engines for trucks and buses in Bombay, and wheat for re-sale to fund an irrigation project in West Bengal and in the Thal in Pakistan. In 1952, quick-thinking members in Canada's Finance Department moved Colombo Plan appropriations to the Canadian Commercial Corporation (CCC), a body that had been set up to manage government-to-government contracts with postwar Europe, and which was now tasked with holding Colombo Plan funds in trust for recipient countries. The Cabinet could thus say that funds had been allocated while the CCC was better able to absorb the consequences of delays in works planned. When dealing with state authorities (e.g. Bombay) in addition to the government of India, the extra layer of bureaucracy almost guaranteed delay.[107]

To have failed in this early task of spending on worthy projects would have given ammunition to sceptics at home in Canada and would have undermined the premise that partnerships in Asia could work. Given that Cavell started with little administrative support and needed to work quickly with bureaucracies still absorbing the implications of the Colombo Plan in India and Pakistan, his early achievement was significant and defining.[108] It also cemented his role at the helm of the IETCD. There, his self-anointed mission blended with the government's new mandate. According to Plumptre, 'His chief assets were his humanity, his unbounded enthusiasm for the cause, his broad and colourful background, his early experience of administration in India, both military and civilian, and his healthy intolerance of anyone he thought was getting in his way.'[109] Historian Greg Donaghy adds that Cavell was not starry-eyed about the capacity of foreign aid to change the circumstances of impoverished Asians, but he was a good fit for others' expectations of his role: 'As an apparently authentic product of colonial India, he helped slot Canada's new development role in Asia into the familiar British Empire, or increasingly Commonwealth, framework . . .' Despite the constant potential for upheaval in Asia, 'Cavell himself was reassuring evidence that Canada's development project represented a secure status quo.'[110]

[107] Ibid., pp. 89–94.

[108] See Spicer, 'The Administration of Canadian Colombo Plan Aid', pp. 174–75.

[109] A. F. W. Plumptre, 'Perspective on Our Aid to Others', *International Journal*, 22 (1967), 488–89.

[110] Donaghy, '"Reasonably Well-Organized"', pp. 58–59.

Cavell's business background meshed comfortably with his internationalism. He spent much of the 1950s agitating for flows of aid to Asia while also trying to cultivate distinctly bilateral Canadian–Asian forms of aid. This meant promoting Canadian-made products such as hydroelectric engineering, train engines chassis and road trucks, while treating bigger multilateral projects with caution – at the same time as listening carefully to Asian civil servants' identification of their needs. It included his railing against the burdensome tensions between the Indian states and central government in New Delhi at the same time as he insisted to anyone who would listen that India's Five-Year Plan must be made to work.[111] He was sympathetic towards Pakistan's development challenges as well as being critical in his 1953 report.[112] He was the flamboyant champion of Canadian aid during the 1950s, travelling for a good part of each year to Colombo Plan countries, in order to ascertain matches between country needs and Canadian capacities, and then badgering those in Ottawa who moved too slowly to respond. His choices of what to fund also reflected his determination that the projects were capable of being managed entirely by Canadians; and on this score, he generally won battles with Canada's High Commissioner in India.[113] This was his modus operandi until his posting as the High Commissioner to Ceylon in 1958, during a time when there was little higher-level thinking about foreign aid, and a strong default setting to assisting Commonwealth countries in particular. From 1950 to 1960, only two per cent of Canadian foreign aid went to non-Commonwealth countries. This was not only due to the popular appeal of supporting the new Commonwealth – although that would reach new heights under Prime Minister Diefenbaker at the end of the decade – but through the recommendations of Cavell who pointed to the existence of multi-year plans,

[111] This theme is explored in Campbell-Miller, 'The Mind of Modernity', pp. 90–91, 110 and passim.

[112] Cavell (Karachi) to Ed Ritchie, External Affairs, 8 May 1953, RG 25 vol. 6577 11038-40 part 11.2, LAC.

[113] For an example of another of Cavell's regional Asian tour reports, see Nik Cavell, 'Report on Colombo Plan Consultative Committee Meeting no. 5' held in Wellington, New Zealand, November 19 to December 8, 1956 and Visits to South and South East Asian Countries by Mr Nik Cavell, Colombo Plan Administrator in Canada and Mr Rodney Grey of the Department of External Affairs, 15 May 1957, RG 25 vol. 7359 11038-5-B-40 part 2 fp 3.2, LAC; Campbell-Miller, 'The Mind of Modernity', pp. 160–72.

planning boards and growing absorptive capacity in countries such as India, Pakistan and Ceylon.[114]

If members' initial responses to the Colombo Plan were very mixed at the outset, then the first two years saw a certain solidifying of commitments plus the addition of new members, the United States, the French Associated States of Laos, Cambodia, Vietnam, then Burma and Nepal, and in 1953, Indonesia. Patterns of diplomacy took shape quickly, including annual meetings of the Consultative Committee where decisions were made unanimously. That the Colombo Plan began to carve out a special niche among other like-focused organizations such as ECAFE owed also to the importance members attached to hosting a meeting and managing the expectations of a curious and sometimes sceptical media. This task of managing expectations would be a constant, requiring even more energies. Navigating these early years was also made possible by a fellowship of mid-to-high-ranking civil servants from both Asian and non-Asian members. The likes of Wilson, Cavell and Narasimhan saw in the Colombo Plan opportunities to further ideals and their careers, and they also spent considerable time explaining the hopes, plans and constraints of Asian and Western governments to all those who would listen.

[114] David R. Morrison, *Aid and Ebb Tide: A History of CIDA and Canadian Development Assistance* (Waterloo: Wilfred Laurier University Press, 1998), pp. 33–35. During the decade, India received $148.4 million (53.4 per cent) and Pakistan $100.6 million (36.5 per cent), the two biggest shares.

3

Flexibility, with Limits

If the Colombo Plan's international status was unclear in its early years, events of the mid-1950s seemed to open all sorts of possibilities, ranging from its being marginal to something more emboldened, possibly even an organization capable of intervening decisively in the Cold War. With flexibility came risks. An informal organization that appeared endlessly malleable was in danger of having little purchase in international diplomacy. The same malleability left it vulnerable to attempted appropriation in the grand schemes of others. The Colombo Plan faced both of these tests in the middle years of the 1950s. As this chapter shows, it survived the tests and emerged from potential controversy mostly unscathed, and indeed, enlarged.

Rapid political changes in Asia, especially in Southeast Asia during the mid-1950s, impacted on how the Colombo Plan was perceived. The triumph of the Viet Minh over the French in Vietnam in May 1954 marked the end of colonial rule in Indochina and the consolidation of a communist stronghold in Southeast Asia. For the Americans, who had been bankrolling the French to the tune of almost three-quarters the cost of their military struggle, it seemed a potential Cold War turning point. Partly in response, they met with Cold War allies at Manila in September that year to sign a new security pact, the South-East Asian Collective Defense Treaty, later known as SEATO. Explicitly anti-communist in its aims, the treaty comprised the United States, Australia, New Zealand, France, the United Kingdom, Thailand, Pakistan and the Philippines. SEATO immediately complicated the Cold War agnosticism of the Colombo Plan as it resembled an anti-communist sub-grouping of the plan. As the Thai and Philippines governments were on the verge of joining the Colombo Plan, France was effectively the only non-Colombo member.

The same year, 1954, saw another key regional conference in Colombo from which there emerged a loose five-power group called the 'Colombo Powers'. Hosted by the Ceylonese government of John Kotelawala, the group comprised the prime ministers of Burma, Ceylon, India, Indonesia and Pakistan. They met at the end of April 1954 to discuss a wide range of issues, including the role of Communist China in regional and international affairs, the Kashmir dispute between India and Pakistan, the war in Korea and the ascendancy of the Viet Minh in Indochina. On these and other matters, they did not search for consensus and readily agreed to disagree. Collectively though, they committed to consolidating and extending recently won freedoms by improving living conditions, giving the peoples of the region greater say in international affairs and preventing outside powers from dictating their fortunes. This was regional assertiveness, 'resurgent Asia' from a starting position of state sovereignty rather than innovative pan-federalism of the kind being considered in decolonizing Africa.[1] The Colombo Powers carried some of this new activism into the Indian-led representations at the Geneva conference in June–July, which eventually arrived at accords recognizing the sovereignty of Cambodia, Laos and Vietnam. They then took their diplomatic momentum into organizing the Asian-African Conference attended by representatives of twenty-nine nations in Bandung, in April 1955.

In addition to the initial meeting and the Bandung conference, there were two further meetings of the Colombo Powers, in Bogor, 28–29 December 1954, preceding Bandung, and in New Delhi, 12–14 December 1956, before they lapsed as a functioning group.[2] Those assembled at Bandung in 1955 called for an end to nuclear testing, disarmament and

[1] Cindy Ewing, 'The Colombo Powers: Crafting Diplomacy in the Third World and Launching Afro-Asia at Bandung', *Cold War History*, 19, 1 (2018), 2 and passim; Tony Ballantyne and Antionette Burton, 'Empires and the Reach of the Global', in Emily S. Rosenberg (ed.), *A World Connecting, 1870–1945* (Cambridge, MA: The Belknap Press of Harvard University Press), 2012, pp. 422–31.

[2] While both the short-lived cohesion of the Colombo Powers and their greatest legacy, the Bandung Conference, rightly attract historians' attention, they were neither the start nor the end of a great conferencing phenomenon in Asia based on common experiences of colonialism. See Ewing, 'The Colombo Powers'; Sally Percival Wood, 'Retrieving the Bandung Conference … Moment by Moment', *Journal of Southeast Studies*, 43, 3 (2012), 523–30; and for different perspectives see contributions in Christopher J. Lee (ed.), *Making a World after Empire: The Bandung Moment and Its Political Afterlives* (Athens: Ohio University Press), 2010.

the prohibition of nuclear weapons. In the same year, the UN gained sixteen new members, and Cambodia, Ceylon and Laos were among them. With three more former colonies from North Africa joining the following year, the UN General Assembly was becoming an arena for anti-colonialism. Recent studies have demonstrated the need to broaden historical understanding of the Bandung 'moment' of 1955 by considering non-official as well as official meetings of those wanting to bring about change and to consider the diplomacy that flowed indirectly as well as directly from the Bandung meeting. Some of the key themes emerging from Bandung flowed into Colombo Plan annual meetings, including representatives' insistence on the end of colonialism, rejection of a system of international relations divided into two camps by the Cold War, respect for human rights and for national sovereignty, the equality of all races, rejection of military alliances and the settlement of international disputes by peaceful means, in accordance with the UN Charter. While absent from the ten-point declaration emerging from Bandung, not least of the matters discussed was the priority of economic development, and the need for post-colonial states to pass on lessons in development to others.[3]

The final communiqué from Bandung also mentioned the significance of peaceful nuclear power for Asian-African countries. In the context of economic development, this was less surprising than at first it appeared. Earlier, on 8 December 1953, US President Dwight D. Eisenhower had taken many by surprise with his so-called 'atoms for peace' speech to the UN General Assembly, arguing for greater application of nuclear power for energy production, agriculture, medical and other uses as a precursor to nuclear disarmament. Thereafter, the Americans embarked on a propaganda campaign on the virtues of the peaceful atom and signed bilateral agreements with several countries, enabling the transfer of technology and materials and sometimes a research reactor. There were clear foreign policy goals attached to these developments, atomic power necessarily being a long-term commitment tying newcomers to American lines of supply and expertise. During the UN General Assemblies of 1954 and 1955, it became clear that the remit of the new International Atomic Energy Agency would include nuclear power as foreign aid. A US-sponsored regional nuclear research centre for Asia was one of the

[3] This theme is explored in detail in Frank Gerits' exploration of what was described in conference literature as 'the brown man's burden': Frank Gerits, 'Bandung as the Call for a Better Development Project: US, British and Gold Coast Perceptions of the Afro-Asian Conference (1955)', *Cold War History*, 16, 3 (2016), 255–72.

proposals that took shape in 1955 in ways that potentially connected with the Colombo Plan.[4]

As this chapter shows, these developments reverberated through the three mid-decade meetings of the Consultative Committee. While navigating them, members demonstrated how valued these annual gatherings were, especially by their hosts, and how expert were the ways by which consensus was made to prevail and controversy avoided.

NAVIGATING CROSS-WINDS

'Asia', wrote Kipling, 'is not going be "civilized" after the methods of the West. There is too much of Asia and she is too old."'[5] This line from Ottawa mayor Charlotte Whitton's welcome to delegates to the 1954 meeting of the Consultative Committee might have provoked mixed reactions, given Kipling's readiness to orientalize the 'East', but it did underline the point that much of Asia was joining the Colombo Plan. From initial uncertainty followed by a hasty mix of Commonwealth and Cold War prerogatives, the Canadian position on the Colombo Plan was having to adjust to the longer-term view by the time of their hosting of the Consultative Committee meeting. This was the first committee meeting outside of Asia, excepting the formative ones in Sydney and London during 1950. It was the mid-point of the initial six-year development plans, and the group was set to grow further, with full membership approved for Japan, the Philippines and Thailand. Broad-minded Canadians wondered in 1954 if it was time that the financial and technical side of the Colombo Plan was matched by something more cultural. After prompting by a professor of comparative religion at McGill University, and cautious endorsement from Canada's high commission in Karachi, External Affairs officials explored the idea of some sort of

[4] There is a growing literature on the atoms for peace initiatives of the 1950s. Among the most significant in relation to atomic energy as foreign aid are: Ira Chernus, *Eisenhower's Atoms for Peace* (College Station, TX: A&M University Press, 2002); Scott Kirsch, *Proving Grounds: Project Plowshare and the Unrealized Dream of Nuclear Earthmoving* (New Brunswick, NJ: Rutgers University Press, 2005); Elisabeth Roehrlich, 'The Cold War, the Developing World, and the Creation of the International Atomic Agency (IAEA), 1953–1957', *Cold War History*, 16, 4 (2016), 195–212; Mara Drogan, 'The Atoms for Peace Program and the Third World', *Cahiers du Monde Russse*, 60, 2–3 (2019), 441–60.

[5] Charlotte Whitton, Mayor of Ottawa, written greeting, 6 October 1954, in minutes of sixth meeting of Consultative Committee on Co-operative Economic Development in South and South-East Asia, 7 October, Ottawa, CRS A10167 item 1954/5 NAA.

educational exchange program with Pakistan and possibly others – not as an element of technical training, the established pathway for student and trainee movement, but more a stand-alone iconic new program.[6] This was a soft power suggestion a little ahead of its time. While the gesture might have been welcomed by Asian members, no one was confident that the steely-eyed economic planners of the region would embrace it. As one keen observer of Colombo Plan meetings warned, there were limits to what could be expected of cultural exchange proposals when the Colombo Plan was handled in Asian countries largely by ministries of finance and economic affairs, and most of the delegations to the Consultative Committee were drawn from these ministries.[7]

By 1954 there were more annual reports to review. In addition to original Commonwealth members, newer members Burma, the three French Indochinese states and Indonesia submitted questionnaires and spoke respectively to their development achievements and challenges. Of the new members joining, the most controversial was Japan. Since the signing of the Japanese Peace Treaty and resulting restoration of Japan's sovereignty in April 1952, the Colombo Plan had been in Tokyo's sights. One of the Japanese government's first challenges was to ease itself back into economic and political connections with Southeast Asia, where recent Japanese conquest, forced labour and other coercions, accompanied by incitement to throw off colonial rule, left a complex and mostly unpopular legacy. The Japanese were still negotiating agreements on reparations with Burma (agreed in 1954), the Philippines (1956), Indonesia (1958) and South Vietnam (1959). Membership of the Colombo Plan as a provider of aid was one of the first logical steps towards Japan's re-emergence in regional politics beyond these wartime legacies.[8]

[6] Wilfred Cantwell Smith, McGill, letter to Prime Minster St Laurent, 25 March 1954, RG 25 vol. 8407 11038-2-40 part 1.1, LAC; A. E. Ritchie, Economic Division, to Under-Secretary, 5 July 1954, ibid; J. Cleveland, Acting High Commissioner for Canada, Karachi, to Secretary of State for External Affairs, no. 845, 29 September 1954, RG 25 vol. 8407 11038-2-40 part 1.2, LAC.

[7] A. E. Ritchie, Economic Division, to Under-Secretary, 5 July 1954, RG 25 vol. 8407 11038-2-40 part 1.1, LAC.

[8] Sumio Hatano, 'The Colombo Plan and Japan: Focusing on the 1960 Tokyo Meeting', in Akita, Krozewski, and Watanabe (eds.), *The Transformation of the International Order of Asia*, pp. 131–32; Hoshiro, 'Reconsidering Japan's War Reparations', pp. 673–702. Japan's war reparations to the Philippines and Burma were paid over the period, 1956–76. Other Colombo Plan members waived claims to formal reparations and/or sought informal favourable economic relations with postwar Japan.

The British made cautious inquiries on behalf of Japan in the lead up to the fourth meeting of the Consultative Committee held in Karachi in March 1952. They quickly backed away in the face of stiff opposition from Australia, New Zealand and most other members. The Americans took up the Japanese cause with greater energy, as Japan became increasingly important strategically in Cold War Asia. Elsewhere, Japan was made an associate member of ECAFE at the start of 1952 and was able to attend meetings in this capacity before full membership was conferred in 1954. As ECAFE's headquarters had settled in Bangkok by this time, Japan's ECAFE representative was also Japan's Ambassador in Thailand, Ichiro Ohta, a double role common to other diplomatic services. Through ECAFE, Ohta sounded out Indian and US representatives about the prospect of being invited to send an observer to the Colombo Plan Consultative Committee meeting in New Delhi in 1953. Both responded positively, but the Americans, conscious of their later joining the committee, deferred to the Indian view. In August, Deputy Foreign Minister B. K. Nehru couched India's support with caution. Potential other supporters, the Canadians and Pakistanis, found it too late to take Japan out of the 'too hard' basket in time for the Delhi meeting.[9] As other members wavered or expressed cautious interest, the Australians expressed direct opposition, citing a combination of public mood, an unresolved pearl fishing dispute with Japan in Australia's northern waters and lack of clarity about Japan's role as a donor or a recipient. This latter point was specious – it was clear that Japan was seeking to join as a donor – but Australian opposition and others' wariness was enough to squash any hopes for Japanese membership when the committee met in New Delhi.

Fortunately for the Japanese, and surprisingly for most others, the Australians undertook a major revision of their attitude towards Japan in the middle months of 1954, conscious of the need for Japan's re-emergence in regional affairs as a counter to China. Given Japan's

[9] Ohta to Okazaki (Foreign Minister), 24 February 1953, no. 159, 'Participation in the Meeting of the Consultative Committee of the Colombo Plan', file E'.4.1.0.12.1, Diplomatic Record Office, Tokyo (hereinafter, DRO); Ohta to Okazaki, 2 April 1953, no. 250, 'Participation in the Meeting of the Consultative Committee of the Colombo Plan', ibid; Nishiyama (Ambassador to India) to Okazaki, 27 September 1953, no. 197, ibid; Nishi (Ambassador to Australia) to Okazaki, 28 September 1953, no. 264, ibid; Yamagata (Ambassador to Pakistan) to Okazaki, 28 September 1953, no. 229, ibid; Iguchi (Ambassador to Canada) to Okazaki, 28 September 1953, no. 139, ibid. See also Ai Kobayashi, 'Australia and Japan's Admission into the Colombo Plan', *Australian Journal of Politics & History*, 60, 4 (2014), 520–22.

substantial reliance on external trade, the West wanted to ensure that the non-communist countries of Asia remained a more attractive group of nations for Japan than Communist China. The Australian position suddenly shifted to one of support; then the Australians even came in with the sponsorship of Japan's membership of the Colombo Plan. In changing their stance, the Australians were influenced by British and American advocacy, and their overarching argument of the now more urgent need to keep Japan in the pro-Western camp. The Menzies government's decision to back Japan's membership was part of an important shift in policy towards Japan in August 1954, envisaging stronger relations between Japan and other non-communist countries of Asia, and expanded trade with Japan. The shift was justified overwhelmingly in a Cold War logic of keeping Japan in the Western camp.[10] Thus, the Australians suddenly became enthusiasts of Japan's membership of the Colombo Plan. Although the Japanese found it more prudent to seek sponsorship from an Asian member, Ceylon, the Australians remained helpful as a seconder, and Japan became a member at the Ottawa meeting in 1954.[11]

The strategic context to Japan's joining in 1954 was pivotal for the Australians and for others who interpreted communist-led successes in Asia through Cold War lenses. The Japanese government of Yoshida Shigeru had, in fact, been keeping open the option of closer trading relations with communist China. The timing was also much considered in Tokyo. Closer relations with regional nations, including more coordinated regional development, was a particular priority for the new Ichiro Hatoyama government of 1954–56. Ministers were aware of tentative US planning, in the wake of the French collapse in Indo China, for renewed spending on Asian security. One idea was a multilateral regional organization that might administer US capital aid, and the Japanese were keen to dovetail their initiatives for regional development with anything that took shape along these lines.[12]

[10] Australian Cabinet Minute, Prime Minister's Committee, 17 August 1954, CRS A4940 C998; Hirokazu Matsui, 'Australia and Japan's Return to International Society: Negotiating Allies and the Afro-Asian Bloc, 1952–56', *Australian Journal of Politics and History*, 69, 2 (2023), 251–53.

[11] Kobayashi, 'Australia and Japan's Admission to the Colombo Plan', pp. 518–33.

[12] Iguchi to Ogata (acting Foreign Minister) 13 October 1954, no. 2525, E'.4.1.0.12.1.1, DRO; Matsudoira (Ambassador to Canada) to Okazaki, 23 November 1954, no. 470, 'Annual Report on the Colombo Plan', ibid. See Hirokazu Matsui, 'Australia–Japan Relations and the International Re-emergence of Japan, 1952–1962', unpublished Ph. D. Thesis, Deakin University, 2024.

There was, in fact, potential for the Colombo Plan to be captured by US policy adjustments as the Korean War ground to an armistice and the French situation worsened in Vietnam. At the end of April 1953, Merrill Gay, the State Department official charged with ECAFE and related matters, wondered if it might be time to be less neutral towards the Colombo Plan, now that its British Commonwealth complexion had been overtaken by the non-Commonwealth Asian membership; and whether it could play the role of administering new injections of US aid for Asia on an explicitly regional basis.[13] A year later, after the French defeat in Vietnam and in the lead up to Ottawa, the State Department was mulling further over possibilities of 'The Colombo Plan as a vehicle for US aid'. Noting its benign qualities, the lack of pressure on participants to live up to promises and meet targets, the 'discussion group' qualities of the Consultative Committee and the strong sense of mutual goodwill, Asian specialist Konrad Bekker admired the Colombo Plan. He marked how it had overcome early suspicions and remained relatively free from political pressure and the taints of Western imperialism and unrequited charity. It was, he thought, a curious success story arising from hopes unfulfilled:

> Some of these characteristics are the unplanned results of the Colombo Plan's failure to gather the momentum – particularly the US support – which its supporters had hoped for. Nevertheless, they have permitted the establishment of an organization which embraces the nations of South and Southeast Asia that would be the major recipients of increased developmental assistance from the US. In particular, the Colombo Plan has the support and confidence of those Asian nations – India, Ceylon, Burma, and Indonesia – whose need for economic development is accompanied by strong sensitivity to the political implications of foreign aid.[14]

Bekker observed that the expansion of the Colombo Plan in ways that encompassed a major US aid program in Asia would be consistent with original hopes for the plan. Now, however, in 1954, such a move would mean 'substantial changes in the existing loose organization'.[15]

[13] Noel Hemmendinger memorandum to Robert McClurkin (both Northeast Asian Affairs), 30 April 1953, 890.00/4-2053, USNA.

[14] Konrad Bekker, DRF, 'The Colombo Plan as a Vehicle for US Aid', 25 August 1954, SEAP D.7, RG 59 Lot 55 D480, box 8, USNA.

[15] Ibid. This preceded the report of an Asian Economic Working Group wrestling with choices between a high impact 'massive aid' effort versus more bilateral and targeted initiatives: Everett F. Drumright memo to Walter Robertson, 4 October 1954, 890.00/9-3021, USNA.

Whether the Colombo Plan could be the vehicle for grand American plans would be more fully tested in the following year. Harold Stassen, Director of the US Mutual Security Agency, gave a hint of what was to come when he appeared at Ottawa and alluded to the desirability of some sort of Asian equivalent of the Organisation of European Economic Community.[16] His appearance stirred press speculation that up to $700 million formerly tied up in military ventures might now be made available for Asia as foreign aid.[17] For the near-term meeting in Ottawa in October 1954, Stassen and his colleagues focused on one recent initiative, inviting Colombo Plan members to accept agricultural surpluses as the basis of counterpart funds. This was another significant outcome from Ottawa. Delegates agreed to the Colombo Plan's availing itself of what became known as PL 480, Public Law no. 480 of 1954. Formally, the Agriculture Trade Development and Assistance Act, PL 480 was the start of a US food aid program that became massive in its reach and proportions around the world. The early operation of PL 480 in the second half of the 1950s involved disposing of large, mostly wheat surpluses in ways that would assist 'friendly nations' and help create new markets overseas. The American PL 480 and Canadian variant of providing accumulated wheat surpluses as aid for Asia were the biggest food-as-aid operations. Both governments acted from strong self-interest (especially the electoral value of maintaining prices for farmers by allowing large crop surpluses) as well as hoping to alleviate food shortages and thicken relationships with Asian governments. Receiving governments accepted food aid with this awareness and with concern for its implications. By way of illustration, in the case of the Indian acceptance of huge dollar loans in the form of Canadian wheat, (as well as the counterpart wheat grants, during 1958–59) Nehru's initial reluctance gave way to the immediacy of a foreign exchange crisis and bad harvests.[18] From the start of the 1960s, food aid grew both under the Colombo Plan and in bigger multilateral forms. It subsequently attracted criticism for a number of reasons ranging from the quality of wheat to its impact on global market prices, commercial trade and on local food production.[19] In Ottawa in 1954, however, at the start of what

[16] US State Department Memo, Saltzman, to American Embassy, Colombo A-58, 29 November 1954, 890.00/10-3059, USNA.

[17] *Globe and Mail* (Toronto), 9 October 1954, p. 1.

[18] Campbell-Miller, 'The Mind of Modernity', pp. 214–20.

[19] See Food and Agriculture Organization, *The State of Food and Agriculture*, 2006, pp. 32–36, www.fao.org/3/a0800e/a0800e03.pdf (accessed 2 September 2022); Barry Riley, *The Political History of American Food Aid: An Uneasy Benevolence* (Oxford:

FIGURE 3.1 Prime Minister St. Laurent welcomes delegates to the ministerial meetings in the House of Commons Chamber, Ottawa, 4 October 1954.
Source: The National Archive (UK) INF 10/88, TNA (and National Film Board of Canada).

would be a long and controversial US food aid program, India's Finance Minister C. D. Deshmukh started the PL 480 ball rolling among Asian countries by welcoming this initiative.[20]

The Philippines and Thailand were the other new full members approved in Ottawa, and welcomed by Canadian Prime Minister, Louis St Laurent (Figure 3.1). Well-foreshadowed and without the wartime opprobrium attaching to Japan, the Philippines and Thailand's memberships were easier decisions for members, completing the jigsaw of South and Southeast Asian membership. Having been nervous about the risk of US bulldozing diplomacy disturbing the geniality of previous meetings, the

Oxford University Press, 2017); Christopher Barrett and Daniel G. Maxwell, *Food Aid after Fifty Years: Reacting Its Role* (Abingdon: Routledge, 2005); Mark W. Charlton, *The Making of Canadian Food Aid Policy* (Montreal: McGill-Queens University Press, 1982).

20 Final Minutes, Fifth Meeting, Consultative Committee on Co-operative Development in South and South-East Asia, 6 October 1954, C.CO. 54-5, CRS A10067 item 1954/5, NAA; *Times of Indonesia*, 11 October 1954, p. 2.

Canadian hosts were happy to have avoided controversy. Radio, newspaper and television programs all gave favourable coverage. Delegates enjoyed the ambience of the capitol's parliamentary buildings where meetings were held, the gothic revival architecture lending weight to the seriousness of their tasks. They also enjoyed the many social functions and the post-conference tours to one of: Montreal–Kingston–Toronto–Niagara Falls; a northern venture by plane to Arvada; or a western provinces tour. Schoolchildren filed in to see the Colombo Plan Exhibition held in the Parliament Building at regular intervals, and the public attended in good number those sessions of committees that were held openly.[21] Narasimhan, whose recollections of Consultative Committee meetings were strongly shaped by the hotels in which they unfolded, was impressed by Thai Foreign Minister and veteran diplomat, Prince Wan, when they met for the first time in Ottawa in 1954. Narasimhan remembered also that the wheels of conversation were well-oiled: 'We were all lodged in the Chateau Laurier Hotel and there was one suite of rooms on the third floor which was set aside as a bar and lounge. This place used to be fairly well patronized from the time that the afternoon session closed till midnight, which was closing time for the bar.'[22]

Between Ottawa and the next meeting of the Consultative Committee in Singapore the following October, there were two major developments in international relations that would affect the Colombo Plan. The first was the meeting of twenty-nine countries predominately from Asia and Africa, at Bandung, Indonesia, in April 1955, where colonially shaped ideas about economic development, including possible knowledge transfers from Asia to Africa, underpinned much that delegates pondered.[23] At a level of powerful rhetoric, Bandung was also a reminder that the implacable condition of colonial rule and the counter-determination for racial equality among new nations inspired solidarity beyond Cold War alliances. Bandung underlined the strong sense of anti-colonial unfinished business that pervaded international conferences of the mid-1950s. Even in drafting what became SEATO in Manila in September the previous year, the Asian

[21] Extracts from a Departmental Assessment of the Colombo Plan Conference held in Ottawa in 1954, no date (1954), RG 25 vol. 7361 11038-5-D-40 part 1.1, LAC. No attendance figures are provided. More fine-grained post conference analysis, including details of the daily tins of cigarettes supplied to delegates are in another Extract called, 'The Conference Room Itself', ibid.

[22] C. V. Narasimhan, 'Reminiscences of the Colombo Plan: From Delhi to Tokyo', *Colombo Plan Newsletter*, pp. 6, 7, 1961, 11, RCS, CUL.

[23] Gerits, 'Bandung as the Call for a Better Development Project', pp. 255–72.

delegates from Thailand, Pakistan and the Philippines tried to include in the treaty an article indicating the commitment by all parties to the principle of self-determination. Only stubborn resistance from Australian, British and New Zealand representatives prevented this from happening, deflecting the ideal of self-determination to the treaty's preamble.[24]

The second was the Soviet Union's launch of a major foreign aid campaign in Asia. In February 1955, the Soviets reached agreement with the Indian government to fund a steel plant at Bhilai in India at a cost of more than $200 million. In the same year, Nehru visited the Soviet Union and Soviet Premier Nikita Khrushchev reciprocated with a tour of India. Bhilai was one of the first proclaimed landmarks of India's Second Five-Year Plan, commencing in 1956, with an emphasis on rapid industrialization and greater readiness to accept external aid. Although well behind the West in quantum of aid provided to India in the mid-1950s, the Soviets proved adept at maximizing the publicity around iconic ventures such as Bhilai. By contrast, the Americans had, to this time, been less project-focused in their provision of capital goods.[25] The British and West Germans provided steel-making competition in India by commencing to aid new mills at Durgapur and Rourkela, respectively, around the same time as Bhilai began. More broadly, Soviet aid consisted of low-interest loans that were repayable in local currency or in exports, something that looked attractive to Asian governments. The sense of contest was suddenly more acute. As the British and Americans were keenly aware, it was hard to argue that their foreign aid efforts in Asia to the middle of the decade had resulted in any 'noticeable betterment of living standards'.[26] In this elevated state of Cold War competition, it was not surprising that the Americans tested out how effectively or otherwise the Colombo Plan might become 'a vehicle' for their plans for foreign aid and security in Cold War Asia.

In February–March 1955, Harold Stassen toured the Asian Colombo Plan countries seeking reactions to his idea for aid provision through a more centralized secretariat, possibly also connected to European donors through the Organization for European Economic Cooperation (OEEC). He had in mind a special fund of some $205 million to be made available

[24] Verbatim proceedings, 4th and 5th sessions, Manila, 7 and 8 September 1954, RG 59 lot 55 D480, box 10, USNA.

[25] Engerman, *The Price of Aid*, pp. 120–28.

[26] British Aide Memoire provided to US State Department, 15 December 1954, 890.00/12-1554, USNA.

for regional institutions and projects that might emerge over and above existing US aid commitments. He found some interest, especially from the Indians, who then organized a conference of regional-only Colombo Plan members in Simla in May, to discuss suitable organization for the utilization of short- and longer-term US aid.[27] The diplomatic path towards convening separately in Simla was not smoothly paved by the Indian government, which issued sudden invitations unaccompanied by the usual ground-clearing work;[28] but the bigger lesson from what happened next was that the Colombo Plan was too valued in its current form and too conveniently flexible to be subsumed within some grander US aid architecture. The Ceylonese and Burmese governments promptly declined their invitations, based on their not being in receipt of US aid at that time. Those attending were India, Cambodia, Indonesia, Japan, Laos, Nepal, Pakistan, Thailand, Vietnam, the Philippines (observer only) and the British Southeast Asian governments of Singapore, Malaya, North Borneo and Sarawak. All the potential reforms on the agenda at Simla were rejected: there was no enthusiasm for a regional organization to better administer US aid; no support for a Japanese-sponsored regional development fund; no enthusiasm for expanding Colombo Plan membership to include European donors – any European country that wanted to provide aid could do so bilaterally without needing to join the Colombo Plan; no demonstrated need for centrally funded regional training facilities; and the time had not yet come for the setting up of a Colombo Plan secretariat.[29]

The opposition to Stassen's plans came from different but complementary perspectives. While greater US foreign aid was generally welcome, most felt that it should not come at the expense of the Colombo Plan's current procedures. By the time of the meeting in Simla, the Indian hosts, led by Deshmukh and B. K. Nehru, had come to the conclusion that most of Stassen's suggestions were misaligned with Colombo Plan progress and what was needed next.[30] Stassen's sudden portfolio shift,

[27] State Department memorandum of Conversation, Stassen, G. L. Mehta, Ambassador of India, and others 30 March 1955, 890.00/3-3055, USNA.

[28] State Department memorandum of Conversation, Murphy and Corbett, Lord Harcourt, Economic Minister, British Embassy and others, 5 May 1955, 890.00/5-555, USNA.

[29] Press Release, Press Information Bureau, Government of India, 'Conference of Asian Countries of Colombo Plan', Simla, 13 May 1955, in DO 35/5751, TNA; Telegram, US Embassy New Delhi, to Secretary of State, 24 May 1955, no. 1838, 890.00/5-2455, USNA.

[30] UK Report of Simla conference (no author), 16 May 1955, DO 35/5752, TNA.

before the Simla conference, from foreign aid to advising President Eisenhower on disarmament matters may not have helped. Looking on, the original donor governments were largely sceptical beyond noting some potential efficiencies in a Colombo Plan secretariat, although mindful of their need to follow Asian inclinations.[31] Nik Cavell was characteristically critical of the Americans for their not understanding the virtues of the Colombo Plan and for their cavalier 'jumping on the Colombo Plan band-wagon'.[32] Cavell need not have worried. Having been discussed and rejected at Simla, the Americans' proposals did not feature in the following meeting of the full Consultative Committee.[33]

The Indian record of the Simla conference revealed, however, that the gathering was valued as an opportunity for reflections about states of development, foreign aid and regionalism by Asian delegates meeting on their own. While welcoming the prospect of greater US foreign aid for Asia, delegates pointed out how some of the US thinking was misaligned with members' conditions and plans. Education, health and agricultural production as components of national plans were the starting points for most members. Everyone welcomed *regional* thinking about development; yet such was the unevenness between members in capacities and needs that they agreed that regional projects based on common starting points might also be a recipe for lengthy delays. A regional development fund used to address the sudden balance of payments problems caused by price fluctuations in exports was, at first glance, attractive, but the large sums needed, including some necessarily from within the region, made this a potential draw on precious capital at the wrong time. Funding for greater inter-regional trade might also be useful, but members were focused more on production than trade. Greater production should lead to more trade, in any case. Members embraced regionalism as a tenet of faith, but with a realistic gradualism about its process, and recognition that bilateral aid was generally a better fit for near-term conditions:

[31] Secretary of State, CRO telegram to UK High Commissioner, Colombo, 2 May 1955, DO 35/5751, TNA.

[32] Note by N. E. Costar, UK High Commission, Colombo, to J. Thomson, CRO, 17 March 1955, TNA.

[33] J. G. Hadwen to Dept of External Affairs, Ottawa, General Report on the [Singapore] Conference Proceedings, 30 October 1955, RG 25 vol. 6601 11038-5-A-40 part 3, fp 2, LAC; HM Treasury Private Paper III, Colombo Plan Consultative Committee Meetings, Singapore, September/October 1955, The Simla Conference, 15 September 1955, TNA.

> The Asian Members of the Colombo Plan Committee firmly believe that the development of every country in the area is closely linked with the development of the region as a whole. They have therefore always been not only willing but anxious to cooperate among themselves in order to aid, in so far as they can, the economic development of the region as a whole. The extent of such cooperation in any region, must, however, depend necessarily on the conditions of the region itself.[34]

The second American foray was a proposal for a regional nuclear research and training centre. They announced this idea at the 1955 Consultative Committee meeting held in Singapore in October, adding that while they were prepared to contribute substantially to its costs, the venture would sink or swim depending on its embrace by Colombo Plan members. Not surprisingly, given the extravagant claims being made in the mid-1950s for power generation by atomic reactors, most regional members showed some interest. The Ceylonese and the Singaporeans put arguments respectively for their credentials to host the facility. Faced with a grand and potentially divisive proposal, the assembled representatives deflected all the discussions to hotel corridors and out-of-session meetings. John Hollister, US delegation leader and director of Washington's new International Cooperation Administration overseeing foreign aid, told the British delegation leader Lord Reading that they were very keen on establishing the centre at Manila. Reading replied that he couldn't think of a worse selection, given the Philippines' close military connections to the United States.[35] As others noted, the Bandung meeting had made a great impression on those who had attended and was constantly referenced in Singapore. According to Raju Coomaraswamy, the Philippines were more isolated in the region, in the wake of Bandung, the common perception being that they had given up too much too easily to the Americans, in return for US aid. The Americans retreated from announcing Manila as the chosen site for a nuclear research centre (but made it clear that this was the direction of their thinking) and left Singapore needing to follow up with individual members, and with little sense of how this adventurous idea might be bolted onto the Colombo Plan.[36]

Thereafter, a team from the US Atomic Energy Commission's Brookhaven Laboratory toured Colombo Plan countries ascertaining

[34] Sri Prem Narian, Summary of the Proceedings of the Conference of Asian Members of the Colombo Plan Committee, 13 May 1955, DO 35/5752, TNA.

[35] 'Asian Nuclear Centre', Working Group Meeting in Washington, July 1957, Brief for the United Kingdom Delegation, undated (June 1957), DO 35/5781, TNA.

[36] J. G. Hadwen to Department of External Affairs, Ottawa, General Report on Conference Proceedings, 30 October 1955, RG 25 vol. 6601 11038-5-A-40 part 3 fp 2, LAC.

levels of support and gathering information as a basis for recommendations on the size and other characteristics of the proposed centre. The team envisaged facilities for research in basic sciences, applications in nuclear sciences and ultimately a demonstration power reactor.[37] While the level of interest in the region was high, the team found very little scientific expertise save for pockets in Japan, India and Pakistan; and also found little enthusiasm for something regional, based in Manila. The Brookhaven Report was passed to all members at the end of 1956.[38] By this time, the proposal was faltering. One reason was the enduring American commitment, made before the Bandung Conference, to base the centre in Manila. For most, the Philippines government's strong pro-American Cold War stance, confirmed in hosting the conference that led to SEATO in 1954, lent a worrying Cold War-strategic complexion to the idea. Should a nuclear research centre be located in a SEATO or non-SEATO country? This was a question pondered by all Colombo Plan members, according to Canadian External Affairs officer Ed Ritchie, in the wake of the Singapore meeting. Excepting the US and the Philippines, all seemed anxious at the potential for the proposed centre to divide the Colombo Plan in an unwanted military-strategic manner.[39] Of all the regional members, the Indian government was the least enthused and not only on Cold War grounds. The Indians had no need to join in a plan to build a nuclear facility as they had just made public their acceptance of an offer of Canadian Colombo Plan aid to build a national research experimental (NRX) nuclear reactor at Trombay near Bombay.[40] The other big problem bedevilling the US idea was the need for specialized personnel to staff any new nuclear training centre. As the Brookhaven report outlined in detail, there were significant commitments needed, at a time when US resources were already stretched across a burgeoning military–industrial

[37] 'Asian Nuclear Centre', Working Group Meeting in Washington, July 1957, Brief for the United Kingdom Delegation, undated (June 1957), DO 35/5781, TNA.

[38] Drogan, 'The Atoms for Peace Program and the Third World', pp. 441–51. The full Brookhaven Report, 'Study for an Asian Regional Nuclear Center', 15 November 1956, favoured the model of CERN, the European Council for Nuclear Research, established with UNESCO encouragement in 1954, for collaboration and sharing of costs and responsibilities: Copy in FO 371/123252, TNA.

[39] US Embassy, Ottawa, despatch to State Department, no. 320, 1 November 1955, 890.00/11-155, USNA.

[40] Memorandum of Conversation, George Springsteen Jr, State Department and N. V. Lough, New Zealand Embassy, 5 September 1956, 890.00/9-556, USNA; John Hollister, Director, US International Cooperation Administration, memorandum for Secretary of State, 11 November 1955, 890.00/11-1155, USNA.

complex, and with uncertainty about which countries might provide the estimated other half of the staffing required.[41]

The Consultative Committee meeting held in Singapore was significant in ways beyond the Americans' testing the waters for new organizational structure around aid and for interest in a nuclear research centre. It was two years before Malayan independence and four years before Singapore's gaining internal self-government and a source of some satisfaction for Singapore's pro-independence Chief Minister David Marshall who was automatically elected Chair. One of Marshall's initiatives was to collect all the ministerial statements, in advance of sessions, for publication. The resulting 189-page booklet was a once-only experiment, partly because it failed in its aim to prevent ministers from launching into speeches additional to those already in print (see Figures 3.2 and 3.3). The meeting testified to the importance of set speech diplomacy and provided a snapshot of how members embraced both the statistical aspect of annual stock-taking on countries progress reports and the chance to reflect on the past, present and future. Some also relished the chance to gesture towards something bigger about the nexus between development cooperation and a better functioning world. India's Shri Gulzari Lal Nanda (Minister for Irrigation and Power), for example, declared his love of statistics. He felt 'there is something magically stimulating in a figure – which crystallizes a whole economic process'[42] but then sobered quickly by suggesting that the regional members had probably not yet recovered standards of living that matched the statistical baseline year of 1937. Meeting the growing aspirations of Indian people was a giant challenge, but then he felt that the Colombo Plan itself was also aspirational in its broader purpose: 'to secure peace of this region and of the whole world – peace based on progress'.[43]

Speaking to the Singapore chapter, Adbul Hamid b. Haji Jumat (Minister of Local Government, Lands and Housing, and Singapore's first minister of Malay descent) approved of the nickname 'Asian watering can' that he had heard economists use for the Colombo Plan,

[41] US State Department memo, Mein to Schaetzel, 15 October 1956, 890.00/10-1556, USNA.

[42] Government of Singapore, *The Colombo Plan for Co-operative Economic Development in South and South-East Asia. Meetings in Singapore of the Consultative Committee 1955: Minutes and Statements of the Consultative Committee, Minutes of the Preliminary Meetings of Officials and Selected Conference Papers, with Minor Editorial Corrections*, Singapore Government Office, 1956, p. 53, in DO 35/5731, TNA.

[43] Ibid, p. 54.

FIGURE 3.2 Delegates' Handbook for the Singapore meeting of the Consultative Committee, October 1955.
Source: The National Archive (UK) DO 35/5730.

Aerial view of Singapore City

CONTENTS

FIGURE 3.3 Delegates' Handbook for the Singapore meeting of the Consultative Committee, October 1955 – Contents page.
Source: The National Archive (UK) DO 35/5730.

because it captured two essential features: it stimulated and integrated local growth, but at the same time it placed on each country the onus of undertaking the major share of planning its own development. This, he felt, was the pattern of development best suited to the needs of Southeast Asia.[44] Canadian Lester Pearson was upbeat about the huge potential of atomic energy and know-how, in announcing the recently concluded agreement for Canada to build an NRX-type reactor in India; and Hollister was even more effusive about atomic futures in setting out the US proposal for a regional centre for research and training. Asian scientists, he said, would be able to use isotopes and other tools of atomic research to study and cure the diseases endemic to Asia and improve the crops most important to Asia.[45]

In the previous year, one of the features in Canadians' preparations for the Ottawa meeting of the Consultative Committee was their determination to 'keep clearly in mind not only the business side of the conference but also the representational and hospitality aspects'.[46] The attention to

[44] Ibid, p. 99. [45] Ibid, p. 123; Pearson at ibid, pp. 115–16.

[46] Memorandum of First Meeting of Colombo Plan Planning Committee, 15 April 1954, External Affairs, 22 April 1954, RG 19 vol. 4273 8055-04-02 (54) part 2, LAC.

hosting was just as strong the following year in Singapore. The Cathay Hotel had sufficient rooms for all the official business. It was also where most delegates stayed, with Raffles and Goodwood Park providing for the remainder. For the first time, a drafting committee of officials preceded other business, again with business expediency in mind. On their third evening, this new group was treated to five short films produced by the Malayan Film Unit, the source of most British-distributed films for the region. The films highlighted three themes: the orderliness of Singapore's first general elections held recently; the varying ways in which local families were getting ahead through thrift and hard work; and the high quality and impact of Singapore's social services. Thereafter, in addition to multiple cocktail parties and drinks receptions, delegates' social activities encompassed an Inter-School Art Exhibition, Singapore's Commemoration Day celebrations (8 October), the opening of Children's Ward in the General Hospital, Rotary-connected events and the option of visiting the Trade Fair at the Happy World Amusement Park. An art exhibition in the delegation offices at Victoria Memorial Hall remained throughout. Such was the entertainment programme for the minor status Drafting Committee. Ministerial members enjoyed comparable opportunities plus a never-ending series of receptions. Hollister confessed to the assembled that he had fallen asleep while trying to read the lengthy draft chapter reports, not on account on their content, but 'from the fine entertainment which the City Council of Singapore had rendered to the Ministers last night'.[47] Delegates seeking post-conference excursions chose between a tour of the Federated States of Malaya and a tour of Sarawak and North Borneo.[48]

All these activities came at a price to the host nation, as they met the bill for most expenses and social activities around the conferences. Something of a climax to the hospitality dimension was reached in 1956 when New Zealand hosted the Consultative Committee. Up to this point, the expenses of delegates meeting at the annual committee meetings had been covered by the host nation. This was in addition to the hosting and entertainment costs incurred. The Canadians had been surprised by the total costs of their hosting ninety delegates in Ottawa in 1954 and prompted discussion prior to meeting in Singapore the following year

[47] Hollister in Government of Singapore, *The Colombo Plan for Co-operative Economic Development in South and South-East Asia* in DO 35/5731, TNA.

[48] Orders of the Day, 28 September–5 October 1955, no author, Commonwealth Relations Office, DO 35/5730, TNA; Colombo Plan conference report, Commonwealth Relations Office, no author, no date (October 1955), DO 35/5741, TNA.

over whether, given the increasing membership of the plan, visiting delegations be invited to cover their own costs.[49] In 1955, the Indian and Ceylonese representatives rejected this idea, the Indians arguing that bearing these costs was '"an exercise in international goodwill"' and the Ceylonese suggesting that each member needed to bear the burden of hosting once before any change was made.[50] But the time commitments, travel and generous proportions of the meeting in Wellington in 1956 ensured that it would be the last time that hosts covered all the delegates' costs. So significant were the expenses that members worried about Asian readiness to host in future years, and they agreed that from 1957 onwards, they would pay their own way in accommodation and many of the conference activities.[51] The meeting in Wellington was the first major international conference of such dimensions hosted in New Zealand. It was also the longest meeting of the Consultative Committee to date. Officially the date range was 19 November to 8 December, the last week being the meeting of ministers or their representatives; but including post-conference excursions, the Wellington conference lasted four weeks. The journey was so long that many officials combined it with tours of the region or other events nearby. If they were lucky, the latter included stopping off at the Olympic Games being held in Melbourne. Limited flight options meant that a Royal New Zealand Airforce military plane was needed to pick up several delegates struggling to find onward flights from Singapore.[52]

The timing was awkward for three reasons. One was the above-mentioned Olympic Games held across almost the same dates as the conference, 22 November to 8 December; the second was the desire by some foreign ministers to be in New York for the opening of the eleventh

[49] While detailed costs are not provided, the level of detail in the Canadian post-meeting evaluation makes clear the scale of providing for delegates: 'Extracts from a Departmental Assessment of the Colombo Plan Conference held in Ottawa in 1954', External Affairs, undated (1955), including details on 'The Conference Room itself', and 'Planning of the Colombo Joint Conference', RG 25 vol. 7362 11038-5-D-40 part 1.1, LAC.

[50] 'Instructions to the Canadian Delegation to the Colombo Plan Consultative Committee Meeting, Singapore, October 1955', undated External Affairs brief (September 1955), RG 25 vol. 7358 11038-5-A-40 part 3 fp1, LAC.

[51] MAC (SA)(57)1, UK Cabinet Mutual Aid Committee, Sub-committee on South and South-East Asia, 'Colombo Plan Consultative Committee Meeting', Wellington, December 1956, note by Commonwealth Relations Office, 15 January 1956, CO 852/1588, TNA.

[52] *The Colombo Plan Newsletter*, vol. 2, no. 1, January–February 1957, p. 11, RCS, CUL.

session of the UN General Assembly on 12 November; and the third and least anticipated was the unfolding consequences of the Suez Canal crisis, with Anglo-French forces still withdrawing from their abortive invasion of Egypt, and sharp criticisms of Britain circulating as the meeting in Wellington began. The *Auckland Star*'s front page featured accounts of British MPs attacking the Eden government for ruining Britain's reputation. Alongside this, a story reported the Prime Minister Sid Holland welcoming ministerial delegates with a pointed reminder of all the help and guidance Britain had provided in New Zealand's development. Holland also provided a familiarly warm embrace of the Colombo Plan as 'an imaginative experiment in international cooperation', adding that it was playing 'a noble part in bridging civilisations of east and west and in reconciling wide differences of history, tradition and race, and in stimulating friendship, mutual respect and understanding among peoples'.[53]

Delegations from twenty-one member countries, representatives from the Colombo Plan Bureau in Ceylon and three observers convened in Wellington to attend meetings held in the capital's Parliament Buildings.[54] A large map showing how much of Asia was being redrawn as a Colombo Plan area formed the backdrop. Delegations joined sight-seeing opportunities in and around Wellington during their stay. They also enjoyed a photographic exhibition of Colombo Plan projects, films about New Zealand or Colombo Plan work and a performance by the New Zealand National Orchestra. One observer wrote that Wellington was 'agog with excitement'. There were many welcomes, both official, and by 'the average Wellingtonian, the farmer in the village and the Maori in his home . . .'[55] At the end of the conference delegates could join, as guests of the New Zealand government, a tour of the South Island, to 14 December, or a tour of the North Island lasting a day longer.

The scale of enterprise was the more remarkable for New Zealand not being a big contributor of aid under the Colombo Plan. A short sketch of New Zealand's aid contributions to November 1956 included, beyond the

53 *Auckland Star*, 4 December 1956, p. 1.

54 The twenty-one members were: Australia, Burma, Cambodia, Canada, Ceylon, India, Indonesia, Japan, Laos, Nepal, New Zealand, Pakistan, Philippines, Thailand, United Kingdom, Federation of Malaya, North Borneo, Sarawak, Singapore, United States and Vietnam. The three observers represented the International Bank of Reconstruction, the UN Technical Assistance Bureau and the UN Economic Commission for Asia and the Far East.

55 *Colombo Plan Newsletter*, January–February 1957, p. 11.

training of students, capital aid funding to earth-moving equipment for Pakistan, dry-farming research, two technical schools and an ambulance launch and dental nurses training for Ceylon, a new medical institute being built in New Delhi, a railway apprentices' school in Cambodia and a trade training school in Indonesia.[56] The government had developed a modest but distinctive profile, especially in relation to dental health and, as is discussed further below, in assisting milk production in the region.

According to Nik Cavell, Wellington passed the hospitality test with some bumps along the way due to physical constraints. Such was the small capacity of Wellington hotels that five had to be used to accommodate delegates, some distance from each other. He also felt that the Parliamentary Buildings did not lend themselves to the kinds of informal discussions sought by delegates (see Figure 3.4). Cavell was convinced that one of the best aspects of Consultative Committee meetings was the time they enabled for delegate discussions outside of the meeting rooms, which tended, in his words, 'to reach its zenith towards the end of a conference when delegates have come to know and trust one another and are therefore more inclined to speak with some freedom'.[57] This, according to Cavell, was harder to do in Wellington, however welcoming the hospitality.

Hotel capacities notwithstanding, the conference was regarded a success. As New Zealand had so little diplomatic representation in the region (in 1956 only Singapore), it was a chance for their officials to do a lot of basic work on a broad spectrum of issues and other delegations did similarly. Around 4,000 New Zealand schoolchildren visited the photographic exhibition accompanying the conference.[58] The hosts won admiration for maintaining the Consultative Committee norm of being a safe space. They sustained the pattern of minimal decision-making, and any decision made by unanimity, while avoiding controversy. At the meeting, the Americans provided an update on their regional nuclear centre proposal, saying that they had decided to base it in Manila, and were waiting

[56] The Singapore meeting also revealed the space for play in these meetings – David Marshall, for example, was not about to restrained by British colonial propriety and set about cultivating better relations with the Indonesians: Statement by Minister for External Affairs, 23 November 1955, in *New Zealand External Affairs Record*, V, 11 (1955), p. 4.

[57] Report on Colombo Plan Consultative Committee Meeting no. 5 held in Wellington New Zealand, November 19 to December 8, 1956 and Visits to South and South East Asian Countries by Mr Nik Cavell, Colombo Plan Administrator in Canada and Mr Rodney Grey of Department of External Affairs, Ottawa, 15 May 1957, RG 25 vol. 7359 11038-5-B-40 part 2 FP 3.2, LAC.

[58] *The Colombo Plan Newsletter*, January–February 1957, p. 10, RCS, CUL.

FIGURE 3.4 The Consultative Committee in session, Wellington Conference, December 1956.
Source: Alexander Turnbull Library, Wellington, Colombo Plan Conference, November 1956, Ref: 1/2/177157-F. Used with permission.

for co-funding offers to emerge from Colombo Plan members. This was simply noted rather than discussed in formal meetings and it would be allowed to die completely the next year.[59] New Zealand joined the club of those nations that had hosted a grand-scale international conference, via the Colombo Plan, and its leaders and newspaper editorials marked the occasion with some pride.[60]

59 MAC (SA)(57)1 15 January 1957, Cabinet Mutual Aid Committee, Sub-committee on South and South East Asia, Appendix 1, report by Lord Munster, CO 852/1588, TNA.
60 Copy of Letter from New Zealand Government, Colombo Plan Consultative Committee 1956, 18 September 1956, DO 35/5727, TNA.

In short, the mid-decade meetings proved that members were protective of what they had built in the Consultative Committee. It was not just big American aid structures that were fended away. A more modest Australian proposal for donor members to meet fortnightly to better coordinate who was providing what to whom was also nipped in the bud by other donors. The bigger Colombo Plan membership including aid recipients was bound to find out, and potentially be affronted, other members decided. In addition, there would be an added burden that would fall on administrations to keep records. So, this Australian proposal, while not quite nuclear power generation, might also best be avoided.[61]

PROMOTING PLAN AND REGION

One of the earliest detailed booklets promoting the Colombo Plan appeared at the end of 1953, in the wake of the Consultative Committee's meeting in New Delhi. It was produced by Geoffrey Bridson of the British Broadcasting Commission, whose tour of Colombo Plan countries in 1952–53 extended to the production of more than just radio broadcasts. Titled *Progress in Asia: The Colombo Plan in Action*,[62] the thirty-six-page booklet was printed in London and contained twenty-three photographs, four tables and three maps (Figure 3.5). Its British roots meant that *Progress in Asia*, while looking to the future, also bore traces of an older voice of enlightened colonialism. The front cover juxtaposed modernity and traditional ways by focusing on a South Asian labourer transporting materials on his head, viewed through a cut-out section of impressive concrete water pipe. It also pointed to a mix of narrative and pictorial forms that would make the Colombo Plan into something more than its bilateral and separable parts.

Beyond the front cover, the first thing the reader met was a map of 'South and South East Asia', with shading marking members of the Commonwealth and members of the Colombo Plan. Only the Philippines and Thailand were unshaded as they belonged to neither in 1953. Both would join the Colombo Plan the following year. The map also conveyed size and scale, with an inset showing Great Britain drawn

[61] State Department memo, 'Australian Proposal for Colombo Plan Coordination', 9 February 1955, 890.00/2-955, USNA.

[62] D. G. Bridson, *Progress in Asia: The Colombo Plan in Action*, Her Majesty's Stationery Office, London, 1953, RCS, CUL.

FIGURE 3.5 G. D. Bridson, *Progress in Asia*, HMSO, London, 1953.
Source: Royal Commonwealth Society collection, Cambridge University Library.

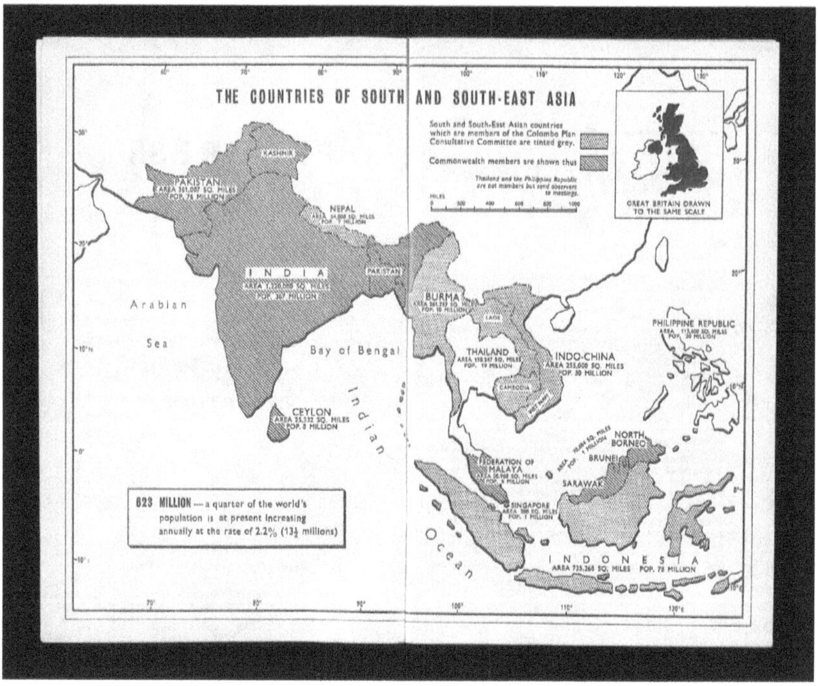

FIGURE 3.6 G. D. Bridson, *Progress in Asia*, HMSO London, 1953, pp. 2–3.
Source: Royal Commonwealth Society collection, Cambridge University Library.

to scale, diminutive by area. Further, a text box informed the reader that the South and Southeast Asia region shown hosted 623 million people, one-quarter of the world's population (Figure 3.6).

The same map appeared in two further forms, one identifying the origins of major exports, including jute, rubber, timber, tin and cotton, and the other denoting the biggest development projects underway. These were primarily multi-purpose hydroelectric schemes, irrigation, new ports, 'new industries' and other electricity-generating projects. Text boxes proclaimed impressive increases of irrigable land or increases in crop production in recent years, complementing the picture of industrial/power stirrings.[63] This and subsequent exercises in heavily visual representations of the Colombo Plan mattered in several ways. In this case, a British production was shaped in a manner that might assist the public recognition of Britain's transition from imperial/colonial power to pre-eminence in the postwar Commonwealth of freely associated nations.

[63] Ibid, pp. 18–19, 34–35.

It was also a form of what might now be called regional branding, building on the Second World War's mapping of Southeast Asia, and much older Asian ideas about interconnections between the states of South and Southeast Asia.[64]

The next major exercises in such work were the result of the Colombo Plan's Information Unit making its mark during 1955–56. Two booklets called *Change in Asia* appeared across the two years, the first being *The Colombo Plan in Pictures* and the second, although still missing some details of activity in certain member countries, conveying more information in text (Figure 3.7 shows the 1955 version). The first was packed with photographs and minimal text beyond a short opening section outlining how 'A Commonwealth Dream Coming True' was transformed quickly into something more international, given the broadening membership, and reminders of the cultural wealth of the region, in the form of photographs of temples, artefacts, gardens and works of art. Thereafter, the sub-headings told of vast enterprise underway: 'Challenge to Hunger'; 'Power for Prosperity'; 'Speedy Ways'; 'Wheels of Industry'; 'Design for Living'; and 'Trained Men'. Photographs from across the region, and occasionally of training within donor countries, conveyed enormous breadth to development work underway.[65] The second, more text-based version published the following year, followed the familiar pattern of invoking ancient glory at the beginning – Mohenjodaro in Pakistan, Sarnath in India, Anuradhapura in Ceylon, Borobadur in Indonesia – and then entering a period of 'stagnation' through lack of independence and the ravages of war. The adroit use of passive tense and generalization enabled the avoidance of who inflicted what harms on whom. A new era of resurgence since the late 1940s brought new hopes and aspirations, according to the story, but with a desperate need for more food, technical knowledge and provisions for a growing population. Snapshot profiles of the member countries enabled readers to learn of major exports, challenges and myriad development projects underway. The multi-year national development plans of various countries were cited, but in the hands of the Information Unit authors, the value of the Colombo Plan was elevated by indirect, vague causation, along the lines of: 'Since the

[64] For further ideas about the history of national and transnational branding as a lens for the study of international history, see Jessica Gienow-Hecht, 'Nation Branding: A Useful Category for International History', *Diplomacy & Statecraft*, 30, 4 (2019), 755–79.

[65] Colombo Plan Information Unit, *Change in Asia: The Colombo Plan in Pictures*, Bureau for Technical Co-operation, Colombo, 1955, in DO35/5761, TNA.

FIGURE 3.7 *Change in Asia: The Colombo Plan in Pictures*, Bureau for Technical Co-operation, Colombo, 1955.
Source: The National Archive (UK) DO 35/5761.

commencement of the Colombo Plan, industrial development has been taken up in many countries of the area ...'[66] This second version of

[66] Colombo Plan Information Unit, *Change in Asia: The Colombo Plan*, Government Press, Colombo, 1956, p. 29 and passim, RCS, CUL.

Change in Asia remained heavily dependent on photographs for conveying the diversity and grandiosity of development activities.

These early hit-outs by the Information Unit worked hard to cover a diverse region, but still relied heavily on British images and information. From the donor countries, the largest complement of information officers focused on or located in South and Southeast Asia were British. Most of the British posts in the region included diplomats responsible for information activities, designed to foster a positive image of Britain's role through print, radio and film. The scale of their activities was significant. Desmond Higgins, a young third secretary serving in the British High Commission in New Delhi in the late 1950s, was charged primarily with information activities. He recalled the 'exotic exercises' of bouncing film vans around the Punjab, Rajasthan and Uttar Pradesh, showing films about Britain. He was both warmly received and well-supported, with over 100 Indian staff engaged in information work. This sustained what he called 'a huge range of activities', including the production and wide distribution of a monthly news leaflet, a local version of that produced by the British Information Service.[67] Higgins and his colleagues had available materials produced by the British Information Service in London, but they were also expected to be pro-active according to local circumstances, placing and producing separate content.

The British attached special attention to film, one of two components (the other being personal contacts, especially Asian correspondents visiting the UK) of what they called 'action propaganda' designed to counter communist appeals and claims and build an atmosphere favourable to UK, Commonwealth and 'free world' policies throughout the region. In the 1950s, information officers held high hopes for the power of film as a medium, not least for its apparent capacity to transcend linguistic barriers and carry narratives of progressive change largely through moving images. The Colombo Plan assumed importance in information activities partly through its suitability as a narrative pivot in an unfolding tale of turning the tide against communist success and of progressive change for the region.[68]

[67] Interview transcript, Desmond Higgins (interviewed by Malcolm McBain, 20 April 2010), British Diplomatic Oral History Programme, Churchill College, Cambridge, pp. 3–4.

[68] Office of the Commissioner General for the United Kingdom in South East Asia to Anthony Eden, Secretary of State for Foreign Affairs, Report of the Information Conference held at Phoenix Park, Singapore, 12–17 January 1953, 23 January 1953, CO1027/26, INF 104/105/03, TNA, accessed through *Cinematic Realism* –

Some of the most substantial Colombo Plan films are discussed in Chapter 6, most of them appearing from the late 1950s onwards. They would draw on different sources. Not surprisingly, given the ongoing struggle against the Malayan Communist Party, the UK Malayan Film Unit worked variations of the anti-communist message into their films.[69] Elsewhere, those making documentary films about the Colombo Plan also drew inspiration from interwar pioneers in the United States, Canada, the Soviet Union and, in the case of Australia and New Zealand, especially Britain where John Grierson and Paul Rotha pioneered distinctive documentary treatments. The head of Australia's Commonwealth Film Unit, Stanley Hawes, trained with Grierson in the 1930s and followed Grierson's style of the authoritative male voice (also called 'the disembodied voice of God'). The tone was one of observing progress, with a liberal humanist gaze and attention for nation-building projects.[70]

The Colombo Plan rated highly among British Information Officers and information services of other donors as a benign and locally identified idea that could work both inside and outside the parameters of the Cold War. From early in the decade, donor governments commissioned tours of Colombo Plan countries by journalists who would, upon their return, brief their governments and generate newspaper articles and radio broadcasts. Early British guidelines for this activity, which set the tone for others, were to produce material that would:

Documentary Film Website, The Documentary Film in South and South-East Asia Research Programme, https://digital.lib.hkbu.edu.hk/documentary-film/ (accessed 30 October 2018).

[69] R. H. Scott, Letter and Reports on the Conference of Information Officers from South-East Asia, 6 to 8 November 1956, 18 December 1956, FCO 141/14841, TNA. And see, more generally, Ian Aitken, 'British Governmental Institutions, the Regional Office in Singapore and the Use of Official Film in Malaya and Singapore, 1948–1961', *Historical Journal of Film, Radio and Television*, 35, I (2014), 27–52; and Tom Rice, '*Merdeka for Malaya*: Imagining Independence across the British Empire', in Ian Aitken and Camille Deprez (eds.), *The Colonial Documentary Film in South and South-East Asia* (Edinburgh: Edinburgh University Press, 2017), pp. 45–62. As film historian Tom Rice has written, with reference to the Malayan Film Unit's work and to other film-making endeavours of its kind, 'Power is visual, and the positioning and organization of personnel (through editing, buildings and events) is one of the ways in which power is transformed into spectacle.' Effective documentary film-making encourages a certain form of viewer hypnosis that discourages contemplation of 'the tensions, frustrations, failings and successes of the colonial era' while it hastens on to the modernizing progress of the present: Rice, '*Merdeka for Malaya*', pp. 58, 60.

[70] Belinda Smaill, 'Promoting Australia: Post-war Documentary and Asia', *Continuum*, 28, 5 (2014), 621; Srirupa Roy, *Beyond Belief: India and the Politics of Postcolonial Nationalism* (Durham, NC: Duke University Press, 2007), pp. 35–39.

(a) cover specific development projects in a topical manner;
(b) give sufficient local background and human interest; and
(c) provide material for use in other types of media.[71]

Bridson's was one of the first such commissioned tours. It was conducted jointly with Loftus Hyde for the Australian Broadcasting Commission. Bridson set out on 10 November 1952 and was joined by Hyde two weeks later for what would be a three-month tour of 'Colombo Plan countries' to enable them to tell the story of development in these countries through local radio broadcasts in Britain and Australia. They would also use the short-wave BBC overseas service and provide transcribed text copies for all Commonwealth countries. The two men began in Ceylon and then moved to Singapore, Malaya, Thailand, Burma, East Pakistan, India and West Pakistan, in that order. They quickly discovered that talking up the Colombo Plan could be problematic. It was a delicate and sometimes unwanted conversation in India and Pakistan where their respective Five-Year and Six-Year Plans were more ambitious in scope, more central to nation-making politics and not to be marginalized. This contrasted with Ceylon where big placards advertised the Colombo Plan, demonstrating how the government enjoyed trading on the name. In Malaya, British authorities wanted to direct all media attention to the struggle against the Malayan Communist Party in the ongoing 'Emergency'. Relaying these experiences to information officers in London after the trip, Bridson likened his experience to looking through the other end of a telescope: 'When you see the Plan in action it is obviously bound to look rather different from what it may look over here.'[72]

Bridson and Hyde adjusted their messages, avoiding the grander and more collective narratives and focusing on the excitement of particular development projects they found. In the case of Ceylon, it was not just the Colombo Plan's obvious brand that appealed but local politicians and engineers spoke of it helping to recover past greatness in irrigation. Some of the main activities to date had been helping to restore the system of water tanks and channels that were engineered two thousand years earlier, but had, for reasons of wars and diseases, fallen into disrepair.[73]

[71] C.P (I.W.P)(52) 2nd Meeting, Notes of a Meeting of Information Officers to Discuss Colombo Plan Publicity', H.M. Treasury, 22 September 1952, DO 35/5755, TNA.

[72] Treasury Reporter 'Notes of a Talk by Mr. Geoffrey Bridson, of the British Broadcasting Corporation, to Information Officers held at H.M. Treasury on Tuesday, 24th February, 1953', DO 35/5755, TNA.

[73] Ibid.

In his search for 'good interesting human material', Bridson found rich pickings at the Gal Oya scheme, where enthusiastic settlers spoke of their new land made possible by jungle clearance. In his broadcasts, he did not exaggerate the modest contributions of the Colombo Plan to national development plans but portrayed it as a stitching together of great programs already underway, 'a plan by which an increasing number of development schemes in Asia can be related and in part co-ordinated – the Five-Year Plan in India, the Six-Year Plans in Pakistan and Ceylon, the Colonial Development and Welfare schemes in Malaya, and so on'.[74] The stitching was the aid being provided by members of the Commonwealth. What also resonated in Bridson's version was the Commonwealth's postwar formula of 'a free association of independent sovereign countries', the symbol of which was the Crown. He concluded, 'The fact that all countries participating in the plan have the same aims and ideals has made their free association in a common cause a practical possibility; the fact that the plan is basically a device for promoting and facilitating Asian self-help is making it a conspicuous success.'[75]

A COLOMBO HUB

The composition of the Colombo Plan Council established in Colombo in December 1950 was determined by those members with diplomatic representation in Ceylon, so there was no New Zealander. It initially found its feet through collecting and disseminating information. The Founding President Raju Coomaraswamy drew on a combination of UN and colonial data sets, UN rates of pay and conditions of employment for experts abroad and the energies of the first Director of the Bureau, Geoffrey Wilson. Much of Wilson's time was spent trying to organize the administration of donor countries' technical aid efforts in ways that could be recorded and coordinated, and securing regular updates on how this was working from donor nations. That there were other technical assistance schemes operating, including the expanding UN one, added to the complications in knowing which gaps were best filled first.[76] The Bureau and Council struggled to keep up with the movement of experts coming

74 Bridson's introduction to his broadcasts, 'Asia Has a Plan', 23 April 1953, DO 35/5755, TNA.

75 Ibid.

76 Memorandum by the Director, 'Co-ordination with Other Agencies', 29 February 1952, Colombo, CRS A1361 item 43/1/6 part 3, NAA; Memorandum by the Director, 'Further Developments in Technical Co-operation', by Wilson, Colombo, 23 June 1952, ibid.

and going under the technical cooperation side of the plan and therefore prodded members to provide these details. They also invited donor governments to consider ways in which going beyond bilateral aid provision might enable more beneficial sharing and coordination of information.[77] Donor members reported twice yearly on their expenditure. Only about half of the £800,000 available for technical assistance in the first two years of the plan was expended, and there was great relief in the Bureau when it was decided, in April 1952, that the technical assistance scheme should run coterminous with the capital aid side of the plan, to the middle of 1957.[78]

Two challenges for the Council that persisted into the middle of the decade were managing popular, especially media, expectations and reminding observers that Asian members were active donors as well as recipients of foreign aid. The first task was the more formidable. Having called the new scheme emanating from meetings in Colombo, Sydney and London a 'Plan' with a capital 'P' raised media expectations. The Marshall Plan, reaching its peak before concluding in 1952, saw the Americans inject $17 billion into European countries, accompanied by the elimination of trade barriers and other measures of integration to make Western Europe function more cohesively as an economic region.[79] To remind journalists that the Colombo Plan was more of an umbrella for many bilateral flows of aid of varying scales, without an overarching agenda of regional integration, was to risk disappointment unless some alternative spectacular features of the Colombo Plan could be quickly instanced. Here, the second challenge of ensuring widespread knowledge of Asian agency and donor efforts was a potential answer. There were examples to point to: by the start of 1953, India had supplied five experts to Ceylon, had taken in trainees from other parts of the region to study statistics, sugar making, customs administration, engineering and broadcasting, and offered fifty-five scholarships in Indian universities and institutes; Ceylon had offered facilities to trainees from neighbouring countries at the newly built Co-operative Training School; and Pakistan had offered training in civil aviation, had hosted a Ceylonese trainee in

77 Minutes of Council Meeting, Colombo, 4 September 1952, CRS A1361 item 43/1/6 part 3, NAA.

78 G. M. Wilson, Council Report for 1952: Memorandum by the Director, 3 March 1953, CRS A 1361 item 43/1/6 part 3, NAA.

79 For details, see the classic study, Michael J. Hogan, *The Marshall Plan: America, Britain and Reconstruction of Western Europe, 1947–1952* (Cambridge: Cambridge University Press, 1987).

dam construction and had provided thirty head of cattle for breeding in Australia's tropical zone.[80] Otherwise, a Regional Training Centre for Railway Operating and Signalling Officials opened in Lahore in April 1954, sponsored by ECAFE and UNTAA, and ECAFE was also sponsoring regional (rather than country) mineral and tectonic maps. But until the Council boasted a separate Information Unit, from 1954, and a widely distributed monthly newsletter from 1956, it had very partial success in raising broader awareness of these endeavours.

As donor country information services cranked up to generate encouraging stories about development activities in Asia, the Colombo Plan's small Bureau also began to initiate and coordinate publicity efforts. Like film, the power of the image in photographic form was eagerly seized on as a way of transcending linguistic differences. The Bridson booklet and other early publicity efforts were templates that could be adapted as Colombo Plan activities expanded. Others engaged in development and humanitarian missions, at state and non-state levels, also demonstrated what might be possible. By the mid-1950s, for example, the Save the Children Fund spent 5 per cent of its annual income on advertising (primarily in newspapers and on radio) and in producing a bimonthly magazine.[81]

In style and substance, publicity for the Colombo Plan shared common roots with that of other international organizations. The middle years of the decade witnessed a growing belief among information workers that good photographs could transcend differences and convey the essence of shared humanity. The image rose in prominence with the rise of the UN. Appeals to the new, public internationalism and to universal values celebrated by UNESCO in its promotion of mutual understanding 'by word and image' found expression in photographic exhibitions such as the well-known *Family of Man* (1955) curated by Edward Streichen. The *Family of Man* toured the world, crossing Cold War lines, inviting crowds to reflect on such universal themes as love, work, birth and death.[82] In UNESCO's own photo magazine *Courier*, image took primacy over text.[83] Similarly, the World Health Organization's newsletter relied

[80] G. M. Wilson, Council Report for 1952: Memorandum by the Director, 3 March 1953, CRS A 1361 item 43/1/6 part 3, NAA.

[81] Alexander Medcalf, 'Between Art and Information: Communicating World Health, 1948–70', *Journal of Global History*, 13 (2018), 100, 94–120.

[82] Ibid, pp. 103–5.

[83] Tom Allbeson, 'Photographic Diplomacy in the Postwar World: UNESCO and the Conception of Photography as a Universal Language, 1946–1956', *Modern Intellectual History*, 12, 2 (2015), 383–415.

heavily on the use of photographs, drawing on both centralized production in Geneva and acquisitions from information officers in regional offices. As the visual message became a key part of the Colombo Plan, the universalism of the UN and the mission of cooperative development mixed with more particular national and imagined regional objectives.

Specialized agencies of the United Nations played a major role in the provision of experts and fellowships. Up to mid-1957, UN agencies provided 3,982 experts for South and Southeast Asia, with the FAO, WHO and UNTAA the largest providers. They also supported 2,440 fellowships. These figures compared with 792 experts provided by Colombo Plan members and 5,622 students who had received training. India hosted 511 of the training places.[84] Thus, while the Colombo Plan could not compete with UN agencies for the provision of experts, it did much better for provision of scholarships/fellowships. Comparison remained difficult, however, as expenditure on technical assistance could include equipment for training and use by experts. That the Americans did not immediately join the Technical Council was accommodated relatively easily by those in the Information Bureau. In updates on the progress in technical assistance, they were adept in mentioning US membership of the Consultative Committee and then glossing over their formal absence from the Technical Council, listing their various impressive statistics relating to training and provision of experts. Up to mid-1957 the United States sent 1,449 experts to the region and offered 4,833 training places.[85]

Both image and statistics were important to donor governments for their own domestic uses. Governments of donor countries such as Canada and Australia needed to show voters that their aid was doing good work, and this was not easy. Both governments emphasized the foreign policy objectives behind giving aid. The Colombo Plan enabled Asia to come into focus for a cohort of Canadian policymakers who recovered from their initial grudging involvement to incorporating it in their sense of Canada's expanding role in world affairs.[86] An early Australian analysis of what they hoped to achieve under the plan listed three related aims of halting the spread of communism, modifying any resentments arising from differences between Australian and Asian living standards, and the broadest one, developing 'amicable political relations' with countries

[84] Ibid. [85] *Colombo Plan Newsletter*, 2, 9, October 1957, p. 4, RCS, CUL.

[86] David Webster, 'Mental Maps and Canada's Post-war Asian Policy', *International Journal: Canada's Journal of Global Policy Analysis*, 75, 4 (2020), 548–62.

involved.[87] Attempts to disburse quickly approved allocations of Colombo Plan funding, to India in particular, met with delays resulting from initial uncertainty about 'best match' forms of aid, logistical issues and, as is discussed further in the following chapter, the tight control wielded by India's Planning Commission. Both the Canadians and Australians used liaison offices to try to expedite the matching of capital with what was needed in India. Ottawa drew on the Canadian Commercial Corporation and Canberra looked to an enterprising trade public servant, J. B. Todd, whose career straddled army service and the Australian Trade Commissioner Service. Todd was made Director of Colombo Plan Supplies in 1951, based in the Department of Commerce and Agriculture.

While Todd enjoyed some early success in matching Australian diesel locomotives to Pakistan's needs,[88] the CCC broke through more spectacularly in India with steam locomotives. After the first two years, only $18 million of the $50 million allocated by the Canadian government had been spent.[89] This prompted some awkward questions in parliament and although the CCC enabled allocations to be shifted and parked, it was still with great relief that Ottawa learned of an Indian appetite for the kind of steam locomotives, WPs, so-called on account of their wide gauge and passenger-bearing purpose, that had traversed Canada. Cranking up a production line that was scheduled to wind down in favour of diesel engines, the Canadian Locomotive Company embraced a last hurrah for steam and shipped 120 WPs to India for re-assembling between March 1955 and September 1956. The WPs entered service quickly and effectively. Their number was soon exceeded by locally built versions and together these trains were a familiar sight over the coming decades. The last Canadian-built WP was withdrawn from service only in 1996. Many of the locomotives were painted in bright colours, or with the Star of India, and given modernist bullet noses, ensuring their iconic status among the travelling public. While it would prove hard for the Canadians to assess

[87] Draft Report, 'The Colombo Plan: An Appraisal', no author (Department of External Affairs), no date (by implication, 1952), CRS A4311 item 145/1, NAA.

[88] Copy of letter no. 1 (HC)/52-1416 Indian Trade Commissioner in Australia to Mharaj Shree Duleepsinhji, High Commissioner in Australia, included with Prem Narian (Minister for Finance) 'Record of Conversation with Francis Stuart, Australian High Commission, and J.S.', 29 July 1952, MEA File F.22-5/51-M (M), NAI.

[89] David McGee and Rian Manson, 'Canada, Communism and the Colombo Plan', in Nina Mollers and Bryan DeWalt (eds.), *Objects in Motion: Globalizing Technology* (Washington, DC: Smithsonian Institution Scholarly Press, 2016), pp. 56, 46–64.

exactly how much brand recognition and goodwill resulted, especially on account of the greater number of Indian-built versions, they were relieved at the early success of such a tangible form of aid. As one interpreter of the episode suggests, Canadian officials concluded that 'big stuff' was what best bridged the expectations of the two governments.[90]

AGENTS ON THE MOVE

The first half of the 1950s revealed how central were the small groups of mid-tier officials to the Colombo Plan's consolidation. In most cases, working in the plan's small bureaucratic headquarters in Colombo also proved career-enhancing. As ECAFE and other UN auxiliaries expanded their operations, and as member governments called on more planners and social scientists to manage their economic growth, innovative thinkers moved readily between Colombo, other international organizations and their home governments. Rajendra (Raju) Coomaraswamy, Oxford BA and keen cricketer, was one of these (Figure 3.8). He entered the Ceylonese Civil Service prior to independence and cut his teeth in the industry, labour and commerce sections. He was Assistant Secretary in Finance in Ceylon for the first half of the 1950s, and his career rode on the back of the Colombo Plan. Three years after the Plan's launch, he was described in a British presentation as knowing more about it than anyone else.[91] By the end of the decade, he had been President of the Colombo Plan Council twice (December 1950–October 1953 and December 1957–January 1959) and was also known for his larger-than-life personality and love of travel. 'Roving Raju' was his nickname. Indeed, he relished the long annual meetings of the Consultative Committee and was opposed to most suggestions aimed at shortening them. In 1958, even when the improving quality of first drafts of the annual country reports seemed to suggest that there might be less need for preliminary working on them, he maintained that 'the work and the struggle entailed in preparing this material [was] an integral part of the conference. Without it, the nature of the conference would be changed, and it would lose much of its reason for being'.[92] After finishing his

[90] Ibid, p. 61.

[91] A. C. B. Symon, 'The Colombo Plan', *Journal of the Royal Asian Society*, 3–4 (1952), 189.

[92] Informal Summary, Third Meeting of the Business Committee, 5 November 1958, Seattle, CRS A 10617 item 1958/4, NAA.

FIGURE 3.8 Rajendra Coomaraswamy.
Source: Open Minds! Site https://nalakagunawardene.com/wp-content/uploads/2015/10/raju-coomaraswamy-and-his-daugher-radhika-coomaraswamy.jpg or Geni www.geni.com/photo/view/6000000043993624020?album_type=photos_of_me&photo_id=6000000043994181123

second term on the Council, he became head of the United Nations Development Program's first Asia and Pacific Bureau in 1961 and later Assistant Administrator of the UNDP in New York.

As the first President of the Colombo Plan Council, Coomaraswamy set the tone for much that followed. Statistics were important, especially those relating to training provided, specialist equipment received and experts loaned. So too was a sense of horizons. In the short term, regional members would necessarily be relying on experience and techniques from abroad. Specialists would always be shared and loaned, even among the most developed countries. In the longer term, Coomaraswamy argued it was crucial that Asia develop its own capacity to train high numbers of qualified workers who could grapple with the enormity of ambitious development. In the annual report by the Council for 1952, Coomaraswamy's voice could be heard figuratively rolling up the sleeves of regional governments and amplifying a tone set by Geoffrey Wilson; 'the medium and lower grade technicians, the agricultural extension workers, the teachers and whole range of non-commissioned officers in every branch of industry and administration, whose role is just as important as that of the qualified professional men and who will be needed in millions rather than thousands, can only be trained in their own countries'.[93]

When he was not President of the Council, Coomaraswamy was the main point of contact for most matters relating to Ceylon's participation in the Colombo Plan, and he represented the government at the Consultative Committee meetings. He made it clear in his negotiations with others that he had considerable delegated authority in representing Ceylon's development needs, and he could therefore change the relative priorities attaching to different projects. Visiting Ottawa in 1953, he put to the Canadians a new project to light the runway at Colombo's Ratmalana Airport. At the same time, he tried to steer the Canadians into thinking their way towards counterpart aid funding through the provision of flour (which they had not contemplated to date) with the funds raised going towards road building. The conversation suggested that the Canadians were nervous about selling this idea in Ottawa. Was lighting for an airport runway a development project as the Canadian people understood development? Finally, Coomaraswamy tested his hosts on the funding of cooperative schools. He found them wary of being seen to support this form of education over other schooling, so Coomaraswamy switched to seeking funding for a Polytechnic Institute on the outskirts of Colombo. This project had narrowly missed out on Ford Foundation money, he said, although they had managed to fund a near-identical one in Pakistan. The Canadians took much greater interest.[94] Very quickly, Coomaraswamy established his authority as the go-to person in relation to Ceylon's aid projects, having been granted a long leash that sat well with his love of deal-making.[95] Indeed, for Canadians seeking to increase their knowledge about political dynamics in Asia, Coomaraswamy became the go-to for all sorts of information: what really transpired at the Bandung Conference in 1955, how close were Filipino politicians to the Americans and so on.[96]

Another important enterprising bureaucrat was the Indian economist Palamadai S. Lokanathan whose work connected directly and indirectly

[93] *The Colombo Plan: Report of the Council for Technical Co-operation in South and South-East Asia for 1952*, February 1953, p. 8, RCS, CUL.

[94] A. E. Ritchie, Minutes of Colombo Group Meeting with Coomaraswamy, 29 June 1953, 1 July 1953, RG 25 vol. 6576 11038-40 part 12, LAC.

[95] Canadian High Commissioner, Ceylon to Secretary of State, External Affairs, 9 December 1954, RG 25 vol. 6595 11038-A-1-40 part 10.1; Coomaraswamy to High Commissioner, Canada, Ceylon, 16 November 1954, ibid.

[96] J. G. Hadwen to Dept of External Affairs, 'Politics at the Singapore Meetings', 30 October 1955, RG 25 vol. 6601 11038-5-A-40 part 3, fp2, LAC.

with the Colombo Plan throughout the 1950s. Lokanathan completed a master's degree in economics at the University of Madras, under the training of English and Indian economists trained at the London School of Economics (LSE). He was appointed a Reader at Madras and wrote on industrial welfare in India before following the path of his mentors and completing a doctorate at the LSE on industrial organization. This was published as *Industrial Organization in India* in 1935 and was widely admired. After returning to the University of Madras, Lokanathan was appointed to several state committees and became editor of the influential Indian periodical *Eastern Economist*. He also worked for Indian business magnate, G. D. Birla, and was one of a select group of economists responsible for the famous Bombay Plan, an ambitious vision of India's postwar development sponsored by Birla and seven other major industrialists. Published in 1944, the plan envisaged significant government intervention and regulation, underpinned by a large public sector, as the basis for India's rapid growth, especially in heavy industry. While not socialist, its core of centralized planning and targets set the direction for India's Five-Year Plans under Nehru.[97]

As described in Chapter 1, Lokanathan was the first Executive Secretary of ECAFE, and largely responsible for ECAFE's survival and semi-autonomy within the UN system. His victories were gained through force of intellect and his preparedness take up a fight, especially against the colonial and great power members of ECAFE whose motives he always suspected. Some of those who worked with him in the ECAFE Secretariat described his leadership style as that of a 'Mughal emperor'.[98] During the second half of 1952, Lokanathan teamed up with his counterpart head of the Economic Commission for Europe, Swedish economist Gunnar Myrdal, to try to have more European countries attend ECAFE conferences to discuss trade. Americans were alarmed at the prospect of (communist) Eastern European countries flooding into ECAFE meetings and they managed to nip these plans in the bud, accompanied by familiar mutterings about those who 'overstepped their authority'.[99] In the mid-1950s Lokanathan continued to push for greater capacity, especially research capacity, in the ECAFE Secretariat in Bangkok, and he looked

[97] Kudaisya, *Tryst with Prosperity*, pp. 71–72.

[98] Singh, *The Politics of Economic Cooperation in Asia*, pp. 97–98.

[99] Merrill C. Gay (US State Dept) memo for Allison and Johnson, 24 September 1952, RG 59, lot file 64D207, box 3, Miscellaneous Economic Records of Bureau of Far Eastern Affairs 1945–61, Merrill C. Gay files, USNA.

always to Asian experts before non-Asians. Nor did he relax his mission to agitate through ECAFE work and the Colombo Plan, for more aid projects of an explicitly regional character.[100] As ECAFE leader, he attended annual Consultative Committee meetings, alongside World Bank, UNTAA and Ford Foundation representatives. In the 1955 Singapore meeting, he gave one of the longest speeches, outlining the new research capacity in ECAFE for economic development studies. Conferences for statisticians and also new working parties on different aspects of development would embark on research that could inform Colombo Plan deliberations, he said. Indeed, important statistically based planning such as countries' population estimates and annual public expenditure on development increasingly became the province of ECAFE. Technical training, said Lokanathan, was becoming more regional, including a UN-sponsored centre for railway operation, an ILO-supported centre for diesel mechanics, and Pakistan's Lahore Railway Training Centre where Colombo Plan scholarships enabled regional students to study. He looked forward to more studies of training and specific industrial activities that could enhance regional cooperation and trade, both intra- and inter-regional.[101]

In the wake of the kind of advocacy and entrepreneurship shown by Narasimhan, Lokanathan, Coomaraswamy and others, those with lesser knowledge and experience followed. Diplomats in donor countries and in regional posts, often on steep learning curves about conditions in Asia, relied on these prominent local experts for deciding what was logical and mutually satisfactory between regional and donor members.[102] The same

[100] Note by E. R. Warner, Foreign Office, of Lokanathan visit, 6 April 1954, FO 371/112587, TNA; Note by E. R. Warner, of Lokanathan visit, on 15 April, 24 April 1954, ibid.

[101] Lokanathan's speech, in Government of Singapore, *The Colombo Plan for Co-operative Economic Development in South and South-East Asia.* Meetings in Singapore of the Consultative Committee 1955, Singapore Government Office, 1956, pp. 73–76, in DO 35/5731, TNA.

[102] A tour by Canadian Minister W. J. Browne of Ceylon, India and Pakistan in 1957 was clearly an eye-opening experience by one on a steep learning curve, and highly dependent on the kinds of exchanges and writings of key officials. In his reports back to Ottawa, it was the Colombo Plan and Commonwealth connectedness that enabled Browne to add order to his wide-eyed observations about impoverished conditions and colourful personalities, and to thread his observations into policy recommendations around future aid actions: W. J. Browne to Sidney Smith, Secretary of State for External Affairs, Ceylon, 8 November 1957, RG 25 vol. 7361 11038-5-c-2-40 part 1.2, LAC; W. J. Browne to Sidney Smith, Secretary of State for External Affairs, India, 9 November 1957, ibid; W. J. Browne to Sidney Smith, Secretary of State for External Affairs, Pakistan, 21 November 1957, ibid.

mid-level professionals played important roles in the preliminary meetings, the working groups, drafting committees and business committees that pored over progress reports, asking questions and filling gaps, for the first weeks of the annual Consultative Committee meetings. In this work, they were at first somewhat constrained by templates and practices derived from colonial eras and postwar reconstruction in Europe, but their efforts were very necessary for the completion of the annual updates and reporting that lay at the heart of the Colombo Plan. If anything, their role grew stronger with the expanding membership. As the following chapters show, the work of the Consultative Committee, in terms of diplomacy addressing region, nation, and global economy, gathered even more momentum in the latter years of the decade. So too did the Colombo Plan's capacity to tell of its own importance and to generate stories for members wanting to demonstrate its success.

4

States, Sovereignty and Story

By the late 1950s, the Colombo Plan had gathered steam and supporters. As this chapter shows, the small Bureau in Colombo attracted talented experts who worked as advocates as much as administrators. Drawn on a rotating basis from donor nations, the directors of the Bureau could be counted on to expand the realms of their work and reporting. For several of the newly joined governments, membership was a step towards higher diplomatic cachet, towards full sovereignty, membership of the UN, or simply higher standing among neighbours. Representatives enjoyed the indulgences granted by long meetings. In addition to lavish hospitality, the annual meetings provided ample space for reflections on the state of 'East–West' relations and on the best paths towards peace and prosperity. Still buoyed by the momentum from Bandung, leaders such as Sukarno relished the chance to again proclaim how the world had changed and how Indonesia would not be moulded into a Western approximation of how a state should function. One grievance that Asian representatives found they had in common with colleagues from Australia and especially New Zealand was the effects of price fluctuations on their main exports.

At the same time, the Cold War intruded into Colombo Plan decision-making regularly. Soviet interest in the region accelerated during the second half of the decade. As outlined below, the forms that Cold War thinking took could vary considerably, but some decisions about aid demonstrated the power of brinkmanship, playing off East against West. Others seemed more like military assistance than development. It was more remarkable, then, that the Cold War was kept at bay in the sessions of the Consultative Committee and surfaced mostly in private meetings. In the Committee, the Commonwealth-borrowed culture of avoiding conflict and reaching decision by consensus prevailed.

There remained a need to find ways of measuring the success of the Colombo Plan, something that was a constant work in progress. Lest there seemed too little to boast about in the way of achievements as the first milestone of six-year plans was reached, donor members created distinctive claims for their efforts. For the New Zealanders, the Colombo Plan rapidly turned into a tale of assisting through dentistry and milk production. They focused especially on dairy expertise, and this became a means by which a government-crafted story of New Zealand leadership was projected into Asia. For others, and especially for the Australians, sponsored students was another compelling story that continued to grow and was easily illustrated with examples of success. Both the case-book nature of the Colombo Plan, producing a rich variety of stories that could be seized on for publicity, and its quiet diplomatic space, reliably welcoming while gesturing to the prospect of some bigger potential, proved key to its endurance.

GROWING STATES

On 16 May 1958, Nik Cavell, Colombo Plan veteran and recently arrived High Commissioner for Canada in Colombo, was summoned to an urgent meeting. He was told that the Colombo Plan could be crucial in helping to address 'a very grave matter concerning the future of Ceylon'.[1] He waited outside the meeting room in Queen's House, the residence of Ceylon's Governor-General, Sir Oliver Goonetilleke, until the American Ambassador, Max Gluck, was led out of the meeting room. Then it was Cavell's turn for an emergency meeting. Goonetilleke, joined by Prime Minister Bandaranaike, the Minister for Finance and the Secretaries of Finance and External Affairs, outlined for Cavell how the political situation had become desperate. Leftists within Cabinet were destabilizing the government, rising unemployment was fuelling discontent, capital projects were delayed, and there was a severe risk that communists would sweep to power in the 1961 elections. If they were to avoid this calamity, the government would need to embark on substantial spending, to the tune of nearly 233 million Sri Lankan rupees. Cavell saw where the conversation was heading and so asked the crunch question: Did they

[1] N. Cavell to Secretary of State for External Affairs, Ottawa, 19 May 1958, RG 25 vol. 7357 11038-3-17-40 art 1, LAC.

want to know how much the US and Canadian governments could provide by means of aid? The answer was yes, and after an awkward 'as much as you can provide' initial response, they settled on requesting $50 million from Canada over the next three years, with no more than $24 million of that in flour (as counterpart funding). A mission would be heading to Ottawa soon to follow up, and the Governor-General implored Cavell to go to Ottawa in advance, adding that his ability to put Ceylon's case would be invaluable.[2]

Cavell protested that his duty was to act as Canada's representative and that it would be impossible for him to go to Ottawa (while noting the flattery in Ceylonese protests that 'I had a long experience in Asia and Ceylon, of which they wanted to make use.').[3] But he, Gluck and other diplomats stationed in Colombo endorsed the sense of emergency; 'this is unquestionably the most critical year Ceylon has experienced since she gained her independence'.[4] The Cold War choice was a real one. Given that the only other source of aid for Ceylon was from 'Iron Curtain Embassies' now was the time for the likes of Canada and the United States to think hard about what needed to be done. There was no guarantee that any amount of money or flour would ensure that an anti-communist government was retained, but Cavell felt 'this may be the last chance the West may have'; and, just as one looked hard at the risk that was being insured against before paying a premium, this was one such premium worth paying.[5]

This was certainly not the first time Cavell had been briefed about the communist menace in Ceylon. Communist influence there had been the subject of conversations in Ottawa preceding his departure for Colombo, including in relation to a huge Colombo Plan Exhibition and Trade Fair planned by the Ceylonese government for 1957. Knowing that the Soviets were going to be mounting exhibits, Cavell and his colleagues readied themselves for a Cold War tussle over hearts and minds at the exhibition. They embarked on deciding what forms of Canadian technological prowess to show, before the exhibition was suddenly abandoned due to budget alarms and rising political unrest in Colombo.[6] In the aftermath of Cavell's dramatic meeting in 1958, the Canadians fended away Goonetilleke and Bandaranaike's brinkmanship while maintaining their various commitments to Ceylon. They resisted seeing the Ceylonese

[2] Ibid. [3] Ibid. [4] Ibid. [5] Ibid.

[6] Minutes of meeting of the Ad-Hoc Interdepartmental Planning Group on the 1957 Colombo Plan Exhibition, 19 January 1956, RG 20 vol. 3103, 950-C1–2 v.3, LAC.

situation as part of a broader blackmailing trend; 'it is not the Asians themselves who ask us to help them so that they will not turn to the Communists. It is the Americans who insist on defining their aid in these terms and it is not surprising therefore if some Asians play upon this theme'. However, the Canadian Cabinet noted, the only Asian country which had blatantly used this argument was a Commonwealth country – Ceylon.[7] Thereafter, Ceylonese politics remained febrile, and Bandaranaike was assassinated on 25 September 1959.

Some forms of foreign aid were more easily deployed for what could be called internal security by recipient governments but might also be accurately described as Cold War or state authoritarian measures. The Australians provided police training and radio equipment to South Vietnam for use by the army.[8] The Canadians confronted a fluid civil–military situation when matching their experience of float planes with the desire of the Sukarno government in Indonesia to open access to remote areas. The Cold War context shaped their decision-making. In the latter months of 1958, they discussed possible Canadian support for a road-building programme in the Celebes but were suddenly gazumped by a Soviet offer. As the Indonesians took delivery of $2 million worth of Soviet road-building equipment in January 1959, the Canadians responded by committing the provision of de Havilland Otter aircraft to improve inter-island connectedness. While knowing that the request came from the Indonesian Air Force, which viewed such aircraft in strategic ways, Canada's ambassador Theodore Newton argued persuasively that the Air Force was destined to always play a developmental role in Indonesia, and that Foreign Minister Subandrio had given assurances about their intended civilian roles. The Otters arrived as gifts under the Colombo Plan and by credit extended. Some months later, Newton was delighted to join a flight flown by an Indonesian pilot trained in Canada that carried President Sukarno smoothly across southern Kalimantan (Borneo).[9]

[7] John Wendell Holmes, memorandum for the Minister, Colombo Plan Program, 7 September 1958, RG 25 vol. 7357 11038-4-40 part 2.2, LAC.

[8] Casey Diary, 3 September 1954, Casey Papers, box 28, MS 6150, National Library of Australia (NLA).

[9] John Diefenbaker, Secretary of State for External Affairs, memorandum for Under-Secretary, 13 November 1958; Theodore Newton to Secretary of State for External Affairs, 30 January 1959, RG 25 vol. 7357 11038-4-40 part 2.2, LAC; Theodore Newton to Secretary of State for External Affairs, 23 September 1959, RG 25 vol. 7357 11038-4-40 part 2.2, LAC.

Both Canadian and Australian governments tried to counter the increasing Soviet propaganda efforts in Asia by planning to send high volumes of books under the Colombo Plan that were intended to convey the virtues of democracy, freedom and the Commonwealth. The more modest Canadian programme sent hundreds of books to public and university libraries, especially in India, Pakistan, Ceylon and Malaya, from the middle of the decade. The Canadians' 1958 list of books comprised more than 100 titles in English and a similar number in French. Chosen for their capacity to 'help build up in the [Colombo Plan] area sympathy for Western thought and institutions, and to compete to some degree with the flood of Communist literature',[10] they were categorized under (English) headings: Economics; Political Institutions and Ideas; Economic History, Economic History – Canadian; General History; Philosophy and General; Canadian History and Biography; General Books on Canada; Sociology.[11] The ambitious Australian 'Cheap Books' scheme envisaged 10,000 copies of selected Australian titles (including Casey's own depiction of Australian–Asian relations, *Friends and Neighbours*); but, with the exception of some sent as gifts, most remained in warehouses as the Australians could not agree on their final list of which books to send.[12]

In the bigger picture, it was hard to demonstrate a broader awareness throughout Asia of Colombo Plan activity through the dissemination of print material, but the Plan and government information officers always tried to do more with their modest resources. The small Colombo Plan Information Unit published in English only, and the print order of its *Colombo Plan* broadsheet newsletter was a modest 13,000 at the end of 1957. By this time, the British had published *Change in Asia* (1955) in Burmese, Chinese, Malay and Romanized Indonesian. The Government of Singapore was working on a Chinese version of the updated *Change in Asia, 1956*, and the Ceylonese government was producing Sinhalese and Tamil editions of *Fifth Year: Progress of the Colombo Plan*. A small

[10] E. R. Bellamare, Under Secretary of State for External Affairs, to Dr Wm Kaye Lamb, National Librarian, 20 December 1957, RG 25 vol. 7797 12569-20-40 part 1.1, LAC.

[11] Wm Kaye Lamb, National Librarian, to Miss M. Q. Dench, External Affairs, 30 January 1958, RG 25 vol. 7797 12569-20-40 part 1.1, LAC; K. A. McVey, External Affairs, Draft Estimates, 'Books for Presentation', 15 July 1957, RG 25 vol. 7797 12569-20-40 part 1.1, LAC.

[12] Minutes of Overseas Planning Committee meeting, 2 February 1962, item 1(b) Cheap Books, 26 January 1962, CRS A1838/287 item 2048/2 part 9, NAA. Full details of Casey's book are, R. G. Casey, *Friends and Neighbours: Australia and the World* (Melbourne: Cheshire, 1954).

publication about the Technical Co-operation Scheme was produced in French for use in Vietnam, Cambodia and Laos.[13]

There was a 'busyness' to much of this work that might be dismissed by those preoccupied with hard power jostling in the Cold War, but from at least several state perspectives, the Colombo Plan's rising profile mattered. It provided opportunities for civilized legitimations of state power that were especially welcomed by those governments emerging, or re-emerging among other states. By narrating progress in publications and by sending delegates to meetings or, even better, hosting a meeting of the Consultative Committee, post-colonial governments were able to add diplomatic and symbolic reinforcement to the apparatus of the state while bolstering their legitimacy. Perhaps not surprisingly then, while the host cities rotated to maximize participation, this was not without politicking by those anxious to display their diplomatic credentials sooner rather than later. In Wellington, the New Zealanders had to manage behind-the-scenes lobbying led by the Japanese for Tokyo to host the next meeting in 1957, but this was too soon for some still carrying strong memories of the war. When momentum shifted towards Pakistan or Vietnam, Raju Coomaraswamy countered that it was Colombo's turn before Karachi could host a second one, and the deadlock was not resolved in favour of Saigon until afterwards.[14] The same conference diplomacy that curtailed American nuclear ambitions also set limits to what might be attempted by way of lobbying for political change. Heavy-handed efforts to claim sovereignty over areas under dispute, as the Indonesians tried with reference to Dutch New Guinea in 1961, were unwelcome and gained no traction in the committee.[15]

Colombo Plan membership proved valuable in opening the door to other formal means of international acceptance. Japan joined the Consultative Committee in 1954 prior to being accepted as a member of the United Nations. In Singapore in 1955, David Marshall was Singapore's first elected Chief Minister and a leading figure in the campaign for Singapore's independence. He only served as Chief Minister for fourteen months, but he made the most of chairing the meeting of the Consultative Committee, conducting himself with diplomatic skill and

[13] 'Report of the Information Committee on the Working of the Colombo Plan Information Unit during 1956–57', undated report from Saigon meeting of the Consultative Committee (November 1957), RG 25 vol. 7360 11038-5-C-40 part 2, fp 2, LAC.

[14] H. A. F. Rumbold (CRO) to UK High Commission, Canberra, 17 December 1956, DO 35/5732, TNA.

[15] Ibid.

exhibiting his confidence in an independent Singapore in the near future. The leader of the Malayan delegation in 1955, Dr Ismail bin Abdul Rahman (Minister for Natural Resources) found the Chief Minister's chairing of the meeting of the Consultative Committee very significant: 'Your presence in the chair today marks in a most fitting manner the great political and constitutional advances which have taken place in Malaya since the last meeting of the Consultative Committee. The Federation of Malaya of course is also embarked on a similar course of evolution ...'[16] Two years later in Saigon, the Malayan government was admitted smoothly as an independent member of the Colombo Plan, just two months after declaring its independence from Britain. Malaya's new Prime Minister, Tunku Abdul Rahman Putra, followed this up by hosting a meeting of ECAFE in March 1958. The Tunku's government of the new Federation of Malaya proved keen to demonstrate its legitimacy through its capacity to manage its population of Malay, Chinese and Indian ethnic composition. When Malaya hosted the Consultative Committee meeting in bustling Kuala Lumpur in 1961, it was not only the motor cars and building activity that guests noted but also the conspicuous nods towards multi-ethnic harmony. Participants immediately registered that the conference Secretariat included Malays, Chinese and Indians.[17]

Meetings of the Consultative Committee held in the region brought opportunities for other host governments to demonstrate worldly thinking at the same time as reinforcing local authority. In 1957, Diem's admiring glance at the Commonwealth as having set the tone for the Colombo Plan was quickly followed by his inviting members to help answer the question, 'How else can we synthesize the best of East and West for the great tasks that this mid-century places before us?'[18] Taking his seat as representative of the newly admitted Federation of Malaya, Raja Tun Mohar (head of Trade within the Ministry of Commerce and Industry) part-answered Diem by saying that the knowledge of the goodwill of the member countries would be a source of confidence to the Federation in carrying out its international obligations. Japan's Deputy

[16] Dr Ismail bin Abdul Rahman, in Government of Singapore, *The Colombo Plan for Co-operative Economic Development in South and South-East Asia. Meetings in Singapore of the Consultative Committee 1955*, Singapore Government Office, 1956, p. 50, in DO 35/5731, TNA.

[17] Lord Lansdowne, Secretary UK Foreign Office, to Duncan Sandys, 15 December 1961, DO 189/327, TNA.

[18] CC VN 57 MM WP 2, 21 October 1957, Consultative Committee, Ministerial Meeting, Inaugural Session, RG 25 vol. 7360 11038-5-C-40 part 2, LAC.

Prime Minister Mitsujiro Ishii declared the Colombo Plan to be one of the most realistic development plans of the time, and integral to prosperity and peace in Asia.[19] Not all attendees enjoyed such indulgences. Canadian diplomat Arthur Menzies, also attending Saigon, his third Consultative Committee meeting, 'marvelled that the participating Governments continued to be willing to send delegations to engage in such an empty exercise'.[20] He felt that most delegates dodged the urgent problems of population pressures, rising demands for better livelihoods and the appeal of communists for faster economic development. But, like others before and after him, he could see advantages in continuing to turn up. From a more Cold War geopolitical angle, he even arrived back at Diem's broad proposition:

> These Colombo Plan Conferences provide a means of maintaining contact between the English speaking countries of the West and the free countries of South and Southeast Asia who are still trying to solve their economic development problems by democratic processes. SEATO provides contacts between the West and the committed countries of the area. But the Colombo Plan as an extension of the free Commonwealth association concept, serves as an important link between the West and the neutralist nations of South and Southeast Asia at a time when their foreign policy spokesman are extolling the virtues of coexistence, praising the Bandung spirit (which spans ideological differences between the free and communist countries), decrying military pacts, and ranting against the vestiges of colonialism. In my view, so long as the countries of South and Southeast Asia continue to try to solve their domestic economic and social development problems by democratic means under representative systems of government, we will have maintained our essential contacts with them despite such differences as may emerge in the foreign policy field. I think, therefore, that from a broad political point of view, we should do nothing to disturb the Colombo Plan conference as it is an important bridge between the West and the neutralist nations of South and Southeast Asia, in particular.[21]

An environment viewed as 'an extension of the Commonwealth' prized state sovereignty as a precondition of development internationalism. 'We are dealing with a state in the making and with a government and its officials faced daily with a multitude of political and executive problems,

[19] 'The Colombo Plan for Co-operative Economic Development in South and South-East Asia: Meetings in Saigon of the Consultative Committee 1957. Minutes, Statements, and Selected Documents of the Meeting of Officials and of the Consultative Committee with Minor Editorial Corrections', Saigon, October 1957, pp. 185, 24, in DO 35/5738, TNA.

[20] Arthur Menzies, External Affairs Memorandum, 'Colombo Plan Conference', 20 November 1957, RG 25 vol. 7360 11038-5-C-40 part 2.2, LAC.

[21] Ibid.

the like of which it is hard for us to appreciate' was Cavell's perspective on Canadian aid provided to Pakistan in 1957.[22] For Cavell, the Colombo Plan benefitted from its part-running parallel, and being part-intertwined with the Commonwealth, which was referenced admiringly by members other than himself during the decade. In 1957, in the wake of Diem's glowing remarks, Canadian Minister without Portfolio W. J Browne said he found it understandable that the Colombo Plan grew from a Commonwealth initiative, 'because we regard the Commonwealth as an association in which free nations of different races, cultures and religions meet on equal terms to engage in friendly, frank and informal discussions which enable them as a group to undertake positive measures for the general good'. Browne flew from Saigon to Ceylon to discuss Canadian aid efforts and discovered that he and Prime Minister Bandaranaike had taken part in a debate on prohibition at the Oxford Union in 1919 during their education in Britain.[23] Indonesian Foreign Minister Dr Subandrio also took up Diem's lead and referred approvingly to the plan's Commonwealth origins.[24]

Those churning out stories in Colombo also felt that some qualities of the Commonwealth had transferred to the organization, not just the family feel but the regard for popular sovereignty and constitutional underpinning.[25] The *Newsletter* of November 1957 proudly reproduced the words of Queen Elizabeth II when opening the Canadian Parliament a month earlier. The Queen expressed her pleasure at the growing membership of the Commonwealth 'as more of us come to share the great inheritance of those institutions and ideals which make our association a quiet but pervasive force for good in an unquiet world'. She added, 'A similar spirit has been evident in the Colombo Plan, which is part of the high venture of the people of South and South East Asia as they move along the path of national development ...'[26] By this stage, the Colombo Plan had also lodged firmly with policymakers in Whitehall, primarily within a

[22] Nik Cavell, 'Report on Colombo Plan Consultative Committee Meeting no. 5 held in Wellington, New Zealand, November 19 to December 8, 1956' and 'Visits to South and South East Asian Countries by Mr Nik Cavell, Colombo Plan Administrator in Canada and Mr Rodney Grey of the Department of External Affairs', 15 May 1957, RG 25 vol. 7359 11038-5-B-40 part 2 fp 3.2, LAC.

[23] William J. Browne, *And Now – Eighty-Seven Years a Newfoundler: Memoirs of William J. Browne* (St Johns: Dicks and Co, 1984), p. 209.

[24] *Colombo Plan Newsletter*, 2, 10, November 1957, p. 12, RCS, CUL.

[25] J. K. Thompson, Director, Colombo Plan Council, to Member Governments, 8 March 1961, RG 25 vol. 5421 11038-S-10-40 part 2, LAC.

[26] *Colombo Plan Newsletter*, 2, 10, November 1957, p. 6, RCS, CUL.

Commonwealth context. The Development Department of Britain's Commonwealth Relations Office was renamed the Colombo Plan Department in 1955. Such was Colombo Plan's dominance in departmental thinking about development. This name lasted until 1960, when it was renamed the Technical Assistance Department and a year later was tweaked further into the Department of Technical Co-operation.

The intertwining of Commonwealth ideals with the Colombo Plan was made more possible by the demonstrable mutability of the idea of the Commonwealth during the 1950s. It was not only expanded membership brought about by the independence of Ghana and Malaya in 1957 and the prospect of more transfers of power to come, but the Commonwealth seemed to stretch in ways that conferred legitimacy on new nation-states without detracting from their independent credentials. As Arthur Menzies suggested, the concept of the 'free Commonwealth association' was one that could be extended. The Commonwealth also managed tensions reasonably adroitly, riding out the Suez crisis and conversations about inner and outer circles, other possible European and African membership, even Cypriot membership in 1960. These developments spoke to a malleability that predated the acrimony and division caused by South Africa's departure from the Commonwealth in 1961, in the face of criticism of its apartheid policy. From London's perspective, accommodations and adjustments to the evolving postwar Commonwealth were constantly being made, while diplomatic civility and controversy avoidance were preserved in prime ministers' meetings. At least until the turn of the decade, the Commonwealth was held to be essential to the maintenance of British prestige, the value of sterling and Britain's standing as a great ally in the Cold War.[27]

In Southeast Asia, even the former British colony that had quickly rejected Commonwealth membership decided that membership of the Colombo Plan was more useful than not. For the Burmese government of U Nu, set on a path of neutralism and not retaining a Commonwealth connection upon independence, the Colombo Plan initially looked unappealing, a subtle but powerful means of drawing recipient nations into the Western orbit. The U Nu government maintained this position for the first year and a half, believing that American sources of aid might be more palatable for their lack of strings, but then got a shock with the passing of the US Mutual Security Act at the beginning of 1952. This

[27] See Frank Henlein, *British Government Policy and Decolonisation, 1945–1963: Scrutinising the Official Mind* (London: Frank Cass, 2002), pp. 128–46, 203–58.

effectively tied US aid firmly to its strategic interests and appeared even more transparently a means of luring neutralist nations to the West. US aid would have been a dangerous choice in a Burmese political environment of strong communist groups waiting to seize upon signs of the government caving in to Western imperialism. Thus, the Colombo Plan's flat structure and subtle ways suddenly became more attractive. The Burmese government joined the Colombo Plan at the Karachi meeting in March 1952 and was a reasonably steady Colombo Plan citizen for the remainder of the decade.[28] In common with other non-Commonwealth members, the Burmese had well-founded suspicions during the early years that they were likely to be placed second in line when decisions about aid were being made.[29] But this suspicion abated in the wake of efforts by donor members to expand their aid distribution. Importantly, the Burmese communists were unable to make capital out of Burma's membership. Burma's governments, including the caretaker one led by Army Chief Ne Win, September 1958 to February 1960, enjoyed aid without obvious 'strings'. As one commentator puts it, 'Their suspicion about the West's motives, as well as their anxiety about the conditionality in Western aid, and the political price they might have to pay, were allayed by the Colombo Plan's distinctive and peculiar architecture.'[30]

For governments such as India's, determined to demonstrate regional leadership and independence, it was also important that the Colombo Plan could be kept in a place secondary to grand state-led development plans. Nehru's governments of the 1950s embraced the Colombo Plan for its malleability and its conformity with state power but also kept it in its place. Centralized control by India's powerful Planning Commission proved formidable, both to potential aid donors and to those Indian state politicians and civil servants who tried to promote projects according to their regional needs. The Planning Commission was charged with oversight of India's first Five-Year Plan, handed down at the end of 1951, and all Colombo Plan considerations were subject to the Five-Year Plan's assumptions and prerogatives. Nothing, including any form of foreign aid, was to be considered outside the framework of the Five-Year Plan. Even an offer of textbooks from the British in 1953 provoked a reminder

28 Ademola Adeleke, 'The Strings of Neutralism: Burma and the Colombo Plan', *Pacific Affairs*, 76, 4 (2003–4), 593–610.

29 L. V. J. Roy, Acting High Commissioner, Ceylon, to Secretary of State for External Affairs, Ottawa, 21 November 1958, RG 25 vol. 7387 11038-G-40 part 5.1, LAC.

30 Adeleke, 'The Strings of Neutralism', p. 603.

to those seeking a quick 'yes, please' that 'all expenditure in connection with Central or State Schemes should be included in the Plan, no matter from where the resources in question are provided'.[31] Similarly, Indian forms of regional leadership were not threatened and, in fact, easily facilitated under the Colombo Plan, wherein they continued to send strong delegations to annual meetings and continued to promote the interests of neighbouring Asian nations emerging from the vicissitudes of colonialism.

REGIONAL PLANNING?

While those regional representatives at Simla in 1955 rejected anything resembling a regionally coordinated approach to uses of US aid or anything like a payments union, the issue of some sort of greater regional collaboration did not disappear from Colombo Plan meetings. The Japanese made clear their keen interest in keeping the idea of a regional development bank alive. ECAFE working groups probed different angles such as payments and especially intra-regional trade during 1957–58. Most of the region's exports moved along lines that today could be described as South–North. ECAFE explored whether there was scope beyond the well-known movements of rice for greater export markets to be found within the region. Not surprisingly, the issue popped up again in the Consultative Committee, with Vietnam's representative at the Wellington meeting suggesting a study of methods to increase intra-regional trade and the stability of commodity prices.[32]

There was no new dawn of declaratory Asian regionalism the next time the Consultative Committee met, in Saigon (Figure 4.1). In an update on their most ambitious initiative, the Americans spoke very briefly to the languishing Nuclear Regional Training Centre, spreading the blame around for the lack of funding secured, and leaving most in no doubt

[31] Y. N. Sukthankar (Secretary, Planning Commission) memorandum, 'Consultation with the Planning Commission before Acceptance of Offers of Foreign Assistance to Ensure that All Foreign Assistance in Accounted for in the Five Year Plan', 11 June 1953, Education File 42-20/52-SIR, NAI.

[32] UK Treasury Note, 'Suggestions for Regional Economic Organisation and Activities in South and South East Asia', for UK Delegation to Colombo Plan Consultative Committee Meetings, Saigon, 1957, 26 September 1957, DO 35/5740, TNA. This Treasury paper concluded with a list of suggested ways in which UK delegates could deflect the subject or make matters seem problematic without being seen to oppose the suggestions being aired.

FIGURE 4.1 Meeting of the Consultative Committee in Saigon, 1957.
Source: The National Archive (UK) DO35/5733.

that it would be allowed to fail.[33] But what continued to bubble away were gestures towards a more regional outlook and modus operandi when the time was right. The Treaty of Rome struck in March 1957, providing for the establishment of the European Economic Community (EEC), initially among six European countries, was a new and important source of impetus. To what extent might the EEC act as a model for Asia? For the first time, ECAFE's *Annual Survey of Asia and the Far East* for 1957 switched from providing country-by-country updates to a regional review of the economic situation, followed by an analysis of particular problems or subjects of common importance. Selected country studies would subsequently appear in greater detail in ECAFE's *Bulletin* or *Survey*.[34] At the same time, the Burmese Minister for Mines, U Raschid (a veteran of Burma's independence movement) successfully pressed at Saigon for there to be a special topic at the next meeting of the Consultative Committee on the prospects and possibilities for greater regional coordination of national development plans. Taking account of

[33] M.A.C. (S.A.) (57) 23 Colombo Plan Consultative Committee Meeting Saigon, October 1957, Report by CRO, 12 November 1957, DO 35/8788, TNA.

[34] Narasimhan, ECAFE Executive Secretary, appears to have a big influence behind the shift to regional reviews: UNESCO, 26th session, ECAFE Annual Report, covering 29 March 1957 to 15 March 1958, *United Nations Official Record* (hereinafter *UNOR*), p. 30.

recent ECAFE work, the committee invited this organization to submit a paper on the subject to the next meeting of the committee held in Seattle in November 1958.

The ECAFE 'Note on the Question of Regional Co-ordination of National Development Plans' for the Seattle meeting considered the question in relation to the eleven national development plans encompassing the broader ECAFE membership (Afghanistan and both the People's Republic of China and the Republic of China being the extras to Colombo Plan membership). Again bearing traces of Narasimhan's work, it pointed out that 'regional' and 'co-ordination' were both terms that operated at varying levels. Not all nations had to align neatly for some valuable measure of coordination to be present. It might be that two or three nations could coordinate activities in productive ways. The recently commenced development of the lower Mekong Basin, including Thailand, Laos, Cambodia and Vietnam, was an example. Nor did all aspects of economic planning have to be present to fulfil the meaning of coordination. One or more aspects of development activity would suffice, such as an Indo-Japanese project to develop iron ore in India's eastern state of Orissa.[35] Thus clarified, there were plenty of examples of regional coordination in place. The report found that geographical contiguity mattered, as suggested by train services from Thailand through Malaya and electricity flowing through the Malay peninsula. The availability of markets mattered, too. Exporting nations were sometimes hindered by smaller populations, as in the cases of Nepal and Singapore, but others were also impacted by low purchasing power in cases such as India. Not much had changed in the composition of the main exports by regional countries, mostly food and raw materials since the end of the Second World War. This, according to ECAFE, was unwelcome and potentially misleading. It fostered a short-sighted view that the economies of the region were persistently non-complementary, and it ignored substantial changes underway, such as Japan's economic recovery and economic re-engagement with the region, the ambitious plans for industrialization, especially in India and mainland China but also in other regional nations; and, in most cases, a modest but discernible postwar trend towards greater trade with other ECAFE countries.[36]

[35] ECAFE, 'A Note on the Question of Regional Co-ordination of National Development Plans', CC 58 0 36, 13 November 1958, CRS A10617 item 1958/4, NAA.

[36] Ibid. The exception was India, whose postwar trade with ECAFE countries had declined to 1957.

Attempting to point out how stronger coordination of national development plans among members of ECAFE might result in stronger economic results involved some extrapolation and assumptions, but the paper ventured examples, suggesting that, with Japan and India bent on increasing their cotton textile exports, it might logically pay for others such as the Philippines to pause rather than embark on an expensive programme of their own self-sufficiency in cotton. Pakistan would be well-placed to meet the expanded demand for raw cotton from Japan and India, rather than rely on markets further afield. Similarly, with established steel production set to expand in Japan, India and China, there was cause to question the expensive establishment or expansion of steel production in other countries such as was planned in Burma, Indonesia and the Philippines. Again, those regional countries exporting iron ore might consider Japan's expanded needs rather than rely on markets elsewhere.[37]

This was at the more adventurous end of regionalism thinking. Less speculative were the acknowledged benefits gained from regular, mutual consultations about each other's plans, including reviews, and the quality of information and administration. The ECAFE paper concluded by noting that extended discussions about forms of regionalism were on the rise in international organizations, especially in relation to agricultural surpluses. They were triggered partly by the creation of the EEC. Some were sensitive to Asia's dependence on more developed countries outside the ECAFE region, and there were too many differences on the subject among regional members to envisage a consensus response on bigger conceptualizations of regionalism: 'the present general tendency appears to be to look with favour on coordination in respect of specific projects or programmes, rather than to embark on more ambitious over-all regional co-ordination of the various national development plans'.[38]

It was a typically ECAFE response to a challenging question: optimistic about agency in post-colonial Asia and the potential for plans to evolve with some synchronicity, but pulling back from outright advocacy, while demonstrating recognition of the limitations and differences among members. At the Seattle meeting, Michael Hoffman, head of the Economic Development Institute of the World Bank, introduced the topic, with some overly forensic observations about development processes and tensions between private and public enterprise.[39] Sri Bali Ram Baghat

[37] Ibid. [38] Ibid.

[39] W. Vawdrey (External Affairs, Australia) note on item 6, 13 November 1958, CRS A10617 item 1958/5, NAA.

(Indian Deputy Finance Minister, attending his sixth consecutive Consultative Committee meeting) opined that there was so much basic developmental work needed in the region that it was hard to envisage an immediate need for elaborate coordination among members, and he felt that other more specialized organizations were better placed to examine the question than the Consultative Committee. Others felt similarly, but with variations: Burmese diplomat U Win and J. M. Jumabhoy, Singapore's Minister for Commerce and Industry, were the most upbeat about what might be possible in intra-regional trade in times to come, and Narasimhan quietly reinforced the paper's main suggestions, but Vu Van Mau (Vietnam's Foreign Minister), Mohammed Ali (Pakistan's Ambassador to the United States) and the US Under Secretary of State for Economic Affairs C. Douglas Dillon all trod very carefully in relation to any regional coordination of planning. Most notable was New Zealand Prime Minister Walter Nash's response. As a representative of a country frustrated by the volatility of prices for commodities on which it depended (the 1958 meeting took place in the wake of some spectacular recent falls in prices for wool and other commodities), Nash saw value in something that provided better value for those producers of raw materials. He wondered if something like a sovereign government for the whole of Southeast Asia might get the same sort of trade results enjoyed by the United States![40] No one else ventured comment on this idea; but Nash's idealism, on display again at the following meeting of the committee in Jogjakarta, was received warmly by Asian delegates.[41] The discussion was more cathartic than conclusive in any direction. With some suitable references to the ongoing work of ECAFE on this question of possible coordination of development plans, the matter rested.

The discussion was a good reminder of how delegates valued the work of ECAFE but also kept it at arm's length from the Colombo Plan. Regional members were pleased that ECAFE, under the vigorous leadership of Narasimhan and others, would provoke thinking beyond the status quo of a global economy wherein Asian governments were too often pigeon-holed as the hewers of wood and drawers of water, where 'complementarity' sounded like continuation of colonial economic conditions. These ECAFE perspectives served as reminders that others viewed

40 G. A. Low (External Affairs, Australia) note on item 6, 13 November 1958, CRS A10617 item 1958/5, NAA.

41 Francis Russell, US Ambassador Wellington, to Secretary of State, 4 December 1959, 890.00/12-459, USNA.

the United States and former/current colonial powers as economic hegemons, but they elicited a broad spectrum of views on regional organization rather than great consensus. They were injected occasionally into the Consultative Committee rather than establishing a mainstream debate.

As indicated by those debating the special topic of regional coordination of plans, the Seattle meeting attracted both senior and experienced country representatives, including seven foreign ministers and a prime minister. Held in late October 1958, some 161 delegates and observers from 21 member countries and 4 international organizations were greeted by a City of Seattle Host Committee comprising business and government representatives and then escorted to the Olympic Hotel where sessions were held. Their excursion activities included visits to the gigantic Boeing Aircraft factory and the nearby Grand Coulee Dam and Columbia river basin, another multi-purpose irrigation-power enterprise that served as an exemplar for similar projects underway in Asia. The Grand Coulee featured a dam wall that was the biggest cement structure in the world.[42] Not only did the United States prove a good host, but President Eisenhower opened the meeting to much fanfare and generally favourable press commentary – the *New York Times* printing Eisenhower's speech verbatim and the *Pittsburgh Post-Gazette* describing the Colombo Plan as 'one of the more successful of the postwar ventures in economic cooperation among free nations'.[43] Eisenhower depicted the struggle against want and suffering in spiritual-libertarian-Cold War terms for which he was well known. Referencing the Divine Creator who cared for all of his children, Eisenhower said that, 'wherever free men lose hope of progress, liberty will be weakened and the seeds of conflict will be sown. In working together to create that hope of progress, we raise barriers against tyranny and the war which tyranny breeds'.[44] While he was not specific, he was resolute in his commitment to an increased aid programme according to five major requirements for economic growth: expanded international trade; technical skills; private investment; normal bankable loans; and financing to cover other sound projects offering the borrower flexibility with repayments. The US president concentrated mostly on the final two requirements. Members were able to note his optimism that the World Bank would be underwriting more bankable loans and his underlining the

[42] *Colombo Plan Newsletter*, 3, 12, December 1958, pp. 7–8, RCS, CUL.

[43] As reported in British telegram, Sir Harold Caccia to Foreign Office, 17 November 1958, CO 1030/622, TNA.

[44] *Colombo Plan Newsletter*, 3, 12, December 1958, p. 2, RCS, CUL.

creation in 1957 of the US Development Loan Fund, providing for repayments of loans for development in local currencies (thus matching Soviet practice) and liaising closely with the World Bank and Export–Import Bank. He also reinforced the concept of the Colombo Plan as constituting something that was geographically and politically defined. Eisenhower mentioned how 'Colombo Plan countries' had received more than half of the Development Loan Fund's loans to date, and how 'Colombo Plan nations' were seeking more assistance.[45] Also pleasingly, from other donor members' perspectives, in the lead up to the meeting, the *Washington Post* was happy to aggregate all US foreign aid to recipient members and declare the $4 billion as 'Colombo-Plan Aid', adding that the United States was ready to do more.[46]

In 1959 the Consultative Committee met in Jogjakarta, Indonesia, at the Gadja Mada University. The English-language *Times of Indonesia* found it fitting that the Ceylonese government, an early supporter of Indonesian independence, installed its first ambassador in Djakarta, at the same time.[47] The meeting in Jogjakarta attracted strong local media interest and unfolded in an atmosphere of assertive and somewhat febrile Indonesian nationalism. The Ministerial sessions began on 11 November, the day after Indonesia's Day of Heroes, commemorating those who were involved in the struggle for independence. President Sukarno channelled the remembrance by greeting delegates in a revolutionary, anti-colonial spirit. His ninety-minute welcome address did not refer to the Consultative Committee but was laced with barbs directed at the West. He warned donor nations not to expect that development assistance would produce an Indonesia 'in their image' as the model of Western democracy could not apply there. Indonesia was witnessing a new confidence and unity, he said, and delegates should take the time to visit past symbols of the country's greatness, such as the ninth-century Buddhist temple at Borabadur or the similarly aged Hindu temple of Prambanan. As delegates admired Indonesia's *high* stage of development when measured spiritually, morally and culturally, Sukarno said they should also remember that the West's imposition of power over the archipelago was 'By an accident of military power.'[48]

Watching Sukarno in full rhetorical flight, Canadian journalist Russell Elman got the message: 'The Westerner is deluding himself if he believes he

[45] Ibid, 3–4.
[46] *Washington Post*, 4 November 1958, p. A12; ibid, 11 November 1958, pp. A1, A8.
[47] *Times of Indonesia*, 11 November 1959, p. 1. [48] Ibid, 12 November 1959, p. 1.

can buy support from these emerging peoples of Asia for his own political system by giving aid.'[49] As for many others, the Cold War contest between communism and democracy still surfaced readily for Elman:

> The citizen of the West, can, however, have some influence in determining which method will win out ... But he needs to do more than enjoy the luxury of winning a few votes on the international hustings by doling out shiploads of surplus wheat or constructing an impressive power station ... He needs to ponder Asia's problems and decide to give and give generously, not out of charity but out of a certain realization that to assist now at the time of great need during the formative years of her newly-independent countries may be, in fact, a privilege and even an obligation.[50]

Following the lead of others in previous meetings, Sukarno seized on the word 'cooperative' in the Colombo Plan's full title and elevated it, claiming that this mode of behaviour underpinned both the past practices and the modern concept of Indonesia.[51] Extending this, Sukarno invoked the Indonesian notion of *gotong royong*, cooperation and mutual assistance. Fourteen years earlier, in 1945, when setting out Indonesia's five foundational principles, the Pancasila, he had added *gotong royong* as the underlying principle binding them together in an organic manner. Much more recently, at the start of a new, authoritarian form of 'guided democracy', Sukarno had drawn again on *gotong royong* during July 1959, dismissing the elected Assembly and forming new legislative bodies, appointing himself as Prime Minister and selecting a so-called *gotong royong* cabinet from different political groups.[52]

None of this impacted on the Consultative Committee or Colombo Plan activities more generally. To the extent that dramatic domestic politics in states such as Indonesia, Burma and Ceylon in the late 1950s influenced donor members' decision-making, it did so only around the timing and extent of aid to be provided.[53] In Jogjakarta in 1959, what was remarkable was how, in the wake of Sukarno's powerful rhetoric, the meetings of the Consultative Committee then unfolded with customary civility, formal and informal talks on matters of regional economy and

49 Russell Elman, *Asian Experiment* (Toronto: Riverson Press, 1961), p. 99.

50 Ibid, p. 101.

51 *Times of Indonesia*, 12 November 1959, p. 1.

52 On the political uses of *gotong royong*, see John R. Bowen, 'On the Political Construction of Tradition: *Gotong Royong* in Indonesia', *Journal of Asian Studies*, 45, 3 (1986), 545–61.

53 Report by the Australian Delegation, 'Colombo Plan: Consultative Committee for Co-operative Economic Development in South and South-East Asia, Djakarta 1959', CRS A1361 item 43/1/6 part 4A, NAA.

security, and avoidance of issues that might prove inflammatory. Foreign Minister Subandrio, who led the conference, was moderate and conciliatory, in contrast to his president. The Committee progressed with the usual eschewing of resolutions and refraining from comment on domestic politics. Problems of expanded economic activity – balance of payments issues and inflation – had become staple subjects of conversation in the late 1950s, in addition to the perennial volatility of export prices. In 1959, there was slightly less anxiety as stronger commodity prices and higher export volumes in the region for the first half of the year helped with the terms of trade for regional members; but several representatives still had it as a top talking point. 'I am convinced that one of the greatest tasks we face in grappling with poverty, hunger, ignorance and disease is the instability of commodity prices' was a declaration that might have easily come from a representative from Southeast Asia but was again the lament of New Zealand's Walter Nash.[54]

OF MILK AND MEN

Nash's repeated interventions spoke to New Zealand's great dependence on export prices for a narrow range of goods. The distinctiveness of the New Zealand economy and its relatively small sums allocated for foreign aid also posed some hard questions, especially early on, about what forms its Colombo Plan contributions might take. A logical focus was one of those industries that caused Nash anxiety for its fluctuating prices – dairy goods. Successive New Zealand governments offered to help build robust milk supply systems in South Asia. One of the main outcomes was the Delhi Milk Supply Scheme, a program to provide citizens of Delhi with regular milk that was initiated locally in the wake of independence but not fully functional until 1959. The Delhi Milk Scheme was, in the first ten years of the Colombo Plan, New Zealand's biggest project in any country to which it contributed both capital and technical training. Come 1962, the New Zealand government made capital assistance grants to India totalling £2.5 million, and of this sum, £1.5 million was spent on dairy

[54] Statement by Walter Nash on the Draft Annual Report, annex to Report of New Zealand Delegation to Eleventh Meeting of the Colombo Plan Consultative Committee, Jogjakarta, 26 October to 14 November 1959, J. Shepherd, November 1959, Sir Walter Nash Papers, International Affairs: Economic-Colombo Plan (R22848896) 1951–58: AEFZ 22618 W5727 83/94/0001-003036/1, ANZ.

development.[55] Essentially, the scheme was a means by which cheap milk could be collected more systematically from rural areas around Delhi, thereby enabling the gradual removal of cows from the city. It involved mixing the local high-fat buffalo milk with skim milk powder (a New Zealand product), thereby reducing the fat content and extending the quantity of milk available. The final product was processed and refrigerated in a new Central Dairy drawing from collection centres and then chilled and distributed to 300 sites throughout Delhi twice daily. In a documentary film produced by the New Zealand National Film Unit in 1962, From *Indonesia to India*, New Zealand's financial aid and knowledge provided by experts was in evidence in every step of the milk production process. The New Delhi Milk Supply, described as a crucial contribution to public health, was the climactic final case study of the nineteen-minute documentary.[56]

Comparable operations also took shape, with New Zealand support, in the Indian cities of Madras, Patna, and Jaipur, and also in Colombo. The Delhi Scheme still operates today.[57] New Zealand experts also helped establish the Indian National Dairy Institute at Karnal, Haryana, and built a hostel at the Aarey Milk Colony near Bombay for those being trained in the industry. Thus, milk flowed from the technical assistance side of the Colombo Plan, complementing the capital provided. Most of the eighty-two students from India who were trained in New Zealand to 1962 undertook courses relating to the treatment, processing and other aspects of dairying.[58]

Different versions of the history of milk production in India serve to remind us that donors and recipients of foreign aid contextualized it in different ways. In the case of Indian dairy activity, as with many other development projects assisted under the Colombo Plan, there was considerable momentum prior to 1951, and New Zealand assistance was one of several factors behind its growth. Much of this history was overlooked, not unusually, in diplomatic reporting at the time and in subsequent summaries of New Zealand's efforts under the Colombo Plan. For

55 NZEAR, *New Zealand and the Colombo Plan*, p. 21.

56 Ibid. The film's full title was, *Some Aspects of New Zealand's Part in the Colombo Plan: From Indonesia to India*, NZ National Film Unit Production, 1962, www.nzonscreen.com/title/from-indonesia-to-india-1962 (accessed 2 January 2020).

57 *Economic Times (India)*, 29 June 2018, https://economictimes.indiatimes.com/industry/cons-products/food/government-to-lease-out-delhi-milk-scheme-for-30-years/articleshow/64787076.cms (accessed 20 January 2019).

58 NZEAR, *New Zealand and the Colombo Plan*, p. 21.

example, another successful dairy venture supported by New Zealand was the cooperative dairy at Anand in Gujarat. The Kaira District Cooperative Milk Producers' Union at Anand transformed in 1956 into the Amul cooperative dairy company and is now a dairy giant of modern India and, indeed, of the world. A New Zealand External Affairs briefing paper from 1958 noted the provision of £23,600 for the dairy and treatment centre and measures to address the seasonal vagaries of production; and the same paper recorded the provision of sixteen rail tankers and four road tankers to transport the milk from Anand to Bombay, some 260 miles away.[59] In very recent years, the New Zealand Ministry of Foreign Affairs and Trade, on its website, credits the Colombo Plan with paving the way for formal diplomatic relations with India, a New Zealand High Commission opening in Delhi at the end of 1958. It mentions New Zealand's support for the All India Medical Institute in New Delhi and the technical assistance aiding India's dairy industry. It singles out Dr Verghese Kurien, one of the founders behind Amul, who 'under the Colombo Plan, studied plant design and dairy engineering at Massey University before returning to India where he founded Operation Flood, the world's biggest dairy development program, launched in 1970, to transform India's burgeoning dairy industry'.[60]

The fuller story of Anand and Amul is connected to the history of cooperatives in India, with progress towards expansion and modernization punctuated by resource shortages and state, local and personal politics.[61] Kurien, who trained first at Michigan State University, was entrepreneurial enough in the early 1950s to secure government support to advance his training overseas. He wanted to be sent to Denmark, known for its cooperatives in dairying. Instead, he was sent by a quick-thinking Indian public servant aware of Colombo Plan traineeships to another country where cooperatives managed dairy plants – New Zealand. For seven months, October 1952 to April 1953, Kurien was at Massey Agricultural College, working with Professor Kelvin Scott, head of dairy engineering and the New Zealand Dairy Research Institute. A historian of the Amul story writes that Kurien enjoyed working closely

[59] External Affairs briefing paper, 'The Colombo Plan: Participation of New Zealand', 17 July 1958, R22848901 1956–60, Walter Nash Papers AE FZ 22618 W5727 84/94/0266-0377 36/2, ANZ.

[60] 'New Zealand High Commission in India', www.mfat.govt.nz/en/about-us/mfat75/75-our-story/new-delhi/ (accessed 3 January 2020).

[61] For the story of the Kaira District Cooperative Milk Producers' Union of Gujarat, see Ruth Heredia, *The Amul India Story* (New Delhi: Tata McGraw-Hill Publishing, 1997).

with Scott, but describes his relationship with New Zealand as 'peculiarly ambivalent.'[62] Soon after he arrived at Massey, Kurien discovered that, in local production, buttermilk was secretly being mixed with skim milk before it was spray dried, in order to extend the quantity of finished skim milk powder. Then it was being sent to India. When Kurien told Scott of his discovery, Scott rang alarm bells with New Zealand authorities and had the practice stopped and then assisted in negotiating a revised price for the product already shipped to India. After averting this potential scandal, the New Zealand government approached Kurien with generous Colombo Plan funding to support his plans for Anand. Later, when Kurien was back in Anand, he needed to demonstrate his capacity to spray-dry buffalo milk on a commercial scale to convince UNICEF officials to fund the dairy's expansion. At the time, the higher fat content of buffalo milk was thought to be a major obstacle to spray-drying into powder form. Another leading New Zealand expert in dairying, Professor William Riddet, one of the founders of Massey, accepted an invitation in 1954 to visit Kurien's operation but advised that spray-drying buffalo milk could not work on a commercial basis. Kurien recalled that Riddet told him he was 'a bloody fool'.[63] Kurien's subsequent success with buffalo milk proved Riddet wrong and enabled UNICEF funds to flow. Reflecting on this episode in an interview in 2007, Kurien wondered whether commerce had compromised scientific advice, whether the value of New Zealand milk powder then being exported to India had influenced Riddet's judgement.[64]

This short sketch of the New Zealand Colombo Plan connection to the Anand–Amul story reveals both significant cross-cultural testing points and possible tensions between scientific and commercial interests. More importantly, it contrasts the simple, narrow 'seed and watch grow' quality of development stories characteristic of donor nations such as New Zealand, Canada and Australia with fuller accounts of development projects generated from their geographic origins. These tell of projects with complex, often partly colonial, histories predating and outliving periods of Colombo Plan funding. Canada funded a dam-building project in West Bengal in the mid-1950s at Mayurakashi that eventually became

[62] Ibid, p. 107.

[63] Interview with Kurien in the *Times of India*, 23 August 2007, https://timesofindia.indiatimes.com/india/Experts-called-me-a-bloody-fool-Verghese-Kurien/articleshow/2302656.cms (accessed 20 November 2019).

[64] Ibid; Heredia, *The Amul India Story*, pp. 112–19; and see Verghese Kurien and Gouri Salvi, *I Too Had a Dream* (New Delhi: Lotus Collection, 2005).

the 'Canada Dam', but the origins of the project dated from the late 1920s.[65] Indian government officials were effusive in their praise for New Zealand assistance at the launch of the Delhi Central Dairy that was a big part of the milk scheme;[66] but it is now hard to find a prominent role for New Zealand in Indian-based or other studies of the scheme.[67] Those who have written from materials and memories in South and Southeast Asia have tended to take the longer time frame and have seen foreign injections of assistance as fleeting parts of a much bigger story. As one environmental history of the Mekong Delta development project in Vietnam puts it, '"Often, new projects are sited directly atop the ruins of earlier abandoned ones."'[68] Nothing that the New Zealand ministry wrote in 1958, or that its successor ministry claimed recently was, or is, wildly inaccurate. But, like most donors, these accounts omitted earlier history and focused on connecting the aid provision with short-term results. Their reports and claims to influence were directed at local taxpayers who needed to be convinced of foreign aid spending as much as they were directed at recipients.[69]

Further, the local, domestic audience within New Zealand was important in another identity-constituting way. One of the greatest strengths of the 'milk for Asia' story was as a narrative of New Zealand as an actor in the region performing a role that was familiar. Having promoted itself as the 'empire's dairy farm' during the interwar years, New Zealand governments introduced free milk for children, the nation-builders of tomorrow. After the Second World War, they adjusted to the expanded expectations of state welfare support by strengthening the idea that the state was now

[65] Campbell-Miller, 'Encounter and Apprenticeship', p. 39.

[66] *NZEAR*, 10, no. 12, December 1960, p. 25.

[67] See Harold Alderman, George Mergos, and Roger Slade, 'Cooperatives and the Commercialization of Milk Production in India: A Literature Review', International Food Policy Research Institute, Washington, DC, 1987. There is no evidence of New Zealand's role being recognized in more contemporary online accounts.

[68] From David Biggs's *Quagmire: Nation Building and Nature in the Mekong Delta* (Seattle: University of Washington Press, 2010), quoted in Hodge, 'Writing the History of Development (Part 2)', 133–34.

[69] The government's proud boast to have welcomed six Ceylonese dental nurses as the first students sponsored under the Colombo Plan omitted its earlier origins. The negotiations behind this initiative began in 1947, when Ceylon's Director of Medical and Sanitary Services, Dr Wickremasinghe, visited New Zealand: Walter Nash, Draft Speech Notes, 'Maharagama Dental Nurses' Training School, Ceylon', undated (1958), R22848901 1956–60, Walter Nash Papers AE FZ 22618 W5727 84/94/0266-0377 36/2, ANZ.

the logical supplier of milk, an essential food.[70] Helping developing Asia – and especially the Commonwealth in Asia – by providing milk where too little was enjoyed by too few, was a bridge between the older, well-remembered imperial narrative and the brave new world in which the state was more activist and more responsive to external changes. It thereby opened a door to the presence of Asia in New Zealand's nation-building history. As historian Tony Ballantyne and others have shown, it was certainly not the case that New Zealanders had shunned economic, cultural and religious links with Britain's Asian colonies, but up to the end of the Second World War, these rich networks of exchange had not been part of the government's own nation-making story.[71]

Dairy work did not constitute all of the New Zealand aid efforts[72] but featured especially strongly in India, the country to which most of its aid flowed. Dairy initiatives elsewhere, such as a similar Milk Scheme for Colombo, were also given special attention.[73] Contrary to hopes, expanded New Zealand exports beyond the mid-1950s levels of skim milk did not follow. Although in many places Indians continued to combine high-fat local milk with New Zealand skim milk for the best health outcomes, the new European Common Market undercut the price of New Zealand's skim milk, through heavy subsidies, and so replaced New Zealand as a source.[74]

Nevertheless, the dairy theme remained an important bridge between tentative engagement with Asia and popular conceptions of New Zealand's role in the world. The New Zealand government could extrapolate to health issues that New Zealanders shared with Asians. An External Affairs information booklet produced in 1962 referred to the development challenges of Asia. Like many official Colombo Plan accounts, it began with a potted history of Asian past civilizational glory, touching extremely briefly on the causes of its demise, and looked

70 Philippa Mein-Smith, 'New Zealand Milk for "Building Britons"', in Bridie Andrew and Mary P. Stephen (eds.), *Medicine and Colonial Identity* (Abingdon: Routledge, 2013), pp. 79–102.

71 Tony Ballantyne, *Webs of Empire: Locating New Zealand's Colonial Past* (Vancouver: University of British Columbia, 2015); Sekhar Bandyopadhyay (ed.), *India in New Zealand: Local Identities, Global Relations* (Dunedin: Otago University Press, 2010).

72 They supported the establishment of the All India Institute of Medical Sciences in Delhi; building the Zealpak Cement Factory was the biggest item of aid for Pakistan, and laboratories supporting dry-farming research was the biggest item for Ceylon.

73 NZEAR, *New Zealand and the Colombo Plan*, passim.

74 New Zealand Ministry of Foreign Affairs and Trade, *The Colombo Plan at 50: A New Zealand Perspective*.

optimistically towards a future of recaptured greatness and modernization through development. This effectively side-stepped the legacies of colonialism and their connections to current economic conditions of the region. The booklet then confidently joined some dots between national and Asian histories:

> The very nature of their [Asia's] problems makes a strong appeal to the humanitarian instincts of New Zealanders, themselves pioneers in the field of social legislation, who ... were already associating themselves with international activities affecting the lives and welfare of the people of the region.[75]

Across the Tasman Sea, the Australians were similarly making claims to distinctiveness in their Colombo Plan aid efforts, especially in relation to their sponsoring Asian students. At the end of 1955, the 1,000th Colombo Plan student arrived in Australia. The designated student was one of 117 Indonesians who were flown to Sydney in a specially chartered plane. He was Entol Soeparman, a twenty-two-year old chemical engineering student who, before departure, enjoyed receptions at the Australian Embassy with Australian Minister for External Affairs, Richard Casey and at the Presidential Palace with Indonesian President Sukarno. Soeparman quickly became a pin-up student for Australian journalists who enjoyed the chance to call him 'superman' and follow his progress when he visited different capital cities on a free air travel ticket during 1956. He seemed to take the publicity in his stride. As a personifying bridge between Asia in transition and Australia, he was especially attractive as he came from Bandung and had been a volunteer worker at the conference of Asian and African nations in April 1955 (Figure 4.2).[76]

The Australians were the most active in generating publicity around their Colombo Plan efforts, sometimes drawing resentment from other donors for their capacity to turn measurably small gestures into a grand story. Casey provided the impetus for much of the information activity, having become attracted to the burgeoning realm of public relations. His department worked closely with the Australian News and Information

[75] The early text includes 'the attainment of independence – in some cases after a period of military struggle ... all afforded evidence of expanded political horizons', NZEAR, *New Zealand and the Colombo Plan*, 1.

[76] Jemma Purdey, 'Scholarships and Connections: Australia, Indonesia and Papua New Guinea', *Alfred Deakin Research Institute Working Papers*, Series Two, 46 (Geelong: Alfred Deakin Research Institute, Deakin University, 2014), p. 14; *Canberra Times*, 29 August 1956, p. 5.

FIGURE 4.2 Entol Soeparman (middle) 1956.
Source: Photograph in possession of the author.

FIGURE 4.3 The 1956 booklet, *My Life in Australia*, was distinctive for its focus on the experiences of a female student, Filipina Minda Feliciano.
Source: Australian Government publication, in possession of the author.

Bureau (ANIB), which soon had a separate Colombo Plan desk that was both generating stories locally and providing material to the Bureau in Colombo. Asian students and trainees sponsored for study in Australia were a particular focus. By 1956, the ANIB had produced two booklets on the experiences of Colombo Plan students: *My Life in Australia* (1956) (Figure 4.3) and *We Look at Australia* (1956).

Multiple copies of these booklets were sent both to Colombo and to diplomatic posts throughout the region. Their regional impact is hard to gauge. It was easier to find them distributed well throughout Australia, in the same manner as the most significant Colombo Plan literature. They had a local print run of at least 20,000 and were sent to a long list of youth and student groups, public libraries, churches, trade unions, banks, employers' groups, business organizations, legal firms, mayors and state parliaments.[77] The year 1956 also marked the start of a new Asian/Australian student magazine, *Hemisphere*, featuring Asian students' reflections on varsity life and Australian culture and society. At this time, Australian newspaper editorial support for the Colombo Plan was generally strong. Editors saw it as a 'gesture of help and goodwill towards our Asian neighbours' and felt that Asian students in Australia were building 'two-way understanding'.[78]

By the middle of the decade the Australians, Canadians and New Zealanders were focusing more on the technical assistance side of the Colombo Plan – students, experts and specialist equipment – in their storytelling. This was partly a response to the balance of payments problems among donor members and delays and difficulties with some of the bigger infrastructure works. It reflected the worrying trend for the gap between development needs and resources appearing to be widening mid-decade through falling export prices and rising populations, among other more specific issues. It was also consistent with an international orthodoxy then growing around the virtues of technical assistance. Pragmatically, too, students and visiting experts generated stories involving fewer components and were therefore easier to control. Especially during the first phase of the plan, the Australians were entitled to boast their special efforts in the field of technical assistance. To the middle of 1956, they had provided more training places (1,610) than any other member, and they had sent to Asia almost as many experts as had

[77] While the record is not conclusive for the distribution of these booklets relating to students, they are likely to have followed this pattern, which applied to both early Colombo Plan information, such as the *New Hope for Asia* booklet (1951) and the 1961 account by Australian journalist, Osmar White, *The Seed of Freedom*: Australia and the Colombo Plan (Australian Government Printing, 1961); Minute from Tange to Casey, 8 June 1951, CRS A 9879 2202/D, NAA; G. N. Upton, DEA to Kevin Murphy, ANIB, 13 March 1961, CRS A6895 N58/164, NAA; Upton to Murphy, 15 March 1961, ibid.

[78] The *Age*, 17 July 1956, p. 2; *The Sydney Morning Herald*, 12 July 1956, p. 13; ibid, 16 July 1956, p. 4.

Britain.[79] Indeed, such was the demand on training places in Australia's small but expanding higher education sector that the Australians announced in Saigon in 1957 that they were struggling to cope.[80]

In small ways, these burgeoning human interactions helped citizens of Colombo Plan countries learn more about each other, albeit with misunderstandings and persisting cultural clashes. They were another arena, in addition to Consultative Committee meetings and especially in the publicity about the Colombo Plan, in which shifting notions of difference and common ground played out.

As Walter Nash illustrated, a popular refrain from the 'frontier' dominions of Canada, New Zealand and Australia in the mid-1950s was that they too faced their development challenges; they were also vulnerable to commodity price fluctuations such was their dependence on a few key exports. This made them even better able to share, to the benefit of recipient nations, their experiences with ambitious development projects. The emphasis on common challenges reflected something of a learning curve for the Canadians and Australians. The Australians tried to connect with regional members in the early years of the plan by extolling the virtues of enlightened colonialism; they would hold themselves up as an example of British influence leaving progressive legacies and wait in vain for fruitful exchanges to follow. By mid-decade, they had dropped the enlightened colonialism story. The shift towards common challenges in narrative strategy also made the External Affairs departments of these donor countries more receptive to stories of reverse flows of expertise, of learning from the developmental experiences of those in South and Southeast Asia.[81] In Australia's case, the student who had been brought to Australia for training but then made breakthroughs to the benefit of the local farming community was a cause celebré. Filipino Nestor C. Vera Cruz, completing a masters degree in agricultural science at the University of Queensland in 1957, suddenly became a friend of farmers and the Australian Commonwealth Scientific and Industrial Research Organisation (and the media) for his discoveries enabling more effective artificial insemination of pigs.[82] In the Canadian case, it resulted in a very

[79] *Colombo Plan Newsletter*, 1, 10, December 1956, p. 7, RCS, CUL.

[80] US Position Paper, Seattle Meeting of Colombo Plan Consultative Committee Agenda Item on Technical Assistance (undated, 1958), State Department, Merrill C. Gay Files, RG 59 Lot File 64D 207 box 3, Miscellaneous Economic Records of Bureau of Far Eastern Affairs 1945–61, USNA.

[81] Lowe, 'Canberra's Colombo Plan', p. 199.

[82] *The Colombo Plan*, Newsletter, 2, 11, December 1957, p. 3, RCS, CUL.

advanced but ultimately unconsummated plan to transport yaks from India to Northern Quebec where they were to assist with animal husbandry for the Inuit peoples there. An imaginative scheme that the *Hindustan Times* reported in January 1954 as 'a pleasant reversal of the Colombo Plan', and the Montreal *Gazette* also applauded, suddenly collapsed in the face of health regulations and fear of foot-and-mouth disease.[83]

In New Zealand, Britain and Canada, stories of Colombo Plan students gained prominence in similar, if lower-key ways to the Australian efforts, fostering a significant public awareness of this aspect of the plan. Diplomatic posts, too, began to note returning Colombo Plan students who rose to government or industry prominence. The Australians counted four former Australian-sponsored students among those representing their governments at the Jogjakarta meeting in 1959.[84] Other overseas posts would welcome alumni groups of former Colombo Plan students taking shape in later years.[85] In Australia's case, as is outlined in Chapters 6 and 7, the Colombo Plan effectively appropriated the big, complex story of overseas students studying in Australia.

BUREAU ON THE RISE

The Jogjakarta meeting of the Consultative Committee in 1959 was notable for its accompanying photographic and poster exhibition, marking an elevated form of national performance in a regional context. Encouraged by the Information Unit, this exhibition was bigger and better attended than previous ones, in part, benefiting from the earlier preparations to hold the huge Colombo Plan Exhibition in Ceylon in 1957 that was then cancelled. The Sultan of Jogjakarta opened the

[83] A. E. Richie, memorandum for Acting Under-Secretary, 'Colombo Plan: Possible Indian Assistance to the Development of the Eskimo Economy', 12 May 1954, RG25 vol. 8407 1108-Y-2-40 part1, LAC; and see Meren, '"Commend Me the Yak"', pp. 364–65 and passim, 343–70.

[84] Report by the Australian Delegation, 'Colombo Plan: Consultative Committee for Co-operative Economic Development in South and South-East Asia, Djakarta 1959', CRS A1361 item 43/1/6 part 4A, NAA.

[85] For example, Malaysian Colombo Plan alumni who studied in Australia have mobilized effectively and have been embraced by the Australian High Commission in Kuala Lumpur; and a similar pattern emerged in Thailand for alumni of New Zealand institutions: Gary R. Hawke, 'The Economic Relationship', in Anthony L. Smith (ed.), *Southeast Asia: A History of Regional and Bilateral Relations* (Singapore: ISEAS and NZIIA and Victoria University Press, 2005), p. 90.

exhibition on 26 October and Sukarno visited two weeks later. The Indonesian President tried to distinguish it from previous such efforts on the grounds that this exhibition was more cooperative than competitive. Local authorities claimed that it attracted 5,000 visitors daily. Such was the widely held view of the exhibition's success that it set the pattern for similar efforts accompanying meetings of the Consultative Committee for the next five years. In other work relating to publicity, delegates at Jogjakarta agreed that 1 July 1961 would be the date marking the Colombo Plan's tenth anniversary, and the time for commencement of various celebrations.[86]

Such activity represented a new high point for the influence of the Colombo Plan Bureau and its Information Unit benefiting from the work of three directors succeeding Wilson – Percy 'Pike' Curtin (September 1953–February 1956), Nathan Keyfitz (April 1956–August 1957), and R. Hunter Wade (August 1957–July 1959). One of the Australians most closely connected to the burgeoning Colombo Plan bureaucracy, Curtin earlier attracted public attention by opening the batting for Western Australia in Perth against the infamous English cricket team's 'bodyline' fast bowlers of 1932–33. Having survived this, he studied economics at the University of Western Australia, where he also completed a law degree. From there, he also took the common empire pilgrimage to the UK for postgraduate study, and in the case of economics, like Lokanathan, to the London School of Economics (LSE). He was a contemporary at the LSE of fellow Australian economist H. C. Coombs. Afterwards, as Coombs rose to prominence in leading public service roles in wartime and postwar Australia, Curtin was recruited to his teams. He was Assistant Director in Australia's Ministry of Post War Reconstruction, 1942–46 and he published in academic journals on the challenges of public policy in Australia. Curtin headed the Colombo Plan's Technical Assistance Bureau on loan from the Australian Prime Minister's Department. After returning from Colombo, Curtin remained engaged on questions relating to finance, economics and development in an era of decolonization. He wrote admiringly of Nehru and of the challenges ahead for India.[87] From the late 1950s, he was charged by

[86] J. K. Thompson, Consultative Committee, 1959, Information Items, 24 November 1959, Colombo, DO 35/9493, TNA.

[87] P. W. E. Curtin, 'India and Her Plans', *Australian Journal of Politics and History*, 2, 1 (1956), 37–45; and see also Curtin's published interview on the Colombo Plan, 'The Effect of the Colombo Plan', *Pakistan Horizon*, 7, 2 (1954), 77–80.

Coombs, then head of Australia's Reserve Bank, with setting up a financial and banking system for Papua New Guinea (under Australian trusteeship).[88] This task would be a long struggle, chiefly against the mixture of colonial and conservative attitudes in Canberra.

Described by a sympathetic contemporary as 'an unorthodox economist of Fabian persuasion',[89] Curtin was preoccupied in Colombo with enabling the Bureau to reach its potential. He arrived after Wilson had started this process, and he also inherited some of the local political tensions. By general agreement, directors of the Bureau were from donor governments, and Presidents of the Council were from the regional members, usually the senior diplomats of governments represented in Ceylon. During Curtin's term, the presidents were C. C. Desai, Indian High Commissioner in Ceylon, and then Haju Abdus Sattar Saith, Pakistan's High Commissioner.

Curtin found that those with grievances vented them with the director. At the Singapore meeting of the Consultative Committee, the Indonesian and Burmese delegations told him that there were two gangs of recipient nations operating, one being the Commonwealth members and the others, Indonesia, Burma, Vietnam, Cambodia, Lao, Nepal, the Philippines and Thailand, the 'poor relations'.[90] While the middle years of the decade saw more concerted efforts by donor governments to extend aid to these countries, the sense of there being an inner and outer circle lingered. Curtin also had to manage the ambitions of the two semi-independent Information Unit officers, Indian B. L. Sharma and Ceylonese L. P. Goonetilleke, who, because they could never cover the vast scope of everything going on, granted themselves great licence in what they did choose to highlight.

Curtin's time coincided with something of an identity crisis for the Bureau. At Simla, had regional members' discussion produced enthusiasm for a serious secretariat, then this would have transformed the Bureau into something much bigger in size and scope. When this suggestion came to naught, the small Colombo team was disappointed and Curtin tried to keep something of the idea alive. A Bureau tasked with information for the Colombo Plan as a whole, and not just technical assistance, he argued,

88 Ron May, *State and Society in Papua New Guinea: The First Twenty-Five Years* (Canberra: Australian National University Press, 2004), pp. 352–78.

89 Ibid, p. 252.

90 Outline of conversation between Dr P. W. E. Curtin, Director, Bureau for Technical Cooperation and L. V. J. Roy, Acting High Commissioner for Canada in Ceylon, 8 November 1955, RG 25 vol. 7387 11038-G-40 part 5.1, LAC.

would be valued also for recording the progress of capital aid projects and facilitating negotiations on capital aid. Providing the Bureau with several advisory technical officers would also mean greater intelligence returning from different locations and enable the director to suggest what was needed next. Both measures would be good for the morale of the small team working valiantly but with resource and remit constraints in Colombo. When Council members recovered from the shock of this expansionist policy proposal, they agreed that Curtin be invited to await further feedback and also test out his ideas at the coming meeting of the Consultative Committee in Singapore.[91] It would take until 1956–57, after he had departed, but Curtin's agitations for a broader remit for the Bureau eventually bore some fruit, made possible by the complete integration of the Information Unit within the Bureau in 1957, with a mandate to report on and promote all aspects of the Colombo Plan.[92]

Curtin and his successors learnt also that they could only go so far in this direction. By the mid-1950s, it was clear that members of the Consultative Committee valued their annual meetings and did not want to see the growth of a powerful secretariat that would undermine the need for diplomatic exchange and decision-making at these. Dr Nathan Keyfitz, the third director of the Colombo Plan Bureau following from Curtin, realized this, too. Majoring in mathematics at McGill, Keyfitz then completed a Ph.D. in Sociology at the University of Chicago. He worked as a demographer for the Canadian Bureau of Statistics, from which he took leave to work in Colombo. Keyfitz served for one and a half years from April 1956 before returning to the Bureau of Statistics, and then taking a chair at the University of Toronto. His academic career flourished as a leading exponent of mathematical demography, including as Director of the Harvard Center for Population and Development Studies, 1978–80. His time with the Colombo Plan, and working with fellow Canadian Cavell, brought frustrations, and shaped

[91] J. Hurley, Canadian High Commissioner, Ceylon, to Under-Secretary of State for External Affairs, 26 July 1955, RG 25 vol. 7387 11038-G-40 part 5.1, LAC; Outline of conversation between Dr P. W. E. Curtin, Director, Bureau for Technical Cooperation and L. V. J. Roy, Acting High Commissioner for Canada in Ceylon, 8 November 1955, RG 25 vol. 7387 11038-G-40 part 5.1, LAC.

[92] These reforms were the result of a review of the Information Unit and Bureau, the recommendations of which were endorsed at the 1957 meeting of the Consultative Committee in Saigon: 'The Colombo Plan for Economic Development in South and South-East Asia: Meetings in Saigon of the Consultative Committee 1957, Saigon, October 1957', pp. 150–54, in DO 35/5738, TNA.

some of his subsequent recommendations. In 1962, he wrote that foreign aid should only be provided to those countries that were adjudged to be near the point of 'take off', using Walt Rostow's description of the point at which economic growth becomes self-sustaining, such is the capability of a country to make use of capital. Or in Keyfitz's terms, 'the composition of elements within the developing societies is such that with some further addition of capital they will reach the critical proportion of factors; they will arrive at a kind of flash-point and explode into development'.[93] Like Rostow, he envisaged a linear continuum of development for nations and he focused on those near, but just to the left of his mid-point of 'take off'. He added that there were probably only between five and twelve countries in the world in this condition, and that one of these might be India. By contrast, 'Whatever the etiquette of international relations, it is nonsense to treat two million shifting cultivators in the jungle – I am describing Laos – as a nation ready to industrialize.'[94] Emergency aid provided to relieve the risks of hunger through drought etc., and particular forms of technical assistance, especially education (here, he mentioned Ceylon), might be exceptions to the rule of concentrating on aid on those poised for take off. Otherwise, the current distribution of foreign aid, as Keyfitz saw it, 'in which all countries get some but none gets enough', had no penalties for waste nor rewards for effective use. The benefits of changing policy along the lines he suggested would be that those countries benefiting from larger sums of foreign aid, by virtue of concentrated efforts on fewer, would take off quickly and soon be able to extend their own aid to others in the queue. But a new mind-set was needed from the current one operating in most donor countries. Neither Cold War considerations nor decisions based on fairness, he argued, would deliver the necessary results.[95]

In his relatively short term as director, Keyfitz made the most of the push for glossy publications to spread the word of the Colombo Plan, securing agreement for a mixture of three specially illustrated, four enlarged and eight ordinary issues of the Colombo Plan *Newsletter* for 1957. The arrival of Indian media expert R. K. Chatterjee to head the Information Unit helped enormously in this effort. Keyfitz admired the growing research capacity informing planning in the region, and in October 1956 he triggered a lengthy discussion in the Council and then

[93] Nathan Keyfitz, 'Foreign Aid Can Be Rational', *International Journal*, 17, 237 (1962), 241.

[94] Ibid, pp. 245, 237–50.

[95] Ibid, pp. 248–50.

in the Consultative Committee about whether evaluations of technical assistance projects might be undertaken. By this stage, chimed a United Nations observer, all UN specialized agencies were required to include evaluations with their reports on technical assistance projects. Council members agreed that it was worth trying to evaluate projects and awaited further views.[96] On a tour of several member countries in mid-1956, Keyfitz was most taken with the quality of work undertaken in India's Statistical Institute and in the ECAFE Secretariat in Bangkok. He was more engaged in research challenges than in managing office politics and delicate egos in the Colombo office. He decried what he saw as the tendency for employees there to act as representatives of their countries rather than as servants of the organization, especially on minor matters.[97]

New Zealander Hunter Wade succeeded Keyfitz as head of the Colombo Plan Bureau in August 1957. Unlike Curtin or Keyfitz, his career was already tied up with the Colombo Plan. He was a diplomat who connected regularly with like-minded counterparts from other Colombo Plan countries and who explained matters for politicians on a steep learning curve.[98] Wade had held diplomatic posts in Delhi, Simla and Canberra during the 1940s and was involved from the very first meeting at Colombo in January 1950. In Delhi, during the war, he had been a member of the Eastern Group Supply Council, a group comprising representatives from Britain, colonial and dominion governments that coordinated the supply of war materials east of Suez. He thus became very familiar with Indian conditions, in a war-colonial context, and with India's very substantial contributions to the war effort.[99]

[96] J. Hurley, High Commissioner for Canada in Ceylon, to Secretary of State for External Affairs, 30 October 1956, RG 25 vol. 7387 11038-G-40 part 6.1, LAC.

[97] Keyfitz (Wellington, attending the 1956 Consultative Committee Meeting) to Ed Ritchie, External Affairs, 1 December 1956, RG 25 vol. 7376 11038-C-40 part 4.1, LAC; Hurley, Canadian High Commissioner in Ceylon, to Under Secretary of State for External Affairs, 30 July 1956, enclosing Keyfitz's tour notes from Madras, Calcutta, Rangoon and Bangkok, 30 July 1956, ibid.

[98] Bio-notes drawn from, New Zealand Ministry of Foreign Affairs and Trade, *The Colombo Plan at 50: A New Zealand Perspective*, New Zealand Ministry of Foreign Affairs and Trade, Wellington, 2001, pp. 9–10.

[99] For a contemporary account of the work of the Eastern Group Supply Council, by the Australian representative, Bertram Stevens, see 'The Eastern Group Supply Council', *Australian Quarterly*, 13, 3 (1941), 9–18. Stevens was impressed by the potential for Indian industrialization and argued that the Supply Council should remain 'a regional economic entity' after the war.

Wade held postings in Washington and Ottawa during the 1950s, before he was appointed to the Colombo Plan Bureau and from there returned to Wellington at the end of 1959 as Director of New Zealand's External Aid section. While Director of the Bureau, as part of the ramping up of information activity, he also claimed to have persuaded the Americans to label more of their aid for Asia as Colombo Plan aid.[100] He was a great enthusiast for technical assistance on 'bang for buck' grounds. At the end of 1957, he wrote for the *Newsletter* that while only 4 per cent of the total value of Colombo Plan aid provided by donor members (excluding the United States) had been given under the Technical Co-operation Scheme, its impact had been huge. The special value of technical assistance lay, he said, in its value for money and its flexibility. Shifts of focüs and sources of aid could be adjusted, including changing practices across different industries. He added that building managerial and technical expertise within a country made it more attractive for further funding, private and public; and that intra-regional training was an exciting trend, whereby countries were both receiving and giving technical assistance.[101]

Among Wade's other boasts was an early one – persuading others at Colombo in January 1950 that this new aid program should be called the Colombo Plan rather than the 'Spender Plan'. As noted, the scale of his achievement might be open to question. When 'Colombo' was suggested rather than something to do with 'spending', there was a stampede to seize it as the better name.[102] His more significant management efforts were towards bedding down the new structure of the Bureau and Council. Thanks to the agitations of his predecessors, Curtin and Keyfitz, a review concluded early in 1957 that the Information Unit should be totally integrated with the Bureau and an Information Committee, which had gathered steam under Sharma and Chatterjee, should be absorbed into the work of the Council. These recommendations were approved at Saigon in October 1957. It did not prove easy to rein in the freewheeling Chatterjee who was enjoying building a mini empire with the plan bureaucracy, but the two co-existed in mostly productive ways.

[100] Bio-notes drawn from *The Colombo Plan at 50: A New Zealand Perspective*, and notes from New Zealand National Library, https://natlib.govt.nz/records/23126977 (accessed 5 January 2019).

[101] *Colombo Plan Newsletter*, 2, 10, November 1957, p. 22, RCS, CUL.

[102] Bio-notes drawn from *The Colombo Plan at 50: A New Zealand Perspective*.

At a meeting of Colombo Plan National Information Officers in Singapore in 1958, the first of its kind, Wade argued that information activity was much more than mere publicity. It was integral to national development. It underpinned the understanding and popular support that would be essential if development activities were to succeed. Wade also wrote lyrically of the Colombo Plan's organic and even spiritual qualities.[103] By 1959, six different members had produced, or were producing documentary films about the Colombo Plan and this medium continued to attract attention for its potential, like that of photographs with minimal text, for attracting broader audiences and transcending literacy and translation issues.[104] When Wade stepped down as director at the end of that year, the Bureau in Colombo was building towards a climax of 1961 when the tenth anniversary of the Colombo Plan was to be celebrated. The pressure on media liaison officers in member countries during the new information campaign of 1959 emerges clearly through the frazzled responses in donor capitals to requests for more photos of farms, dams, mills, more smiling students – nowhere more so than in New Zealand where the grudging need to keep up with the public relations-savvy Australians was an added irritant.[105] Ironically for harassed New Zealanders, it was their countryman Hunter Wade who led the campaign and fuelled the need for more stories and images of New Zealand's efforts to assist development.

Thus, Wade's term concluded at a high point of preparing for celebrations and gearing up for a continuation of the Colombo Plan beyond ten years. What lay beyond 1961 was the special topic considered at the Jogjakarta meeting. All members quickly indicated that they wanted the plan to continue. There was some division over the period of extension prior to another review, with the UK, United States and Canada more

[103] *Colombo Plan Newsletter*, 2, 10, November 1957, p. 22, RCS, CUL.

[104] The Colombo Plan Conference of National Information Officers, Singapore, 9–12 September 1958, Summaries of proceedings, texts of speeches and messages, and conference papers, Colombo Plan Bureau 1958, CRS A6895 item N58/137, NAA; P. H. Gore-Booth British Embassy, Rangoon, to P. F. Grey, FO, 13 September 1956, FO 953/1638 P1061/47, TNA. The results owed some of their form and intent to colonial, wartime and postwar efforts as well as the new energy around the Colombo Plan. The mentoring of interwar British documentary-maker John Grierson, for example, was evident in Australian films.

[105] R. K. Chatterjee (Information Officer, Colombo) to G. C. Burton, Technical Assistance Unit, Department of External Affairs, 6 February 1959, EA 1 W2824 118/7/17/4 part 1, NZ; Sid Odell to G. C. Burton, 25 March 1959, ibid; Sid Odell to Press Attache, New Zealand High Commission, Singapore, 9 December 1959, ibid.

inclined towards five years, while India and a number of others, mostly recipients, were more inclined to ten years. The Australians suggested indefinite extension. Outside of formal proceedings, Australian, Canadian, Indian and New Zealand delegates arrived at a compromise formula that was accepted by all. The Colombo Plan would extend for another five years, from 1961 to 1966, on the understanding that the 1964 meeting of the Consultative Committee would consider a period of further extension.[106] While some might still puzzle over how the Colombo Plan survived without seeming to chalk up major successes, it was an organization that had lodged in different imaginations in ways that ensured its ongoing support.

[106] Report by the Australian Delegation, 'Colombo Plan: Consultative Committee for Co-operative Economic Development in South and South-East Asia, Djakarta 1959', 4 February 1960, CRS A1361 item 43/1/6 part 4A, NAA.

5

So Much Useful Work at So Small a Cost

As the Colombo Plan neared its tenth anniversary, its members could point to growing examples of intra-regional cooperation. By the end of 1958, the mutuality of aid among Colombo Plan members was more demonstrable. No other regional members approached India's sponsorship of nearly 900 trainee students and capital aid for Nepal, but on more modest scale, Ceylon, Burma, Pakistan, Indonesia, the Philippines and Thailand had all sponsored training places and/or experts in development-related industries.[1] At the end of July 1961, three members – Malaya, the Philippines and Thailand – created the first region-only organization, the Association of South-East Asia (ASA), designed to foster joint efforts in economic and cultural fields. ASA was inspired also by opposition to communism. Its short history proved turbulent, but it served as a valuable precursor to the broader-based Association of South-East Asian Nations (ASEAN) formed in 1967.[2]

While regional bonds were quietly thickening, the original host vehicle for the Colombo Plan, the Commonwealth, was thinning to the point of hard questions being asked. Such was the acceleration of transfers of political power in Africa – seven former colonies in seven years, 1957–63 – and elsewhere, accompanied by Commonwealth membership, that British officials regarding the Commonwealth's diversity were wondering what the common factors were beyond English language and colonial pasts. South Africa left the organization in 1961 in the face of

[1] *Colombo Plan Newsletter*, 3, 12, December 1958, p. 19, RCS, CUL.

[2] Vincent K. Pollard, 'ASA and ASEAN, 1961–1967: Southeast Asian Regionalism', *Asian Survey*, 10, 3 (1970), 244–55.

Asian and African hostility to its government's racial segregation laws. In the same year, the British government made its first, unsuccessful, application to join the European Economic Community. By 1962, as Commonwealth historian Philip Murphy summarizes: 'Thoughts of the Commonwealth as a military or economic block had long since been abandoned. The sterling area was in terminal decline. The notion of a common citizenship was steadily being stripped of any practical value. The Commonwealth was no longer bound together by common allegiance to the Crown.'[3] These blows to the Commonwealth's authority impacted the Colombo Plan, just not as sharply as they aggregated in hindsight. The Commonwealth did not lose its appeal to members overnight, as they regarded it as a vaguely helpful mooring and source of mysterious functionality. British Treasury officials might have exaggerated in the middle of 1959 when they described the Colombo Plan as being 'only comprehensible if one remembers its Commonwealth origins'; but they were accurate in reminding of the similarities: 'it is an association without formal agreement or binding obligation which aims at commonly inspired individual action resting on a frank and informal exchange of views'.[4]

This chapter examines the Colombo Plan's progress towards something of a climax, its tenth anniversary in 1961, and the following year. The sense of climax arose not only from anniversary preparations and activities but also through expanded efforts in both capital aid for grand nation-building projects and training and education. Both forms of aid generated multifarious forms of publicity. The lead up to the tenth anniversary also sharpened the hitherto occasional musing about how to evaluate aid efforts and how to measure progress. When members decided this was something the Colombo Plan should do beyond the selective use of statistics and compelling case-study narratives, they were staying true to form. This was consistent with past practice, but it was also starting to draw attention to the plan's limitations. At the beginning of the 1960s, as expectations grew around the evaluation of foreign aid in standardized ways, the Colombo Plan's wonderful lack of rules loomed as a source of weakness rather than one of strength.

[3] Philip Murphy, 'Britain and the Commonwealth: Confronting the Past – Imagining the Future', *The Round Table*, 100, 414 (2011), 269, and 267–83.

[4] Henry Jenkyns (Treasury) to Norman Costar (CRO), Draft paper, 'The Future of the Colombo Plan', 1 July 1959, DO 35/8783, TNA.

EMBRACING AND COMPLICATING REGION

Almost immediately in the wake of their joining the Colombo Plan in 1954, the Japanese were keen to host a meeting of the Consultative Committee.[5] That they had to wait until 1960 was frustrating, but that did not stop them from testing levels of enthusiasm in the region for what they called 'open regionalism', a stronger sense of regional coordination matched by cooperation with other parts of the world. On the first occasion that Japan joined in a full meeting of the Consultative Committee meeting, in 1955, delegation leader T. Ishibashi (Minister of Trade and Industry) suggested that the Colombo Plan was 'surely the most suitable set-up for promoting and fostering such a type of "open regionalism"' and warned against the waste of capital resources if all regional countries tried to develop with the same template.[6] Like the Americans, the Japanese were disappointed that the Simla initiative of 1955 came to naught. In 1957 Prime Minister Nobuo Kishi visited the governments of South and Southeast Asia to promote the idea of an Asian Development Fund to complement the more bilateral flows of specific aid under the Colombo Plan. He pitched this proposed regional financing organization as a force for greater regional integration and a new financial buttress against the appeal of communism. Not incidentally, the fund would smooth paths for greater Japanese access to Southeast Asian markets and, he hoped, appeal to the Americans from a Cold War perspective. Kishi's efforts did not immediately yield fruit, stymied by the lack of support from the Americans who preferred to promote the use of World Bank finance. This was even before regional governments could express their concerns at the possible re-emergence of an economic hegemon, memories of Japan's wartime Co-Prosperity Sphere proving slow to fade. Kishi won some US admiration for his general attempt to provide leadership however, and he arguably laid some of the groundwork for the later creation of the Asian Development Bank, with Japan at the helm, at the end of 1966.[7]

[5] H. A. F. Rumbold (CRO) to UK High Commission, Canberra, 17 December 1956, DO 35/5732, TNA.

[6] T. Ishibashi, Minister for Trade and Industry, In Government of Singapore, *The Colombo Plan for Co-operative Economic Development in South and South-East Asia. Meetings in Singapore of the Consultative Committee 1955*, Singapore Government Office, 1956, p. 66, in DO 35/5731, TNA.

[7] Indian Foreign Secretary Subimal Dutt recorded Nehru's lack of enthusiasm when Kishi visited New Delhi. Dutt added, 'At the Simla Conference of 1955 a similar proposal was

For Japanese leaders trying to convince their South and Southeast Asian counterparts that Japan's economic regionalism was mutually beneficial and unconnected to its earlier imperial ambitions the late 1950s were testing times in several ways. The Colombo Plan remained a valuable means by which they could build a new image of economic strength that avoided war memories. By the time of their hosting the annual Consultative Committee meeting in 1960, they had settled on a narrative of Japan as a model for the rest of developing Asia. The adoption of Western technology and industrial models post the Meiji Restoration, combined with the more recent recovery from war, was a success story that others could follow. Japan's growth was also made possible by values of thrift, savings and hard work. Such was the message of welcome by recently elected Prime Minister Hayato Ikeda to Committee delegates gathered in Tokyo in November 1960.[8]

The Japanese hosts of the Consultative Committee meeting proved skilled at impressing delegates. The meeting included the usual formidable round of receptions hosted by various delegations and a photographic exhibition in the auditorium of the Gaimusho, Japan's Ministry of Foreign Affairs. Ikeda, especially, would have been pleased by the British assessment of the Tokyo meeting. Delegation leader Lord Lansdowne stressed how the Asian participants must have noted how a modern economy could be created in an Asian country that was over-populated and limited in natural resources. He felt that others increasingly looked to Japan as a 'dynamic industrial power and a potentially valuable trading partner'.[9] His colleague and Britain's Director of Technical Assistance, Hugh Humphrey, agreed, venturing that the conference must have helped Japan re-establish a leadership position in the region, 'and in reviving, although in a different pattern, her pre-war

put forward by Japanese Delegates. Other Asian countries did not react favourably to it. The Government of India also did not favour it.' Dutt letter to Gundevia (Colombo), 20 May 1957, Subimal Dutt Papers, Subject File no. 49, April–June 1957, NMML.

[8] Lord Lansdowne's Report on the 12th Session of the Consultative Committee of the Colombo Plan held at Tokyo during November 1960, 13 December 1960, DO 198/12, TNA; Hatano, 'The Colombo Plan and Japan', pp. 131–42; Saori N. Katada, 'Japan's Foreign Aid after the San Francisco Treaty', *The Journal of American–East Asian Relations*, 9, 3–4 (2000), 204–6. Ministers such as Tanzan Ishibashi (Trade and Industry) and civil servants Tatsunosuke Takasi (Head, Economic Planning Agency) were to the fore in promoting 'open regionalism'.

[9] Lord Lansdowne's Report on the 12th Session of the Consultative Committee of the Colombo Plan held at Tokyo during November 1960, 13 December 1960, DO 198/12, TNA.

conception of a Co-Prosperity Sphere', a comment that was clearly for British eyes only.[10] In the wake of the meeting at Tokyo, the Japanese government provided its first officer to a senior post in the Colombo Plan bureaucracy. Sashichiro Matsui became Director of the Bureau in December 1961, serving for a little over two years. Matsui championed technical assistance in ways described further below. While the Japanese had pressed their case for occupying the role in 1959, opposition from the Australians, who remained nervous about Japan's ventures towards regional development organization, had forced them to put their bid on ice for a couple of years (and another British Director, J. K. Thompson was appointed).[11] By 1961, no further delay was possible without unwanted diplomatic repercussions for the one donor country yet to provide a director.

In Tokyo, the information and publicity workers were focused on the big ten-year anniversary events to unfold in 1961. There were two controversial aspects of the Consultative Committee meeting. One was another manifestation of that sense by some non-Commonwealth members that they were still the poor relations of the Colombo Plan. Despite efforts by donor countries to spread their aid around more widely from the mid-1950s onwards, the nagging feeling by some that they were second in line persisted. Felixberto Serrano, Secretary of Foreign Affairs for the Philippines, supported by Burma's Raschid, already an activist in this regard, argued for less bilateralism and more centralization. Serrano suggested that donor countries might meet twelve months in advance to discuss the aid they could provide, and then the Colombo Plan Bureau could be tasked to allocate this to the best-fitting needs. His foray attracted some support from Laotian and Vietnamese delegates, but not from India or Pakistan. The unanimous opposition from donor countries to disturbing the bilateralism of foreign aid allocation ensured its failure – with good grace, as usual.[12] The other source of tension was the presence of Afghanistan representatives, Abdul Karim Hakimi, Deputy Finance Minister, and Abdulla Jan Yaftali, General Director of Statistics in the Ministry of Planning, as observers. While not all those who had been

[10] Colombo Plan Conference, Tokyo, 1960, Note by the Leader of the United Kingdom Official Delegation (A. H. P. Humphrey), 18 November 1960, DO 198/12, TNA.

[11] Perry Ellis, First Secretary, US Embassy, Colombo, to Department of State, reporting conversation with Director, Hunter Wade, 14 July 1958, 890.00/7-1458 USNA.

[12] Lord Lansdowne's Report on the 12th Session of the Consultative Committee of the Colombo Plan held at Tokyo during November 1960, 13 December 1960, DO 198/12, TNA.

observers at Consultative Committee meetings had then sought membership, it was nevertheless a first possible step down this path, the convention to date being that observers might become full members of the plan, if they wished, two years after first attending as observers. The lack of the always-needed Asian sponsor in 1961 meant that there was no guarantee, but the British felt that Afghanistan membership soon seemed likely. What this meant for the imagined region, for the 'Colombo region' that had become part of publicity, was hard to foresee. If Afghanistan could join, then which other countries might argue their cases?[13]

This sense of a membership growing beyond expectations challenged a vaguely shared sense, rarely explicated, that economic development mapped onto geography in ways that had been made workable and were best not to disturb. At the following year's meeting of the Consultative Committee meeting in Kuala Lumpur, the membership question was sharpened by the presence of representatives from the Republic of Korea (RoK) as observers, and observers whose membership intentions were clear. The meeting's host Malayan Prime Minister Tunku Abdul Rahman could dodge what lay down the track, and he did so gladly. In fact, he was keen to draw attention to another regional development. He welcomed the delegates by sketching the Colombo Plan as a haven of cooperation in a world growing more tumultuous through talk of war and the proliferation of increasingly powerful bombs and rockets. Malaya had benefited especially from the technical assistance side of the plan, he said, aided by 135 experts who had lived in Malaya and 700 sponsored traineeships and fellowships for Malayans studying in other countries; and he was proud that Malaya had also turned host to training others in fields such as rubber technology, rice agronomy and veterinary work. He was especially delighted at the recently launched ASA. The Tunku had just concluded hosting the Economic Committee of the ASA in Kuala Lumpur prior to the meeting of the Consultative Committee. He claimed that, 'The Philippines, Thailand and Malaya have come together in this association in the true spirit of the Colombo Plan which in fact is the prime source of inspiration for our desire to foster greater regional cooperation in South-East Asia.'[14] Hoping that more members would soon

[13] Ibid. Some delegates wondered whether Afghanistan membership would necessitate their supporting others who had expressed interest, but who had, to date, been discouraged on geographical and other grounds, such as South Korea.

[14] Text of opening speech by Tunku Abdul Rahman Putra, 13 November 1961, in UK High Commission, Kuala Lumpur telegram to CRO, 12 November 1961, no. 91, FO 371/160016, TNA.

join, he added that the same non-political and non-ideological spirit as characterized the Colombo Plan now underpinned the ASA but 'on a more intimate basis for the benefit of countries in this region who are immediate neighbours'.[15] This was a Malayan leader riding high on the back of his leading role in ASA's formation. The Tunku was generous in how much the Colombo Plan had inspired all forms of progress, including ASA, and he was ambitious on behalf of fellow regional governments. He even returned to the tricky question of regional coordination of development plans but left this worthy aim in the hands of ECAFE and a recently constituted Asian Economic Planners group.[16]

As befitted a government staking claim to leadership in the region, Malayan hospitality was generous. One British official, new to such meetings, suggested there were eight Federation functions that were 'musts' and then each of the twenty delegations added two, one for officials and one during the ministerial meetings.[17] (One of the Malay functions was, for the first time, organized by former Colombo Plan students, hosted in the university.) This was before one counted the smaller luncheons and cocktail parties and so on. Hospitality remained a reason why the three-week period for meetings was hard to shorten.[18] The other, very special feature of the meeting in Kuala Lumpur was that it coincided with the tenth anniversary of the plan and therefore invited a taking of stock on a grander scale, the main features of which are discussed further below.

One year later, in October 1962, Australian Prime Minister Robert Menzies welcomed the 175 delegates from twenty-one nations to a meeting of the Consultative Committee in Melbourne. Menzies opened with reflections on how much had been achieved in the Colombo Plan's first ten years, but emphasized also how serious remained the challenges of those nations, including Australia, that required capital for development and stable markets for their exports.[19] Nineteen sixty-two had not been a

[15] Ibid. [16] Ibid.

[17] M. J. Moynihan, Acting UK High Commissioner, Kuala Lumpur, to Richard Omerod, CRO, 24 November 1961, DO 189/327, TNA.

[18] Peter Jenkins, UK High Commission, Kuala Lumpur, to Leslie Heptinstall, CRO, 23 November 1961, DO 189/327, TNA. Britain's delegation leader at official level, Hugh Humphrey, attended eighteen luncheons, seventeen cocktail parties, fourteen dinner parties and two tea-time functions in the three weeks: A. H. P. Humphrey, UK Department of Technical Co-Operation, to Sir Algernon Rumbold, CRO, 19 December 1961, DO 189/327, TNA.

[19] *Colombo Plan Newsletter*, 7, 11, 1962, p. 3, RCS, CUL.

good year for commodity prices, with combined trade deficits of the Colombo Plan area increasing by around 13 per cent.[20] For Menzies and for leaders of Asian countries, it was a case of trying to remain upbeat about development progress achieved while reminding powerful friends of the structural problems that persisted. The leader of the US delegation was Deputy Administrator for Operations in the one-year-old Agency for International Development, Frank M. Coffin, who reflected on the complexity that now necessarily accompanied all thinking about development. Coffin was attending his first Consultative Committee meeting, but he had past annual reports on hand. He seized on members' consciousness-raising efforts towards planning as *the* story of the Colombo Plan; 'In a deep sense one of the greatest contributions of Colombo Plan members to the world has been their pioneering in the processes of development.'[21]

The Australians, eager to rekindle a sense of policy leadership among members in the wake of the tenth anniversary, proposed changes to the technical cooperation side of these processes. They built on previous conversations about improving training opportunities within the region. In 1960, a Ford Foundation-sponsored survey by a British Council officer and regional educator H. R. Mills explored how to make better use of training facilities that had emerged within the region. While 16 per cent of training places were awarded within the area by 1960, Mills argued that this figure should be rising, given the recent building of technical colleges and the like.[22] The Mills Report confirmed a desperate need in most countries for more technicians. It was at this level of technician training, added the report, that local training centres were likely to achieve best results. The report also pointed to shortfalls in training facilities for particular craftsmen and technologists. Having been commended at Kuala Lumpur and discussed in Colombo and among members through 1961–62, the state of regional training seemed ripe for policy intervention. But, twelve years after Australia's Percy Spender had blazed an undiplomatic path towards the formation of the technical cooperation side of the Colombo Plan, his successors struggled to reform its minimalist structure. They argued, during 1962 and into the following year, that the addition of specialist field officers to the Bureau would better enable a

[20] Communiqué summary, ibid, 6. [21] Ibid, 7.

[22] Record of Conclusions of the Twelfth Meeting of the Consultative Committee on Economic Development in South and Southeast Asia, Report of the Subcommittee on Technical Assistance, CC 60 MM 4, 14 November 1960, DO 198/12, TNA.

more centralized approach (including a proposed new directory of information and a standing committee) to identifying the currently underutilized training opportunities in the region and placing trainees accordingly. In the main, they were rebuffed. Asian members were unwilling to surrender their oversight of trainee selection and only one new appointee to the Bureau was approved. The issue was explored further but not resolved in Melbourne. As discussions continued into 1963, some compromises emerged, as everyone agreed with Mills that action was needed, but the Australians had to retreat from their more substantial challenge to bilateralism and, instead, tread a more careful diplomatic line.[23]

The Melbourne meeting was most notable for the addition of the RoK and Bhutan as members. The government of the Republic of Korea had noted Japan's successful bid to join the Colombo Plan as a step towards strengthening relations with other governments in South and Southeast Asia. RoK leaders wanted to emerge as a discrete diplomatic entity, unhindered by their split from the North, and build on their minimal diplomatic relationships with only a handful of other governments through the 1950s. In 1957, RoK representatives began pressing the British and Americans for support for their own membership, but unlike Japan, the RoK government was wanting to join as an aid recipient more than as a donor. This, plus questions it raised over boundary definitions of the Colombo Plan, made the British uneasy, and with palpable hesitation from founding members India and Ceylon, the matter of RoK membership was set aside. The Koreans returned in 1961, having established diplomatic relations with Thailand, the Federation of Malaya and Australia between 1958 and 1961. The RoK ambassador to Thailand attended the Consultative Committee in Kuala Lumpur planning on seeking membership and lobbying other members in advance of formal proceedings. This unprecedented behaviour shocked most members, with the Indonesians issuing an especially sharp statement, and was managed only by members agreeing that RoK could appear as an observer. The Koreans then successfully sought observer status again for the Melbourne meeting the following year, and in the meantime embarked on a diplomatic offensive to secure stronger support. With the Ceylonese and

[23] The episode is summarized in British Delegation Brief for Colombo Plan Consultative Committee Meeting, Bangkok, October 1963, CPCC (63) 12 Final, Technician Training in S. and S.E. Asia, October 1963, FO 371/169957, TNA; Government of Australia, 'Colombo Plan: Proposals for Expansion of Technician Training within South and South East Asia', submitted to Colombo Plan Bureau, 5 March 1963, RG 59 Central Foreign Policy File, box 3298, USNA.

Indonesians abstaining from what had suddenly become something more akin to a majority 'vote', other members agreed to full membership for RoK in Melbourne.[24] Thus, the Colombo Plan now had a clear presence in Northeast Asia. While Japan's membership had been geographically neutralized on account of its being a donor member, Korea joined as an intending recipient of aid. The big maps generated for Consultative Committee meetings showing how the Colombo Plan helped define a new entity called 'South and South-East Asia' suddenly looked redundant.

Cartographically less testing but attracting more media attention than the RoK membership in Melbourne was the attendance of Bhutanese representatives for the first time and their surprise elevation as full members.[25] Having gained independence in 1947 at the same time as India, Bhutan only gradually embraced a separate international identity, the government taking its lead from India in external affairs. With the agreement of other members, the Australians invited the prime Minister of Bhutan, Jigme Palden Dorji, to attend the Melbourne meeting as an observer. As Jigme and his delegation were about to depart for Melbourne, the Sino-Indian war broke out and the Prime Minister was compelled to remain in his suddenly threatened country. Instead, he sent his sister, Ashi Tashi Dorji, with an all-women delegation that also included his wife, Tessla Dorji.

During the 1950s, Tashi Dorji, a member of the Bhutan royal family, won admirers for her leading land reforms, marshalling men to the ranks of the army and administering penicillin to leprosy sufferers. In Melbourne, she impressed her hosts and other representatives with her energy and grace, aided by the romanticism attached to her small country making its way into world affairs. The Melbourne meeting was only the second international conference at which Bhutan was represented. A short memoir of Tashi Dorji's time in Australia testifies to her excitement at attending and the sense of Australia and the Colombo Plan facilitating Bhutan's emergence in international society. It is interlaced with invitation cards for receptions and excursions to the National (art) Gallery and a sheep farm, and photographs and notes of appreciation.[26]

[24] Ademola Adeleke, 'The Diplomacy of Programme Boundaries: The Republic of Korea and the Colombo Plan', *International Journal of Developing Societies*, 2, 2 (2013), 73–77.

[25] The Bhutan delegation was especially well photographed, for example, *Canberra Times*, 20 November 1962, 3 and reported in *New York Times*, 18 November 1962, 74.

[26] Undated memoir by Tashi Dorji, https://colombo-plan.org/wp-content/uploads/2020/03/Ashi_Tashi_Doriji.pdf (accessed 2 August 2022).

Such was the impact that Tashi Dorji and her colleagues had on delegates, and such was the plight of Bhutan at that time, that, with some advocacy by New Zealanders and the Australian hosts, delegates agreed to waive the conventional two-year wait time and admit Bhutan to membership of the Colombo Plan immediately. That the South Koreans managed to secure membership without the usual wait time no doubt helped, but Tashi Dorji's grace and beauty among the typically masculine group, and the story of small, plucky Bhutan facing up to aggression were important. Tashi Dorji's acceptance speech, in which she offered safe haven in Bhutan to any delegates who encountered problems for having exceeded their diplomatic instructions in agreeing to Bhutanese membership was, according to a British delegate, 'the best thing of the Conference'.[27]

Did this comment also suggest that something of a peak had been reached and that the annual meetings were less valued? In part, probably yes, but British archness should not be mistaken for a general mood or a sudden slide in how they were viewed. The three meetings of the new decade had all been slightly shorter, with greater upfront efficiency in drafting annual reports and tighter discipline around the number and length of ministerial speeches. Researcher Lalita Prasad Singh circulated among those at the Melbourne meeting and found that delegates were in a hurry to finish the formal work of meetings to preserve time for informal consultations.[28] Informal diplomacy in hotel rooms and receptions was still cherished. One of the biggest changes was that some of those who had best oiled the wheels were no longer appearing. Two ministerial stalwart supporters and attendees, Australia's Casey and Britain's Lord Reading, were gone, Casey having resigned from parliament in the middle of 1960 and Reading ejected as Minister of State for Foreign Affairs by the new British Prime Minister Harold Macmillan in 1957. The last time the two were together was the great Wellington meeting of 1956. Casey was not only the 'patron saint' of the Colombo Plan in his advocacy within Australia, but he could also be counted on to regale others of its virtues in his travels overseas. His woolly liberalism could sound myopic and trite, but he always demonstrated an eagerness to connect with leaders of post-colonial Asia:

[27] Annex A in British Report of Consultative Committee Conference, Melbourne, 1962, by Hugh Humphrey no date (December 1962), DO 189/308, TNA.

[28] Singh, *The Politics of Economic Cooperation in Asia*, p. 200.

We ourselves are a young country engaged in the absorbing and difficult task of developing our own land. Without the latest technology to aid us, our task would be almost as difficult as that of the pioneers who came to Australia 169 years ago. I believe that our developmental experience over these years has been most useful in enabling us to understand the developmental needs of other countries and to be able to help them in a practical way.[29]

Casey's dedication to the Colombo Plan and his old-school faith in talkative diplomacy sat well with the broader assembly. Reading shared Casey's concern for good publicity. He welcomed the innovation, from 1955, of a much stronger section in annual public reports on the future of the region. The work of a drafting committee meant that these reports appeared sooner, too, so he was better able to interest journalists bent on news that was current or future-oriented.[30] That ministerial stalwarts such as Casey and Reading embraced the annual meetings so eagerly also reflected the quality and dependability of the civil servants and experts who they relied on and whose adroit straddling of colonial and post-colonial worlds continued after their ministers' departures.[31]

The Consultative Committee's gradual slippage resulted more from organizational initiatives all around it. While American and Australian inclinations to bolster the authority and resourcing of the Bureau in Colombo struggled to gain support, the burgeoning ranks of development experts went elsewhere, into ECAFE or another of the UN auxiliary bodies, or one of the new donor country bureaucracies focused specifically on foreign aid. As is outlined below, it was becoming harder for the Committee to maintain a principled agnosticism on measuring success and lack of success in foreign aid at a time when most donor members were setting up specialized bureaucracies to do just this, and when the

[29] *Colombo Plan Newsletter*, 2, 1, January–February 1957, p. 1.

[30] Reading in Government of Singapore, *The Colombo Plan for Co-operative Economic Development in South and South-East Asia. Meetings in Singapore of the Consultative Committee 1955*, Singapore Government Office, 1956, p. 70, in DO 35/5731, TNA.

[31] Colombo Plan Conference, Tokyo, 1960, Note by the Leader of the United Kingdom Official Delegation (A. H. P. Humphrey), 18 November 1960, DO 198/12, TNA. Reading and Casey helped set a British Commonwealth tone to civilized diplomacy that grew from the gentlemanly capitalism of empire and was underpinned by its enduring legacies present with others who assembled. For example, in the British report on the Tokyo meeting of the Consultative Committee, there was a customary assessment of other delegations' respective performances, among which was the self-satisfied comment that both Sen Gupta of the Indian delegation, and Mr Qarni (A. G. L. Kazi), Official Leader of the Pakistan delegation, were in the Indian Civil Service when the Indian subcontinent was under British control.

Organisation of Economic Co-operation and Development (OECD) was calling for standardized measures by which to measure aid.

TRAINING AND TEMPLES

Donor governments made most of the mistakes imaginable in sending experts into the region and learned quickly from the poor results. Early ventures included experts who were simply unprepared or ill-suited to the rigours of what they faced in parts of Asia, often working in remote locations with little support. Other experts in particular industrial or mechanical skills made fleeting appearances that were not long enough for locals to be trained to the requisite standard; and those sent prematurely or sent to situations where local obstacles ranged from neglect and obstructionism to severe misunderstandings were destined for failure.[32] The conditions of South Asian roads proved testing for expert visitors on the move, and at least in one early case, fatal. The *Colombo Plan Newsletter* for December 1957 carried the sad news that a Japanese expert in automatic bottling techniques, Katsumi Ishizuka, had been killed in a car accident while advising a glass factory in Ceylon.[33]

While noting the successes of New Zealand-sponsored dairy work in India and Ceylon, bovine projects seemed especially susceptible to trouble, the abortive plans to send Indian yaks to Canada included. The Australians sponsored an unsuccessful cattle breeding programme in Sarawak, British Borneo, a Sarawak representative lamenting that 'A fine Hereford bull from Australia failed to produce any calves and remained like a white elephant – an honoured but unproductive guest.'[34] On a bigger scale, the Australians encountered several problems in trying to set up an experimental dairy farm at Ben Cat in Vietnam. The South Vietnamese government failed to ensure that enough local workers were available to assist, and while the Jersey cows settled well enough, the

[32] Reports by donor country aid overseers identified these types of problems, in addition to more specific ones relating to the suitability of machinery etc. See, for example, Nik Cavell, 'Report on Colombo Plan Consultative Committee Meeting no. 5 held in Wellington, New Zealand, November 19 to December 8, 1956' and 'Visits to South and South East Asian Countries by Mr Nik Cavell, Colombo Plan Administrator in Canada and Mr Rodney Grey of the Department of External Affairs', 15 May 1957, RG 25 vol. 7359 11038-5-B-40 part 2 fp 3.2, LAC.

[33] *Colombo Plan Newsletter*, 2, 11, December 1957, p. 2, RCS, CUL.

[34] Minutes of Second Meeting of Officials, Wellington, 19 November 1956, DO 35/5734, TNA.

whole endeavour was also made much harder by the entrenched local preference for tinned (and cheaper) milk.[35]

But stories of experts having a transformational impact were also readily found. The best reported were also those that captured the imagination of the reading public. Canada's aerial surveys of Ceylon enabled planners there to fully appreciate the hydrology of the Kirindi Oya River in 1956;[36] Australian plastic surgeon Benjamin Rank completed a successful program of surgery in Malaya and Singapore in 1954, including thirty-nine operations, and then followed up with similar visits to Ceylon and India the following year. With Casey's support, the Royal Australasian College of Surgeons swung in behind these visits to provide teaching and examinations for those training in Singapore and Malaya.[37] By the end of the decade, most had come to appreciate the value of the integrated project: the provision of equipment accompanied by experts but also linked to training in situ and/or scholarships for training in the donor country. Given that engineering dominated the technical assistance, in terms of both numbers of students sponsored and experts provided, the joining of training and capital assistance happened most often in relation to big, multi-purpose projects.[38]

As noted, host countries included those within South and Southeast Asia. From the outset, the Indian government was determinedly a source of training expertise and provided capital assistance to Nepal for a hydroelectric project. *The Colombo Plan Newsletters* ensured that others knew of the Indian Army engineers taming hostile landscape in the Himalayas in building the Indo-Nepal Road; and by early 1958, the newsletters were adding to India's impressive training opportunities a smaller number sponsored by the governments of Pakistan, Singapore, Ceylon, Malaya, Indonesia and Thailand.[39]

Even more than experts in developing Asia, the students hosted by donor members provided great examples of sponsored internationalism;

[35] Report by American Embassy, Saigon, Weekly review, 27 October 1959, 890.00/10-2759, USNA.

[36] *Colombo Plan Newsletter*, 1, 9, November 1956, pp. 1–3, RCS, CUL.

[37] *Canberra Times*, 4 September 1954, 2; Douglas Miller, 'The History of the Royal Australasian College of Surgeons', *The Australian New Zealand Journal of Surgery*, 41, 4 (1972), 308.

[38] Canadian Embassy, Djakarta to Under Secretary of State for External Affairs, 11 July 1958, reporting on discussions with Australians, RG 25 vol. 7357 11038-4-40 part 2.1, LAC.

[39] *Colombo Plan Newsletter*, 2, 1, January–February 1957, p. 2, RCS, CUL; ibid, 3, 3, March 1958, 7.

and as their social circulation inevitably went beyond educational settings to other members of host societies, they helped add a more vernacular form of internationalism around the Colombo Plan.[40] Inevitably, students and trainees moved in host countries in ways that broadened the forms of human interactions beyond the ranks of politicians and public servants invested in the Plan. Some would meet racism, rudeness and be insufficiently equipped to meet the training requirements. But, according to the sources available, a majority of Asian students had positive, even transformative, experiences in their host countries.[41] Media organizations in host countries and the Information Unit in Colombo were ready to churn out positive tales of cross-cultural discovery and knowledge translating into innovations and progress in students' home countries. Not surprisingly, then, these were the prevailing narratives.

While local authorities in South and Southeast Asia oversaw student selection, sponsoring governments controlled the arrival and settlement of incoming students. The British were the most practiced at this, utilizing the skills of the British Council, described as the 'foster mother' of Colombo Plan trainees. By the middle of 1958, the Council had shepherded some 2,000 sponsored students to their lodgings and training institutions.[42] British Council officials remained involved in all aspects of students' training and well-being. In addition to ensuring that students settled quickly, the pragmatically titled 'Programme Organisers' wanted students to 'enjoy their leisure time, have opportunities for sightseeing and for meeting British families, and adapt themselves to two of the greatest mysteries for a visitor to Britain – the British climate and the British diet'.[43] In Australia, External Affairs liaison officer Max Berman played a key role, being the first point of contact for many incoming students, and the liaison with their educational institutions and places of accommodation. Berman was one of the few who kept tabs on students and was able to report on the state of play around Australia. In 1959, he provided comprehensive lists of returned students and trainees to

40 Making a strong case for international students to play a greater role in our understanding of foreign policy, from a US perspective, is Paul Kramer, 'Is the World Our Campus? International Students and U.S. Global Power in the Long Twentieth Century', *Diplomatic History*, 33, 5, November 2009, 775–806.

41 Most studies of student experiences note the difficulties of self-selective bias, that is, those students who had positive experiences in host countries tend to be more identifiable and accessible to researchers than those who had less good experiences.

42 *Colombo Plan Newsletter*, 3, 7, July 1958, p. 4, RCS, CUL. 43 Ibid.

Australian journalist, Osmar White, in preparation for White's tour of recipient nations, detailed in the following chapter.[44]

Prevailing gendered expectations and the predominance of engineering training ensured that students and experts were overwhelmingly male. In coordinating accommodation and pastoral care for students, however, several women and women's groups emerged as champions of internationally minded hospitality. More than departmental officials overseeing the selection and placement of students, those at the interface between students and host families did much to humanize the experiences of Asian students. In Wellington, New Zealand, Margaret Wallis rose to prominence as a student liaison officer who brought to her task a strong commitment to providing distinctive hospitality and pastoral care.[45] Significantly, ongoing checks and pastoral care for sponsored students began to contrast with the lack of concern for the far more numerous private Asian students in Australia. Women community leaders sometimes bridged the gap between Colombo Plan and other students. In Australia, the Country Women's Association (CWA), in addition to hosting summer vacation tours by students, was active in monitoring standards around student accommodation and ensuring that students saw more than universities and the four walls of their dwellings. 'How can they get a true impression of Australian democracy from the inside of hostels and boarding-houses, which are alike the world over?' cried the New South Wales president of the CWA, Mrs. W. H. Cullen.[46] The CWA was one of the mainstays of the Australian Organisations' Coordinating Committee for Overseas Students, created in the 1950s to oversee student accommodation placements. Energetic individuals also rose to the challenge. External Affairs officers noted that a Mrs Tuckett in Melbourne took on a self-appointed role to oversee the welfare of students housed in private homes, following up students who ran into debt, or went missing from their classes or encountered other personal problems.[47]

In New Zealand, similar coalitions of women, mostly middle class and Christian, celebrated their country's hosting of Asian students.

[44] Record of External Affairs Officers' meeting with Osmar White, 26 November 1958, by R. D. Sturkey, CRS A6895 item N58/134 part 1, NAA.

[45] Jenny Collins, 'Perspectives from the Periphery? Colombo Plan Scholars in New Zealand Universities, 1951–1975', *History of Education Review*, 41, 2 (2012), 139.

[46] 'Hospitality Wanted for Asian Students – How Rotary Plan Works', *The Land*, 1 October 1954, p. 40.

[47] R. H. Gardner, Private Secretary for Casey, minute for Minister, 8 October 1956, CRS A10302 item 1960/36, NAA.

The Christchurch Federated Business and Professional Women's Club joined with the local Young Women's Christian Association to host an 'International Night' in February 1953. Themed 'Every Right Entails a Duty', the evening featured candle-lighting by Colombo Plan students, singing and exhortations by leading women to extend the forms of hospitality shown to Asian students.[48] In 1956, the Christchurch branch of the Pan-Pacific and South-East Asia Women's Associations introduced a hospitality committee to meet and greet students and host events for them.[49]

These unofficial realms of vernacular internationalism increasingly featured women, in contrast to the official stories generated by governments and the Bureau. Diplomatic pioneers such as Eleanor Hinder to one side, women seldom featured in official accounts of the Colombo Plan beyond secretariat and hospitality roles associated with large meetings. The two exceptions were in the information bureaucracies of donor countries and occasional stories of training relating mostly to nursing. In the first category, the British Information Unit based in Singapore included Barbara Fell, who in 1958 was back in London still working on Colombo Plan matters as a more senior information officer. Four years later she was sentenced to a jail term for passing secret documents to communist agents. In the second group, the Ceylonese dental nurses sponsored to study in New Zealand in 1951 was a rare cohort of well-known women students, and in their aftermath the New Zealand government sent dental nurses into the region for what was described as 'new waves of teaching that will benefit millions of young people'.[50] Fortuitously, New Zealand's 800th sponsored student was a woman, Miss Moertini from Indonesia, who, in 1961, was training to become an English language teacher.[51] There was a sprinkling of other story-worthy examples, such as Australian nurse Kathleen Thompson sent to Ceylon's School of Nursing in 1956–57 to advise on the treatment of tuberculosis, and Canadian Pearl Isaacs working as a village officer in Gal Oya, Ceylon, in 1960.[52]

48 *Press* (Canterbury), vol. LXXXIX, issue 26973, 24 February 1952, p. 2.

49 Ibid, vol. XCIV, issue 28125, 14 November 1956, p. 2.

50 *Colombo Plan Newsletter*, 3, 1, January 1958, p. 2, RCS, CUL.

51 Ibid, 3, 8, August 1961.

52 Ibid, 2, 9, October 1957, 16. Three Australian nurses specialising in tuberculosis treatment who had also assisted in Ceylon featured in a story about boosting nursing capacity in Malaya in 1958: ibid, 3, 8 August 1958, 1; Elman, *Asian Experiment*, pp. 16–18.

These developments in non-government activities reflected the expansion more broadly of civic-minded organizations and institutions established in the interwar years. Many found international students logical foci for their missions of service and promotion of mutual understanding. The Rotary Clubs of Australia organized vacation activities for Colombo Plan students over the summer holidays, specializing in taking individuals or small groups into small country towns on overnight excursions. The students would be expected to give short talks on aspects of their homeland to Rotary members, in return for which they would be fed, housed and shown the local industry and sights. This formula made for sometimes eclectic itineraries, such as the one for two students, an Indian and a Malayan, in 1953, visiting the outback town of Wellington, New South Wales. As reported by the local newspaper, 'during their visit, they saw shearing taking place, hunted kangaroos, played golf and inspected [the] Wellington telephone exchange'.[53] In fact, something of a friendly competition over who could best host Asian students emerged. Before Rotary began to mobilize, the locally founded community organization Apex (1930) boasted that it pioneered the holiday excursion/hosting of Asian students in 1952; and in 1964, the national Apex leadership decreed that each club branch should host Asian students in homes in every year.[54] This was a 'ground-up' dimension of the Colombo Plan that compelled governments to follow. By the mid-1950s, governments in Australia, Canada and New Zealand were liaising directly with the likes of Rotary and church groups to better coordinate the activities of sponsored students over their summer breaks.

At the end of the decade, host countries such as Australia and New Zealand were struggling to accommodate Colombo Plan and the more numerous private Asian students. Host families were still taking most students, but authorities bemoaned the lack of a campus-based experience and embarked on hostel building and conversion projects as quickly as budgets would allow. Sometimes this involved adding to existing student accommodation or repurposing existing buildings. In New Zealand, for example, there were such hostels for international students in Wellington (the first such building was completed in 1957) and Auckland in 1961,

[53] The was an Apex Club hosted visit – 'Asian Students Entertained by Apex Club', *Wellington Times*, 27 August 1953, 1.

[54] 'Echuca Apex Started National Move', *Riverine Herald*, 17 May 1952; 'Apex Plans for Asians', *Canberra Times*, 31 March 1964, 10; and for further examples see, David Lowe and Anna Kent, 'Sponsored Students and the Rise of "the International" in Australian Communities', *Journal of Australian Studies*, 43 (2019), 487–502.

when around 300 Colombo Plan students were in situ. The government also contributed to the expansion of hostel capacities at Otago and Christchurch Universities and at Massey Agricultural College.[55] The more spectacular response was to build new, dedicated international student houses, wherein international students enjoyed domiciled internationalism, sharing their building with an agreed quota of domestic students.[56]

Unlike students, who could be interviewed, grand development projects in developing Asia were more easily captured in images with short celebratory text, and more readily construed as cooperative nation-state-building than as episodes in humanized internationalism. The Colombo Plan's bigger multi-purpose projects unfolded with delays and sometimes fractious relationships among stakeholders that were clear to those who looked closely but which remained suppressed in public accounts. Some of the projects revealed the limits of mutual understanding and cooperation in a climate shaped by financial and Cold War competition. Others were delayed by the diversity of personnel brought together in bigger infrastructure projects, many motivated less by Colombo Plan ideals than contractual obligations and opportunities. Project case studies outlined briefly below also reveal the problems that subsequent critiques of post-war development have laid bare in detail: the capacity for a political elite to utilize funds in ways benefiting particular social/ethnic groups at the expense of others; the new forms of colonialism played out in relations between donor country experts and local workers employed on large projects; and the cultivation of continued dependency flowing from encouragement of raw material exports in a capitalist global economy, and instruction in particular forms of technology and techniques

[55] *Press* (Canterbury), vol. C, issue 29498, 27 April 1961, p. 8.

[56] Kate Darian-Smith and James Waghorne, 'Australian-Asian Sociability, Student Activism and the University Challenge to White Australia in the 1950s', *Australian Journal of Politics and History* 62, 2 (2016), 203–18; L. R. Humphries, *Of Many Nations: A History of International House* (Melbourne: Melbourne University Press, 2004); Jon Piccini, *Fifty Years of Friendship: A History of International House, Brisbane, 1965–2015* (St Lucia: University of Queensland Press, 2015); Basil Shaw, *From Many Nations: A History of International House, University of Queensland, 1955 to 1994* (St. Lucia: International House, 1995). In fact, an international student house project, to foster mutual understanding across cultures, took shape internationally well before the Colombo Plan forced hard thinking about student accommodation. The first international student house was erected in New York in 1924, and the second in Tokyo. Some of the same community organizations fostering student experiences outside of their studies, such as Rotary, joined in campaigning for, and fundraising for, the building of new international student houses.

accessible only from the respective donor countries. The Colombo Plan's featured iconic projects were repeatedly referenced in publicity, but descriptions of their progress failed to mention that they were far from immune to these types of problems.

In Ceylon, for example, the Gal Oya project grew bigger and attracted multiple forms of aid in the late 1950s. As it grew, lines of ethnic tension became clear. Initial migrants to the region were mostly Tamils and Muslims from nearby areas, the east being a celebrated, if also contested, site of earlier Tamil settlement and at the time occupied primarily by Tamils. But then, Sinhalese from central and other provinces followed in numbers that soon marginalized Tamils. The later settled Sinhalese were spatially separated from others, receiving the better land plots further upstream where the flow and quality of water from the new dam was more reliable, and they were quickly resented by local Tamils. Sinhalese colonists soon outnumbered Tamils, thereby challenging recent and historical claims to regional distinctiveness. The officials and bureaucrats overseeing the development programme lived in the best conditions of all, adding another layer of differentiation and grounds for resentment.[57] The tensions generated also drew directly on ethnic politics in Colombo, where, in 1956, the new Sri Lankan Freedom Party won power partly on the basis of anti-Tamil policies, and then passed the Official Language Act declaring Sinhala the one official language. Tamil protests sparked violent counteractions from Sinhalese in Colombo, and the rioting, fuelled by rumour, spread to the Eastern Province, including the Gal Oya Valley and nearby Batticaloa, where there were up to 200 estimated deaths.[58] Rioters were all the more mobile and dangerous for their commandeering of vehicles and other equipment from the Gal Oya Authority. It was the worst affected area by the communal violence of mid-1956. Two years later, it was again a hotspot in another outbreak of communal rioting and violence.[59] In short, the colonization of Gal Oya very quickly became hard to interpret purely in developmental terminology. It was seen as one dimension of an increasingly comprehensive government effort to deny

57 Stanley J. Tambiah, *Leveling Crowds: Ethnonationalist Conflicts and Collective Violence in South Asia* (Berkeley: University of California Press, 1996), pp. 82–94. Tambiah reproduces his notes of the riots penned at the time he was in Gal Oya area.

58 Ibid; James Dana Fearon and David D. Laitin, 'Sons of the Soil, Migrants, and Civil War', *World Development*, 39, 2 (2011) 202–3.

59 James Manor, *The Expedient Utopian: Bandaranaike and Ceylon* (Cambridge: Cambridge University Press, 1989), pp. 287–97.

Tamil claims for autonomy and/or equality by rendering them minorities in lands they claimed to have been, historically, rooted in Tamilness.[60]

None of this featured in Colombo Plan reports of Gal Oya's progress. Nor did widespread criticism from across the political spectrum of Ceylon's first Six-Year Plan, which conveyed no sense of priorities and, in providing little direction for government departments, seemed to change little from colonial times.[61] Separate reports by a British scientist, Canadian aid chief Nik Cavell, a Canadian journalist and several updates on Gal Oya appearing in news distributed from the Colombo Plan Bureau all dwelt on the rapid progress made according to indices such as forest cleared, roads laid, colonists settled and land accessing irrigated water.[62] Cavell visited Gal Oya for the fourth time in 1957 and briefly noted resettlement 'problems' in language consistent with that of the Ceylonese government reports.[63] At the time, Canadians were assisting there mostly through agricultural training and providing high-capacity electricity transmission lines. The Canadian journalist, Russell Elman, was typical of others in his admiration for the arrival of modernity at Gal Oya, likening it to a Tennessee Valley Authority in Ceylon, such that 'Within ten years the one-thousand-square mile valley was transformed into a thriving community of more than one hundred thousand people'; and this was matched with the romance of the genuine reclamation at work – the 2,000-year-old ancient tanks and channels of the ancient Sinhala kingdom that had once enabled human habitation there were again being called into use alongside the modern methods, thanks to the restoration efforts of Australia and New Zealand engineers.[64] Elman visited the area in 1959, less than a year after the second wave of violence there.

Among projects that appealed to donor and recipient governments alike for their metaphorical impact were transport ones. New machines

[60] See also Dagmar Hellmann-Rajanayagam, 'The Politics of the Tamil Past', in Jonathan Spencer (ed.), *Sri Lanka: History and the Roots of Conflict* (London: Routledge, 1990), pp. 115–17.

[61] Manor, *The Expedient Utopian*, p. 220.

[62] Railston, 'Britain and the Technical Development of Eastern Commonwealth Countries', 656; Elman, *Asian Experiment*, pp. 6–18.

[63] Nik Cavell, 'Report on Colombo Plan Consultative Committee Meeting no. 5 held in Wellington, New Zealand, November 19 to December 8, 1956' and 'Visits to South and South East Asian Countries by Mr Nik Cavell, Colombo Plan Administrator in Canada and Mr Rodney Grey of the Department of External Affairs', 15 May 1957, RG 25 vol. 7359 11038-5-B-40 part 2 fp 3.2, LAC.

[64] Elman, *Asian Experiment*, pp. 6, 9.

SPECIAL ISSUE

The Colombo Plan

Vol. 4 No. 9 — Registered as a Newspaper at the G. P. O., Colombo — THE COLOMBO PLAN BUREAU, COLOMBO — OCTOBER, 1959

SPEEDIER MOVEMENT

Transport and Communications in South and South-East Asia

One of the 1,500 new locomotives acquired by the Indian Railways in their current development programme. The Indian Railway system is the fourth largest in the world, with a total route mileage of 34,500 miles.

SOME SPECIAL FEATURES

- Railway Development in India by Hon'ble Shri Jagjivan Ram
- Telecommunications System in Pakistan by C. W. C. Richards
- Post-war Reconstruction of Burma Railways
- Dieselisation of Malayan Railways by Chan Peng Kheun
- Progress of Telecommunications in Philippines by Florencio Moreno
- The Kambarangan Story
- Road Development in Nepal by H. Lal
- Khmer-American Friendship Highway.

Wider transport and communications facilities are essential for rapid development. In recent years, most of the countries of South and South-East Asia have launched national plans of development in which they have given high priority to the development of transport and communications. External assistance rendered under the Colombo Plan and other aid programmes is helping in the implementation of these programmes.

In this issue we are presenting to the readers of *The Colombo Plan* some of the highlights in the progress of transport and communications in the countries of South and South-East Asia. Specially contributed articles from authoritative sources, appearing in this issue, have focussed attention on the growth of these facilities, the needs for further development, and the role which external assistance has already played in the promotion of such development.

In the South and South-East Asian region as a whole, development in the field of transport during the last ten years has been considerable. The railways which were overworked during the war, and also damaged in some countries, have been largely rehabilitated. Extensive additions of new railway lines have been made and more amenities provided to the passengers. Roads, and road transport, have received considerable attention and are playing an increasingly effective role in the movement of goods and passengers.

Civil aviation has received high priority in many of the countries where, before the war, aviation was in its infancy. In some countries, mainly on account of disturbed internal security, air journeys constituted for some time the only means of communication between different

FIGURE 5.1 *The Colombo Plan Newsletter*, vol. 4, no. 9, October 1959. *Source*: Royal Commonwealth Society Collection, Cambridge University Library.

smashed distances and visually announced the arrival of modernization. Asia was being picked up and transported into the modern era, according to front covers of the *Colombo Plan Newsletter* (Figure 5.1).[65]

[65] For examples, *Colombo Plan Newsletter*, 3, 4, 1958, p. 1, diesel locomotives for Ceylon; ibid, 3, 7 (1958), 1, Ships in Calcutta port, ibid, 4, 9, 1959, 1, new locomotives for Indian

FIGURE 5.2 Stamp commemorating the Consultative Committee meeting in Jogjakarta, 1959.
Source: Indonesian postage stamp in public domain.

An Indonesian postage stamp commemorating the Consultative Committee meeting in Jogjakarta blended sleek ships, trains, truck and powerlines (Figure 5.2). The Canadian provision of older steam locomotives to India was also an example of how a chance match-up between availability and need could transform into something iconic. Here too, however, there were risks that donor actions supporting growth could fuel inequality or ethnic tension as in Gal Oya. In another Canadian example already cited, specialist Beaver and Otter waterways aircraft sent to Indonesia ended up being used more by the Air Force than for civil purposes – at a time when Djakarta was determined to suppress separatist movements throughout the archipelago.[66]

Arguably, the most potent engineered statement of the future was the Trombay nuclear reactor for India, sponsored by Canada. Nik Cavell set the ball rolling in Ottawa early in 1955, ever alert to something that might capture the public imagination and generate goodwill in both India and

Railways. This last listed *Newsletter* was one of the longest ever, a forty-four-page issue devoted to transport and communications in South and Southeast Asia.

[66] T. F. M. Newton, Canadian Ambassador, Djakarta, to Secretary of State for External Affairs, Ottawa, 30 January 1959, RG 25 vol. 7357 11038-4-40 part 2.2, LAC.

Canada. While Cold War politics made the proposal politically palatable, Canadian scientific commercial interests soon swung in behind the idea. The Canadians were wanting to carve out some space in nuclear energy and make the most of their uranium deposits. Given the high-profile nature of the suggestion, the idea soon warranted executive-level exchanges. Nehru, guided by his charismatic nuclear scientist Dr Homi Bhabha, agreed slowly and with caveats, maximizing the benefits and minimizing any restrictions attached to the products of the Canada–India Reactor beyond the recycling of fuel rods back to Canada. Some of the detail, including policy around the generation of plutonium, was pushed back to be sorted out later in order for a public announcement of the project to be made on 16 September 1955. By this time, the Canadians had agreed to add extra funding to the Colombo Plan allocation earmarked for the project, and the Indians had covered a range of costs, while securing a good degree of control over how the plant operated and which scientists would be approved to work there.[67] Cavell was captivated when he visited in 1957, a little over a year after excavation work had begun. On the one hand, there was concrete pouring from Indian labourers' head baskets to produce what Cavell said was a superior strength product and then there was the brilliance and diverse interests of Homi Bhabha who Cavell described as 'simply amazing'.[68] The Canada–India Reactor went into operation on 10 July 1960, in time for it to feature on the front cover of the Colombo Plan Bureau's tenth anniversary booklet, *The Colombo Plan Story* (Figure 5.3).[69]

Two of the most-celebrated British-sponsored projects were also in India: the building of the Durgapur steel plant in West Bengal and the New Delhi College of Engineering and Technology, which soon transformed into a national priority Indian Institute of Technology (IIT). In both cases, British support squarely met the Colombo Plan mission of assisting growth and development; but the bigger international picture and longer-term implications for British–Indian relations were also important in decision-making. In both cases, the Cold War was a

[67] Campbell-Miller, 'The Mind of Modernity', pp. 191–206.

[68] Nik Cavell, 'Report on Colombo Plan Consultative Committee Meeting no. 5 held in Wellington, New Zealand, November 19 to December 8, 1956' and 'Visits to South and South East Asian Countries by Mr Nik Cavell, Colombo Plan Administrator in Canada and Mr Rodney Grey of the Department of External Affairs', 15 May 1957, RG 25 vol. 7359 11038-5-B-40 part 2 fp 3.2, LAC.

[69] Colombo Plan Bureau, *The Colombo Plan Story: Ten Years of Progress, 1951–1961*, Colombo Plan Council, Colombo, 1961, RCS, CUL.

FIGURE 5.3 *The Colombo Plan Story: Ten Years of Progress, 1951–1961*, Colombo Plan Council, Colombo, 1961.
Source: Royal Commonwealth Society Collection, Cambridge University Library.

prominent factor. The agreement for the Durgapur steel plant was signed in June 1958, one of three state steel plants required under India's second Five-Year Plan and funded with external assistance. The other two had already been signed off with backing from West Germany (at Rourkela) and the Soviet Union (Bombay). Durgapur also met the Consultative

Committee's goal of connecting technical assistance to capital investment wherever possible. Britain was already providing training places for engineers, technicians and other plant workers under the technical cooperation side of the Colombo Plan and was able to send back some 200 'ready' workers for Durgapur by 1960 (though the plant would not be fully operational until 1963).[70]

Prior to Indian independence, analysis of the state of technical training had revealed the urgent need for facilities that would produce engineers capable of meeting ambitious industrialization plans. This was the basis for India's national priority Indian Institutes of Technology (IITs), prestigious centres of training, legislated as national priority institutions in 1961. Before the British efforts transformed into the New Delhi IIT, the Soviet Union sponsored the establishment of an IIT in Bombay (1958), West Germany sponsored the IIT in Madras (1959) and Americans sponsored the IIT in Kanpur (1960). All four sponsoring nations had contributed to the first one established in Kharagpur in 1951, and the Soviet contributions in both of their ventures were channelled through UNESCO.

A detailed study of the IIT at Kanpur highlights the influence of Massachusetts Institute of Technology (MIT) as both model and partner for two-way flows of ideas and people.[71] Both in relation to Kanpur and more generally, the attraction to US institutions was technological, based on the prowess and excitement of US science and technology ushering in a new era of modernization, more than merely a crude alignment with the West in Cold War political terms.[72] The attraction to MIT stemmed also from the model of structuring engineering learning through scientific pathways and from watching how this approach had successfully tapped military funding in the United States through its claims to a nexus with

[70] Katsuhiko Yokoi, 'The Colombo Plan and Industrialization in India: Technical Cooperation for the Indian Institutes of Technology', in Akita, Krozewski, and Watanabe (eds.), *Transformation of the International Order of Asia*, p. 55. The arrival of the first three parties of steelworks trainees in the UK in 1958 attracted considerable press interest: S.E.A (58)10 (Revise), Cabinet Committee on South and South-East Asia, 'Colombo Plan – Publicity', note by the Commonwealth Relations Office, 17 October 1958, DO 35/5757, TNA.

[71] Ron Bassett, 'Aligning India in the Cold War: Indian Technical Elites, the Indian Institute of Technology at Kanpur, and Computing in India and the United States', *Technology and Culture*, 50, 4 (2009), 783–810.

[72] These arguments are developed more fully in Ron Bassett, *The Technological Indian* (Cambridge, MA: Harvard University Press), 2016.

national security.[73] British officials responded positively to an Indian suggestion that they help set up the Delhi Engineering College as they learned of the American involvement in the Kanpur project. The British were conscious of the 'great danger that when the present generation of students comes to have influence in Indian industry, they will have become accustomed to the methods and equipment of our competitors and that our share in India's imports of technical equipment will be affected'.[74] Cold War competition added extra urgency, especially when the British learned that that the Russians were not only sponsoring an IIT for Bombay but were also offering something like 100 free scientific textbook titles, translated into English for mass reproduction and distribution.[75]

The British funding of Delhi Engineering College/IIT was more modest than that of other IITs, but the College was planned as being of smaller size; and the hope was that, located in New Delhi, it would punch above its weight in showcasing British educational and industrial expertise. Under the Colombo Plan, the government promised to fund nine professorial research leaders and two training supervisors for a number of years, in staggered appointments. The estimated cost was around £250,000. In an agreement illustrative of the sub-state institutional investment in orderly decolonization, the Commonwealth Relations Office arranged for a group of British industry leaders to set up an appeal and trust fund that gathered equipment for Delhi of closer to £300,000 in value.[76]

Durgapur Steel eventually proved successful as one of the five steel plants that were fundamental to Nehru's industrialization plans – somewhat akin to his 'temples', the term he used to describe new dams. The British provided a £15 million credit for its building under terms that enabled it to be categorized as Colombo Plan provision, and British banks a further £11.5 million.[77] Again, the Durgapur works also involved British private industry in a substantial way as they were built in

[73] Ibid. See also, Dhruv Raina, 'Engineering Science Education and the Indian Institutes of Technology: Reframing the Context of the "Cold War and Science" (1950–1970)', *Contemporary Education Dialogue*, 14, 1 (2017), 49–70.

[74] Delhi Engineering College Trust, memo by W. G. Wormal, 10 May 1960, DO 35/8754, TNA.

[75] W. Nicoll (CRO) note to A. Parsons, 8 May 1960, DO 35/8754, TNA.

[76] Delhi Engineering College Trust, memo by W. G. Wormal, 10 May 1960, DO 35/8754, TNA. The British sub-state financial interest in orderly decolonization is explored in detail in Stockwell, *The End of the British Empire in Britain.*

[77] 'United Kingdom Aid to India', Draft Brief for Mr Alport, June 1959, DO 35/8528, TNA.

partnership between thirteen British firms that formed the company Indian Steelworks Construction Company Ltd (ISCON) and the Indian state-owned Hindustan Steel. The Government of India's contract with ISCON amounted to £105 million, roughly half of which was spent in India and half on the British plant.[78]

To train a large number of men for a single project – the target for Durgapur was 300 – was unprecedented, and the British ensured that it attracted attention. Journalist Guy Ramsay profiled the 'stupendous scheme' that was Durgapur and wrote that the project had 'caught the imagination of British labour'.[79] This was a reference to the agreement by trade unions to allow trainees in Britain to work at the bench and on production processes so that they gained the hands-on experiences necessary for their anticipated managerial roles. Moving from the importance of getting hands dirty, Ramsay reminded readers of the care taken, by the British Council initially, in enabling Indian trainees of all religions and castes to adjust to English circumstances after their arrival. Ramsay offered a hymn to the virtues of enlightened business: 'Industry has opened the way to real democracy in India: and the democracies of the West regard it as a privilege to assist in a practical way the movement towards the co-operation of all classes and castes.'[80] Durgapur would, in fact, suffer from recurring Hindu–Muslim communal violence in the 1960s.

Before then, Durgapur quickly became iconic for the British. Along the way, however, the construction of the plant revealed some of the forms of friction that could easily detract from the narrative of cooperative progress that underpinned the Colombo Plan and claims made for development initiatives more generally. That there were delays and some construction errors was not so unusual, although it generated unwanted publicity.[81] More problematic were three issues that also affected other large construction projects. One was the politics of labour. From early on, there were Indian concerns that insufficient local (Bengali) labour was being employed, a criticism that was partly rebutted with figures and partly explicable by the need for specialist staff for at least the initial

[78] *Times*, 11 July 1960, in DO 189/115, TNA.

[79] Guy Ramsay, 'Training Steel Workers of Durgapur', *Colombo Plan Newsletter*, 3, 3, March 1948, pp. 39–40, RCS, CUL.

[80] Ibid, p. 40.

[81] For example, see Indian *Blitz Newsmagazine*, 6 June 1959, DO 35/8528, TNA.

FIGURE 5.4 Commemorative teaspoons marked the completion of the steel mill.
Source: Photograph in author's possession.

phase.[82] Related to this was the operation of two different social clubs frequented by those working on the project. Junior workers, all Indian, joined a club subsidized by Hindustan Steel while others, English and some of the more senior Indian technicians, attended another club run by ISCON (Figure 5.4). General W. H. Bishop from the UK High Commissioner's office in Calcutta was sensitive to the seniority/segregationist feel, but could not foresee a merging of clubs: '... I do not see the young British technicians engaged at the site, and their wives, taking readily to any such suggestion. We have to face up to the fact that it is by no means universally held by these people that it is part of their function to be "ambassadors of good will" towards the Indians.'[83]

The tensions arising from the segregation of different groups of workers on large construction sites were not unique to Durgapur. Similar resentments surfaced during the building of the Warsak Dam in

[82] *New Statesman*, 7 August 1958, DO 35/8528, TNA; Record of C. M. Anderson's Visit [to Durgapur], February 1959, ibid.

[83] W. H. A. Bishop, UK High Commissioner's Office, Calcutta, to J. M. C. James, UK High Commission, New Delhi, 5 March 1959, ibid.

Pakistan, one of Canada's signature contributions. An ambitious irrigation and hydroelectric project, the dam plans were approved in 1951 and the Canadian government became a major sponsor the following year. A Canadian firm, Angus Robertson, was awarded the contract to build the dam and Canadian firms won the subsequent contracts for power turbines, generators and plant. Canada's External Affairs Secretary Lester Pearson detonated the first explosive charge to start the build in November 1955. By 1957, there were around 300 Canadians, workers and their families, living onsite in what became a 'little Canada' of segregated library, school, tennis court, church, hospital and bowling alley. The Warsak project progressed much more slowly and expensively than the Canadians had hoped, and Cavell in 1957 tried to inject new urgency into the Pakistan government's commitment. He agitated for greater action while meeting with the Canadian workers who, he knew, had suffered from 'culture shock' during their initial stay.[84] By the mid-1960s, some 10,000 Pakistani men had been employed on the project.[85] In the middle of 1959, Mian Ahmed Hayaud Din, the son of the head of Pakistan's military mission in Washington, reported rising tensions in 'little Canada' and surrounding villages as a result of fraternization between the spouses of Canadian workers and Pakistani engineers during rare social interactions. If such social consequences were foreseeable, then the Western managers did not appear to always manage them effectively.[86]

Nor did technicians foresee at Warsak that by the end of 1965 the reservoir would silt up to the spillways, thereby sending tons of sediment into the power turbines, causing extensive damage.[87] Equipment was not

[84] Nik Cavell, 'Report on Colombo Plan Consultative Committee Meeting no. 5 held in Wellington, New Zealand, November 19 to December 8, 1956' and 'Visits to South and South East Asian Countries by Mr Nik Cavell, Colombo Plan Administrator in Canada and Mr Rodney Grey of the Department of External Affairs', 15 May 1957, RG 25 vol. 7359 11038-5-B-40 part 2 fp 3.2, LAC.

[85] Extract from (British) Peshawar Fortnightly Report, 13–26 June 1956, DO 35/8582, TNA; F. A. K. Harries (Peshawar), Note of Visit by E. L. Miller, 27 April 1957, ibid; Keith Spicer, *A Samaritan State? External Aid in Canada's Foreign Policy* (Toronto: University of Toronto Press, 1966), p. 127.

[86] Rénald Fortier, 'Frankly, My Dear, We Did Give a Dam: Canada and the Warsak Dam in Pakistan', *Ingenium Channel*, 24 January 2021, https://ingeniumcanada.org/channel/articles/frankly-my-dear-we-did-give-a-dam-canada-and-the-warsak-dam-in-pakistan (accessed 7 July 2021).

[87] Ibid. Another Canadian project featuring similar displacement of local inhabitants and tensions between donor and recipient was the multi-purpose dam at Mayuraskhi in India, as is described well by Campbell-Miller, 'The Mind of Modernity', pp. 180–91.

the only thing under threat by grand projects such as Warsak. Beyond the scope of this study is detailed analysis of the long-term environmental impact of great dam-building, land-taming and people-moving projects such as Gal Oya and Warsak that were among the proudest boasts of the Colombo Plan and other foreign aid programs. But this growing field of historical inquiry is revealing how damaging were, in the words of one commentator, these 'vast technology-based environmental and social reconfigurations'.[88] According to historians, the Cold War competition added urgency and intensity to transformational Western efforts to literally reshape the world.[89] It is only by delving deeper into the impacts of roads, population relocations, new technologies such as irrigation, pesticides, new seeds and medicines that we can better appreciate the longer-term ecological dimensions of development projects under the Colombo Plan.

The third issue bedevilling some of the bigger projects was the pervasive sense of Cold War competition. As historian David Engerman has shown in relation to India, this was multi-dimensional in domestic and international politics. From the mid-1950s, Indian ministers and senior officials tied their ambitions and political fortunes to either Soviet or US sources of foreign aid. The competition was also bureaucratically drawn, with certain Indian ministries allying themselves to powerful aid brokers in the United States and Soviet Union in ways that might partly circumvent or preempt Cabinet and India's powerful Planning Commission. It could include both hiding negotiations over a project from the less-involved department and playing foreign governments off against each other in what resembled horse trading.[90] Durgapur was not exempt from these dynamics. In 1959, after news of delays in making the plant operational reached Indian Minister of Steel, Mines and Fuel, Swaran Singh, he told an ISCON representative that he no intention of 'being fleeced' in

[88] Thomas Robertson, 'Cold War Landscapes: Towards an Environmental History of US Development Programmes in the 1950s and 1960s', *Cold War History*, 16, 4 (2016), 418 and 417–41.

[89] Ibid; Cullather, *The Hungry World*. Richard Tucker provides a good survey of ambitious US dam-building projects of the 1950s and 1960s, including two pertinent to Colombo Plan members, the Indus Valley projects for India and Pakistan, and the Mekong River project: Richard P. Tucker, 'Containing Communism by Impounding Rivers: American Strategic Interests and the Global Spread of High Dams in the Early Cold War', in J. R. McNeill and Corinna Under (eds.), *Environmental Histories of the Cold War* (New York: German Historical Institute, Washington, DC and Cambridge University Press, 2010), pp. 139–63.

[90] Engerman, *The Price of Aid*.

paying for more British technicians and that the Russians had offered to run the plant. While British authorities found such blackmail deplorable, they also scrambled to find more Colombo Plan funds that might support the extra help, for fear of failing, or appearing to fail, at Durgapur.[91] The more complicated aspects of building Durgapur to operational status included British government relations with ISCON and the divided responsibilities between ISCON and Hindustan Steel. The project also needed additional credits provided by Western powers and the World Bank (the British share being £38.5 million out of a total of £125 million) to smooth over an Indian foreign exchange deficit that made foreign assistance more urgent and triggered negotiations towards financing its extension beyond initial start-up capacity.[92]

A further problem afflicting grand schemes like Warsak and Durgapur was the lack of neat transitions for those trained overseas under the Colombo Plan for related specialist roles at home. These trainees often found themselves idle or under-utilized upon their return. It was an aspect of foreign training that animated Indian Prime Minister Nehru who called, in 1955, for greater tracking of students who had been trained abroad, either sponsored or unsponsored. Soon afterwards, he argued that 'we should more or less guarantee employment to every Government scholar who is sent abroad'.[93] The British trainee schools and the UK government providing the scholarships felt the same. The *Birmingham Times*, in 1960, talked up the benefits of midlands training of 350 (the target number) Indian technicians for Durgapur: 'Their stay in this country has been one of great opportunity to learn the art of maintenance ... and also to establish a relationship with their shop floor instructors, which will make them, if not exactly pro-British in their outlook, at least eager advocates for the products this country has to offer when they return home.'[94] But keeping track of these technicians once they returned

[91] UK High Commission, Delhi to CRO, no. 1169 SECRET, 3 August 1959, DO 35/8528, TNA.

[92] 'United Kingdom Aid to India', Draft Brief for Mr Alport, June 1959, ibid; Minute by L. H. Robinson, 10 January 1961, DO 189/115, TNA. The London finance market could not be mobilized for financing the planned extension, so a tied government loan from the British government was secured: Cyril E. James to Frank Lee (Treasury) 4 July 1960, DO 189/115, TNA; E. L. Phillips, Brief for the Secretary's Meeting with Mr Shrinagesh on Monday, 12 June 1961, 9 June 1961, T 317/13, TNA.

[93] Nehru's note for Cabinet, 20 August 1956, T. T. Krishnamachari Papers, subject file no. 18, 1956, NMML; Nehru to Minister of Education, 31 July 1955, K. D. Malaviya Papers, subject file no. 10, 1954–56, NMML.

[94] *Birmingham Post*, 8 August 1960, in DO 189/115, TNA.

to India proved hard, and ensuring all of them work that made the most of their training was even harder.

Training, which was a fraction of the value of grand dam-building, power generation and other projects, retained its special attraction for its relatively fast results and the media-friendly human faces it featured. Extolling the virtues of training was easier to do than assessing whole development programmes as the accounting was simpler. There were some grey areas, such as when the one expert spent time in different countries, but generally, the Bureau was able to report confidently on numbers of students/trainees sponsored and numbers of technical experts loaned. But training opportunities and outcomes continued to worry governments. As the Mills Report confirmed in 1960, how to expand and manage regional training was one of the most vexing and recurring subjects of the late 1950s to early 1960s. The Australian proposals to add a new centralized means of selecting trainees, while too much for other members, added urgency to the Mills recommendations.

The issue of training dominated Matsui's term as Director of the Bureau. At the Melbourne meeting, Matsui updated members on this aspect of regional cooperation, a theme with which he was by this time very familiar. Prior to joining the Bureau, Matsui was the Counsellor for Japan in the Bangkok Embassy where he encountered regional diplomacy primarily as Japan's permanent representative at ECAFE meetings. A fluent English speaker, after his Bureau tenure finished in 1961, his diplomatic career flourished, initially in development-related work, including the UN's first two Conferences on Trade and Development, 1964 (Geneva) and 1968 (New Delhi), and then as Ambassador in Afghanistan, then Ceylon and Nigeria. In Melbourne, Matsui spoke to the Council's recent publication of a *Handbook of Training Facilities at the Technician Level in South and South-East Asia*, a venture prompted by the Mills Report and discussion it generated. The *Handbook*, Matsui hoped, would be a valuable snapshot of technical capacity. It would go some way towards more accurate knowledge about training capabilities and opportunities in different countries. But although renowned for not shirking a diplomatic fight, Matsui deferred to those worried about mandating the Bureau with a new centralized agency in training.[95] It would take until 1973 for a comprehensive regional technical training

[95] S. Matsui's Report on the 14th Meeting of the Colombo Plan Consultative Committee held in Melbourne, Commonwealth of Australia, from 30 October–16 November 1962 – Technical Co-operation Items, 6 December 1962, FO 371/169956, TNA Matsui joined

centre to be set up, the Colombo Plan Staff College for Technician Education, in Singapore.

MEASURING PROGRESS

Consensual imprecision was key to harmonious annual meetings of the Consultative Committee at which members reported on their achievements. The questionnaires on which annual reports were based were tweaked throughout their first decade of use, but this did not prevent differences between national accounting efforts. One of the key tasks of the assembled Committee members every year was to strike a balance between wanting to see greater accuracy in statistics and accepting sufficient flexibility such that all members felt that the exercise continued to be valuable. The rotating chair of the drafting committee played an important role in tolerating differences in how measurements were taken among the 'country chapters' and some opaqueness at times over whether achievements reported were those of the last reporting year (mid-year points being the marker) or were more cumulative over a longer period. The 'general chapters' providing the overviews and aggregations were more challenging, as there was too little standardization in the approaches to reporting to be confident about accurately adding up things such as megawatts of power developed, railway track laid etc. The result was the Colombo Plan reporting template of a very generalized account accompanied by highlights and case studies.

Although civil conflict was a big factor for countries such as Vietnam, Indonesia and Burma, this was too inflammatory to be mentioned in the general reports. Over the years, the 'Conclusions', which led to the publicly released reports of 'The Task Ahead', featured a determinedly balanced tone of 'urgency but not emergency' in development needed and reminded readers that external aid was very important but not as essential as local efforts. All of the annual 'Conclusions' added general and uncontroversial advice about the need for increasing agricultural productivity,

Japan's diplomatic service in 1935. He had experience in Japan's own needs after the war, working with the Allied Supreme Command on matters relating to food supply. Matsui served as a diplomat in Portugal, Brazil, Germany and Austria. Even before his appointment to the Bureau, he had proven his willingness to have his views heard. Attending an early conference of the International Atomic Energy Agency in Vienna, he was overlooked by the chair of session. The next day, an angry Matsui returned, ensured an invitation to speak, and then expounded continuously for two hours: *Yomiuri Shimbun*, 23 July 1961, 2; *Colombo Plan Newsletter*, 6, 12, 1961, p. 8 RCS, CUL.

improving taxation methods, encouraging savings and so on. In Wellington in 1956, the Americans took umbrage in some nations including in their annual reports details of foreign aid provided by the Soviet Union and/or China. Delegates defused the tension by adjusting annual questionnaires so that very general, uncategorized aid might be listed. In the following Consultative Committee meetings in Saigon and Seattle, when the growing significance of Sino-Soviet aid to some members was very apparent, members adjusted again, not requiring recipient nations to list all sources of foreign aid but suggesting they provide one or two sources as examples.[96]

Occasionally, journalists offered a critical interpretation of how the Colombo Plan was not doing enough to bring about change, drawing on figures to demonstrate the slowness of progress in agricultural output, irrigation or food consumption. This was a source of frustration for members, as the long-term nature of many of the bigger multi-purpose projects made it hard to show quick results. For those most invested in the plan's reputation, such as Australia's Casey, this made it even more important to keep gathering evidence and advertising progress in the multidimensional idea of 'standard of living'. Casey urged that members be able to show how a significant percentage of total regional development investment (the Ottawa meeting in 1954 estimated something like 18 per cent) came from Colombo Plan efforts. Being able to retain the statistical high ground, argued Casey in 1955, was key to safeguarding the Colombo Plan's reputation:

> Whatever the figure may be, or even if we have to rely on upper and lower limits of figures, that would be something, so as to enable us to get a figure that we can use and that will mean something to the ordinary man who is not technical about the Colombo Plan. I know the difficulties of doing it, I know the problems of anything like accurate statistics coming out of this area, or for that matter I suppose any other area – statistics are very difficult to get out quickly and to be able to use without a multitude of footnotes and side references. But after all, nobody is going to argue with us very much; we can take a stab at the best figure our officers can reach and nobody can produce any better figures than that.[97]

[96] 'Operation of the Consultative Committee and Guidance on Australian Attitude', External Affairs brief for Tokyo meeting of Consultative Committee (no date, September 1960), CRS A4311/2007 item 359/3, NAA.

[97] Government of Singapore, *The Colombo Plan for Co-operative Economic Development in South and South-East Asia. Meetings in Singapore of the Consultative Committee 1955*, Singapore Government Office, 1956, p. 68, in DO 35/5731, TNA.

The Colombo Plan literature never shied from taking a stab at figures. Even in the early 1960s, after a decade of templated questionnaires, the annual progress reports arrived with varying approaches to statistical accuracy and completeness. By then, delegates had the benefit of ECAFE annual and other surveys and would increasingly refer to them. The ECAFE annual survey for 1958, for example, highlighted the worrying gap between food production and current and projected population growth in the region (ECAFE including the two Chinas and Japan). This was a recurring issue in discussions in the Consultative Committee meeting in Jogjakarta in 1959 and in the following years.[98]

The tone of ECAFE surveys was different, and as the decade wore on, the survey authors grew more confident in the veracity of their statistics, thus posing more questions about the standing of the Colombo Plan. Produced by well-trained economists based in the Bangkok office, the *Introductions* to ECAFE annual surveys mixed largely Keynesian analysis of recent and longer-term economic trends with advocacy for regional perspectives. The 1959 survey pointed to disadvantages endured by export-dependent regional members that could not be explained away by depression and war. While ECAFE members watched their import prices rise and their grain needs grow beyond local production, they also noted wealth continuing to accumulate in the industrial world. Looking at the three decades since 1928, the authors concluded that 'The study of these long-term trends leads inescapably to the conclusion that the chronic balance of payments difficulties of the primary exporting countries of the ECAFE region have not been caused by accidental or short-term factors, but are the result of fundamental economic changes, that is, changes in the supply and demand factors in world production and trade.'[99] In fact, the unpredictability of prices for basic commodities, such as rice, rubber, tin and cotton, on which regional members were dependent, was one of the most constant complaints through Colombo Plan and other multilateral meetings of the 1950s and 1960s. It figured in the booklet of collected speeches from the Singapore meeting of 1955. In Kuala Lumpur six years later, the Tunku's warm greeting to delegates contrasted with his frustration at the movements of rubber prices, a sore wound into which salt had been rubbed by the recent British and US

[98] *Colombo Plan Newsletter*, 4, 10, 1959, p. 4, RCS, CUL; ECAFE, *Economic Survey of Asia and the Far East, 1958*, Bangkok, 1959, pp. 1–6, RCS, UCL.

[99] ECAFE, *Economic Survey of Asia and the Far East, 1959*, Bangkok, 1960, p. 4, and 1-4, RCS, UCL.

agreements for the disposal of their rubber stockpiles.[100] Such was their vexation over prices that the regional Asian members gathered at Simla in May 1955 even toyed with the idea of proposing that any extra US funding now available for development needs not be used for a coordinated aid fund but be pooled to offset severe price fluctuations over coming years.[101]

Noting both the more robust statistical work of ECAFE and the impact of these bigger structural problems for growing economies, how then, could success in Colombo Plan efforts be measured? By the time of the tenth anniversary in 1961, members remained wedded to their own statistical reports documenting different forms of development but were also very conscious of the limitations of statistics without narrative, and of a growing push for greater efforts towards measuring projects' successes and shortcomings. At Kuala Lumpur in 1961, the chapter reports and the outlook, 'The Task Ahead', demonstrated how members had managed these tensions to date, but also how hard it had become to constantly tweak a message of impressive results in spite of persistent problems, plus optimism attached to the hard work ahead.

In brief, the ten-year anniversary was a necessary lens but, as had been the case at the inception of the Colombo Plan in mid-1951, it did not match up neatly with plans unfolding in different countries. It was at least useful to be able to document big increases in production of vital products associated with growth over the ten years. Crude petroleum production, for example, rose from 10.8 million tons to 26.5 million tons; coal from 35 million to more than 54 million tons; steel from 1.3 million tons to more than 3 million tons.[102] But any proportional sense of spending on development, the great task, had to be considered in relation to prices that were unstable, year to year, and growing budget deficits in some countries. Development plans were now the norm, but the ten-year view sat awkwardly with how individual countries implemented them. Burma and

[100] Government of Singapore, *The Colombo Plan for Co-operative Economic Development in South and South-East Asia. Meetings in Singapore of the Consultative Committee 1955*, Singapore Government Office, 1956, in DO 35/5731, TNA; Peter Jenkins, UK High Commission, Kuala Lumpur, to Leslie Heptinstall, CRO, 23 November 1961, DO 189/327, TNA.

[101] Press Release, Press Information Bureau, Government of India, 'Conference of Asian Countries of Colombo Plan', Simla, 13 May 1955, in DO 35/5751, TNA.

[102] Drafting Committee, Draft Chapter 1, 'Review of Economic Progress', in T. L. Laister, British Information Service, Kuala Lumpur, to C. R. P. Landon, CRO, 10 November 1961, DO 189/328, TNA.

Cambodia both launched new economic plans in 1961. India, likewise, launched its third Five-Year Plan in 1961, the Federation of Malaya its second Five-Year Plan, and the Philippines its first such Five-Year Plan, while Indonesia started an eight-year version. Ceylon was in the early stages of a Ten-Year Development Plan started in 1959 and Pakistan was in the second year of its second Five-Year Plan.[103]

The near $10 billion of external capital assistance provided to countries of South and South-East Asia between 1951 and 1961 was only one quarter of the money poured into development plans by the regional governments themselves.[104] The draft 'Task Ahead' prepared for public dissemination quoted the very first report of 1950 gesturing to the region's '"incalculable capital in the form of traditions of civilizations which are older than history itself"' and described the Colombo Plan as 'an unparalleled attack on hunger and want, ignorance and disease'.[105] In an area of such diversity, there was no single basis for measuring progress or for comparison of the different countries' economic development, but it was clear that 'firm foundations' had been laid and that increased food production and per capita incomes were encouraging signs for the future. But then population growth had exceeded all expectations, partly as a product of health and medicine initiatives aided by the Colombo Plan. An estimate in 1950 was that the region's population of around 570 million would reach 720 million in 1970; but it had surpassed this figure by 1960.[106] Sharp price fluctuations in the region's key commodities plus civil strife and skill shortages were persisting problems that had been hard to foresee. Development efforts by regional governments had been heroic and benefiting hugely from the expertise and resources of donor Colombo Plan members. 'The task ahead' for regional members, however, brought little comfort. It lay in hard choices between investing in agriculture and industry, or between investment and consumption, specialist education for a few or lower levels for many, and so on. While taking pride in what had been achieved in ten years, the report concluded that much remained to be done. Indeed, chapter one of the report, the economic review, regarded as the greatest single achievement

[103] Ibid. [104] Remme, *Britain and Regional Cooperation*, p. 215.

[105] Drafting Committee, Draft Chapter 2, 'The Task Ahead', in T. L. Laister, British Information Service, Kuala Lumpur, to C. R. P. Landon, CRO, 10 November 1961, DO 189/328, TNA.

[106] Ibid.

to date the growing *awareness* throughout the region and elsewhere of the urgent need for more rapid development![107]

The urge to identify success and failure was even more acute with technical assistance where shorter timelines and more distinct efforts might better lend themselves to evaluation. At Jogjakarta, members suggested that each recipient country select two sample projects for 'comparing and appraising the unit efficiency of technical assistance injected'.[108] Those gathered in a technical assistance sub-committee at Tokyo the following year recognized the impossibility of defining a commonly acceptable unit of technical assistance for use in measurement; but they maintained that internal reviews by receiving countries were valuable. In careful language, they did not think that evaluations by an outside agency should occur, but hoped that 'countries would make information obtained from these evaluations available to other countries through the Bureau, at least in general terms, so that experience could be profitably pooled. An important point was that the evaluation agency in each country should work in close co-operation with those in charge of negotiating and administering technical cooperation in that country'.[109]

The in-house, collaborative and cooperative features of the recommendation were characteristic of the technical assistance sub-committee and of Colombo Plan reports generally. Information sharing and a flexible approach to assessing outcomes were preferable to more steely-eyed evaluations of success and failure. The emphasis was on how to maximize what seemed to be working well.

Success, while resisting verifiable and comparable measurement, resembled modernization meeting restoration. 'The Task Ahead' concluded by circling back to that same juxtaposition, present in the very earliest public messages of the Consultative Committee, between past civilizational greatness and the work to come: 'Member countries will go forward with renewed determination to improve the living conditions of the peoples of the vast region of South and South-East Asia so that they may achieve a standard of material well-being matching their great

[107] Drafting Committee, Draft Chapter 1, 'Review of Economic Progress (my italics)', in T. L. Laister, British Information Service, Kuala Lumpur, to C. R. P. Landon, CRO, 10 November 1961, DO 189/328, TNA.

[108] Record of Conclusions of the Twelfth Meeting of the Consultative Committee on Economic Development in South and Southeast Asia, Report of the Subcommittee on Technical Assistance, CC 60 MM 4, 14 November 1960, DO 198/12, TNA.

[109] Ibid.

cultural traditions.'[110] One of the strongest recurring themes in Colombo Plan publicity, this appeal to restoration entwined with modernization was, in reality, one of the most problematic in practice. As critic Arturo Escobar has argued, the aid and development policies of the 1950s and 1960s more often called for the destruction of local traditions rather than their veneration. Village mentalities stood in the way of bigger production methods, suspicion of modern medicine prevented better health and so modernization was thwarted.[111] Even Colombo Plan literature occasionally suggested as much.[112]

After the Melbourne meeting of 1962, the distinctive and valued features of the Consultative Committee did not fall away suddenly, nor did the diminishing prestige of the Commonwealth result in sharp changes of behaviour. Indeed, the Committee's capacity to sail around international tensions and maintain its loose shape in a world that was transforming international debates and modalities for international development was remarkable. An appraisal by M. J. Marks in the State Department in 1963 summed it up well. US objectives at meetings of the Consultative Committee had been 'broad gauged', he noted, based on presenting US views in the best possible light to Asian ministers and senior officials in an arena less shaped by Cold War and the legacies of colonialism. Marks noted that eleven ministers of Cabinet rank and numerous senior diplomats and experts had attended the Melbourne meeting. He reflected: 'Notwithstanding grandiose intentions at its inception, the Colombo Plan has since evolved into an organization with few, if any, substantive functions . . . Organizations without significant functions tend to deteriorate, and, to a considerable degree, this has been true of the Colombo Plan.' 'Paradoxically', he added, 'the Colombo Plan continues to enjoy high esteem among many of its members.'[113]

110 Drafting Committee, Draft Chapter 2, 'The Task Ahead', in T. L. Laister, British Information Service, Kuala Lumpur, to C. R. P. Landon, CRO, 10 November 1961, DO 189/328, TNA.

111 Arturo Escobar, *Encountering Development: The Making and Unmaking of the Third World* (Princeton, NJ: Princeton University Press, 1995).

112 See, for example, Colombo Plan Information Unit, *The Task Ahead: Progress of the Colombo Plan for Co-operative Economic Development in South and South-East Asia*, Information Unit, Colombo, 1956, pp. 3–4, RCS, CUL.

113 US State Department CPB Paper by M. J. Marks, no. 20, 16 September 1963, 'Colombo Plan Fifteenth Consultative Committee Meeting, Bangkok, October 30–November 15, 1963, Objectives of U.S. Delegation', RG 59, Central Policy File 1963, box 3296, Aid (Colombo Plan), USNA.

This conception of a successful paradox was like a New Zealand appraisal four years earlier that evoked an elusive genius in the international organization, in spite of its seeming fragility. It concluded that the Colombo Plan's success to date resulted largely from its not having tried to be or do too much. It had so little in the ways of rules and permanent structure, 'Yet there are few institutions in the modern world that do so much useful work at so small a cost.'[114] These appraisals did not sufficiently account for the different interests of other, especially Asian, representatives but they conveyed just how important was the sense of successful informality and the broad appreciation of the conversational spaces opened up by meetings of the Consultative Committee. From the time of Marks' general appraisal in 1963, however, these qualities began to matter less, and the organization was overtaken by other initiatives in foreign aid and diplomacy described in the following chapter.

From a regional perspective, the reasons for the decline of the Colombo Plan's standing can be outlined briefly. In very broad terms, two profound changes – the stretching of membership beyond the community imagined for the Colombo Plan's first twelve years and the rise of East Asian economies coinciding broadly with the end of the Cold War – diluted the distinctiveness of the three essential ingredients of development internationalism as a programme. Development-driven state-making, internationalism and regionalism persisted in various ways but less conjoined and increasingly driven by developments outside of the Colombo Plan. The Plan lost its 'South and Southeast Asia' shape. Iran became a member in 1966, Fiji in 1972 and Papua New Guinea in 1973. In 1975, other countries in Europe (and the EEC) and the Middle East were invited to attend the Consultative Committee meetings. In 1977, members changed the programme's name to the *Colombo Plan for Cooperative Economic and Social Development in Asia and the Pacific*. During the 1980s, the main activities settled on training at the Staff College, relocated from Singapore in 1987 to Manila, and a Drug Advisory Programme, as donor members allocated more of their foreign aid under different schemes. As one organizational self-history puts it:

[114] New Zealand Department of External Affairs, 'The Colombo Plan: Participation of New Zealand', 17 July 1958, Sir Walter Nash Papers, International Affairs: Economic-Colombo Plan (R22848896) 1951–58: AEFZ 22618 W5727 83/94/0001-003036/1, ANZ.

By the 1980s, several South and South East Asian member countries had progressed to such an extent that they were fast developing economies. By this time also, the global international cooperation system had matured. The United Nations had established more specialised organizations which mirrored the work of the Colombo Plan and the Colombo Plan donor member countries were beginning to place emphasis on their own bilateral technical cooperation programmes. At the same time, other aid agencies were also set up, many emulating the principles or ideals of the Colombo Plan. The Colombo Plan's relevance as a multilateral aid agency was thus severely challenged. Reflecting these changing times, by 1989, the scholarship programme came to a slow and grinding end. Donor countries felt, perhaps justifiably, that recipient countries no longer needed such intense and committed aid.[115]

At the beginning of the 1990s, the organization seemed in danger of winding up. Crucially, two founding members, Britain and Canada, withdrew from it in 1991. Its original raison d'être seemed to have gone. What the World Bank described as the 'East Asian miracle' was based on markets and the private sector rather than injections of development capital. New forms of regional economic cooperation were being mooted, but the Colombo Plan was no model for post-Cold War regionalism in this new dynamic era of globalization.[116]

Against the odds, the Colombo Plan survived. After a soul-searching reappraisal during 1991–92, members sought to build on the Drug Advisory and training work in a revitalized format. An Eminent Persons Group comprised of six experts from the expanded region recommended at the thirty-fifth meeting of the Consultative Committee in Seoul, in 1994, that members concentrate on a few regular and permanent programmes and that these be formulated on a project-by-project basis. Public administration, private sector development and South–South technical cooperation were added to the focus on Drug Advisory work. The RoK provided donor leadership and a $500,000 injection in this transition phase, its new International Cooperation Agency taking the lead in articulating the new human resources-based agenda. Having collapsed in the 1980s, a new scholarship scheme recommenced from 2005. In the fiftieth anniversary booklet produced in 2001 by the Colombo Plan Secretariat (i.e. what had formerly been the Bureau), there were strong messages of South–South cooperation in what the Colombo Plan stood for.[117]

115 Colombo Plan Secretariat, *The Story of the Colombo Plan: Resource Book 2012* (Colombo: Colombo Plan Secretariat, 2012), p. 36.

116 Adeleke, 'The Diplomacy of Programme Boundaries', 77–78.

117 Ibid; Colombo Plan Secretariat, *The Colombo Plan for Co-operative Economic and Social Development in Asia and the Pacific: 50th Anniversary 1951–2001* (Colombo: Colombo Plan Secretariat, 2001), pp. 40–44.

The South–South theme has grown stronger in subsequent publications.[118] Recent literature generated from Colombo speaks to the Plan's revitalization. A sharp critic might choose 'resuscitation' and suggest that the modern-day Colombo Plan is an emaciated form of its former self. Either way, those invested in the Colombo Plan in the revised form have joined with those who celebrate the work of the earlier body in a coalition of active remembrance. As the following chapter demonstrates, they have considerable material to work with and sustain a story-making side of the Colombo Plan's development internationalism that has endured.

[118] See Colombo Plan Secretariat, *A Legacy of Excellence: The Story of the Colombo Plan* (Colombo: Colombo Plan Secretariat, 2010) and updated version 2014.

6

Projecting the Plan

Given the Colombo Plan's mix of bilateral aid accompanied by gestures towards something collectively bigger than the sum of its parts, its shape and value invited constant crafting by those invested in it. Overall, the crafters were remarkably productive, given their meagre resources. Whereas the Marshall Plan administrators used 2 per cent of all counterpart funds to produce 'the greatest propaganda operation ever seen in peacetime',[1] the information activities of the Colombo Plan drew on miniscule funding for the Information Unit that became part of the Bureau in Colombo plus the goodwill and variable resources available in member countries.[2] Some of the main media forms were similar to those deployed in the Marshall Plan and, from 1957, the European Community's efforts to instil a European civil consciousness: pamphlets, photographic exhibitions, film-making, radio documentaries and essay or photo competitions.[3] Both the small team in Colombo and member country information officers and journalists involved in generating

[1] David W. Ellwood, 'Italian Modernisation and the Propaganda of the Marshall Plan', in L. Cheles and L. Sponza (eds.), *The Art of Persuasion: Political Communication in Italy from 1945 to the 1990s* (Manchester: Manchester University Press, 2001), p. 23; Sherly Kroen, 'Negotiations with the American Way: The Consumer and Social Contract in Post-War Europe', in John Brewer and Frank Trentman (eds.), *Consuming Cultures, Global Perspectives: Historical Trajectories, Transnational Exchanges* (Oxford: Berg, 2006), p. 252.

[2] The budget for 1957 was 840,00 Ceylonese rupees.

[3] A similar range of activities was undertaken in Europe in what has been described as the popularist phase of activity to create a European civil consciousness: Jackie Harrison and Stefanie Pukallus, 'The European Community's Public Communications Policy 1951–1967', *Contemporary European History*, 24, 2 (2015), 233–51.

Colombo Plan stories embraced their pioneering status and ran as hard as they could with resources to hand.

For many, there was a sense of participation in a virtuous enterprise that was more gestured to than defined through the activities the Colombo Plan, that enterprise defined by internationalism, development harnessed to state-making and experimental regionalism – what I have called development internationalism. The Cold War battle against communism was an important motivation for some, more often donors, recurring persistently amidst the more liberal internationalist justifications by donor governments. There emerged also a shared concern to level out any suggestions of unevenness in the amount of aid given. This was addressed through adjustments to aid allocations and through astute publicity. '"Face"' was important, began a note in 1955 produced in the British Treasury, a ministry not renowned for soft power sensitivity. Those non-Commonwealth members of the plan wondering about the benefits of membership needed to feature in stories, continued the note, and to appreciate the benefits of greater public interest in Colombo Plan activities.[4] The stories mattered. As communication scholars have argued, rather than seeing film, photography, radio and print sources as mere tools of postwar development programs, the two phenomena might better be seen as symbiotically entwined under the heading of modernization.[5] Those producing Colombo Plan publicity materials from the late 1950s anticipated this later generation of scholars by suggesting exactly the same. Knowing how easily the Colombo Plan was disassembled into its bilateral component parts, they built something that could appear much bigger and could endure as a rallying cry for at least some of its key members.

Both the bigger virtuous concept and the easy disassembly to suit particular national perspectives remained distinctive features of the Colombo Plan. Even before the early 1960s, as previous chapters have shown, the self-interest behind donors' particular forms of aid giving and the savvy of aid recipients choosing the best deals they could get were apparent. Indian officials, for example, were quick to realize that, as an extension of the Commonwealth, the Colombo Plan enabled them a form

[4] Note by UK Treasury, 'Colombo Plan: Publicity for the Singapore Meeting', 9 September 1955, DO 35/5728, TNA.

[5] On this point see, among other commentary, Rosaleen Smyth, 'Film as Instrument of Modernization and Social Change in Africa: The Long View', in Peter J. Bloom, Stephan F. Miescher, and Takyiwaa Manuh (eds.), *Modernization as Spectacle in Africa* (Bloomington: Indiana Press, 2014), pp. 65–88.

of regional diplomatic leadership. Those providing them with aid had both internationalism and Cold War imperatives in mind. The value of capital aid provided by Australian, British, Canadian and New Zealand governments was small, in the context of India's needs, and much came in the forms of repaid debts (Britain) or counterpart funds generated by India's sale of Australian or Canadian foodstuffs. But these could be acknowledged modestly and folded quietly into India's successive Five-Year plans, which remained the bigger story.

This chapter explores in detail the story-making efforts of those most invested in the Colombo Plan's reputation. Those staffing the Information Unit and Bureau in Colombo, including the talented Indian media experts Brij Lal Sharma and Rama Krishna Chatterjee, set standards in the production of text, image and film. Some donor members proved better than others in this activity, and the chapter includes the successful case study of a government-sponsored tour of the Colombo Plan region by Australian journalist Osmar White, with cameraman, James Fitzpatrick. It also picks up the story of the Colombo Plan past the height of its standing in the early 1960s to near dissolution in the 1980s. Rather than fade completely, as we have seen, a new, less ambitious version of the plan emerged in the 1990s, working in ways that helped to keep some legacy of the original plan alive.

THE STORY FROM COLOMBO

The early meetings of the Consultative Committee up to the end of 1953 attracted mostly favourable publicity, but there was a sag in journalists' interest in between the meetings, and it was not easy to convey a sense of the day-to-day work going on. When the Information Unit was set up in Colombo in 1954, one of its main tasks was to keep public interest simmering.[6] Another of its guiding principles was to stress the cooperative nature of the plan and the relationships it fostered, rather than get locked into a succession of nation-state profiles and updates. In this task, it was mostly successful, though, perhaps understandably, it continued to rely on a fall-back position of 'for example, admire this project or these groups of trainees/experts'. Given the bilateral modus operandi of the plan, the big stories often featured two nations or sometimes more where there were multiple partners – the Thal farming project

[6] M. Dell, UK Treasury, to Stanley Fingland, CRO, enclosing Treasury Note, 16 June 1953, DO 35/5758, TNA.

in West Pakistan was continually promoted as the Commonwealth farm, given the contributions by all founding members.[7] In either case, the tone of collaboration was uppermost and increasingly featured instances of self-help and inter-regional cooperation. In fact, the very earliest reports of the Council featured the sub-heading of 'Intra-regional Assistance' and made clear the offers by India, Ceylon and others for specialist training opportunities. That sub-heading became a fixture, and many of the promotional moments stressed the growth of regional training activity. So for example, in the tenth anniversary year of 1961, the Colombo Plan Council produced *The Colombo Plan Story* booklet highlighting: Philippines fisheries experts training in India recently; a health officer from Sarawak undertaking training in malaria prevention in the Philippines; fourteen railway officials from Burma, Malaya, North Borneo, the Philippines and Vietnam attending the Regional Railway Training Centre in Lahore; and representatives from the Philippines and Vietnam training at Ceylon's Gal Oya Technical Training Institute.[8] By 1961, India had supplied 1,279 training places, which was more than New Zealand's 738, close to Canada's 1,374, and sat respectably with the British and Australians who had each provided over 3,000.[9]

In addition to intra-regional cooperation, the information team in Colombo was immersed in engineering. They told of the vast engineering works underway, usually with pictorial grandeur. They practised their own engineering in the crafting of stories in particular ways. This small group of media public servants swapped stories, copy, film and photography and they forged important connections with government news agencies, such as Indonesia's Antara Agency and the Philippine News Service, to distribute Colombo Plan news more widely. They became expert at making the most of the flexible nature of the Colombo Plan's operation and, in the era before strict standards applied to how one measured foreign aid, presenting the Colombo Plan story in the best possible light. One of the biggest factors in their decision-making around narratives was US aid. As the Americans joined the Consultative Committee quickly, a lot of US aid could be counted as Colombo Plan aid, to spectacular effect, even if it had actually flowed from one of: the US

7 *The Colombo Plan Story*, Colombo Plan Bureau, 1961, Colombo, p. 24, Bevin papers, II, 6/18, Churchill College Cambridge.

8 J. K. Thompson, Director, Colombo Plan Council, to Member Governments, 8 March 1961, RG 25 vol. 5421 11038-S-10-40 part 2, LAC.

9 *The Colombo Plan Story*, p. 10.

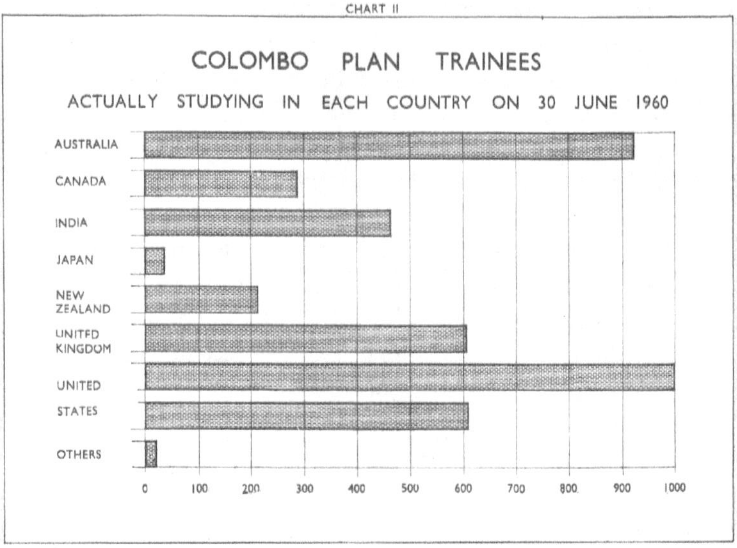

FIGURE 6.1 Colombo Trainees to June 1960, *The Colombo Plan Story: Ten Years of Progress*, Colombo Plan Bureau, Colombo, 1961.
Source: Royal Commonwealth Society Collection, Cambridge University Library.

Mutual Security Program, credits by the Export–Import Bank, Atoms for Peace and the Agriculture Trade Development and Assistance Program – none of which were connected to Colombo Plan origins and evolution. Oblique wording in newsletters and other publicity papered over this lack of Colombo Plan linkage. This sophistry was double-edged, however, as it was hard to avoid the impression of outsized sums of US aid dwarfing the rest. By the end of 1957, a *Colombo Plan Newsletter* noted that the Americans had provided more than $3,000 million of the total $3,500 million provided for the region by donor governments since 1950.[10]

The Americans only joined the Council and technical assistance side of the Plan in 1958, thus presenting both complications and opportunities in reporting. The 1961 booklet mentioned that, of the 21,000 Asian technicians trained in other countries to date, about half had been trained in the United States, an interpretation based on imaginative reverse engineering to capture the pre-1958 (and pre-US membership) years. When it came to depicting the story in graphic form, the authors were able to have the best of both worlds, providing a snapshot from 1960 to include the grand US figure in one graph (Figure 6.1). But in another graph, they started US

[10] *Colombo Plan Newsletter*, 2, 10, 1957, p. 18, RCS, CUL.

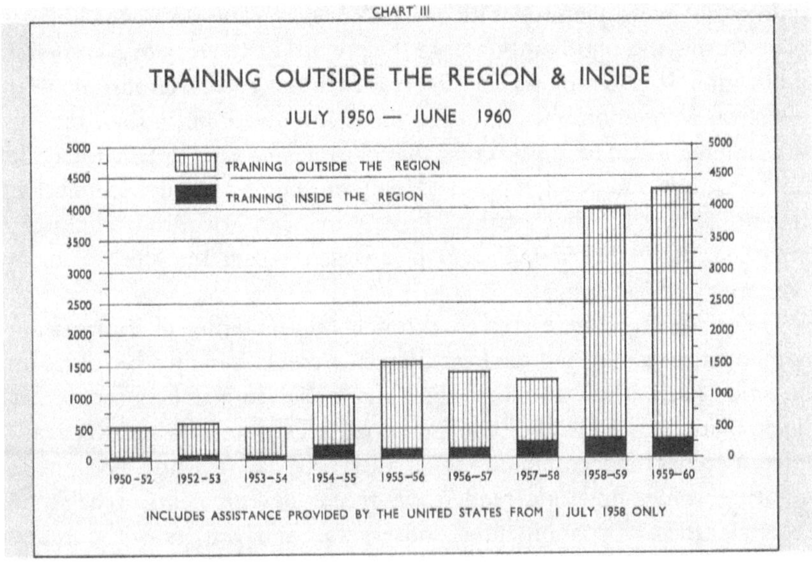

FIGURE 6.2 Training outside the region and inside *The Colombo Plan Story: Ten Years of Progress*, Colombo Plan Bureau, Colombo, 1961.
Source: Royal Commonwealth Society Collection, Cambridge University Library.

training in mid-1958, thus highlighting the respectable level of inter-regional training before then (Figure 6.2).[11]

Such creativity was becoming more necessary in a story that was always in danger of being lost in statistics, a mass of data that could resemble anything from gigantic stock-take to mundane, regular reports. Described further below, in 1961 a new body, the Development Assistance Committee (DAC) of the Organization for Economic Co-operation and Development (OECD), began to establish rules for the measuring of foreign aid; and donor members of the Colombo Plan joined the DAC over the next five years. Prior to this standardizing and definitional rigour around what was foreign aid and how to count it, and prior also to the professionalization of development bureaucracies, there remained considerable licence for the Information Unit officials.

From its launch in March 1956, the *Colombo Plan Newsletter* was especially effective in providing strong visual stories, both literally thanks to the work of liaison officers in various countries who the Bureau badgered to send constant supplies of photographs, and through its

[11] *The Colombo Plan Story*, pp. 15, 18.

fondness of word-pictures. The 1961 *Colombo Plan Story* was able to select stories and photographs from the previous five years of *Newsletter* publication. It began by placing the reader in the Tjurig Aerodrome near Djakarta, where donor aircraft and instructors were busy; then readers were invited to 'Jump now across the South China Sea' to Sihanoukville on the Cambodian coast, a port suddenly benefiting from new connectivity through the building of the Khmer–American Friendship Highway; and then they flew to India, to be taken through the steelworks of Durgapur in West Bengal.[12]

The newsletters were created through the gathering of information from member countries, and writing and commissioning by those in Colombo itself. They were then distributed back to members for further dissemination. The blend of content varied according to what was available: speeches and communiqués if meetings had recently been held; country profiles updating readers on recent developments; articles by experts; articles by anonymous 'observers'; and articles without any attribution at all. In Wellington, 1956 the Consultative Committee welcomed the newsletter's early achievements and decided that it should feature four special issues per year in its monthly programming, leaving some flexibility for what theme or event might be explored at greater length.[13] The longest and most comprehensive of these special features was an issue in March 1958 devoted to 'Industrial Progress in South and South-East Asia.' Running to forty-four pages, with fifty-two photographs, it was a wide-angled snapshot of all forms of industrial activity and the training happening throughout the region (Figure 6.3).[14]

Much of the momentum behind the newsletter came from the Indians who, from early on, campaigned for a strong information and publicity dimension to the Bureau.[15] They originally pressed for the new Information Unit to be based in Delhi but gave way to other members pointing to the need for integration with Bureau work in Colombo.[16]

12 *The Colombo Plan Story*, pp. 1–2.

13 As reported by Casey: *Colombo Plan Newsletter*, 2, 1, January–February 1957, p. 1, RCS, CUL.

14 *Colombo Plan Newsletter*, 3, 3, March 1958, RCS, CUL.

15 Undated (1953) Indian paper, 'A Scheme for Setting up an Information Organisation of the Colombo Plan to Be Considered at the Next Meeting of the Consultative Committee', EA 1 W2619, 118/8/11, NZNA; Secretariat Communique, New Delhi Conference, 17 October 1953, ibid.

16 The Indian paper outlining the case for the Information Unit and staff, and their expected work, left open the question of where the unit would be located and envisaged a director independent of the Bureau in Colombo: T. K. Nandi for Secretary, External Department,

FIGURE 6.3 *The Colombo Plan Newsletter*, vol. 3, no. 3, March 1958.
Source: Royal Commonwealth Society Collection, Cambridge University Library.

They supplied some of the most active media officers, including the first two heads of the unit, Brij Lal Sharma and Rama Krishna Chatterjee, both of whose careers were entwined with the Colombo Plan. Sharma and

High Commission of India, London, to Permanent Under Secretary of State, CRO, 31 August 1953, DO 35/5758, TNA; Acting UK High Commissioner in India to CR, 7 September 1953, DO 35/5758, TNA.

Chatterjee were publicity men who brought to the Colombo Plan a strong familiarity with centralized information and the need for development programmes to work at a popular level. Through post-independence state institutions such as the Films Division and All India Radio, the Indian government cultivated an embrace of modernization overriding village mentality, what one commentator has called the 'hegemony of the developmentalist imaginary'.[17] In the first decade after independence, the need to overcome the lack of development took precedence over communalism, issues of caste conflict and other problems in India. In Colombo, Sharma and Chatterjee extended their developmentalist imaginary from nation-making to international organization-making. Sharma and his colleague, Ceylonese second in command, L. P. Goonetilleke (another British-trained government information officer who oversaw much of the 1952 Colombo Plan Exhibition work), quickly gained a reputation for their skill, judgement and capacity to punch above their two-man weight.[18] Sharma was thrust into the role as a result of the Indian government making sure of its leadership in the information arena and wanting to see its recommendations for a newsletter, journal, pamphlets and photographs and films fully realized. He was seconded from the senior role of India's Principal Information Officer in its Press Information Bureau, responsible for overseeing all press publicity for the Indian government. Having spent time on Fleet Street in the late 1920s and early 1930s, he worked with the *Times of India* before joining the Press Information Bureau during the war years. Before rising to become the head of the Indian Bureau, he oversaw publicity on the sensitive policy issue of Kashmir and other aspects of India's external affairs.[19] Expecting greater levels of working independence, and probably also reflecting his dedication to media in the service of nation-making as well as internationalism, Sharma clashed with Curtin, his Colombo Plan Bureau Director. The latter's inexperience in Asia and inclinations

[17] Roy, *Beyond Belief*, p. 49 and for extended discussion of the Films Division of India, pp. 32–65.

[18] Canadian High Commissioner and Council Representative, James Hurley noted the high regard in which Sharma and Goonetilleke were held and suggested that their work leant support to the idea of a stronger secretariat being formed in Colombo: J. Hurley to Under-Secretary of State, 26 July 1955, RG 25 vol. 7387 11038-G-40 part 5.1, LAC.

[19] R. L. Canerkeratne, Secretary Colombo Plan Bureau, note, 'Appointment of Information Officer', 5 December 1953, DO 35/5758, TNA; N. E. Costar, UK High Commission, Ceylon, to J. Thompson, CRO, 9 September 1954, DO 35/5759, TNA; P. W. E. Curtin, 'Colombo Plan Information Unit', 28 October 1953, DO 35/5758, TNA.

towards British modes of authority did not help, and the two men continued to challenge each other. The Information Unit actually became crucial to Curtin's ambitions, realized at the end of his term, for a Bureau that covered capital aid and well as technical assistance. One of his strongest arguments was that it did not make sense to be reporting and publishing on purely technical assistance. Sharma could go along with this campaign, as it gave him more scope and eventually some more resources, enabling a higher output of print materials (further examples of the *Colombo Plan Newsletter*, Figures 6.4 and 6.5).[20]

When Chatterjee took over from Sharma in 1956, he pushed ahead of Council expectations for the new bulletin/newsletter. He went straight to monthly rather than quarterly production and demanded, successfully, that additional staff and budget help match his pace (Figure 6.6). Chatterjee had studied economics and political science at Calcutta University before joining the Home Department of the Government of India in 1936, moving later to Information and Broadcasting and then, like Sharma, to the Press Information Bureau in the post-independence government. Chatterjee produced publicity for India's first Five-Year Plan and attended the Consultative Committee meeting in New Delhi (1953) and then the last four meetings of the decade, 1956–59 as well as the conference held in Simla in 1955.[21] As the Colombo Plan's Information Officer, he ruffled feathers at times. Donor representatives accustomed to bilateral stories of their aid in action were less attuned to collective regional stories and bristled at Chatterjee's ventures in this direction.[22]

20 My interpretation of the relationship is based on the observations of others. British diplomat in Colombo, Norman Costar, wrote that the Consultative Committee's instructions about the relationship between the Information Unit and the Director of the Bureau were 'somewhat obscure'. He added that 'Sharma is very much an Asian, and Curtin has told me in the past that he has been able, by exercising his authority, to tone down some of the wilder Asian nationalistic flights which have appeared in early drafts of Sharma's work': N. E. Costar to J. Thomson, CRS, 30 November 1954, DO 35/5763, TNA; H. A. P. Rumbold to J. Thomson (CRO), 13 October 1955, DO 35/5763, TNA; and UK Treasury Briefing Paper, 'Colombo Plan Consultative Committee Meetings', Singapore, September/October 1955, The Colombo Plan Information Unit, 22 September 1955, DO 35/5763, TNA.

21 *Colombo Plan Newsletter*, 4, 9, 1959, p. 44, RCS, CUL.

22 'Tenth Meeting of the Colombo Plan Consultative Committee, held in Seattle, 20 October to 13 November 1958, Report of New Zealand Delegation', NZ Department of External Affairs, 22 December 1958, Sir Walter Nash Papers, International Affairs: Economic-Colombo Plan (R22848896) 1951–58: AEFZ 22618 W5727 83/94/0001-003036/1, ANZ.

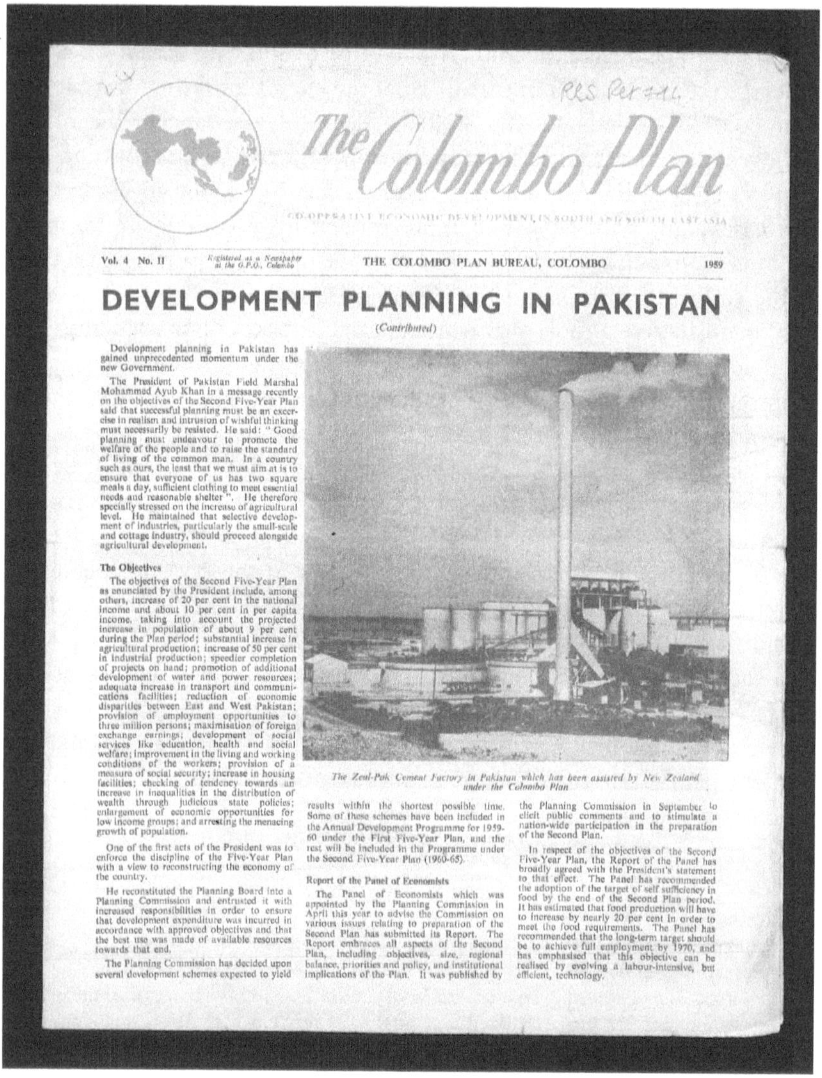

The Colombo Plan

CO-OPERATIVE ECONOMIC DEVELOPMENT IN SOUTH AND SOUTH-EAST ASIA

Vol. 4 No. 11 *Registered as a Newspaper at the G.P.O., Colombo* THE COLOMBO PLAN BUREAU, COLOMBO 1959

DEVELOPMENT PLANNING IN PAKISTAN

(Contributed)

Development planning in Pakistan has gained unprecedented momentum under the new Government.

The President of Pakistan Field Marshal Mohammed Ayub Khan in a message recently on the objectives of the Second Five-Year Plan said that successful planning must be an excercise in realism and intrusion of wishful thinking must necessarily be resisted. He said: " Good planning must endeavour to promote the welfare of the people and to raise the standard of living of the common man. In a country such as ours, the least that we must aim at is to ensure that everyone of us has two square meals a day, sufficient clothing to meet essential needs and reasonable shelter ". He therefore specially stressed on the increase of agricultural level. He maintained that selective development of industries, particularly the small-scale and cottage industry, should proceed alongside agricultural development.

The Objectives

The objectives of the Second Five-Year Plan as enunciated by the President include, among others, increase of 20 per cent in the national income and about 10 per cent in per capita income, taking into account the projected increase in population of about 9 per cent during the Plan period; substantial increase in agricultural production; increase of 50 per cent in industrial production; speedier completion of projects on hand; promotion of additional development of water and power resources; adequate increase in transport and communications facilities; reduction of economic disparities between East and West Pakistan; provision of employment opportunities to three million persons; maximisation of foreign exchange earnings; development of social services like education, health and social welfare; improvement in the living and working conditions of the workers; provision of a measure of social security; increase in housing facilities; checking of tendency towards an increase in inequalities in the distribution of wealth through judicious state policies; enlargement of economic opportunities for low income groups; and arresting the menacing growth of population.

One of the first acts of the President was to enforce the discipline of the Five-Year Plan with a view to reconstructing the economy of the country.

He reconstituted the Planning Board into a Planning Commission and entrusted it with increased responsibilities in order to ensure that development expenditure was incurred in accordance with approved objectives and that the best use was made of available resources towards that end.

The Planning Commission has decided upon several development schemes expected to yield results within the shortest possible time. Some of these schemes have been included in the Annual Development Programme for 1959-60 under the First Five-Year Plan, and the rest will be included in the Programme under the Second Five-Year Plan (1960-65).

The Zeal-Pak Cement Factory in Pakistan which has been assisted by New Zealand under the Colombo Plan

Report of the Panel of Economists

The Panel of Economists which was appointed by the Planning Commission in April this year to advise the Commission on various issues relating to preparation of the Second Plan has submitted its Report. The Report embraces all aspects of the Second Plan, including objectives, size, regional balance, priorities and policy, and institutional implications of the Plan. It was published by the Planning Commission in September to elicit public comments and to stimulate a nation-wide participation in the preparation of the Second Plan.

In respect of the objectives of the Second Five-Year Plan, the Report of the Panel has broadly agreed with the President's statement to that effect. The Panel has recommended the adoption of the target of self sufficiency in food by the end of the Second Plan period. It has estimated that food production will have to increase by nearly 20 per cent in order to meet the food requirements. The Panel has recommended that the long-term target should be to achieve full employment by 1970, and has emphasised that this objective can be realised by evolving a labour-intensive, but efficient, technology.

FIGURE 6.4 *The Colombo Plan Newsletter*, vol. 4, no. 11, 1959.
Source: Royal Commonwealth Society Collection, Cambridge University Library.

On one occasion, Chatterjee's reference to 'haphazard' efforts by governments' publicity efforts resulted in an argument with Pakistan's First Secretary in Colombo, Dr Reyazul Hasan.[23] Generally, though,

[23] J. Hurley, High Commissioner for Canada in Ceylon, to Secretary of State, 30 October 1956, RG 25 vol. 7387 11038-G-40 part 6.1, LAC.

The Colombo Plan

CO-OPERATIVE ECONOMIC DEVELOPMENT IN SOUTH AND SOUTH-EAST ASIA

Vol. 6 No. 3 — Registered as a Newspaper at the G.P.O., Colombo — THE COLOMBO PLAN BUREAU, COLOMBO — 1961

THREE MAJOR POWER PROJECTS IN PAKISTAN: CANADIAN ASSISTANCE

The huge Warsak Dam on the Kabul river, 30 miles from Peshawar in West Pakistan. This multi-purpose project completed early this year was built with Canadian assistance.

SPOTLIGHT ON WARSAK

The week commencing 25 January went down as "power week" on Pakistan's new year calendar with the addition of 190,300 k.w. of more electric power to the national power supply; the inauguration of the gigantic power supply project at Warsak — (160,000 k.w.) within five days the Shadiwal project — (13,500 k.w.) and Goalpara projects — (16,800 k.w.) — all three power stations becoming operational.

On the morning of January 27, ended a costly five-year old battle with the subjugation — for the first time — of the River Kabul, now harnessed to bring fertility to 150,000 acres of waterless land besides providing 160,000 k.w. of electric power.

(Continued on page 3)

COLOMBO PLAN DAY — 1 JULY

TENTATIVE DIARY OF MAJOR EVENTS

Member countries of the Colombo Plan celebrate Colombo Plan Day on 1 July 1961 to mark the completion of the 10th Anniversary of the Colombo Plan. This day will be regarded as the focal point of the decennary celebrations which, according to national wishes and opportunities, may extend over a longer period; member countries are finalising arrangements which include photographic and other exhibitions, film shows devoted to Colombo Plan activities and National development themes; radio and television programmes, newspaper features and supplements; essay competitions, issue of commemorative postage stamps and the use of special cancellation dies, receptions and social functions, etc.

Colombo Plan Stamp

The new 1/- postage stamp featuring a design significant of the Colombo Plan will be issued in Australia on Friday the 30 June, 1961. This stamp will replace the 1/- Platypus stamp which, however, will remain on sale concurrently until stocks are exhausted, states the Post-master-General's Department, Australia.

This stamp is being introduced into the definitive series to show Australia's continuing

(Continued on page 2)

FIGURE 6.5 *Colombo Plan Newsletter*, vol. 6, no. 3, 1961.
Source: Royal Commonwealth Society Collection, Cambridge University Library.

Chatterjee enjoyed his director Keyfitz's support and blazed a new trail of publicity that also jolted member-based media units into action. He toured Pakistan, India and Nepal in March–April 1957, updating himself with the progress of key projects and returning to recommend that a new Colombo Plan documentary film be made. *New Horizons*,

MR. R. K. CHATTERJEE

FIGURE 6.6 R. K. Chatterjee.
Source: Colombo Plan Newsletter, Royal Commonwealth Society Collection, Cambridge University Library.

discussed further below, was the immediate result, and other documentary ventures followed.[24]

MOBILIZING JOURNALISTS

In November 1956, twenty-one British Information Officers from Southeast Asian posts met in Singapore, where they agreed that the public lacked detailed knowledge about the Colombo Plan. They struggled at times to distinguish the Colombo Plan's apparent strengths from its weaknesses. The view was that few people realized it was a label covering a series of bilateral programmes rather than something grander and more centralized. This, however, was probably also one of the reasons for its appeal. Nor, they felt, was the relative modesty of expenditure under the Colombo Plan when measured against what had been spent on Europe's

[24] Percy Ellis, US Ambassador Ceylon, to State Department, 20 May 1957, 890.00/5-2057, USNA.

postwar recovery, or when considered against the area's needs, necessarily a problem. For its goodwill earned, agreed the assembled British officers, the Colombo Plan delivered. The host of the conference, veteran British diplomat and Commissioner-General for Southeast Asia, Malcolm MacDonald, urged more efforts to promote activities occurring under the aegis of the Plan, more encouragement of Asian countries to promote it and support for the Bureau in Colombo to ramp up publicity through production of its recently launched journal, including by making copies available by posts in local languages.[25] To date, the British Regional Office (in Singapore) had produced vernacular versions of the (1956) *Change in Asia* booklet. Most of the officers present enthused about more information activities being linked to the Colombo Plan, including, among other things, pictures and wall sheets of images for Malaya, stories with a sense of its regional purpose in Laos, the benefits accruing to trainees in Burma, and radio stories and a film for Sarawak.[26]

For all their resources and training, however, the British struggled to cut through with Colombo Plan stories in the same way that other countries managed. At a fundamental level, the Colombo Plan was less central to British projections of its image in Asia than was the case for governments finding their way in Asia, namely Australia, New Zealand and Canada. In addition, it was hard to make extravagant claims for noble-mindedness when the reality was that by far Britain's greatest spending under the Colombo Plan was the release of the debt owed to some countries, especially to India. There were also other reasons. An exasperated information officer in Kuala Lumpur complained to London in 1959 that interviews with Malayan students hosted by Britain were unimaginative and ill-targeted, especially by comparison with the more adroit Australian reporting of how Malay students were thriving in social and family settings there. In the hands of reporters in Britain, he said, 'Interviews with Malayans seem to be conducted on a stereotyped pattern – do you like Britain; is the course of value to you; what advantages will derive from it when you return home?' He continued:

[25] R. H. Scott, Letter and Reports on the Conference of Information Officers from South East Asia, 6 to 8 November , 1956, 18 December 1956, FCO 141/14841, TNA, accessed through *Cinematic Realism – Documentary Film Website*, The Documentary Film in South and South-East Asia Research Programme, https://digital.lib.hkbu.edu.hk/documentary-film/ (accessed 30 October 2018).

[26] Ibid.

This kind of approach is not only dull but it is useless for our purposes and could be positively damaging to our reputation if we were to offer the product to our newspapers. The Malayan guest in the United Kingdom is obliged to praise Britain and is often led to making statements about himself and his work which label the whole thing as propagandist and could damage his reputation with his own Government and his friends on his return here.[27]

It was not that the British neglected to publicize the Colombo Plan. In 1960 the Central Publicity Office was distributing Colombo Plan material to more than 16,000 clubs, associations, newspapers, unions and other groups. Special stories such Britain's funding towards the Durgapur steelworks appeared in another regular broadsheet, *Commonwealth Today*. A Commonwealth Exhibition touring the UK in 1960 had a section devoted to the Colombo Plan. What was needed, agreed information officers in the Commonwealth Relations Office in London, was more publicity about those trained in Britain after they had returned home.[28]

At the Saigon meeting of the Consultative Committee in 1957, the collective agreement to sign off on the first six years of the Colombo Plan and prepare for a new phase was accompanied by a proselytizing spirit. Members agreed on the need to do more information work across all media forms, including, where possible, television.[29] The national information officers of seventeen member countries, plus representatives from the UN Department of Information, the World Health Organization (WHO) and the Colombo Plan Bureau were mobilized as a new group and met first in Singapore in September 1958. As had been the case in 1955 when Singapore hosted the Consultative Committee, lavish hospitality was a feature. Opening the meeting, Lim Yew Hock, Singapore's Chief Minister, mused that information officers might logically be given honorific titles, 'your intensities'. By the end of the meeting, three and a half days later, it was the intensity of the dining, ten-course Chinese meals at the end of each day, that was more the talking point.[30]

[27] J. S. Ellis, Director UK Information Services, Kuala Lumpur, to Jack Hughes (CRO, Information Directorate), 24 September 1959, DO 35/9493, TNA.

[28] Colombo Plan Information Working Party, Meeting of the Colombo Plan Consultative Committee, Tokyo – 1960, Colombo Plan Publicity, Draft CRO note, 8 September 1960, DO 35/9625, TNA.

[29] The Colombo Plan Conference of National Information Officers, Singapore, 9–12 September 1958, Summaries of proceedings, texts of speeches and messages, and conference papers, Colombo Plan Bureau, 1958, CRS A6895 item N58/137, NAA.

[30] Ibid.

At the meeting, Phillip Jones, a British Information Officer based in participating Sarawak, expressed frustration at what he saw as a lack of appreciation about Colombo Plan successes. The main problem, he said, was 'the Plan's lack of glamour, drama and apparent humanity'. Comparing it to the UN, he said, it had, 'no glass tower on the East River, no flag, no stamp, no [Dag] Hammarskjoeld'.[31] Jones would not have to wait long for the flag and stamp, and the meeting was held on the eve of the release of the first major documentary film on the Colombo Plan. As head of the Colombo Bureau, Hunter Wade took up the challenge at the Singapore meeting, setting out the case for information activity as 'an integral part of the machinery of national development':

> To the extent the information activity in an under-developed country can help mobilize popular support for a vigorous programme of economic and social development, it is a productive activity of the utmost importance. In the same way, the work of information officers in the more highly developed countries can help to build up public support for a programme of technical assistance and capital aid to the less developed countries. Both of these aspects of information work are of concern to the Colombo Plan which, in its widest sense, consists of the application of a blend of national effort and external aid to the development programmes of the countries of the Colombo Plan area.[32]

Like Diem at the meeting of the Consultative Committee the previous year, Wade thus celebrated and built on what he regarded as the glue that held the umbrella of aid activities together. In his mind, the plan may have exhibited Diem's 'enduring and universal values of good-will' but it also depended on more manufactured efforts, the constant work of information experts, to sustain it over the long haul. The information officers departed Singapore agreeing that even more publicity efforts were needed, in print, poster, film and radio.[33]

Information was also crucial to the desired transformation of how the plan could be seen as something more than just a postwar experiment, but rather something more like an enduring series of partnerships between

[31] Note by Phillip Jones on Information and Broadcasting Services of the Government of Sarawak on Colombo Plan Publicity in ibid.

[32] Wade's remarks and vote of thanks at Opening Ceremony, Conference of National Information Officers, Singapore, 9 September 1958, Summaries of proceedings, texts of speeches and messages, and conference papers numbers, 11–12, 50, Colombo Plan Bureau, 1958, CRS A6895 item N58/137, NAA.

[33] Summaries of proceedings, texts of speeches and messages, and conference papers, 9–12 September 1958, Colombo Plan Bureau, 1958, CRS A6895 item N58/137, NAA.

donor and recipient nations.[34] However many heads nodded at Diem's and others' affirmations, it was much harder to make big inroads into communications in those Asian countries where journalism was in its infancy and the infrastructure around communications was one of the development projects underway. Nor was it wise to badger regional news services to tell of Western aid. As Pakistan diplomats pointed out, clumsy announcements of Western aid could result in odious comparisons with other countries or even envy by unaided local groups who argued they were just as needy. The British report from the Singapore Information Conference reminded: 'Popular publicity in recipient countries must deal almost wholly with national undertakings and it is most effectively carried out by national information services. The stress they can be expected to lay on international bilateral assistance is small.'[35] Donor countries continued to explore new angles that might be more palatable, and film became especially attractive. As noted above, by 1959, several members were eagerly engaged in documentary film making, hoping that this might elevate the Colombo Plan's visibility.

The Singapore meeting was the first of a series that formalized information sharing and heightened coordination. Prior to September 1957, there had been considerable comparing and competing among those responsible for communications. The British discussions in Singapore in November 1956 acknowledged the success of Australian information efforts in the region, noting in particular that their assistance provided to Asian students was extensive and 'backed by vigorous and effective publicity'.[36] This comment reflected intensified publicity efforts in Australia. Having decided in 1955 to focus most publicity on the hosting of Asian students, the Department of External Affairs worked closely with the Australian News and Information Bureau to generate content and disseminate it in multiple formats.[37] For budget reasons too, they borrowed formats from elsewhere and looked to stronger connections

[34] Ibid.

[35] S.E.A. (58)10 (Revise), Cabinet Committee on South and South-East Asia, 'Colombo Plan – Publicity', note by the Commonwealth Relations Office, 17 October 1958, DO 35/5757, TNA.

[36] R. H. Scott, Letter and Reports on the Conference of Information Officers from South-East Asia, 6–8 November 1956, 18 December 1956, FCO 141/14841, TNA.

[37] Formed in 1950, the Australian News and Information Bureau was the successor to the Australian Department of Information. Unlike British, Japanese and Canadian governments, neither Australians nor New Zealanders had the major engineering equipment that might underpin multi-purpose projects, nor did they see their aid as leading to possible trade.

within the region for some of this new work. Noting the success of a Kodak exhibition of photographs about development projects provided by the UN in 1957, External Affairs reproduced this format, organizing a collection of photographs of Australian Colombo Plan activities for exhibit in Melbourne and Sydney later that year. It featured both student-life images and country-specific sections, so that it could then pack and reassemble easily for the next meeting of the Consultative Committee in Seattle the following year for the now-established exhibition accompanying the annual meeting.[38]

The Australian Colombo Plan budget provided for a team of regional ('non-SEATO' countries) journalists to tour Australia in 1957. While in fact this was the fourth recent tour of Australia by Asian journalists,[39] it was of higher profile than those previous and included Durga Das, Chief Editor of the *Hindustan Times* in India. Das, who recorded some of his observations and experiences in his 'Editor's Note-Book' column, was impressed by the intent behind the tour. He encountered plenty of Eurocentrism, ignorance and cloistered thinking among the politicians and others he met, but still reported positively about the Australians' training of students from the region, and, for the most part, the broad-mindedness of the people with whom they mixed. Australian journalists were apologetic for their failure to raise awareness of India, which at least suggested potential for change.[40] Thereafter, Australia's sponsorship of students increasingly drew in those studying journalism, with thirty-two from thirteen countries training in Australia between 1958 and 1960.[41]

38 D. Dexter (DEA) memo for Assistant Secretary, 'Colombo Plan Display of Photographs by Kodak' (Melbourne) 2 July 1957, CRS A1838/294 item 20148/2 part 7, NAA; Mel Pratt, Acting Director ANIB, letter to Mr R. D. Sturkey, 8 January 1959, ibid; *The Colombo Plan*, Newsletter, 2, 11, December 1957, p. 4, RCS, CUL.

39 A number of Indian journalists were among the first to be sponsored. In 1950, E. P. W. da Costa, editor of *Eastern Economist* and the founder of the India Institute of Public Opinion, toured Australia. Frank Moraes, editor of *Times of India*, visited in the same year; and in the following year, an international press delegation, including Indian J. N. Sahni, covered the Jubilee of Australia's Federal Parliament. Their visits, and their reflections, are discussed in Amit Sarwal, '"A Kangaroo and Bradman": Indian Journalists' Visits to Australia under the Colombo Plan, 1950–57', *Journalism Studies*, 18 (2018), 1–17; *Colombo Plan Newsletter*, 2, 4, 1957, p. 4, RCS, CUL.

40 Ibid, pp. 10–13. Durga's columns in *The Hindustan Times* were called 'India and the World'.

41 Undated notes (1960) prepared by ANIB officers in preparation for 1960 Colombo Plan Conference of National Information Officers, CRS A6895 item N60/29, NAA. See also, Amit and Sarwal and David Lowe, '"Behind the White Curtain"': Indian Students and Researchers in Australia, 1901–1950', *History of Education Review*, 50 (2021), 212–25.

The UN continued to provide a lead on how to generate stories from experts sent to Colombo Plan countries. In September 1958, the Australians noted how slow they had been by comparison with UN efforts, at tapping into the experts' and students' stories. From that point, they began more determinedly to seek out students who had returned to their home countries for their recollections.[42] It was similar in Canada where it took until 1960–61 for a good collection of student stories and photos to be gathered despite pleas from representatives in Asian capitals.[43] Relying on students and universities to take photographs themselves produced patchy results, one External Affairs officer in Ottawa noting that in some shots, 'the supposedly hard-working trainee is either passively standing by watching the diligent antics of his teacher, or worse yet, is engaged in the somewhat social occupation of bending the elbow'.[44] The accumulation of suitable student photographs in Canada, as elsewhere, proceeded with the recruitment of more journalists and a stronger editorial eye.

IMAGE

From their early days in the mid-1950s, the Colombo Plan *Newsletters* helped to generate more demand for details, especially more images. Regional newspapers, whether in donor or recipient countries, tended to be especially conscious of the human-interest aspect and demanded photographs of smiling trainees or impressive engineering works before running stories.[45] The staff of the Information Unit enjoyed adding distinctiveness to an increasingly broad tableaux of development projects. In 1956, they devised a Colombo Plan crest that began appearing on most of their publications. The crest comprised two sheaves of corn and a

[42] This formed part of the brief for the tour by Australian journalist Osmar White, described below in this chapter: Colin Moodie (DEA) to Australian posts in South and Southeast Asia, 'Colombo Plan – Visit by Journalist to South and South East Asia', 19 September 1958, CRS A6895 item N58/134 part 1, NAA.

[43] Arthur Menzies in Kuala Lumpur bemoaned his lack of success despite repeated calls for photographs and stories of Malayan students who had studied in Canada and returned to Malaya: Menzies to Under Secretary of State for External Affairs, 19 May 1961, RG 25 vol. 5419 11038-S-40 part 5, LAC.

[44] Memo, D. M. Miller to I. W. Robertson, 18 May 1961, RG 25 vol. 5419 11038-S-40 part 5, LAC.

[45] P. H. Gore-Booth British Embassy, Rangoon, to P. F. Grey, FO, 13 September 1956, FO 953/1638 P1061/47, TNA. The results owed some of their form and intent to colonial, wartime and postwar efforts as well as the new energy around the Colombo Plan.

FIGURE 6.7 *The Fifth Year: Progress of the Colombo Plan*, Colombo Plan Bureau, 1956.
Source: Churchill College, Cambridge, Bevin Collection.

wheel of industry, representing the basic economy as well as development needs of the region This was combined with a torch representing light, knowledge and assistance. It began appearing with the logo, 'Planning for Prosperity' (Figure 6.7). The Consultative Committee considered the crest at its meeting in Saigon in 1957 and decided that while there was no need to adopt an official crest, it would be acceptable to continue to use it. And use it, the Colombo publicity men did![46]

Photographic exhibitions accompanied most of the meetings of the Consultative Committee. They were of a small scale at first, but, as noted

[46] 'Report of the Information Committee on the Working of the Colombo Plan Information Unit during 1956–57', undated report from Saigon meeting of the Consultative Committee (November 1957), RG 25 vol. 7360 11038-5-C-40 part 2, FP 2, LAC.

in Chapter 3, they quickly became more central to the annual meetings. The 4,000 schoolchildren marched by their teachers through Wellington's special photographic exhibition on the Colombo Plan in November 1956 were witness to the image-led internationalism joining dairy know-how and public health with development. They were to be followed by successive waves of schoolchildren and publics in the years to come. Information officers were attempting new heights in preparing for the exhibition that was to have been held in Colombo in 1957. Although that event was aborted, preparations were not wasted, as was clear from the scale and quality of the exhibition accompanying the Consultative Committee meeting in Jogjakarta at the end of 1959 (visited by an estimated 5,000 visitors). From there, Information Unit officials and liaison officers in the member countries concentrated on the tenth anniversary in 1961. Thereafter, exhibitions accompanying meetings of the Consultative Committee stayed at elevated levels for the following three years before returning to more modest proportions. By this stage, too, the stock of publications and images being collected in the small Bureau library in Colombo had grown, aided by the inauguration events around some of the bigger projects such as dam construction, railway locomotives in action, irrigation and power generation. In 1958, the Bureau library had gathered around 900 publications. Geography seemed to play a big part in which countries sent the most, with India (406), Ceylon (106) and Pakistan (81) well ahead of other members, suggesting that the 'pulling' power of the Bureau was geographically determined.[47] By 1961, the Australians, British and Canadians all had commissioned special tours of the Colombo Plan area by journalists whose efforts always included photographs and increasingly included film.

The tenth anniversary was greatly celebrated in multifarious forms. The Canadians prepared 8,000 copies of the booklet *Canada and the Colombo Plan* for sending to: all those receiving its monthly *External Affairs* news bulletin; another mail list receiving Colombo Plan information; and around 900 copies for overseas posts.[48] Otherwise,

[47] The figures for other members were: Philippines (38), Burma (29), Indonesia (28), USA (39), Canada (33), Japan (16), UK (15), Australia (13) and New Zealand (12): R. K. Chatterjee, 'Information Officers' Conference, Singapore', to R. I. Hall, CRO, 27 August 1958, DO 35/9626, TNA.

[48] N. F. H. Berlis, Information Division, External Affairs, memorandum, 26 April 1961, RG 25 vol. 5420 11038-S-2-40 part 2, LAC; Canadian Department of External Affairs in Cooperation with the External Aid Office, *Canada and the Colombo Plan, 1951–1961* (Ottawa: Queen's Printer, 1961).

FIGURE 6.8 Vietnamese stamps commemorating the hosting of the 1957 Consultative Committee meeting in Saigon.
Source: Vietnamese postage stamps in public domain.

photographs, films and displays were the standard items, and the Colombo Plan crest was a defining feature of many representations. Postage stamps depicting scenes of development had already been struck by Vietnamese and Indonesian host meetings of Consultative Committee Meetings, in 1957 (Figure 6.8) and 1959, respectively, and they became a feature of the 1961 celebrations.

For the anniversary year of 1961 Australia, Canada, the Philippines and the Consultative Committee host nation, Malaya, produced commemorative postage stamps (Australian stamp, Figure 6.9). Despite their tiny size, these stamps invited attention to members' commitments and involvement in changes underway in Asia growing from the Colombo Plan. They projected the state both internally and overseas. The Colombo Plan stamps conveyed faith in modernization and the intermingling of nationalism with a new internationalism that was characteristic within the Commonwealth and among newly independent nation-states in the middle of the century.[49] Canada's version featured two figures holding a project blueprint in front of a massive hydroelectric project. One figure wore Western clothes and the other was turbaned, depicting a South Asian man. The Canadian government printed 30 million for sale in post offices from 28 June 1961, the eve of the tenth anniversary.[50] First-day

[49] See for the political representational and semiotic value of stamps, D. Altman, *Paper Ambassadors: The Politics of Stamps* (Sydney: Angus & Robertson, 1991); Yehil Limor and Ilan Tamir, 'The Neglected Medium: Postage Stamps as Mass Media', *Communication Theory*, 31 (2021), 491–505; Jack Child, *Miniature Messages: The Semiotic and Politics of Latin American Postage Stamps* (Durham, NC: Duke University Press, 2008); Michael Mahoney, '"One of the Best Advertising Mediums the Country Can Have." Postage Stamps and National Identity in Canada, New Zealand and Australia', *Material Culture Review*, 77–78 (2013), 21–38.

[50] *Colombo Plan Newsletter*, 6, 4, 1961, p. 1, RCS, CUL.

FIGURE 6.9 Australian stamp commemorating tenth anniversary of Colombo Plan, 1961.
Source: Photograph in author's possession.

covers depicted several extra scenes, including one celebrating a decade of the Colombo Plan with scenes of 'Canadians in Asia', and another showing an appreciative South Asian man, again turbaned, looking out over some building blocks depicting agricultural, transport and industrial progress (Figure 6.10).

The Philippines produced five-cent and six-cent versions, all depicting a human helping hand bearing the Colombo Plan crest, with the region of Southeast Asia (to the near exclusion of India, Pakistan and Ceylon) in the background. Envelopes bearing first-day issues added images ranging from a strong worker bearing a Colombo Plan box of aid to a more explicit message honouring the Colombo Plan and, in another, a contrast between village thatch huts and modern agricultural machinery (Figure 6.11).

There were also ceremonies in most member countries, new commemorative booklets, photo exhibitions, films/TV programmes and a dinner in London featuring the Duke of Edinburgh as guest speaker.

FIGURE 6.10 Canadian stamps commemorating tenth anniversary of the Colombo Plan, 1961.
Source: Canadian postage stamps in public domain.

These publicity efforts, with their occasional effusive allusions to the impact of foreign aid in Asia, shaped how the Colombo Plan would be remembered. Through the 1960s, Colombo Plan Day, 1 July, marking when the plan officially commenced in 1951, was a low-key anniversary event in the foreign ministries of Britain, Australia, Canada and New Zealand, prompting at least a speech or short news article.[51] Cumulatively, such activities and paraphernalia built a contemporary official history and reinscribed an overarching sense of community and common purpose in a Colombo Plan that was always simultaneously being invoked with grandeur, while its operations were accounted more modestly.

[51] For example, see speeches by Canadian and Australian ministers on 1 July 1965, *Colombo Plan Newsletter*, 10, 7, July 1965, p. 2.

FIGURE 6.11 Philippines stamps commemorating the tenth anniversary of the Colombo Plan, 1961.
Source: Philippines postage stamps in public domain.

STORIES OF SEEDS AND FRUIT

The Cold War battle for hearts and minds in Asia recurred in decisions around information campaigns. After the Viet Minh's victory over the French in Indochina in 1954, Western governments redoubled their efforts to inspire and enlighten those parts of Asia deemed vulnerable to communist influence through propaganda measures. Russian books, cheaply produced and widely distributed throughout Asia in the mid-1950s, added to the urgency of the task. The new organization SEATO aimed at countering communist propaganda as well as providing a security treaty. Australian aid efforts inflected by the Cold War stand out on account of Casey's fascination with public relations and propaganda, which he also brought to the Colombo Plan in the middle years of the decade. External Affairs began to work more closely with Radio Australia and a modestly expanding team of information officers with Asian-language proficiency. Australia's Colombo Plan budget included English-language broadcasts on Radio Australia and sponsoring teachers of English to train others in the region. 'English is a weapon', noted Casey in his diary in September 1955, 'that I believe we have not used enough'.[52] His sponsored publication of an Asian/Australian student magazine, *Hemisphere*, flourished, as did English teaching and broadcasts. At the same time, he approved, under Colombo Plan spending, some harder-edged training of police and security forces in Thailand and Malaya and the provision of electricity generation for radios used by the Army of the Republic of Vietnam.[53]

Australian posts were instructed to show an understanding of how tackling Asia's development challenges would be led by Asian peoples, while pointing out the dangers of communism. They were also to stress the value of voluntary cooperation on development, social welfare, defence and with the work of the United Nations. The all-Asian posts directive, from November 1955, also repeated the message that Casey began cultivating as a better alternative than talking up the benefits of enlightened colonialism, namely that Australians might acknowledge their 'relatively advanced development but at the same time indicate that we have many economic development problems in common with neighbouring Asian countries'.[54]

52 Casey Diary, 29 September 1955, CRS M1153 item 37, NAA (Melbourne repository).

53 See Christopher Waters, 'A Failure of Imagination: R.G. Casey and Australian Plans for Counter-subversion in Asia, 1954–1956', *Australian Journal of Politics and History*, 45, 3 (1999), 347–61; Errol Hodge, *Radio Wars: Truth, Propaganda and the Struggle for Radio Australia* (Melbourne: Cambridge University Press, 1995), pp. 31–79; Minute for Overseas Planning Committee, 2 February 1962, item 1 (b), 'Cheap Books', 26 January 1962, CRS A1838/287 item 2048/2 part 9, NAA.

54 External Affairs Guidance Savingram 19 to all posts, 10 November 1955, CRS A5462 item 2/4/2, NAA; 'Cold War – Outline Notes – Working Paper' (author unknown), 23 September 1955, CRS A7452 item A359, NAA; and see generally, Alan Fewster, 'Cold War, Soft Diplomacy', *Inside Story*, 14 January 2014, https://insidestory.org.au/

In addition to Bureau-led initiatives, Casey wanted a leading Australian journalist to undertake a long tour of Colombo Plan countries and report back, emphasizing the human-interest stories that would engage the Australian public and counter critics of spending. He hoped that the material generated might also be suitable for a booklet prepared for use in Asia. His department secured agreements for the syndication of reports from Colombo Plan countries in most of the Australian daily newspapers. In 1958, Casey recruited renowned war correspondent Osmar White and cameraman James Fitzpatrick to the task.[55] Following in the footsteps of Chatterjee eighteen months earlier, the two started in Pakistan in December 1958 and by the time they finished their travel six months later, they had taken in all but two of the countries (Laos and Brunei) to which Australia was providing aid. As the most extensive and arguably the most productive journalist venture with the Colombo Plan, the White–Fitzpatrick tour and its outcomes bear closer examination.

Both White and Fitzpatrick were experienced travellers but also strong-willed and did not hold back in writing to their respective bosses about the gruelling nature of the trip.[56] Fitzpatrick recounted his attempts at photography and hand-held moving picture filming amidst being 'whisked off on another bloody tiring trip some 500 miles to the north [of Bangkok] by jeeps, lorries and little planes'.[57] In addition to meeting Casey's brief, Fitzpatrick compiled film for the Colombo Plan Bureau, most likely at the urging of Chatterjee whom he met in Colombo early in the tour. White joined in this extra work. Noting the amount of improvised help he provided to make filming possible, he described the pair as 'the only two-man cinema circus extant'.[58]

cold-war-soft-diplomacy/ (accessed 20 January 2017). Casey's earlier habit of talking up the benefits of enlightened colonialism can be found in a lecture from 1952 in *Current Notes on International Affairs*, 23, 9, 1952, 477–78.

[55] Record of Conversation in Department of External Affairs, 'Visit of Journalist and Photographer to South and South East Asia', 4 November 1958, CRS A6895 item N58/134 part 1, NAA. For more details of the White/Fitzpatrick tour see, David Lowe, 'Journalists and the Stirring of Australian Public Diplomacy: The Colombo Plan towards the 1960s', *Journal of Contemporary History*, 48, 1 (2013), 183–87.

[56] Lowe, 'Journalists and the Stirring of Australian Public Diplomacy', 183–87; Fitzpatrick letter to M. Pratt, Bangkok, 9 April 1959, ibid; O. White, 'Colombo Plan Survey for Australian Press', 3 December 1958 to 1 June 1959, CRS A10302 item 1959/170 part 2, NAA.

[57] Fitzpatrick letter to M. Pratt, Bangkok, 9 April 1959, CRS A6895 item N58/134 part 1, NAA.

[58] R. K. Chatterjee letter to Kevin Murphy, ANIB, 9 March 1959, CRS A6895 item N58/134 part 2, NAA; White letter to Kevin Murphy, 27 February 1959, ibid.

White's long reports for the Australian External Affairs Department illustrated how hard it was to come to generalized conclusions about the Colombo Plan, given just how different were the experiences he had. White struggled with both bureaucratic obstructionism and the clear signs of waste and neglect connected to some aid initiatives. The sight of earth-moving machinery lying neglected in India and Pakistan were stark images that stuck with him. In these instances, he often blamed both Australian authorities, for their poor choices or poorly timed shipments of machines, and recipient officials for unnecessary delays, lax maintenance and corruption. Australia's embassies, he wrote, were usefully embarked on a broadening range of contacts with Asian officials on account of their connection with Australian-sponsored projects. But not all the diplomats were well equipped to deal with the specialist technical expertise that was needed to provide strong oversight.[59] The same diplomats tried to collect data on various programmes that might feature in White's account, but with similarly patchy outcomes. Burmese trainees who had studied nursing, agriculture, forestry, journalism and education expressed their gratitude to Australia but the seventy who had trained in mining had not been able to find work upon return and had mostly disappeared from view.[60] Chancing his arm, White ventured that, overall, at an official level, the Colombo Plan had 'done much to offset resentment of the Commonwealth's traditional policy on Asian immigration [i.e. the white Australia policy]'. But, whether measuring goodwill or opportunities for future trade, the details mattered: 'Where utilisation [of equipment] has been high (e.g. telecommunications projects) a favourable climate for future trade development has been created. Where unsuitable or defective equipment has been supplied, the Australian reputation has suffered (e.g. certain earth moving machinery, tractor tools and rail wagons supplied to India).'[61]

The reports also exposed White's lack of experience in Asia and his racial and ideological leanings. He found little goodwill flowing from the receipt of Australian aid in Indonesia and India, not coincidentally two countries of challenging proportions and diversity where he and Fitzpatrick struggled to make their way quickly. White found the attitude

59 Osmar White's summary of conclusions, 'Colombo Plan Survey for Australian Press', 3 December–1 June 1958/59, CRS B142 item 58/31, NAA.

60 R. N. Birch, First Secretary, Australian Embassy, Rangoon, to Secretary External Affairs, 23 September 1959, memo 768, CRS B142 item 58/31, NAA.

61 Osmar White's summary of conclusions, 'Colombo Plan Survey for Australian Press', 3 December–1 June 1958/59, CRS B142 item 58/31, NAA.

to foreign aid in India 'at almost all levels, to be ungracious and at times obliquely contemptuous'.[62] By contrast, he was more sanguine about goodwill generated by aid to Pakistan, the recipient of roughly one-quarter of Australia's Colombo Plan aid at the time of his visit, notwithstanding some ill-chosen equipment and his characterization of aid there as 'handing out baksheesh to keep Pakistan in the Western camp'.[63] Officers in External Affairs grew understandably nervous about what White might publish upon return. After a personal struggle with his journalistic instincts to reveal all, played out while enjoying some respite at the Galle Face Hotel in Colombo, he arrived at a compromise of remaining upbeat while reporting on problems he saw and anticipating their resolution soon. Casey bore the brunt of some of his unrestrained opinions but was also successful in encouraging him to see the longer view and to accentuate the positives.[64]

Overall, White's syndicated stories in Australian newspapers during 1959 met the brief of reporting fulsomely and positively, with Fitzpatrick's accompanying photos and human stories from the region dotted throughout. White's formula of featuring innovation in engineering or food production brought about by collaboration between donor and recipient scientists was well-suited to news stories. Where there was waste, he wrote, it was unavoidable during the early stages of what was an enormously exciting experiment.[65] His stories circulated widely in Australia, but, except for syndicated efforts in Pakistan and Burma, they

[62] White to Casey, 28 February 1959, CRS A1032 item 1959/170 part 2, NAA.

[63] Quoted in 'Message Number 1788: Colin Moodie to Casey', 24 December 1958, CRS A10302 item 1959/170, part 2, NAA.

[64] White's unpublished report for the department detailed some of his reservations and his warning that it would only be the long haul of matching the human interest significance of aid with 'a skilled, long term programme of publicity and information': O. White, 'Colombo Plan Survey for Australian Press', 3 December 1958 to 1 June 1959, CRS A10302 item 1959/170 part 2, NAA; O. White, 'Colombo Survey for Australian Press' (undated, 1959), CRS B142 item 58/31. To a colleague in the Australian News and Information Bureau White vented his frustrations in semi-jocular Kiplingesque language of his 'white man's burden' tour but concluded, 'CP [Colombo Plan] and other aid is about the only effective weapon our mob has against the Comms in the Mysterious East ...' White's letter to Kevin Murphy (ANIB), 27 February 1959, CRS A6895 item N58/134 part 2, NAA.

[65] For examples, see, White, 'Daring Bombay Plan Hits Jackpot' about milk production, *Beverley Times* (Western Australia), 9 April 1959, p. 1; White, 'Colombo Waste Unavoidable', *Melbourne Herald*, 16 September 1959.

were not picked up in recipient countries.[66] The planned booklet was *The Seed of Freedom*, published in 1961, featuring eighty-one photographs in forty-eight pages. The distribution of 50,000 copies to leaders and organizations around Australia bore signs of Casey's thoroughness in shaping public opinion. Trade unions, junior and high schools, banks, churches, state parliaments and mayors were deluged with copies. Within the region, the English-language friendly countries of Malaya, Singapore and Britain's Borneo Territories took 20,000 copies.[67] It is hard to gauge the impact of this latter regional batch but the Australian-focused booklets did much to convince Australians of their noble efforts in Asia, and that any Asian student seen in Australia must surely be Colombo Plan sponsored (whereas, by 1961, 3,500 Colombo Plan students were dwarfed by more than 10,000 private students having studied in Australia).[68]

The Seed of Freedom surveyed projects in recipient nations with a breathlessness matching the pace of White and Fitzpatrick's trip. The framing of the stories was carefully put by White in the opening pages. He decried both the old form of exploitative internationalism linked to imperial rule in Asia and the new form of communist internationalism, abolishing all freedom of choice. He found hope in a new version, connecting international organization to development:

> The post-war world, in which man himself emerged as the greatest threat to his own species, presented a new challenge. But different peoples, in their different ways, struggled, and still struggle, to meet that challenge.
>
> The older and more technologically advanced nations are groping their way towards reorganization on an international scale. The newer, less technologically advanced nations are searching for the best way to establish their independent political regimes on a sound economic basis.
>
> The heartening thing, amidst all the war-caused waste of life and energy, was the emergence of a new concept of internationalism, based on practical rather than utopian considerations. The Colombo Plan is one example of this new thinking.[69]

[66] Kevin Murphy, ANIB, report on the Second Colombo Plan Conference of National Information Officers, for Secretary Department of External Affairs, 9 September 1960, CRS A6895 item N60/29, NAA.

[67] G. N. Upton (DEA) to Kevin Murphy (ANIB), 13 March 1961, CRS A6895 item N58/164, NAA; Upton to Murphy, 15 March 1961, ibid.

[68] Lyndon Megarrity, 'Regional Goodwill, Sensibly Priced: Commonwealth Policies towards Colombo Plan Scholars and Private Overseas Students, 1945–72', *Australian Historical Studies*, 129 (2007), 88–105.

[69] Osmar White (with photographs by James Fitzpatrick), *The Seed of Freedom*, p. 6.

White's text contained frequent references to the agency of Asian peoples working for their betterment as well as pointing to their urgent needs. Women made up nearly half the workforce of those building a dam across the Krishna River, southeast of Hyderabad in India. The Australian government had contributed £50,000, in the form of an excavator and earth-moving equipment to the dam building at Nagarjuna Sagar, but much of the labour was still undertaken by hand. Nehru laid the foundation stone for the dam in December 1955, making it the first of his huge 'modern temples'. While this ceremony did not feature in White's account, the journalist noted that the dam-building was part of India's second Five-Year Plan, recently concluded: '... of £6,000 million spent on development during that time, £3,000 million came from taxation and loans, and £1,218 million from external aid, including the Colombo Plan'.[70] Thus, Australian efforts, India's overarching agency and ownership, and a vague and somewhat inflated sense of the Colombo Plan's role all ran together.

This was the kind of formula that worked throughout the booklet. Most of Australia's Colombo Plan spending to date had gone to India and Pakistan, so these countries logically loomed large. Given that much of this aid consisted of counterpart funding in the form of wheat and flour, it made good sense that food and development remained closely connected. There were niche public health projects such as tuberculosis clinics for Ceylon and rehabilitation equipment for Indonesia,[71] but Australian expertise was especially celebrated for its land-taming by engineers and its space-conquering developments in radio, transport and other forms of communication. Iconic projects led by other donor nations occasionally appeared, such as Canada's sponsorship of the Warsak Dam in Pakistan. The Warsak project was even more attractive for its proximity to the Khyber Pass, well known in Australia in tales of imperial derring-do.[72] The other important ingredient, common to much publicity, was the human face of students and trainee stories. In *The Seed of Freedom*, White reminded readers that developmental expertise also flowed from Asia to donor nations: 'Many brilliant young men and women have liberally repaid any debt they may have incurred as our Colombo Plan guests.' His three examples were: two Filipinos, one working on soil and

[70] Ibid, pp. 11–12. [71] Ibid, pp. 23, 26.

[72] Proximity to the Khyber Pass enabled White to write of the involvement of martial Pathans, better known for their fearsome abilities as 'fighters and raiders', Ibid, pp. 14–16.

pasture fertility and the other, Nestor D'Cruz already a cause celebré through work on pig husbandry; and a Pakistan researcher of wheat specialization.[73]

By the middle of the decade, there were advanced conversations occurring among British officials about the best form and content of films, that were increasingly in the vanguard of anti-communist and pro-British propaganda efforts.[74] The first two films about the Colombo Plan were Japanese and Indian composites, drawing on material gathered by the Colombo Plan Information Unit and footage provided by members. The first, *New Horizons*, was produced by Chatterjee and his colleagues in the Government of India Films Division during 1957–58 and released in 1959; and the Japanese-led *Skilled Hands* followed in the same year.[75] By 1962, eleven members had added their own films 'on Colombo Plan themes' including newsreels. Those most directly addressing the Colombo Plan were:

Australia – *Across the Frontier; Asian Students in Australia; Australia, Friend and Neighbour; The Builders*

Britain – *Colombo Plan Stories of the First Ten Years; Training of Engineers and Key Operators in Britain for India's Durgapur Steel Project;* and *Colour Cartoons on the Colombo Plan* (English and Sinhalese)

Canada – *Hands Across the Sky; Getting together with Overseas Friends; Colombo Plan Truck Shipment; Ten Years from Colombo* (English and French)

Ceylon – Various government film newsreels

Federation of Malaya – *Ulu Langat Water Supply; Presentation of Diesel Railways; Faculty of Agriculture, University of Malaya* (English, Malay and Chinese)

Indonesia – Two newsreels on various Colombo Plan activities; *Consultative Committee Meeting in Jogjakarta*

[73] Ibid, p. 41.

[74] R. H. Scott, Letter and Reports on the Conference of Information Officers from South-East Asia, 6 to 8 November 1956, 18 December 1956, FCO 141/14841, TNA. And see, more generally, Aitken, 'British Governmental Institutions, the Regional Office in Singapore'; and Tom Rice, '*Merdeka for Malaya*: Imagining Independence across the British Empire', in Ian Aitken and Camille Deprez (eds.), *The Colonial Documentary Film in South and South-East Asia* (Edinburgh: Edinburgh University Press, 2017), pp. 45–62.

[75] CP (IWP) (59) 1, Colombo Plan Publicity: COI Output July 1958–December 1958, 30 January 1959, DO 35/5757, TNA.

Japan – *Hope for Tomorrow*; *Asia Marches On; Planning for Prosperity*
New Zealand – *South-East Asia Is Our Neighbour*; *New Zealand Colombo Plan Aid Projects*
Philippines – One newsreel, *Colombo Plan and You*
United States – *Forging Ahead* (Ceylon); *Planning for Plenty* (India); *River Valley Projects* (India)
Vietnam – *Consultative Committee Meeting in Saigon*[76]

The Australians joined in the rush to make films, embracing the era of developmentalism in documentary film-making.[77] Australian films produced in the 1950s and early 1960s covered both the infrastructure and training work taking place in donor countries and the experiences of sponsored students in idealized Australian settings. Of the former, *The Builders*, a thirty-minute film released in 1959 was the best promoted and distributed. *The Builders* was the bonus product of the White–Fitzpatrick odyssey of 1958–59. In lugging around his film camera, Fitzpatrick initially had only short clips in mind. The meeting with Chatterjee at the Colombo Plan Bureau helped the idea of more expansive filming take wings, and he returned with thousands of hours of footage. He then secured funds for a commentary and a musical score by the Sydney Symphonic Orchestra and *The Builders*, released towards the end of 1959, was the result.[78]

Not surprisingly, *The Builders* showcased many of the same stories and accompanying narrative that featured in *The Seed of Freedom*. A new sense of interconnectedness made possible by air travel required viewers to appreciate that Asian and Australian destinies were entwined. In addition to dam-building and earth-moving, the Australians were helping, in a manner that punched above their weight, to chip away at the constant gnawing of hunger in over-populous Asia by generating more food. 'It is to achieve this', said the narrator, 'that the "noisy little Australian pumps and engines are chugging away on the banks of Asian rivers" – for by grafting modern techniques on to the traditional pattern of Asian farming, numberless families can be assured of full rice bowls – tomorrow.' The narration ended on a strong note of Cold War modernity:

[76] S. Matsui, Report on Colombo Plan Information Activities during 1962/63 and the Programme for 1963/64, 19 September 1963, FO 371/169957, TNA.
[77] Smaill, 'Promoting Australia', pp. 619–26.
[78] Transcript of interview with James Fitzpatrick by David Lowe, Sydney, 24 September 2003.

> So the people of South, and of South-East Asia, are climbing out of the valley. Out of the valley of the past into a future of their own building …
>
> A building in which we, their friends and neighbours, are playing a part.
>
> This future has its roots and foundations in freedom … Freedom to worship, each after his own fashion; to give praise and thanks for the gift of life in a world of widening horizons.[79]

Australian schools were again beneficiaries of this new way of learning about the Colombo Plan. The Australians were also successful in syndicating its distribution overseas. It showed in fifteen European countries and shorter extracts screened in Britain, Japan, France, the Netherlands, Switzerland, the United States and Mexico.[80] Most of the Plan's member nations received copies, with the invitation to dub local language, though it was not embraced by the Australian High Commission in New Delhi, on the grounds that there was virtually no footage of India, in contrast to generous coverage of Pakistan.[81] As with all of the Colombo Plan films produced, it is hard to find evidence of its reception. It was likely that the broad survey approach made it more appealing to Australians than Asian viewers. A rare New Zealand analysis of its own compilation film, *New Zealand Colombo Plan Aid Projects*, suggested that the sweeping format did not land well in Asia. The verdict was that it 'attempted to cover activities in a number of Asian Colombo Plan countries and consequently succeeded in pleasing none of them'.[82] *The Builders* was likely to have enjoyed similar reception in recipient countries, while landing more solidly at home. In the bigger picture of Australia's relations with Asia, it helped shift Australian opinion towards greater interest and openness towards regional neighbours.[83]

DECLINE

As noted, after 1962, it became harder to argue that the Colombo Plan was in the driving seat of developmental innovation and activity. Similarly, the reach of the story-makers in their pamphlets, photographs,

79 Text of *The Builders*, 1959, in CRS A6895 item N58/165 part 2, NAA.

80 Undated notes (1960) prepared by ANIB officers for the 1960 Colombo Plan Conference of National Information Officers, CRS A6895 item N60/29, NAA.

81 John Murray (ANIB) to Lionel Wigmore, Australian High Commission, New Delhi, 14 September 1960, CRS A6895 item N58/165 part 2, NAA.

82 New Zealand Department of External Affairs, Briefing Paper, 'Four Power Conference in Information Activities in South East Asia and Oceania', Canberra, October 1966, 30 September 1966, EA1 W2824 item 118/7/17/1, ANZ.

83 See Oakman, *Facing Asia*, passim.

newspaper features and films peaked in the early 1960s after which the Colombo Plan's claims to distinctiveness and productive informality began to date quickly.[84] Other initiatives and modes of development storytelling began to take over. The UN General Assembly rhetorically seized the mantle of development with its resolution in December 1961 that the 1960s would be the 'decade of development' and called on economically advanced states to adopt trade and investment policies that would enable developing countries to accelerate their economic growth and self-sufficiency. The General Assembly resolved that the developing countries should have an annual growth rate of 5 per cent in aggregate national income by the end of the decade.[85]

Less than three years later, from 23 March to 16 June 1964, the UN also hosted the first Conference on Trade and Development (UNCTAD) in Geneva. This new forum on connections between trade and development developed into a regular North–South dialogue, meeting every four years. It became a logical focal point for the many governments, including Colombo Plan members, focused on the nexus between development and trade conditions. At the same time, the means by which development assistance would be promoted, measured and monitored were standardized. Anticipating the formation of the OECD on 30 September 1961, a Development Assistance Committee took shape during 1960–61. The DAC began annual reviews and reporting of each member's development assistance in 1962 and established a Working Party on UNCTAD issues after the first UNCTAD meeting in 1964. By this time, the DAC membership included Colombo Plan members – the United States, Britain, Japan and Canada. Australia joined in 1966 and New Zealand in 1973.[86] Financing development in the region also gained a new impetus and focus. In December 1966, the persistence of Japan's leaders was rewarded with the formation of the Asian Development Bank in Manila, under Japanese leadership, to promote regional finance and development.

[84] In addition to output as measured from Colombo and member governments, another indicator of this late 1950s to early 1960s peak is stories in regional newspapers. Those Singapore newspapers electronically searchable for the frequency of 'Colombo Plan', such as *The Straits Times*, *New Nation* and *Singapore Free Press*, show a peak of 399 hits for 1961 (and 304 for 1959, 325 for 1960), falling to below 300 thereafter: Singapore National Library newspaper database: https://eresources.nlb.gov.sg/newspapers/ (accessed 20 December 2020).

[85] Unger, *International Development*, p. 100.

[86] DAC Directorate, OECD, *DAC in Dates: The History of the OECD's Development Assistance Committee* (Paris: OECD Publications, 2006).

Coinciding with these developments, the membership of the Colombo Plan's Consultative Committee broadened in ways that disturbed the accepted modes of behaviour and stretched the meaning of region. The Koreans forced their membership in 1962, against the wishes of Indonesians and Ceylonese. The Bhutanese did similarly, albeit in a unique style. Although delegates of Indonesia and Ceylon abstained from voting on Korea rather than continue to voice concerns, this broke the norm of unanimity. It was the first time a vote on membership had been taken, previous new members having been agreed unanimously prior to the annual conference. Challenged, the Consultative Committee drew on its capacity for self-regulation and healing. Was it the case now that the unofficial unanimity rule needed to be considered, asked one member? There was no need to answer this question was the consensus: 'we did not wish to start laying down rules for an international gathering which had hitherto been successful largely because it had no rules of procedure'.[87] But the Korean coup posed uncomfortable questions over the definition of the Colombo Plan region. Clearly, members had different senses of the region shaped by history, geography and commitments, and there was a collective reluctance to open this can of worms, but nor was it for donor countries to oppose such discussion.[88] Afghanistan's membership in 1963 and Iran's in 1966 confirmed that the more bounded sense provided by neatly drawn maps of members of the 1950s was no longer holding. At the same time, the Commonwealth's splintering on the issue of race made it less able to lend indirect diplomatic cachet to the workings of the plan.

From the second half of the 1960s, even those donor governments that had leveraged their international reputations through Colombo Plan contributions had to acknowledge its slip in status. In addition to the above-mentioned changes, this was partly due to noises from within. Whereas for most of the long 1950s foreign/external affairs bureaucracies in donor countries had managed the provision of foreign aid, by 1964, there were separate foreign aid departments in the United States, Canada,

[87] A. H. P. Humphrey, UK Department of Technical Co-Operation, to Sir Algernon Rumbold, CRO, 19 December 1961, DO 189/327, TNA; Peter Jenkins, UK High Commission, Kuala Lumpur, to Leslie Heptinstall, CRO, 23 November 1961, DO 189/327. TNA.

[88] J. M. Dutton, UK High Commission, Canberra, to Leslie Heptinstall, CRO, 19 September 1961, DO 189/308, TNA; UK High Commission, Wellington, to CRO, no. 469, 25 October 1961, ibid; L. B. Walsh Atkins, CRO, to E. N. Larmour, UK High Commission, Canberra, 4 October 1962, ibid.

Japan and Britain. These new aid agencies bristled at the information successes of the Colombo Plan with its brand-stamped machinery, photo-shoots, magazine stories and so on. They grew quickly tired of an umbrella organization like the Colombo Plan claiming the credit and sometimes diluting the stories of bilateral aid. The same trend extended to other donor nations where aid remained in the remit of External Affairs but was now becoming more specialized. New Zealand diplomat John Ryan recalled that in the late 1960s all the files in New Zealand's External Aid Division were re-labelled from 'Colombo Plan' to 'Bilateral Aid Programme'.[89]

In the context of such changes, member governments remained committed to the Colombo Plan meetings, but without their earlier conviction (at least for some) that the Colombo Plan would remain an encompassing rationale for their foreign aid giving/receiving. The international reputation building accruing from hosting a meeting of the Consultative Committee grew less important over time, as other opportunities for diplomatic standing appeared. It was a steady slide in the Colombo Plan's reputation rather than a sudden dive, made more constant by the lack of vigorous rear-guard defensive efforts from any member. One factor that had initially worked to members' satisfaction but then left a reputational gap when advocacy might have been welcome was the US approach. Even when the Americans had warmed to the Colombo Plan and saw it as possible vehicle for new policies for Asia in the mid-1950s, the Bureau of Public Affairs in the State Department was careful not to promote it strongly. To do so would have been to dominate all other donors, given the magnitude of US assistance for Asian members, and to risk politicization in ways that were unwelcome. Instead, the US Information Agency provided a very modest supply of aid stories to the Colombo Plan Bureau. There was also the domestic US public to consider, and the importance of the Mutual Security Program, under which most US aid was justified, often in anti-communist terms.[90]

What were some of the essential characteristics that made the Colombo Plan loom significantly in international and regional relations during the long 1950s but less so thereafter? One was the extent to which it opened meeting spaces, both literal and metaphorical, for diplomatic exchanges

[89] New Zealand Official Development Assistance, *The Colombo Plan at 50*, p. 11.

[90] US State Department Position paper, 'Colombo Plan Consultative Committee, Officials Meeting, October 31–November 12, 1960, Ministerial Meeting, November 14–17, 1960', 24 October 1960, RG 59 Lot File 64D207, box 3, USNA.

among a particular group of countries invested in the future of decolonizing Asia. Within this diverse group from North America, Britain, Asia and Oceania, there was a common faith among the elites in a modernist assumption that technological progress was the basis of development. As historian of India Gyan Prakash has observed, science, nation-making and imagination worked together metaphorically across North–South lines as well as in development projects.[91] Some developmentalist diplomats stood out for their activism aimed at regional leadership. Newcomers to the Consultative Committee meetings in the late 1950s and early 1960s were struck by the high regard in which Indian delegates were held by other regional representatives.[92]

Indian and other representatives such as New Zealand's Walter Nash and Burma's U Raschid were able to gain attention partly on account of the long meetings and high civility attached to them, but also because members relied on these meetings – especially in the 1950s when most of the members, donor and recipient alike, were still building up their diplomatic representation in Asian capitals. New Zealand's diplomatic representation in Indonesia began in 1957 with a Colombo Plan mission, before building to Consulate-General status in 1961.

For the most part, the Commonwealth was a model and source of strength, its diplomatic procedures and practices laying the basis for a consensual mode of diplomacy within the broader Colombo Plan family. But it never quite threw off the taint of inner and outer family circles which, to some extent, carried through to the Plan. Even in 1960, the British were aware that their preferencing Commonwealth members for capital assistance caused disappointment among others, such as the Thais.[93] At the time, the simmering sense of division between old and new Commonwealth was about to reach a climax over South African apartheid. In 1961, when South Africa's withdrawal dealt the Commonwealth

91 Gyan Prakash, *Another Reason: Science and the Imagination of Modern India* (Princeton, NJ: Princeton University Press, 1999). This is also a central argument of Jill Campbell-Miller in relation to Canadian foreign aid for India, but it applies more generally: Campbell-Miller, 'Encounter and Apprenticeship', p. 46.

92 Peter Jenkins, UK High Commission, Kuala Lumpur, to Leslie Heptinstall, CRO, 23 November 1961, DO 189/327, TNA.

93 'If we fail to provide a convincing token of our interest in these friendly non-Commonwealth countries', wrote Lord Lansdowne, 'I think that not only will our own influence and standing in the Colombo Plan area decline, but we shall run the risk of seeing the Colombo Plan split up into Commonwealth versus the rest': Lord Lansdowne's Report on the 12th Session of the Consultative Committee of the Colombo Plan held at Tokyo during November 1960, 13 December 1960, DO 198/12, TNA.

a heavy blow, this reverberated and drew further diplomatic attention to Africa. The fortunes of the Colombo Plan and the Commonwealth remained loosely intertwined.

The meetings of the Consultative Committee were structured, with evaluation, planning and revising of country reports and a version of 'the task ahead' being drafted by officials before ministerial meetings commenced. They were also renowned for their length and no matter how often attendees suggested ways in which to reduce them – the plea for shorter ministerial speeches being one of the most repeated and least successful – they remained drawn-out affairs. As there was no secretariat and as the composition of working groups examining the annual reports adjusted for rotations among members each year, there was no continuous oversight by the same experts possible. The Colombo-based Council was charged with managing technical cooperation activities only, and the Bureau initially likewise, but it expanded its reach to provide information on all aspects of the plan. As the Council relied for its membership on local diplomats, those without diplomatic representation in Ceylon (e.g. New Zealand) missed out. Thus, for several reasons, the annual meeting of the Consultative Committee was where much of the aid work was done.

These meetings were also vital as demonstrations of international standing for host nations. Governments of newly independent nations such as Ceylon, India, Pakistan, Indonesia and South Vietnam took the opportunity to demonstrate their hospitable internationalism, but so too did governments of smaller donor nations such as Australia and New Zealand, the latter rising to host what was arguably the most elaborate meeting of the Consultative Committee in 1956.

The annual meetings enabled productive airings of regional policy, providing opportunities for ambitious politicians with new ideas about economic and political coordination to test them out. ECAFE remained a valued stalking horse for the Colombo Plan in this regard, its Indian leaders in particular pressing for ways to elevate the sense of a regional collective while building up economic and statistical expertise that increasingly found its way into Consultative Committee meetings. Members watched ECAFE's occasional forays towards regional behaviour and its preparedness to wage campaigns against the West over commodity price instability. They also welcomed its increasingly robust reporting capabilities. When conversation on regionalism tested the strict politeness boundaries of the Consultative Committee, it could be referred back to the more rambunctious realms of ECAFE meetings and watched again with interest. ECAFE has attracted some historical attention, noting that it too underwent reevaluation and transformation in the 1970s. It was enlarged geographically and socially from 1976 into the Economic and Social Commission for Asia and the Pacific (ESCAP). Recently, it was, with the four other UN regional commissions, the focus of an edited book in a UN Intellectual History Project.[94] In his introduction, editor Yves Berthelot bounced off Lokanathan's claim of 1954 that ECAFE was 'the Economic Parliament of Asia' and argued it provided what he calls 'a profound sense of the necessary unity of the region' prior to ECAFE's transformation and loss of intellectual drive with its transformation into ESCAP.[95]

The Colombo Plan took shape in a region navigating tensions between East and West. The Cold War was a constant factor, both in the donor motivations behind the Colombo Plan and the nature of aid provided. The competition between East and West enabled recipients to play off Russians against the West in funding for grand development projects, and gave regional bureaucrats different angles to work with their governments. Some of the influential agents among donors were more Cold War-minded than others. In 1957, at the end of his four-month tour of the Colombo Plan region, Cavell seethed at having had to trail in the wake of what he called 'a triumphal tour' by Chinese Premier Chou En-lai. 'The West', he wrote, 'has a long way to go to catch up'.[96] The Cold War competition mattered more to Cavell than some others, but it was always close to the surface, even as members prided themselves at how effectively they worked around it.

The information professionals driving the Information Unit in Colombo were led by Indians such as Chatterjee and Sharma who had cut their teeth in Nehru's new republic, where information was harnessed to the task of state-making and modernization. They brought with them

[94] Yves Berthelot (ed.), *Unity and Diversity in Development Ideas: Perspectives from the UN Regional Commissions* (Bloomington: Indiana University Press, 2004).

[95] Ibid, p. 5.

[96] 'We were several times at the same places where My Chou En-lai was making his triumphal tours with the pomp and ceremony of many motorcycle escorting police, decorated streets, vast audiences and a travelling circus consisting of Chinese entertainers of various kinds. Everywhere, it seemed to us, his entourage was impressive and the method of his approach and propaganda very clever.' Nik Cavell, 'Report on Colombo Plan Consultative Committee Meeting no. 5 held in Wellington, New Zealand, November 19 to December 8, 1956' and 'Visits to South and South East Asian Countries by Mr Nik Cavell, Colombo Plan Administrator in Canada and Mr Rodney Grey of the Department of External Affairs', 15 May 1957, RG 25 vol. 7359 11038-5-B-40 part 2 fp 3.2, LAC.

their zeal for connecting the great project of development to villages. The information experts helped enable a broad-based appreciation of the Colombo Plan's unusual qualities. Through their efforts, the Colombo Plan gestured towards ideals of regional cooperation within a broader internationalism in ways that continued to attract its regional members even as they were clear-eyed about its practical limitations. State-making was such a high priority for regional members that region-making often came second, even as it retained its appeal.

One of the reasons for the Colombo Plan's embrace during the long 1950s and its persistence in popular remembering in more recent decades was, and still is, this shape-shifting quality. Greater than the sum of its component parts when needed for publicity and promotional reasons, it could also dissemble easily into discrete bilateral relationships or forms of aid such as iconic projects or the flows of sponsored students. As critiques of foreign aid programmes accumulated from the mid-1960s onwards, its benign character and fading significance spared it from becoming the subject of the sharpest attacks. Perhaps the person who best anticipated this was Nehru, who is remembered for so much other than his role in the early meetings that established the Colombo Plan. At the conclusion of that very first meeting in Colombo in January 1950, Nehru reflected that those gathered were never likely to have solved the world's problems, and the world indeed faced serious problems. But it was significant to have looked at them without fear, maintaining tempers and with a view to adapting to some of them. To expect too much from such conferences, said Nehru, was wrong, but nor should they be belittled:

> These conferences perform a useful function. They help us to keep together, to keep on the right path, to tone each other down a little perhaps in our attitudes, which may tend to incline in one direction or another and thus, at least, to set an example of peaceful discussion, thought and co-operation between people who do not and need not think alike or even act alike occasionally.[97]

The small cast of development internationalists he spoke to then grew in number over the next twelve years and beyond. They joined in new ways of peaceful deliberation and attempted cooperation, including state-making in an age of internationalism and a formative sense of region, made more achievable through foreign aid.

[97] Proceedings of the public session held in the Senate Chamber on 14 January 1950, Colombo, CRS A10617 1950/1, NAA.

Coda

Partial Remembering

The Colombo Plan lives on in ways that partly celebrate but also obscure some of its diplomatic efforts in development internationalism during the long 1950s. It grew two identities – the early pioneering experiment that has been the focus of this book and the less glorious thereafter. Both identities attracted supporters, sometimes in connected ways, the earlier pioneering status proving useful later to those seeking to maintain the Colombo Plan in revived form. It became and remains a site of memory, especially attractive as a historical project capable of being wielded for political purposes.[1] We therefore need to make something of a gear shift to appreciate what has happened to the Colombo Plan in its remembering. This is especially necessary in order to appreciate why it is primarily remembered in narrow and partial ways: either as little more than a curious lesser tier foreign aid venture or an early hit-out in soft power diplomacy especially focused on international students; and in either case, generally assumed to feature only a handful of member nations. In its partial remembering, however, both versions of the Colombo Plan,

[1] The remembering is partly what memory scholars describe as *shared* memory: certain groups remembering the same event, where that event might be an educational or training experience, or perhaps the construction of a dam. To some extent, the remembering is also *common*, wherein unrelated groups share in remembering cognate experiences, such as milestone moments in the Colombo Plan and those building, farming and educational legacies that remain relatable today. These concepts were developed in T. G. Ashplant, Graham Dawson, and Michael Roper, 'The Politics of War Memory and Commemoration: Contexts, Structures and Dynamics', in T. G. Ashplant, Graham Dawson, and Michael Ropers (eds.), *The Politics of War Memory and Commemoration* (Abingdon: Routledge, 2000), pp. 18–19.

original and revived, continue to convey stories of development internationalism.

Like the histories of other development plans, the Colombo Plan story needs to incorporate the politics of memory through which projects and practices are retrospectively given meaning.[2] Much of its remembering sits at the intersection of *communicative* and *cultural* memory, where communicative memory depends on the actions of those participants and observers of a particular time/episode, and cultural memory prevails after that generation has died. Cultural memory depends on the energies of those working with texts, pictures, oral accounts, relics, statues and other forms of evidence from that era. The two forms of remembering can be contested, and they intermix from the outset, even before the generation of participants and observers is gone. Given the longevity of the Colombo Plan, and its continuation today in lesser form, the communicative and cultural aspects of its remembering continue to jostle. As this study focuses on the long 1950s, the communicative dimension, dependent on those alive at that time, is rapidly weakening. Cultural remembering, the remembering of what is left from this period, increasingly carries the heavier load. It lies behind most of what we might call 'working memory', a term suggested by literary scholar of memory, Ann Rigny: remembering that 'is continuously performed by individuals and groups as they recollect the past selectively through various media and become involved in various forms of memorial activity'.[3]

As we have seen, the information activities connected to the Colombo Plan built a memory-making legacy. Efforts to remember it continued to be led by the industrious members of the Bureau even as its lustre began to fade. Official publications from the mid-1960s increasingly invoked the 1950s as the glory days of pioneering efforts.[4] Advocates strained to bolster its ongoing value and legacy, British Prime Minister Harold

[2] Cullather, *The Hungry World*, p. 9. I suggest that practices are important, in addition to projects, which, depending on how they are defined, risk missing the diplomacy of development internationalism.

[3] Ann Rigny, 'Plenitude, Scarcity and the Circulation of Cultural Memory', *Journal of European Studies*, 35, 1 (2005), 17; and for further historiographical discussion see, Carola Lentz and David Lowe, *Remembering Independence* (Abingdon: Routledge, 2018), pp. 13–39; and David Lowe and Tony Joel, *Remembering the Cold War: Global Contest and National Stories* (Abingdon: Routledge, 2013), pp. 1–22.

[4] For example, the *Colombo Plan Newsletter* of December 1963 carries a story by Stanley Mayes, headed, 'The Colombo Plan Pioneers the Way', which began with the story of the six Ceylonese dental nurses sponsored to train in New Zealand: *Colombo Plan Newsletter*, 8, 12, December 1963, p. 8, RCS, CUL.

Wilson even claiming in November 1964 that it closely resembled, in structure and intent, the Marshall Plan.[5] Thereafter, the Bureau's *Newsletters* struggled to identify points of distinctiveness beyond student/training stories. They became caught between recalling pioneer status and struggling to maintain relevance, between wanting to celebrate the legacies of earlier work and a need to engage with all aspects of the huge international enterprise that was unfolding in the 1960s under the heading of development. The final issues of the Colombo Plan's now glossy and colour news magazine in 1969 illustrated the 'worn out' feeling of the organization. Even the ingenuity of information officers in Colombo had its limits, and relying on hard-pressed media liaison officers in member countries was a recipe for repetition and patchiness over time.

Some ventures proved successful and enduring in a manner that were news-worthy. In 1969, the magazine revisited New Zealand's sponsoring of the Delhi Milk Scheme ten years earlier, for example, updating the story to highlight its impact (and we can note that the Delhi Milk Scheme, headquartered in West Patel, Nagar, New Delhi, continues to provide milk and other products today).[6] Donor country updates arrived in different forms. Tellingly, the US profile continued to take the form of a loosely applied Colombo Plan filter over the vast US development-related aid for Asia. This was implausible grandeur by semantics, phrases such as 'Colombo Plan countries' and the 'Colombo Plan region' signifying the hazy sorting by which massive aid figures were arrived at.[7]

The last issue of the magazine for 1969 contained familiar stories of training. New Zealand aerial spraying techniques that might be used in Thailand, profiles of Filipino and Indonesian students studying architecture in Britain, increased training programmes occurring within the region and so on. Editors highlighted the need to match fields of education with identified needs generated as part of the 'green revolution', the reforms in agriculture built on education in new techniques and science. Population control was the other big theme of the issue, including an article penned by Dr John Edlefson, an American population expert based

[5] *Colombo Plan Newsletter*, 9, 12, December 1964, p. 1, RCS, CUL. Wilson claimed this as he opened the sixteenth meeting of the Consultative Committee in London, November 1964.

[6] *The Colombo Plan Magazine*, 14, 3, 1969, pp. 5–6, RCS, CUL. As at February 2019, http://dms.nic.in/Home.aspx (accessed 20 February 2019). Its Colombo Plan connection and New Zealand sponsorship are not identified on this Delhi Milk Scheme webpage.

[7] *The Colombo Plan Magazine*, 14, 3, 1969, pp. 7–12, RCS, CUL. Surrounding issues departed from aid to more general news, too. The front cover and lead story of one was the appointment of Sir Paul Hasluck as Australia's new Governor-General: Ibid, pp. 1–3.

at the Colombo Plan Bureau. This was supplemented by stories of Colombo Plan meetings on this theme and sponsored educational programmes rolling out in schools of the region. Both the green revolution and population control were grand-scale issues involving UNESCO, ECAFE and other funding bodies too, as editors acknowledged. The latest dimensions of development work in South and Southeast Asia, namely scientific experimentation, planning and measuring, human resources work and even critiques, emerged largely outside of the Colombo Plan. It was with some relief that editors were able to list on page one an update from the British-sponsored IIT in New Delhi: £1.15 million had been spent by the British government to date, with some of this fostering a special relationship between the IIT and London's Imperial College of Science and Technology.[8]

It was becoming harder to disguise the cherry-picking of development stories. Anything that could be seen as having a link to earlier development work was fair game, but new and weighty subjects such as population control and environmental concerns could not be anchored in the long 1950s. The membership changes and restlessness within new foreign bureaucracies eager to narrate their own prowess made the story from Colombo less appealing. As a New Zealand retrospective later declared, 'By the 1970s . . . the Colombo Plan had lost momentum and was entering a long period in the doldrums.'[9]

AT FIFTY AND BEYOND

When the Colombo Plan turned fifty in 2001 the Koizumi government in Japan announced it would mark Japan's fiftieth anniversary of membership beginning in 1954, by designating the joining date, 6 October, as an 'International Cooperation Day'. For three months, commencing on 1 September 2004, Japanese government agencies and financial institutions joined in a celebratory programme of lectures, seminars, exhibitions and television broadcasts reflecting on fifty years of Japan's promotion of social and economic development in Asia. Coming at a time when the Japanese government was attracting criticism for its recent reductions in foreign aid, in the wake of Japan's economic downturn, the fiftieth anniversary provided an opportunity for officials and commentators to reflect on their history of foreign aid provision. Japan had led the world in

8 *The Colombo Plan Magazine* 14, 11, 1969, p. 3, and passim, RCS, CUL.

9 New Zealand Official Development Assistance, *The Colombo Plan at 50*, p. 5.

Official Development Assistance efforts during the 1980s and 1990s, but was now in second place to the United States, and the future of Tokyo's foreign aid was under greater consideration.[10] The Japanese government was, with the Koreans, to the fore in breathing new life into the flagging remnants of the Colombo Plan in the early 1990s, providing new funds for a very targeted series of training programmes which became the basis of the revived smaller operations.[11] Although recent budget cuts blunted the impact of celebrations in 2001, the broader point was important: the Colombo Plan had facilitated Japan's return to 'international cooperation' in 1954. This was recalling the language of Colombo Plan newsletters. In helping keep a diminished Colombo Plan alive in the 1990s when it was endangered, the Japanese also kept alive this foundational narrative. While not to the fore in subsequent projections of Japanese foreign aid, the Colombo Plan provided a foundational story when needed. Just as the Colombo Plan's earliest milestones and anniversaries (especially its tenth) had generated proclamations, ephemera, events and publicity, so too did its fiftieth anniversary yield opportunities for the enactment of development internationalism. Which of the other members responded to the fiftieth anniversary was instructive. The New Zealand government produced a commemorative booklet with the assistance of the revived Colombo Plan Secretariat (replacing the Bureau in Colombo at the end of 1994). Prime Minister Helen Clark celebrated New Zealanders' active role from the outset into the 1980s, especially the hosting of sponsored students and the provision of experts to members in Asia. The Colombo Plan, she wrote, 'helped create links which today we take for granted. It helped bring an awareness that New Zealanders and the people of Asia are close neighbours, and that our destinies are inevitably intertwined'.[12] Clark found it remarkable that the Colombo Plan endured beyond what was originally intended as fulfilling a short-term need in the 'turbulent' postwar era, thus adding to the chorus of those who have simultaneously admired and puzzled over of the organization's persistence. The bulk of

[10] Colombo Plan Secretariat, *The Colombo Plan for Co-operative Economic and Social Development*, p. 13; Ministry of Foreign Affairs of Japan Notice, 'The 50th Anniversary of Japan's International Cooperation', www.mofa.go.jp/policy/oda/cooperation/anniv50/seminar0411.pdf (accessed 2 November 2021); see also minutes of a seminar held as part of the commemoration at United Nations University, Tokyo, 'The 50th Anniversary of Japan's International Cooperation Symposium: The View on the Japanese ODA in the Recipient Countries', 15 November 2004, www.mofa.go.jp/policy/oda/cooperation/anniv50/seminar0411.pdf (accessed 2 November 2021).

[11] *The Colombo Plan at 50*, p. 12. [12] Ibid, p. 3.

the booklet was given to former Colombo Plan scholars reflecting on their times in New Zealand. These included Charmion Drieberg, one of the original six dental nurses from Ceylon in 1951, and Verghese Kurien, the pioneering figure in milk production in India, after his time spent at Massey University.[13]

Not surprisingly, the Australian higher education sector was active in remembering the Colombo Plan at fifty. The Malaysia–Australia Foundation produced a photography-rich commemorative booklet celebrating fifty years of Malaysian–Australian cooperation under the plan.[14] It was largely produced by an Australian alumni expert, Geoffrey Sauer, Director of Alumni Relations at Adelaide University from 1985 to 2000, during which time he developed a special interest in the history of connections between Malaysian students and the university, and with other Australian universities. Coinciding with the Colombo Plan anniversary, the turn of the century saw a flurry of international alumni initiatives from Australian universities of which this was one. The record-keeping of many organizations had been lax, and administrations realized the importance of being able to point to solid evidence of continuous connections with Asia as they sought to increase numbers of high-fee-paying international students. Several Australian vice-chancellors gathered in Kuala Lumpur at an event connected to the Malaysian alumni publishing venture. The recently formed Malaysia–Australia Foundation supported it, as did the Australian High Commission in Kuala Lumpur, where one of the most active alumni of Australian universities groups remembered the Colombo Plan as a special feature of Australian–Malaysian relations. In his foreword, Australian Minister for Education, Training and Youth Affairs, David Kemp, struck a similar tone to that of Helen Clark, recalling how Colombo Plan students educated Australians about Asia and its people, laying the basis for deeper forms of engagement. He noted also how many scholarship holders had returned to play leadership roles in their respective countries. His other observation was that students under the plan had charted a course for Australian universities: 'The Colombo Plan Scholars were pioneers in the internationalization of Australian education. From an Australian point of view, international students are now an integral part of Australian education, and our

[13] Ibid, pp. 14, 19–20.

[14] Geoffrey Sauer (ed.), *The Colombo Plan for Cooperative Economic Development in South and South East Asia 1951–2001: The Malaysian–Australian Perspective*, Malaysia–Australia Foundation (Adelaide: Openbook Print, 2001).

institutions have benefited enormously from this experience. They are more socially and academically vibrant places today, thanks in part to the presence of international students.'[15]

As a case study of how selectively the Colombo Plan is remembered, the Malaysian venture illustrated mnemonic connections between the past and present. It was a tale of many lasting friendships, of people-to-people connections forged between Australia and Malaysia. At a broader level, it demonstrated how human capital development could be harnessed to mutual benefit, whereby Malaysians trained in Australia returned to assume leadership roles in nation-building and left Australians better aware and more appreciative of their regional neighbours. Of the impressive seventy-nine interview summaries and submitted recollections, nearly one-third (twenty-five) declared that their children were sent, or would be sent, to Australia for education, and/or now lived there.[16]

A short supplementary reflection by Australian journalist Tim Bowden at the end of the book pointed to some reasons why Malaysians might be especially suited to recalling their Colombo Plan student days favourably. One was language. In 1950s and 1960s Australia, speaking good English, as most Malaysians did before arrival, was an enormous help in cultural adjustment. Another was an understanding of development and modernization shaped by the Cold War, and a benevolent appreciation of decolonization rather than revolution. Bowden had just undertaken a tour of South and Southeast Asia to interview former Colombo Plan students for a radio documentary. He recalled being in Singapore in 1960 where Prime Minister Lee Kuan Yew had heaped fulsome praise on the Colombo Plan, adding mischievously that it enabled him to send pro-communist or radically inclined students to Australia knowing that the Australian experience would convert them into comfortable members of the bourgeoisie.[17] While Bowden did not venture that this pertained also to Malayan/Malaysian students, it was the case that all students accepting a position in Australia had to provide a written guarantee that they would refrain from involvement in political activities. The anniversary moment provided fond reminiscing within a warm context of people-to-people internationalism, which was just as important in 2001, if not more

[15] Ibid, p. 3. [16] Ibid, pp. 16–94.

[17] Ibid, p. 96. Bowden added that those students who learnt English for several years, and those students who completed undergraduate degrees over three or four years were more likely to have stronger memories and more enduring connections with their host countries, pp. 97–98.

important than in the 1950s. Significantly too, as the case study of Australia–Malaya/Malaysia relations demonstrated, regional thinking and student-led internationalism continued to be shaped so that they did not endanger state building and state security.

During the 1950s and 1960s countries such as New Zealand, Canada and Australia progressively met some of the training needs of Malaysia and Singapore as the British gradually withdrew administrative and other forms of control. In facilitating some of this, the Colombo Plan provided, and continues to provide, a softening lens to the processes of decolonization. The decline of European influence in Asia appears more managed when conferred the aura of planning, and alumni groups are living evidence of planning and state-managed connectedness. A Canadian Alumni Group formed in Singapore in 1979. In 2023 it proudly featured profiles of those who returned from their sponsored study in Canada to 'serve in various government bodies contributing to the development of Singapore'.[18] The Canadian High Commissioner to Singapore was a member of the group's advisory board. In a Colombo Plan Secretariat publication, an eminent Malaysian forest researcher, Francis S. P. Ng, recalled: 'All through the 1960s, the returning Colombo Plan scholars took over professional positions from departing British officers in the technical departments dealing with public works, agriculture, forestry, utilities and so on.'[19]

Rigny's working memory involves selective recollection and remembering activity that reinvigorates and/or reshapes how something is remembered. In 2001, the recently formed Malaysian–Australian Alumni Council also initiated a special round of Malaysia–Australia Colombo Plan Commemoration (MACC) Scholarships for Malaysian citizens to study in Australia, with the support of the Australian High Commission. The MACC scholarships have been offered every year since 2001.[20] More prominently, the Australian government launched with great fanfare, in 2013, the 'New Colombo Plan' (NCP), a scheme under which Australian undergraduate students were sponsored to spend time in partner Asian and Pacific countries as students or in internships with industry. Although two-way flows of students between the region and

[18] Canadian Alumni Network SG (Colombo Plan Scholars), www.cansg.com/colombo-plan-scholars (accessed 8 January 2023).

[19] Colombo Plan Secretariat, *The Story of The Colombo Plan: Resource Book 2012*, p. 25.

[20] Full details from the website of the Malaysian Alumni Chapters of Australian Universities and other Higher Learning Institutes, www.emaac.org/?ch=emaac_eng_application&pg=how_to_apply&ac=AC_BVm3Tws2_20140527112019 (accessed 2 July 2022).

Australia were referenced, the emphasis was now on outbound Australians, reversing the norm of the original Colombo Plan. It would enable young, bright Australians to better understand the Indo-Pacific region and 'connect to Australia's future'.[21] The pilot year of 2014 saw forty Australians sponsored for up to one year, and 1,300 sponsored for short-term 'mobility' experiences in the Indo-Pacific. By 2022, the number of sponsored students had grown to 10,000 a year, spending time in one of forty locations, including Mongolia in the north and the Cook Islands in the Pacific.[22] Under the NCP, Australian universities assist students in some of the longer-term study options. They also compete with each other for funding in the more numerous short-term cohort experiences.

Such is the importance of international education to the Australian economy – worth A$37.6 billion, and 27.3 per cent of total revenue of Australian universities in the pre-COVID year of 2018–19 – that universities and governments, federal and state, align eagerly in celebrating the lineage between 'old' and new Colombo Plans, a thread of continuity marking Australian–Asian connectedness through student movements.[23] Two forms of appropriation unfold in this selective remembering and celebration of the original Colombo Plan, namely Australia's prominence among other members, and within that, the experiences of Asian students rather than development projects, as defining what the plan was about. While scholarly studies have also featured interviews with former Colombo Plan students who speak of positive, transformative experiences, it remains a methodologically complex field as the most forthcoming students will generally be those with the more positive stories to tell.[24]

Student connections persist as one of the most accessible reminders of regionalism and internationalism harnessed to the growth of states after

21 Australian Department of Foreign Affairs and Trade, Public Diplomacy Strategy 2014–16, www.dfat.gov.au/public-diplomacy/public-diplomacy-strategy.html (accessed 20 September 2014).

22 As summarized on the Australian Department of Foreign Affairs and Trade website: www.dfat.gov.au/people-to-people/new-colombo-plan/about (accessed 28 January 2023).

23 Hazel Ferguson and Harriet Spinks, 'Overseas Students in Australian Higher Education: A Quick Guide', Australian Parliamentary Research Paper, updated 22 April 2021, www.aph.gov.au/About_Parliament/Parliamentary_Departments/Parliamentary_Library/pubs/rp/rp2021/Quick_Guides/OverseasStudents (accessed 20 November 2022).

24 For an introduction to the importance of international students as a source of 'soft power', see Kramer, "'Is the World Our Campus?', 775–806. On some of the methodological problems in how international students are attracted to overseas countries, see Natalie Laifer and Nicholas Kitchen, 'Making Soft Power Work: Theory and Practice in Australia's International Education Policy', *Politics and Policy*, 45, 5 (2017), 813–40.

the Second World War. With the exception of a 1971 book on dams and irrigation,[25] and the continuing efforts in Colombo to track accumulative indices on power generation, food production, steel output and so on, it is the student stories that have dominated. The sponsorship of Colombo Plan students and trainees persisted through the troubled times of the 1970s and 1980s, concluding only in 1989. By this time some 175,000 scholarships to universities and institutes had been granted since 1951. Adding the myriad of short training programmes enabled the Colombo Plan Secretariat to claim 'more than 465,781 programmes and scholarships'.[26] These figures appeared in a remarkable book produced by the Secretariat in 2010 and updated in 2014, as the Plan completed sixty years. Comprising 100 pages and 150 photographs and illustrations, it was the most lavish commemorative volume yet. Two-thirds of *A Legacy of Excellence: The Story of the Colombo Plan* covered the 1950–90 period, and the final third focused on the revitalized Colombo Plan since the mid-1990s. The book featured recurring plates of brightly coloured tapestry and weaving, setting the tone of chapters that were titled: The Colombo Plan Connection: Designing Pathways to Prosperity; Ties that Bind: Partnering for Progress; Interlacing Development for Peace, Harmony and Mutual Help; Fashioning a Framework for Meaningful Collaboration; Leaving an Imprint on the Fabric of Life; Weaving a Tapestry of Success; Towards Self-Reliant and Close-Knit Communities; and The Colombo Plan Leadership.[27] Sri Lankan President Mahinda Rajapaksa wrote in his foreword that the Colombo Plan founding fathers carved out a special design for regional prosperity: 'They erased all colonial notions to establish for the first time in history a multinational aid programme that placed donor and recipient nations side by side, as partners in the ensuing saga of development.'[28]

Like so many Colombo Plan publications, the book was rich in stories of projects, students and indices of growth. Again, like many, it strained at times to foreground the Colombo Plan in grand claims ('In many ways, the Colombo Plan paved the way towards an Industrial Revolution in the region.').[29] The overarching metaphor of woven tapestry was worked to its limits: 'If one were to compare the member countries to blank yarns,

[25] The book on dams was written by the longest-serving member of the Information Unit/Bureau, Lionel Perera Goonetilleke, *Dreams Come True: Dam Construction in the Colombo Plan Region* (Colombo: Colombo Plan Bureau, 1971).

[26] The Colombo Plan Secretariat, *A Legacy of Excellence* (updated in 2014), p. 45.

[27] Ibid, p. 5. [28] Ibid, p. 7. [29] Ibid, p. 56.

FIGURE C.1 The Colombo Plan Secretariat, *A Legacy of Excellence: The Story of the Colombo Plan*.
Source: Colombo Plan Secretariat, Colombo, 2010 and updated in 2014.

the Colombo Plan can be said to have left an indelible imprint on them that would forever change their fabric of life.'[30] Connecting old and re-born versions of the plan was important to the tone of pride and positive outlook. On the book's final page was a strong gesture to the original Colombo Plan and its legacy in supporting educational opportunities. The Colombo Plan's Scholarship Programme 'was its hallmark from its inception until 1989', and it took on a fresh look and focus in 2005 with new masters-level scholarships being made available for study in Korea, Malaysia, Singapore and Thailand (Figure C.1).[31]

[30] Ibid, p. 58. [31] Ibid, p. 91.

Thus, despite the array of formidable critiques of development programmes, there remain Colombo Plan projects and particular narratives that serve contemporary political purposes. When, in recent times, Canadian, New Zealand or Australian politicians have wanted to draw on the Colombo Plan as an early expression of engagement with a changing region, they have had plenty of material to hand. When Japanese commentators have wanted to chart their nation's re-emergence into the international community and region, they have turned to easily-accessed foundations, sketching lines from donor efforts in the Colombo Plan through to their leadership of the Asian Development Bank, created in 1966, and then to more recent provisions of aid and investment. Australians, Canadians and New Zealanders seek to highlight the long histories of hospitality towards international students who now come in greater numbers as vital fee-payers.

In selectively remembered forms, the Colombo Plan endures. Development internationalism has evolved to being defined increasingly through human movements connecting countries, and their remembering. The current Secretariat understandably wears its origins proudly.[32] Thanks to government initiatives such as Australia's New Colombo Plan and the work of active alumni groups, it is invoked with intent. In addition to these particular legacy boosts, there have grown, in recent years, more ways for governments and researchers to make connections between its glory days and current political and economic imperatives. The digitization of easily searched newspapers and other journals beyond the major dailies favoured by political historians affords greater insights into the experiences of Colombo Plan students (sometimes hosted by community organizations) in the regional communities of their host countries. Institutional histories, especially of universities, other training facilities and international houses, provide added texture to the experiences of students and sometimes technical experts. As with newspapers and journals, these publishing genres also tend to feature photographs as essential accompaniments to text. And the third source of active remembering is by students and occasionally experts more directly. Whether interviewed by researchers or sought out by universities writing their histories and celebrating anniversaries, the first two decades of Colombo Plan-sponsored students have generated plenty of copy. At least, this is the case for those who enjoyed their experiences in host

[32] See the history summary on the Secretariat website: https://colombo-plan.org/history/ (accessed 5 March 2023).

countries and whose careers benefitted as a result. Recent efforts by foreign affairs departments, especially Australian and New Zealand, to cultivate alumni organization among more recent cohorts of sponsored students complement the work of universities.[33]

How the Colombo Plan continues to be researched remains to be seen, but it has proven its diplomatic and economic value in how it is wielded by the governments and educational institutions invested in its reputation. In this active remembering, they are joined by the Colombo Plan version II Secretariat. What is less remembered are its credentials as an experiment in new possibilities of foreign relations and cautious regionalism in Cold War Asia in an age of development. Without overstating the case for direct lineage between current-day international organizations and the Colombo Plan, its Consultative Committee practices of generous time for discussion, decision-making by consensus and diverting the most controversial content to other forums, find echoes in the ways of ASEAN. In its recurring discussions about region, acknowledgement of Cold War dynamics, and the potential for regional action through North–South cooperation, the Colombo Plan might also be regarded as a staging post towards the more recent embrace of the 'Indo-Pacific'. In the history of development, the Colombo Plan, while constrained in its operation by legacies of colonialism and Cold War alignments, also enjoyed a certain licence during the long 1950s before standardized aid measurement and the professionalization of foreign aid bureaucracies caught up with it. It enabled member countries to tell stories about themselves for regional readers and viewers.

More generally, the Colombo Plan functioned as a foreign relations laboratory in which knowledge about other peoples and places could accumulate, new professional networks could be built and ideas could be tested. We do well to extend our understanding of the Colombo Plan for its grappling with the more generous rendering of development internationalism, with ideas about development and state-making, region and internationalism in the complex processes of postwar decolonization in Cold War Asia.

33 For more detail on the theme of 'vernacular internationalism' resulting from sponsored students, and the influence of the relational turn in research underpinning this, see the Australian case study; Lowe and Kent, 'Sponsored Students and the Rise of the "International" in Australian Communities', pp. 487–502.

Bibliography

SECONDARY SOURCES

Acharya, Amitav, 'Studying the Bandung Conference from a Global IR Perspective', *Australian Journal of International Affairs*, 70, 4, 2016, 342–57.

Adas, Michael, *Dominance by Design: Technological Imperatives and America's Civilizing Mission*. Cambridge, MA: Harvard University Press, 2006.

Adeleke, Ademola, 'The Diplomacy of Programme Boundaries: The Republic of Korea and the Colombo Plan', *International Journal of Developing Societies*, 2, 2, 2013, 73–79.

'The Strings of Neutralism: Burma and the Colombo Plan', *Pacific Affairs*, 76, 2003, 593–610.

Agnew, John A., *Globalization and Sovereignty*. Lanham, MD: Rowman & Littlefield, 2009.

Aitken, Ian, 'British Governmental Institutions, the Regional Information Office in Singapore and the Use of the Official Film in Malaya and Singapore, 1948–1961', *Historical Journal of Film, Radio and Television*, 35, I, 2015, 27–52.

Akami, Tomoko, 'Imperial Polities, Intercolonialism, and the Shaping of Global Governing Norms: Public Health Expert Networks in Asia and the League of Nations Health Organization, 1908–37', *Journal of Global History*, 12, 1, 2017, 4–25.

Akita, S., G. Krozewski, and S. Watanabe, eds., *The Transformation of the International Order of Asia: Decolonization, the Cold War, and the Colombo Plan*. Routledge Studies in the Modern History of Asia, 97, First issued in paperback. Abingdon: Routledge, 2015.

Alderman, Harold, George Mergos, and Roger Slade, 'Cooperatives and the Commercialization of Milk Production in India: A Literature Review', International Food Policy Research Institute, Washington, DC, 1987.

Allbeson, Tom, 'Photographic Diplomacy in the Postwar World: UNESCO and the Conception of Photography as a Universal Language, 1946–1956', *Modern Intellectual History*, 12, 2, 2015, 383–415.

Altman, Dennis, *Paper Ambassadors: The Politics of Stamps*. North Ryde, Sydney: Angus & Robertson, 1991.

Ampiah, K., *The Political and Moral Imperatives of the Bandung Conference of 1955: The Reactions of the US, UK and Japan*. Folkestone: Global Oriental, 2007.

Anderson, Robert S., *Nucleus and Nation: Scientists, International Networks and Power in India*. Chicago: The University of Chicago Press, 2010.

Ashplant, T. G., Graham Dawson, and Michael Roper, 'The Politics of War Memory and Commemoration: Contexts, Structures and Dynamics' in *The Politics of War Memory and Commemoration*, T. G. Ashplant, G. Dawson, and M. Roper (eds.). Abingdon: Routledge, 2000, pp. 3–85.

Atkinson, Harriet, *The Festival of Britain: A Land and Its People*. London: Bloomsbury, 2021.

Ballantyne, Tony, *Webs of Empire: Locating New Zealand's Colonial Past*. Vancouver: University of British Columbia, 2015.

Ballantyne, Tony, and Antoinette Burton, 'Empires and the Reach of the Global' in *A World Connecting, 1870–1945*, Emily S. Rosenberg (ed.). Cambridge, MA: The Belknap Press of Harvard University Press, 2012, pp. 422–31.

Bandyopadhyay, Sekhar, ed., *India in New Zealand: Local Identities, Global Relations*. Dunedin: Otago University Press, 2010.

Barrett, Christopher, and Daniel G. Maxwell, *Food Aid after Fifty Years: Recasting Its Role*. Abingdon: Routledge, 2005.

Bassett, Ron K., 'Aligning India in the Cold War: Indian Technical Elites, the Indian Institute of Technology at Kanpur, and Computing in India and the United States', *Technology and Culture*, 50, 2009, 783–810.

The Technological Indian. Cambridge, MA: Harvard University Press, 2016.

Bayly, Christopher, *Empire and Information: Intelligence Gathering and Social Communication in India, 1780–1870*. Cambridge: Cambridge University Press, 1996.

Berthelot, Yves, ed., *Unity and Diversity in Development Ideas: Perspectives from the UN Regional Commissions*. United Nations Intellectual History Project, 2. Bloomington: Indiana University Press, 2004.

Biggs, David, *Quagmire: Nation Building and Nature in the Mekong Delta*. Seattle: University of Washington Press, 2010.

Bose, Sugata, and Kris Manjapra, eds., *Cosmopolitan Thought Zones: South Asia and the Global Circulation of Ideas*. Houndmills: Palgrave Macmillan, 2010.

Bowen, John R., 'On the Political Construction of Tradition: *Gotong Royong* in Indonesia', *The Journal of Asian Studies*, 45, 3, 1986, 545–61.

Browne, William J., *And Now – Eighty-Seven Years a Newfoundler: Memoirs of William J. Browne*. St Johns: Dicks and Co, 1984.

Campbell-Miller, Jill, 'Encounter and Apprenticeship: The Colombo Plan and Canadian Aid in India, 1950–1960' in *A Samaritan State Revisited: Historical Perspectives on Canadian Foreign Aid*, Greg Donaghy and David

Webster (eds.), 1st ed. University of Calgary Press, 2019, www.jstor.org/stable/10.2307/j.ctvnjbf57 (accessed 24 March 2023).

'The Mind of Modernity: Canadian Bilateral Foreign Assistance to India 1950–60', unpublished PhD Thesis, Canada, University of Waterloo, 2014.

Carr-Gregg, John R. E., 'The Colombo Plan: A Commonwealth Program for Southeast Asia', *International Conciliation*, 3, 60, 1951, 1–55.

Carr-Gregg, John R. E., and Anne Winslow, *The Colombo Plan: The Commonwealth Program for Southeast Asia*. Whitefish, MT: Literary Licensing, 2013.

Carter, James M., *Inventing Vietnam: The United States and State Building, 1954–1968*. New York: Cambridge University Press, 2008.

Charlton, Mark W., *The Making of Canadian Food Aid Policy*. Montreal: McGill-Queens University Press, 1982.

Chernus, Ira, *Eisenhower's Atoms for Peace*. Library of Presidential Rhetoric, 1st ed. College Station, TX: A&M University Press, 2002.

Child, Jack, *Miniature Messages: The Semiotic and Politics of Latin American Postage Stamps*. Durham, NC: Duke University Press, 2008.

Collins, Jenny, 'Perspectives from the Periphery? Colombo Plan Scholars in New Zealand Universities, 1951–1975', *History of Education Review*, P. Rushbrook (ed.), 41, 2, 2012, 129–46.

Cooper, Frederic, *Citizenship between Empire and Nation: Remaking France and French Africa, 1945–1960*. Princeton, NJ: Princeton University Press, 2014.

Colonialism in Question: Theory, Knowledge, History. Berkeley: University of California Press, 2005.

Craggs, Ruth, 'Hospitality in Geopolitics and the Making of Commonwealth International Relations', *Geoforum*, 52, 2014, 90–100.

Cullather, Nick, *The Hungry World: America's Cold War Battle against Poverty in Asia*. Cambridge, MA: Harvard University Press, 2010.

Darian-Smith, Kate, and James Waghorne, 'Australian-Asian Sociability, Student Activism and the University Challenge to White Australia in the 1950s', *Australian Journal of Politics & History*, 62, 2016, 203–18.

Derek McDougall, and Antonia Finnane, eds., *Bandung 1955: Little Histories*. Monash Papers on Southeast Asia, 69. Melbourne: Monash University Press, 2010.

Donaghy, Greg, '"Reasonably Well-Organized": A History of Early Aid Administration' in *A Samaritan State Revisited: Historical Perspectives on Canadian Foreign Aid*, Greg Donaghy and David Webster (eds.), Beyond Boundaries: Canadian Defence and Strategic Studies Series, no. 10. Calgary: University of Calgary Press, 2019, pp. 53–65.

Drogan, Mara, 'The Atoms for Peace Program and the Third World', *Cahiers du monde russe*, 60, 2–3, 2019, 441–60.

Eggers, Nicole, Jessica Lynne Pearson, and Aurora Almada e Santos, eds., *The United Nations and Decolonization*. 1st ed. Abingdon: Routledge, 2020.

Ekbladh, David, *The Great American Mission: Modernization and the Construction of an American World Order*. America in the World. Princeton, NJ: Princeton University Press, 2010.

Ellwood, David W., 'Italian Modernisation and the Propaganda of the Marshall Plan' in *The Art of Persuasion: Political Communication in Italy from*

1945 to the 1990s, L. Cheles and L. Sponza (eds.), Manchester: Manchester University Press, 2001.

Elman, Russell, *Asian Experiment*. Toronto: Riverson Press, 1961.

Engerman, David C., 'Development Politics and the Cold War', *Diplomatic History*, 41, 1, 2017, 1–19.

The Price of Aid: The Economic Cold War in India. Cambridge, MA: Harvard University Press, 2018.

Escobar, Arturo, *Encountering Development: The Making and Unmaking of the Third World*. Princeton, NJ: Princeton University Press, 1995.

Ewing, Cindy, 'The Colombo Powers: Crafting Diplomacy in the Third World and Launching Afro-Asia at Bandung', *Cold War History*, 19, 1, 2018, 1–19.

Fearon, James Dana, and David D. Laitin, 'Sons of the Soil, Migrants, and Civil War', *World Development*, 39, 2011, 199–211.

Ferguson, Hazel, and Spinks, Harriet, 'Overseas Students in Australian Higher Education: A Quick Guide', Australian Parliamentary Research Paper, update 22 April 2021, www.aph.gov.au/About_Parliament/Parliamentary_Departments/Parliamentary_Library/pubs/rp/rp2021/Quick_Guides/Overseas Students (accessed 20 November 2022).

Fettling, David, *Encounters with Asian Decolonisation*. Melbourne: Australian Scholarly Press, 2017.

Fewster, Alan, 'Cold War, Soft Diplomacy' *Inside Story*, 14 January 2014, https://insidestory.org.au/cold-war-soft-diplomacy/ (accessed 20 January 2017).

Filipova, Marta, ed., *Cultures of International Exhibitions: Great Exhibitions in the Margins*. Abingdon: Routledge, 2015.

Forclaz, Amalia Ribi, 'From Reconstruction to Development: The Early Years of the Food and Agriculture Organization (FAO) and the Conceptualization of Rural Welfare, 1945–1955', *The International History Review*, 41, 2, 2019, 351–71.

Fortier, Rénald, 'Frankly, My Dear, We Did Give a Dam: Canada and the Warsak Dam in Pakistan' *Ingenium Channel*, 24 January 2021, https://ingeniumcanada.org/channel/articles/frankly-my-dear-we-did-give-a-dam-canada-and-the-warsak-dam-in-pakistan (accessed 7 July 2021).

Frey, Marc, Sönke Kunkel, and Corinna R. Unger, eds., *International Organizations and Development, 1945–1990*. Basingstoke: Palgrave Macmillan, 2014.

George, A. K., 'Asian Regionalism & India's Early Initiatives: The Two Asian Conferences', *India Quarterly: A Journal of International Affairs*, 27, 3, 1971, 238–43.

Gerits, Frank, 'Bandung as the Call for a Better Development Project: US, British and Gold Coast Perceptions of the Afro-Asian Conference (1955)', *Cold War History*, 16, 3, 2016, 255–72.

Getachew, Adom, *Worldmaking after Empire: The Rise and Fall of Self-Determination*. Princeton, NJ: Princeton University Press, 2019.

Gienow-Hecht, Jessica, 'Nation Branding: A Useful Category for International History', *Diplomacy & Statecraft*, 30, 2019, 755–79.

Goonetilleke, Lionel Perera, *Dreams Come True: Dam Construction in the Colombo Plan Region*. Colombo: Colombo Plan Bureau, 1971.

Gorman, Daniel, 'Britain, India, and the United Nations: Colonialism and the Development of International Governance, 1945–1960', *Journal of Global History*, 9, 3, 2014, 471–90.

Goscha, Christopher E., and Christian Ostermann, eds., *Connecting Histories: Decolonization and the Cold War in Southeast Asia, 1945–1962*. Stanford, CA: Stanford University Press, 2009.

Goswami, Manu, 'Imaginary Futures and Colonial Internationalisms', *American Historical Review*, 117, 5, 2012, 1461–85.

Greene, Graham, *The Quiet American*. London: William Heinemann, 1955.

Greenhalgh, Paul, *Fair World: A History of World Fairs and Expositions from London to Shanghai, 1851–2010*. Winterbourne, UK: Papadakis, 2011.

Guardian Newspaper, 'Guardian Obituary, Dir Geoffrey Wilson', *The Guardian*, 20 July 2004, www.theguardian.com/news/2004/jul/19/guardianobituaries (accessed 2 July 2021).

Hack, Karl, *The Malayan Emergency: Revolution and Counterinsurgency at the End of Empire*. Milton Keynes: Open University, 2022.

Haines, Daniel, 'A "Commonwealth Moment" in South Asian Decolonization', in *Decolonization and the Cold War: Negotiating Independence*, L. James and E. Leake (eds.), New Approaches to International History. London: Bloomsbury, 2015.

Harrison, Jackie, and Stefanie Pukallus, 'The European Community's Public Communications Policy, 1951–1967', *Contemporary European History*, 24, 2, 2015, 233–51.

Hatano, Sumio, 'The Colombo Plan and Japan: Focusing on the Tokyo Meeting' in *The Transformation of the International Order of Asia: Decolonization, the Cold War, and the Colombo Plan*, Shigeru Akita, Gerald Krozewski, and Shoichi Watanabe (eds.), Routledge Studies in the Modern History of Asia, 97. Milton Park: Routledge, Taylor & Francis Group, 2015, pp. 131–42.

Hawke, Gary R., 'The Economic Relationship' in *Southeast Asia: A History of Regional and Bilateral Relations*, A. L. Smith (ed.). Singapore: ISEAS and NZIIA and Victoria University Press, 2005.

Hellmann-Rajanayagam, D., 'The Politics of the Tamil Past' in *Sri Lanka: History and the Roots of Conflict*, J. Spencer (ed.). London: Routledge, 1990.

Henlein, Frank, *British Government Policy and Decolonisation, 1945–1963: Scrutinising the Official Mind*. London: Frank Cass, 2002.

Heredia, Ruth, *The Amul India Story*. New Delhi: Tata McGraw-Hill Publishing, 1997.

Hobbins, A. J., 'Eleanor Roosevelt, John Humphrey – And Canadian Opposition to the Universal Declaration of Human Rights: Looking Back on the 50th Anniversary of UNHDR', *International Journal*, 53, 1998, 325–42.

Hodge, Errol, *Radio Wars: Truth, Propaganda and the Struggle for Radio Australia*. Melbourne: Cambridge University Press, 1995.

Hodge, Joseph M., 'Writing the History of Development (Part 1: The First Wave)', *Humanity: An International Journal of Human Rights, Humanitarianism, and Development*, 6, 3, 2015, 429–63.

'Writing the History of Development (Part 2: Longer, Deeper, Wider)', *Humanity: An International Journal of Human Rights, Humanitarianism, and Development*, 7, 1, 2016, 125–74.

Hogan, Michael J., *The Marshall Plan: America, Britain and Reconstruction of Western Europe, 1947–1952*. Cambridge: Cambridge University Press, 1987.

Hoshiro, Hiroyuki, 'Reconsidering Japan's War Reparations and Economic Re-Entry into Southeast Asia', *Diplomacy and Statecraft*, 34, 4, 2023, 673–702.

Humphries, L. R., *Of Many Nations: A History of International House*. Melbourne: Melbourne University Press, 2004.

Immerwahr, Daniel, *Thinking Small: The United States and the Lure of Community Development*. First Harvard University Press paperback edition. Cambridge, MA: Harvard University Press, 2015.

Iriye, Akira, *Global Community: The Role of International Organizations in the Making of the Contemporary World*, 1st ed. Berkeley: University of California Press, 2002.

James, Leslie, and Elisabeth Leake, eds., *Decolonization and the Cold War: Negotiating Independence*. London: Bloomsbury, 2015.

Katada, Saori N., 'Japan's Foreign Aid after the San Francisco Treaty', *The Journal of American–East Asian Relations*, 9, 3–4, 2000, 197–220.

Kirsch, Scott, *Proving Grounds: Project Plowshare and the Unrealized Dream of Nuclear Earthmoving*. New Brunswick, NJ: Rutgers University Press, 2005.

Kobayashi, Ai, 'Australia and Japan's Admission into the Colombo Plan', *Australian Journal of Politics & History*, 60, 4, 2014, 518–33.

Kothari, Uma, 'Authority and Expertise: The Professionalisation of International Development and the Ordering of Dissent', *Antipode*, 37, 3, 2005, 425–46.

'Spatial Practices and Imaginaries: Experiences of Colonial Officers and Development Professionals' in *Empire, Development & Colonialism: The Past in the Present*, Mark Duffield and Vernon Hewitt (eds.). Suffolk: James Currey, 2009, XXVII, pp. 161–75.

Kott, Sandrine, 'International Organizations – A Field for Research for Global History', *Zeithistorische Forschungen/Studies in Contemporary History*, 8, 2011, 446–50.

Kramer, Paul, "'Is the World Our Campus?' International Students and U.S. Global Power in the Long Twentieth Century', *Bernath Lecture, Diplomatic History*, 33, 5, 2009, 775–806.

Kroen, Sheryl, 'Negotiations with the American Way: The Consumer and Social Contract in Post-War Europe' in *Consuming Cultures, Global Perspectives: Historical Trajectories, Transnational Exchanges*, John Brewer and Frank Trentman (eds.). Oxford: Berg, 2006.

Kudaisya, Medha M. *Tryst with Prosperity: India Business and the Bombay Plan of 1944*. Haryana: Penguin Random House, 2018.

Kumarasingham, Harshan, *A Political Legacy of the British Empire: Power and The Parliamentary System in Post-colonial India and Sri Lanka*. International Library of Twentieth Century History, 54. London: I. B. Tauris, 2013.

'The "Tropical Dominions": The Appeal of Dominion Status in the Decolonisation of India, Pakistan and Ceylon', *Transactions of the Royal Historical Society*, 23, 6th series, 2013, 223–45.

Kurien, Verghese, and Gouri Salvi, *I Too Had a Dream*. New Delhi: Lotus Collection, 2005.

Laifer, Natalie, and Nicholas Kitchen, 'Making Soft Power Work: Theory and Practice in Australia's International Education Policy', *Politics and Policy*, 45, 5, 2017, 813–40.

Lederer, William, and Eugene Burdick, *The Ugly American*. New York: W.W. Norton, 1958.

Lee, Christopher J., ed., *Making a World after Empire: The Bandung Moment and Its Political Afterlives*. Athens: Ohio University Press, 2010.

Lentz, Carola, and David Lowe, *Remembering Independence*. Abingdon: Routledge, 2018.

LePan, Douglas, *Bright Glass of Memory: A Set of Four Memoirs*. Toronto: McGraw-Hill Ryerson, 1979.

Limor, Yehiel, and Ilan Tamir, 'The Neglected Medium: Postage Stamps as Mass Media', *Communication Theory*, 31, 2021, 491–505.

Lowe, David, *Australian between Empires: The Life of Percy Spender*. London: Pickering & Chatto, 2010.

'Australia's Cold War: Britishness and English-Speaking Worlds Challenged Anew' in *Rediscovering the British World*, P. Buckner and R. D. Francis (eds.). Calgary: University of Calgary Press, 2005, pp. 361–80.

'Australia's Colombo Plans, Old and New: International Students as Foreign Relations', *International Journal of Cultural Policy*, 21, 4, 2015, 448–62.

Canberra's Colombo Plan: Public Images of Australia's Relation with Post-Colonial South and Southeast Asia in the 1950s', *South Asia*, 25, 2, 2002, 183–204.

'From War to Postwar: Ted Williams in Canberra, 1946–52' in *Diplomats at War: British and Commonwealth Diplomacy in Wartime*, C. Baxter and A. Stewart (eds.). Leiden: Martinus Nijhoff, 2008, pp. 275–93.

'Journalists and the Stirring of Australian Public Diplomacy: The Colombo Plan towards the 1960s', *Journal of Contemporary History*, 48, 1 (2013), 183–87.

Lowe, David, and Anna Kent, 'Sponsored Students and the Rise of "the International" in Australian Communities', *Journal of Australian Studies*, 43, 2019, 487–502.

Lowe, David, and Tony Joel, *Remembering the Cold War: Global Contest and National Stories*. Abingdon: Routledge, 2013.

Loy-Wilson, Sophie, '"Liberating" Asia: Strikes and Protest in Sydney and Shanghai, 1920–39', *History Workshop Journal*, 72, 1, 2011, 74–102.

'White Cargo: Australian Residents, Trade and Colonialism in Shanghai between the Wars', *History Australia*, 9, 3, 2012, 154–77.

Macekura, Stephen J., *Of Limits and Growth: The Rise of Global Sustainable Development in the Twentieth Century*. New York: Cambridge University Press, 2015.

Macekura, Stephen J., and Erez Manela, eds., *The Development Century: A Global History*. Global and International History. Cambridge: Cambridge University Press, 2018.

Mahli, Amrita, 'Race, Space and the Malayan Emergency: Expelling Malaya Muslim Communism and Reconstituting Malaya's Racial State, 1945–1954', *Itinerario*, 445, 3, 2021, 435–59.

Mahoney, Michael, '"One of the Best Advertising Mediums the Country Can Have." Postage Stamps and National identity in Canada, New Zealand and Australia', *Material Culture Review*, 77–78, 2013, 21–38.

Manor, James, *The Expedient Utopian: Bandaranaike and Ceylon*. Cambridge: Cambridge University Press, 1989.

Matsui, Hirokazu, 'Australia–Japan Relations and the International Re-emergence of Japan, 1952–1962', unpublished Ph.D. Thesis, Deakin University, 2024.

'Australia and Japan's Return to International Society: Negotiating Allies and the Afro-Asian Bloc, 1952–56', *Australian Journal of Politics and History*, 69, 2, 2023, 248–65.

Maul, Daniel, *The International Labour Organization: 100 Years of Global Social Policy*. Berlin and Geneva, Switzerland: in association with International Labour Office, de Gruyter Oldenbourg, 2019.

May, Ron, *State and Society in Papua New Guinea: The First Twenty-Five Years*. Canberra: Australian National University Press, 2004.

McFadden, C. H., 'The Gal Oya Valley: Ceylon's Little TVA', *Geographical Review*, 44, 2, 1954, 271–81.

McGee, David, and Rian Manson, 'Canada, Communism and the Colombo Plan' in *Objects in Motion: Globalizing Technology*, N. Mollers and B. DeWalt (eds.). Washington, DC: Smithsonian Institution Scholarly Press, 2016.

McKinnon, Malcolm, *Independence and Foreign Policy: New Zealand in the World since 1935*. Auckland: Auckland University Press, 1993.

McNeill, J. R., and Corinna Unger, eds., *Environmental Histories of the Cold War*. Washington, DC and New York: German Historical Institute and Cambridge University Press, 2010.

Medcalf, Alexander, 'Between Art and Information: Communicating World Health, 1948–70', *Journal of Global History*, 13, 2018, 94–120.

Medcalf, Rory, *Contest for the Indo-Pacific: Why China Won't Map the Future*. Carlton: La Trobe University Press and Black Inc, 2020.

Megarrity, Lyndon, 'Regional Goodwill, Sensibly Priced: Commonwealth Policies towards Colombo Plan Scholars and Private Overseas Students, 1945–72', *Australian Historical Studies*, 129, 2007, 88–105.

Mein-Smith, Philippa, 'New Zealand Milk for "Building Britons"' in *Medicine and Colonial Identity*, B. Andrew and M. P. Stephen (eds.). Abingdon: Routledge, 2013, pp. 79–102.

Meren, David, '"Commend Me the Yak": The Colombo Plan, the Inuit of Ungava, and "Developing" Canada's North', *Histoire sociale/Social History*, 50, 2017, 343–70.

Miller, Douglas, 'The History of the Royal Australasian College of Surgeons', *The Australian New Zealand Journal of Surgery*, 41, 4, 1972, 302–9.

Moffat, Susan M., '"A Bold Experiment": The New Zealand School Dental Service and the Colombo Plan', *Journal of the Royal Society of New Zealand*, 50, 1, 2020, 47–66.

Moon, Suzanne, *Technology and Ethical Idealism: A History of Development in the Netherlands East Indies*. Studies in Overseas History, 9. Leiden: CNWS Publications, 2007.

Moore, Robin J., *Making the New Commonwealth*. Oxford: Oxford University Press, 1987.

Morrison, David R., *Aid and Ebb Tide: A History of CIDA and Canadian Development Assistance*. Waterloo: Wilfrid Laurier University Press, 1998.

Murphy, Philip, 'Britain and the Commonwealth: Confronting the Past – Imagining the Future', *The Round Table*, 100, 414, 2011, 267–83.

Muschik, Eva-Maria, *Building States: The United Nations, Development, and Decolonization, 1945–1965*. Columbia Studies in International and Global History. New York: Columbia University Press, 2022.

'Towards a Global History of International Organizations and Decolonization', *Journal of Global History*, 17, 2022, 173–90.

Nakazato, Nariaki, 'The Transfer of Economic Power in India: Indian Big Business, the British Raj and Development Planning, 1930–1948' in *The Unfinished Agenda: Nation Building in South Asia*, Mushirul Hasan and Nariaki Nakazato (eds.). New Delhi: Manohar Publishers & Distributors, 2001, pp. 247–307.

Narasimhan, C. V., *The United Nations at 50: Recollections*. Delhi: Konark Publications, 1996.

Oakman, Daniel, *Facing Asia: A History of the Colombo Plan*. Canberra: Australian National University Press, 2004.

O'Malley, Alana, *The Diplomacy of Decolonisation: America, Britain and the United Nations during the Congo Crisis 1960–1964*. Manchester: Manchester University Press, 2018.

Paddle, Sarah, '"For the China of the Future": Western Feminists, Colonisation and International Citizenship in China in the Inter-war Years', *Australian Feminist Studies*, 16, 36, 2001, 325–41.

Pederson, Susan, *The Guardians: The League of Nations and the Crisis of Empire*. Oxford: Oxford University Press, 2015.

Peebles, Patrick, 'Colonization and Ethnic Conflict in the Dry Zone of Sri Lanka', *The Journal of Asian Studies*, 49, 1990, 30–55.

Percival Wood, Sally, 'Retrieving the Bandung Conference … Moment by Moment', *Journal of Southeast Asian Studies*, 43, 3, 2012, 523–30.

Pernet, Corinne A., and Amalia Ribi Forclaz, 'Revisiting the Food and Agriculture Organization (FAO): International Histories of Agriculture, Nutrition, and Development', *The International History Review*, 41, 2, 2018, 345–50.

Piccini, Jon, *Fifty Years of Friendship: A History of International House, Brisbane, 1965–2015*. St Lucia: University of Queensland Press, 2015.

Pieris, Anoma, *Architecture and Nationalism in Sri Lanka: The Trouser under the Cloth*, Abingdon: Routledge, 2012.

Plumptre, A. F. W., 'Perspective on Our Aid to Others', *International Journal*, 22, 1967, 488–89.

Pollard, Vincent K., 'ASA and ASEAN, 1961–1967: Southeast Asian Regionalism', *Asian Survey*, 10, 3, 1970, 244–55.

Prakash, Gyan, *Another Reason: Science and the Imagination of Modern India*. Princeton, NJ: Princeton University Press, 1999.

Purdey, Jemma, Scholarships and Connections: Australia, Indonesia and Papua New Guinea. *Alfred Deakin Research Institute Working Papers*, Series Two. Geelong, Victoria: Alfred Deakin Research Institute, Deakin University, 2014.

Railston, W., 'Britain and the Technical Development of Eastern Commonwealth Countries under the Colombo Plan', *Journal of the Royal Society of Arts*, 107, 1959, 656.

Raina, Dhruv, 'Engineering Science Education and the Indian Institutes of Technology: Reframing the Context of the "Cold War and Science" (1950–1970)', *Contemporary Education Dialogue*, 14, 2017, 49–70.

Raza, Ali, Franzisak Roy, and Benjamin Zachariah, eds., *The Internationalist Moment: South Asia, Worlds and Worldviews, 1917–1939*. New Delhi: Sage India, 2014.

Reid, Anthony, 'New Zealand's Unexpected Opening to Asia: John Reid and the Making of the Colombo Plan, 1949–52', *New Zealand Journal of Asian Studies*, 21, 1, 2019, 19–38.

Remme, Tilman, *Britain and Regional Cooperation in South-East Asia, 1945–49*. London: Routledge, 2016

Reynolds, David, *Summits: Six Meetings that Shaped the Twentieth century*. New York: Basic Books, 2007.

Rice, Tom, '*Merdeka for Malaya*: Imagining Independence across the British Empire' in *The Colonial Documentary Film in South and South-East Asia*, Ian Aitken and Camille Deprez (eds.). Edinburgh University Press, 2017, pp. 45–62.

Rigny, Ann, 'Plenitude, Scarcity and the Circulation of Cultural Memory', *Journal of European Studies*, 35, 1, 2005, 11–28.

Riley, Barry, *The Political History of American Food Aid: An Uneasy Benevolence*. Oxford: Oxford University Press, 2017.

Robertson, Thomas, 'Cold War Landscapes: Towards an Environmental History of US Development Programmes in the 1950s and 1960s', *Cold War History*, 16, 4, 2016, 417–41.

Roehrlich, Elisabeth, 'The Cold War, the Developing World, and the Creation of the International Atomic Energy Agency (IAEA), 1953–1957', *Cold War History*, 16, 2016, 195–212.

Rolfe, Jim, 'Coming to Terms with the Regional Identity' in *Southeast Asia and New Zealand: A History of Regional and Bilateral Relations*, A. L. Smith (ed.). Singapore and Wellington: Institute of Southeast Asian Studies and New Zealand Institute of International Affairs, in association with Victoria University Press, 2005, pp. 32–56.

Rostow, Walt W., *The Stages of Economic Growth: A Non-Communist Manifesto*, 3rd ed. New York: Cambridge University Press, 1960.

Rotter, Andrew, *The Path to Vietnam: Origins of the American Commitment to Southeast Asia*. Ithaca, NY: Cornell University Press, 1987.

Roy, Srirupa, *Beyond Belief: India and the Politics of Postcolonial Nationalism*. Durham, NC: Duke University Press, 2007.

Sanger, Clyde, *Malcolm MacDonald: Bringing an End to Empire*. Montreal: McGill-Queen's University Press, 1995.

Sarwal, Amit, '"A Kangaroo and Bradman": Indian Journalists' Visits to Australia under the Colombo Plan, 1950–57', *Journalism Studies*, 18, 2018, 1–17.

Sarwal, Amit and David Lowe, '"Behind the White Curtain"': Indian Students and Researchers in Australia, 1901–1950', *History of Education Review*, 50, 2021, 212–25.

Sauer, Geoffrey, ed., *The Colombo Plan for Cooperative Economic Development in South and South East Asia 1951–2001: The Malaysian–Australian Perspective*. Adelaide: Malaysia-Australia Foundation, Openbook Print, 2001.

Sayward, Amy L., *The United Nations in International History*. New Approaches to International History. London: Bloomsbury, 2017.

Schenk, Catherine R., *Britain and the Sterling Area: From Devaluation to Convertibility in the 1950s*. Abingdon: Routledge, 1994.

Shaw, Basil, *From Many Nations: A History of International House, University of Queensland, 1955 to 1994*. St Lucia: International House, 1995.

Shimazu, Naoko, 'Diplomacy as Theatre: Staging the Bandung Conference of 1955', *Modern Asian Studies*, 48, 1, 2014, 225–52.

'Places in Diplomacy', *Political Geography*, 31, 2012, 335–36.

Siegel, Benjamin, '"The Claims of Asia and the Far East": India and the FAO in the Age of Ambivalent Internationalism', *The International History Review*, 41, 2, 2019, 427–50.

Sinclair, Guy Fiti, *To Reform the World: International Organizations and the Making of Modern States*. The History and Theory of International Law, 1st ed. Oxford: Oxford University Press, 2017.

Singh, Lalita Prasad, *The Politics of Economic Cooperation in Asia: A Study of Asian International Organizations*. Columbia: University of Missouri Press, 1966.

Sluga, Glenda, *Internationalism in the Age of Nationalism*. Philadelphia: University of Pennsylvania Press, 2013.

Sluga, Glenda, and Patricia Clavin, eds., *Internationalisms: A Twentieth-Century History*, 1st ed. Cambridge: Cambridge University Press, 2017.

Smaill, Belinda, 'Promoting Australia: Post-war Documentary and Asia', *Continuum*, 28, 5, 2014, 616–28.

Smyth, Roslyn, 'Film as Instrument of Modernization and Social Change in Africa: The Long View' in *Modernization as Spectacle in Africa*, P. J. Bloom, S. F. Miescher, and T. Manuh (eds.). Bloomington: Indiana Press, 2014.

Spender, Percy, *Exercises in Diplomacy: The ANZUS Treaty and the Colombo Plan*. Sydney: University of Sydney Press, 1969.

Spicer, Keith, 'The Administration of Canadian Colombo Plan Aid', *International Journal*, 16, 169, 1961, 169–82.

'Clubmanship Upstaged: Canada's Twenty Years in the Colombo Plan', *International Journal: Canada's Journal of Global Policy Analysis*, 25, 1, 1969, 23–33.

A Samaritan State? External Aid in Canada's Foreign Policy. Toronto: University of Toronto Press, 1966.

Staples, Amy, *Birth of Development: How the World Bank, Food and Agriculture Organization, and World Health Organization Changed the World, 1945–1965*. New Studies in U.S. Foreign Relations, 1. Kent: Kent State University Press, 2006.

Stockwell, Sarah, *The British End of the British Empire*. Cambridge: Cambridge University Press, 2018.

Stokke, Olav, *The UN and Development: From Aid to Cooperation*. Bloomington: Indiana University Press, 2009.

Suares, Julie, 'Engaging with Asia: The Chifley Government and the New Delhi Conferences of 1947 and 1949', *Australian Journal of Politics & History*, 57, 4, 2011, 495–510.

Tambiah, Stanley J., *Leveling Crowds: Ethnonationalist Conflicts and Collective Violence in South Asia*. Berkeley: University of California Press, 1996.

Tan, See Seng, and Amitav Acharya, eds., *Bandung Revisited: The Legacy of the 1955 Asian-African Conference for International Order*. Singapore: National University of Singapore Press, 2009.

Tarling, Nicholas, *Britain, Southeast Asia and the Onset of the Cold War, 1945–1950*, 1st ed. Cambridge: Cambridge University Press, 2007 [1998].

'The United Kingdom and the Origins of the Colombo Plan', *The Journal of Commonwealth & Comparative Politics*, 24, 1, 1986, 3–34.

Thakur, Vineet, 'An Asian Drama: The Asian Relations Conference, 1947', *The International History Review*, 41, 3, 2019, 673–95.

Tomlinson, B. R., '"The weapons of the Weakened": British Power, Sterling Balances and the Origins of the Colombo Plan' in *The Transformation of the International Order of Asia: Decolonization, the Cold War, and the Colombo Plan*, Shigeru Akita, Gerold Krozewski, and Shoichi Watanabe (eds.), Routledge Studies in the Modern History of Asia, 97. Abingdon: Routledge, 2015, pp. 34–48.

Tonks, Paul, and Laavanyan Michael Ratnapalan, 'Ideologies of the New Commonwealth', *The International History Review*, 43, 4, 2021, 887–905.

Tucker, Richard P., 'Containing Communism by Impounding Rivers: American Strategic Interests and the Global Spread of High Dams in the Early Cold War' in *Environmental Histories of the Cold War*, J. R. McNeill and Corinna Unger (eds.). Washington, DC and New York: German Historical Institute and Cambridge University Press, 2010, pp. 139–63.

Unger, Corinna R., *International Development: A Postwar History*. New Approaches to International History. London: Bloomsbury, 2018.

'The United States, Decolonization and the Education of Third World Elites' in *Elites and Decolonization in the Twentieth Century*, J. Dülffer and M. Frey (eds.). Houndmills, Palgrave Macmillan, 2011, pp. 241–61.

Uphoff, N., *Learning from Gal Oya: Possibilities for Participatory Development and Post-Newtonian Social Science*. Ithaca, NY: Cornell University Press, 1992.

Waters, Christopher, 'A Failure of Imagination: R.G. Casey and Australian Plans for Counter-subversion in Asia, 1954–1956', *Australian Journal of Politics & History*, 45, 3, 1999, 347–61.

Webster, David, 'Developing the World in Canada's Image: Hugh Keenleyside and Technical Assistance' in *A Samaritan State Revisited: Historical*

Perspectives on Canadian Foreign Aid, G. Donaghy and D. Webster (eds.), Beyond Boundaries: Canadian Defence and Strategic Studies Series, no. 10. Calgary, University of Calgary Press, 2019, pp. 73–99.

Fire and the Full Moon: Canada and Indonesia in a Decolonizing World. Vancouver: University of British Columbia Press, 2009.

'Mental Maps and Canada's Post-war Asian Policy', *International Journal: Canada's Journal of Global Policy Analysis*, 75, 4, 2020, 548–62.

'Modern Missionaries: Canadian Postwar Technical Assistance Advisors in Southeast Asia', *Journal of the Canadian Historical Association*, 20, 2, 2009, 86–111.

Westad, Odd Arne, *The Global Cold War: Third World Interventions and the Makings of our Times*. Cambridge: Cambridge University Press, 2005.

Westwater, C. G., 'Foreign Intervention in the Planning and Execution of National Development in an Underdeveloped Country: A Case Study of Pakistan', unpublished Thesis for Master of City Planning, MIT, 1972.

Wheelhouse, Frances, *Eleanor Mary Hinder, an Australian Woman's Social Welfare Work in China between the Wars*. Sydney: Wentworth Books, 1978.

Wightman, David, *Toward Economic Cooperation in Asia: The United Nations Economic Commission for Asia and the Far East*. New Haven, CT: Yale University Press, 1963.

Wilmington, Martin W., *The Middle East Supply Centre*, 1st ed. New York: State University of New York Press, 1971 [1961].

Wint, Guy, *What Is the Colombo Plan?* Bloomsbury: The Batchworth Press, 1952.

Yamaguchi, Ikuto, 'The Development and Activities of the Economic Commission for Asia and the Far East (ECAFE), 1947–65' in *The Transformation of the International Order of Asia: Decolonization, the Cold War, and the Colombo Plan*, Shigeru Akita, Gerold Krozewski, and Shoichi Watanabe (eds.), Routledge Studies in the Modern History of Asia, 97. Abingdon: Routledge, 2015, pp. 91–108.

Yao, Souchou, *The Malayan Emergency: A Small, Distant War*. Copenhagen: Nordic Institute of Asian Studies Press, 2016.

Yokoi, Katsuhiko, 'The Colombo Plan and Industrialization in India: Technical Cooperation for the Indian Institutes of Technology' in *The Transformation of the International Order of Asia: Decolonization, the Cold War, and the Colombo Plan*, Shigeru Akita, Gerold Krozewski, and Shoichi Watanabe (eds.), Routledge Studies in the Modern History of Asia, 97. Milton Park: Routledge, Taylor & Francis Group, 2015.

PRIMARY SOURCES

Archival Sources

Archives New Zealand
- File Series
  - EA 1
  - Walter Nash Papers AE

British Library
  Newspapers
Cambridge University Library, Royal Commonwealth Society collection
Churchill College, Cambridge
'The Colombo Plan: Report of the Council for Technical Co-operation in South and South-East Asia for 1952', 1953.
Colombo Plan Bureau, *The Colombo Plan Story: Ten Years of Progress, 1951–1961*, Colombo Plan Council, Colombo, 1961.
The Fifth Year: Progress of the Colombo Plan, Colombo Plan Bureau, Colombo, 1956.
Colombo Plan Information Unit, *Change in Asia: The Colombo Plan*, Government Press, 1956.
Colombo Plan Newsletter/Magazine, 1956–69.
Economic Commission for Asia and the Far East, *Economic Survey of Asia and the Far East*, 1948–63.
(Ernest) Bevin Papers
Desmond Higgins, Interview Transcript, 2010, British Diplomatic Oral History Programme
Japan Diplomatic Record Office
  E' Series
Library and Archives Canada
  File Series
    RG 19
    RG 20
    RG 25
National Archives of India
  File Series
    1(20) UN
    Education F. 42
    MEA F. 5
    MEA F. 22
  Abilekh Patal (online National Archives of India)
  Sardar Patel Collection
    Education F. 15
National Archives of Australia
  File Series
    A 621
    A 1361
    A 1838
    A 4311
    A 4638
    A 6895
    A10067
    A 10167
    A 10302
    B 142
    M 1153

National Library of Australia
Casey Papers MS 6150
National Library of New Zealand
K. D. Malaviya Papers
McIntosh Papers MS 6759
Nehru Memorial Museum and Library
Subimal Dutt Papers
T. T. Krishnamachari Papers
The National Archives (UK) series
File Series
CAB 134
CO 852
CO 1030
DO 35
DO 189
DO 198
FCO 141
FO 371
FO 953
T317
United States National Archives
File Series
RG59
RG84
Decimal series 890.00

PUBLISHED PRIMARY SOURCES

Annual Survey of Asia and the Far East, 1957.

Asian Relations Organization, *Being Report of the Proceedings and Documentation of the First Asian Relations Conference, New Delhi*, March–April, 1947. New Delhi: Asian Relations Organization, 1948.

Australian Department of Commerce and Agriculture, 'Australia at Colombo Exhibition', *Overseas Trading (Journal of the Australian Department of Commerce and Agriculture)*, 4, 12, 1952, 1.

Australian Department of Foreign Affairs and Trade, 'New Colombo Plan', as summarized on the Australian Department of Foreign Affairs and Trade website: www.dfat.gov.au/people-to-people/new-colombo-plan/about (accessed 28 January 2023).

Bridson, Douglas G., *Progress in Asia: The Colombo Plan in Action*. London: Her Majesty's Stationery Office, 1953.

Canadian Department of External Affairs in Cooperation with the External Aid Office, *Canada and the Colombo Plan, 1951–1961*. Ottawa: Queen's Printer, 1961.

Casey, Richard Gardiner, *Friends and Neighbours: Australia and the World*. Melbourne: Cheshire, 1954.

Colombo Plan Secretariat, *A Legacy of Excellence: The Story of the Colombo Plan*. Colombo: Colombo Plan Secretariat, 2010.

The Colombo Plan for Co-operative Economic and Social Development in Asia and the Pacific: 50th Anniversary 1951–2001. Colombo: Colombo Plan Secretariat, 2001.

The Story of The Colombo Plan: Resource Book 2012. Colombo: Colombo Plan Secretariat, 2012.

Commonwealth Consultative Committee, *The Colombo Plan for Cooperative Economic Development in South and South-East Asia*. London: HMSO, October 1950.

Current Notes on International Affairs. Canberra: Department of Foreign Affairs, 1936–72.

Curtin, P. W. E., 'The Effect of the Colombo Plan', *Pakistan Horizon*, 7, 1954, 77–80.

'India and Her Plans', *Australian Journal of Politics & History*, 2, 1956, 37–45.

Documents on Canadian External Relations, 16, 1950, https://gac.canadiana.ca/view/ooe.b2217569F_016/1 (accessed 3 November 2020).

Dorji, Tashi, 'Undated Memoir'. 2022, https://colombo-plan.org/wp-content/uploads/2020/03/Ashi_Tashi_Doriji.pdf (accessed 2 August 2022).

Food and Agriculture Organization, *The State of Food and Agriculture, 2006*, www.fao.org/3/a0800e/a0800e.03.pdf, pp. 32–64.

Keyfitz, Nathan, 'Foreign Aid Can Be Rational', *International Journal*, 17, 1962, 241.

Ministry of Foreign Affairs of Japan, *The 50th Anniversary of Japan's International Cooperation*, www.mofa.go.jp/policy/oda/cooperation/anniv50/seminar0411.pdf (accessed 2 November 2021).

New Zealand External Affairs Record (*NZEAR*).

'New Zealand High Commission in India', 2020, www.mfat.govt.nz/en/about-us/mfat75/75-our-story/new-delhi/ (accessed 3 January 2020).

New Zealand Ministry of Foreign Affairs and Trade, *The Colombo Plan at 50: A New Zealand Perspective*, 50th Anniversary of the Colombo Plan 1951–2001. Wellington: New Zealand Official Development Assistance, 2001.

OECD, *DAC in Dates: The History of the OECD's Development Assistance Committee* (Paris: OECD Publications, 2006).

Royal Commonwealth Society, *New Horizons in the East*. Cambridge University Library, 1950.

Some Aspects of New Zealand's Part in in the Colombo Plan: From Indonesia to India. NZ National Film Unit Production, 1962, www.nzonscreen.com/title/from-indonesia-to-india-1962 (accessed 2 January 2020).

Stevens, Bertram, 'The Eastern Group Supply Council', *Australian Quarterly*, 13, 1941, 9–18.

Symon, A. C. B., 'The Colombo Plan', *Journal of the Royal Asian Society*, 39, 3–4, 1952, 188–99.

The 50th Anniversary of Japan's International Cooperation Symposium: The View on the Japanese ODA in the Recipient Countries. United Nations University, Tokyo, 15 November 2004, www.mofa.go.jp/policy/oda/cooperation/anniv50/seminar0411.pdf (accessed 2 November 2021).

UN Digital Library, UN Economic and Social Council Resolution 37 (IV), 28 March 1947, document E/405, 4th session, 1947, https://digitallibrary.un.org/record/211438?ln=en (accessed 5 July 2019).

UNESCO, 26th session, ECAFE Annual Report, covering 29 March 1957 to 15 March 1958. *United Nations Official Record.*

White, Osmar (with photographs by James Fitzpatrick), *The Seed of Freedom: Australia and the Colombo Plan.* Australian Government Printing, 1961.

FILM

The Builders (Canberra) 1959
New Horizons (New Delhi and Colombo) 1959
Skilled Hands (Tokyo and Colombo) 1959

NEWSPAPERS

Age (Melbourne)
Argus (Melbourne)
Auckland Star
Bangkok Post
Beverley Times (WA)
Canberra Times
Daily News (Sri Lanka)
Daily Telegraph (Sydney)
Dawn (Karachi)
Economic Times, India,
Globe and Mail (Toronto)
Hemisphere
Melbourne Herald
Montreal *Gazette*
New Nation
New York Times
Pittsburgh Post-Gazette
Press (Canterbury)
Riverine Herald
Singapore Free Press
Singapore National Library newspaper database
Sun (Sydney)
Sydney Morning Herald
The Land (Australia)
The Straits Times
Times
Times of Ceylon
Times of India
Times of Indonesia

Washington Post
Wellington Times (NSW)
Yomiuri Shimbun

ORAL HISTORIES

James Fitzpatrick, transcript of interview with David Lowe, 2003.

Index

For EU product safety concerns, contact us at Calle de José Abascal, 56–1°, 28003 Madrid, Spain or eugpsr@cambridge.org.

www.ingramcontent.com/pod-product-compliance
Lightning Source LLC
LaVergne TN
LVHW091525200926
848483LV00002B/309
9781009600736